Dyslexia, Fluency, and the Brain

Dyslexia, Fluency, and the Brain

edited by Maryanne Wolf

YORK
PRESS

Typography by Type Shoppe II Productions Ltd.
Printing and Binding by McNaughton & Gunn, Inc.
Cover design by Joseph Dieter, Jr.

Library of Congress Cataloging-in-Publication Data

Dyslexia, fluency, and the brain / edited by Maryanne Wolf.
        p. cm.
    Includes bibliographical references and index.
    ISBN 0-912752-60-2
        1. Dyslexia. 2. Reading disability--Physiological aspect. 3. Brain. I. Wolf, Maryanne.
RC394.W6 D958 2001
616.85'53--dc21   2001026557

Dedication

To my parents, Frank Wolf and Mary Beckman Wolf,
and my teachers, Jeanne Sternlicht Chall and Norman Geschwind.

Contents

PREFACE:
Seven Dimensions of Time

Out in the middle of the wine-dark sea
there is a land called Crete,
a rich and lovely land,
washed by the sea on every side;
and in it are many peoples, and ninety cities.
And there one language
mingles with another.
Among the cities is Knossos, a great city;
and there Minos was nine years king
the boon companion of mighty Zeus

—Homer, Odyssey, Book Nineteen

In the year 2000 on the legendary island of Crete, a small group of researchers from around the world came to discuss a relatively new set of ideas: how the time it takes for the brain to process written language may impede the development of reading. Beginning with this introduction, seven dimensions of time are considered within this volume 1) as an historical factor in the evolution of writing; 2) as a basic property of neurological function; 3) as a developmental component of all cognitive and linguistic processes; 4) as a potential source of disruption in developmental disorders of reading and language; 5) as an outcome in reading fluency; 6) as a critical aspect of psychometric measurement; and 7) as a key dimension of intervention in reading fluency. This book represents a first approximation of what an approach to dyslexia might be that emphasizes multiple dimensions of time.

In the preface, I introduce the reader to the underlying questions that motivated this effort and the themes that emerged from it. But first, I would like to use the unique history of Crete to place the themes of the book within the first dimension of time discussed here: that is, the broader context of the history of written language—in particular, the contributions of Crete and the ancient Greek world to the evolution of writing.

In so doing, I hope to ground the relatively new questions about time, dyslexia, and the human brain that are raised in this volume within the sweeping, humbling context of the history of efforts the species has made to become literate. In addition, within this history, I wish the modern reader to confront and be reminded of the reasons one of the foremost apologists of oral language, Socrates, felt written language would irrevocably change our species—to its detriment.

The historical facts that connect the island of Crete to any study of written language continue to unfold. We now know that Crete was the home of at least three ancient writing systems. Linear A, a hieroglyphic system, was used in 19th-18th centuries BCE and continues to elude decipherment. Linear B was used around 1450 BCE and was discovered at Knossos at the turn of the twentieth century by Sir Arthur Evans. Evans spent more than 40 years of his life trying to decipher it, only to fail. At last deciphered by a young scholar named Michael Ventris, the elaborate story of the decipherment of Linear B is one of the great intellectual tales of the 20th century (see Coe 1999; Daniels and Bright 1996).

But the real story in the history of written language is the creation of the Greek alphabet, that was traced back at least to the eighth century BCE in Crete and two other sites. Until recently, many scholars (myself included) believed the Greek alphabet was the first "true alphabet" (Havelock 1976), an argument still made by some classicists. More recent archeological evidence changes our whole understanding of early alphabets (see Daniels and Bright 1996) and comes from places whose very names evoke a sense of the ominous (e.g., Wadi el Hol in Egypt physically looks like and linguistically translates as the Gulch of Terror). This evidence makes it far more probable that the first alphabet was a Semitic system, used by scribes in and out of Egypt in the 19-18th Century BCE, at least a full millennium before the Greeks!

That acknowledged, there is probably no people in the history of the world who came closer to being the world's first speech-perception researchers than the scholars who created the first Greek alphabet. To be sure, the concept of letters was something the Greeks borrowed from the Phoenicians, who had, in turn, borrowed their system from Semitic scripts. But, to accomplish what the Greeks attained required an unimaginably precise analysis of the Phoenician sound system and the Greek sound system (Swiggers 1996). The result was a system capable of matching every Greek sound (i.e., phoneme) with a letter. The extraordinary alphabet that the early Greek scholars on Crete produced was an achievement of a millennium, reflected in the fact that the Greek alphabet is the basis of most alphabets today, including our own (Threatte 1996).

The stunning cognitive and linguistic breakthroughs that the Greek alphabet represented have been historically underappreciated, beginning with the time of its creation. For the Greeks gave more complex twists to the history of writing than the creation of the Greek alphabet; they raised timeless and deeply critical questions about written language that are as thought-provoking now as then. It is a good thing for the modern reader to pause and be quietly astounded not only by the intellectual and epistemological revolution that the first Greek alphabet represented for our species' evolution, but also by their reasons for initially rejecting it. It took, in fact, more than three and a half centuries for the Greek alphabet to come into regular use in the schools.

This is because the Homeric-driven Greece of the first half of the first millennium BCE possessed one of the most highly developed oral cultures that the world has ever known. Plato's Dialogues were one of the most perfect examples of orality captured in text (that is, they were neither speech nor prose) (Klein 1965). Paradoxically, The Dialogues recorded the most prescient arguments against literacy that have ever been made, before or since (see Nussbaum 1997). Within the Dialogues, Socrates scorned written language and tried, unsuccessfully, to limit its use.

At the heart of Socrates' protestations was his fear and belief that the appearance of permanence in written text would give readers the false "conceit of wisdom" (Plato, Phaedrus, 275b) and lead them away from a rigorous, ongoing examination of the essence of words. That is, the learner would confuse the permanence of print with truth and not feel the need either for the ongoing examination of words or the storage of oral passages in memory. To Socrates, only "living speech" could be questioned, probed, and then transformed into human memory, personal knowledge, and the earnest pursuit of wisdom. This entire process—from the examination of word and thought through its embodiment in the learner's memory—was considered the basis of virtue in the individual and society. Socrates' deep-seated concerns over his society's shift to the mode of literacy were profound and deserving of our attentiveness today, as we make our own shift from text to the visual, image-dominated mode of a technologically based society.

To those of us who spend our lives in the service of words and their accessibility to all young humans, Socrates may be an unusual ally and "gadfly." I would like to invoke and re-fashion three of Socrates' objections to literacy and use them as guideposts for the reader before encountering the material in this book: first, that the earnest examination of words should be vigilantly attended to (in this case, specifying with care to the terms related to time); second, that there are critical ways of learning from "living speech" that may increase our understanding and teaching of written language (as in our intervention); and third, that many human beings (for example, children and adults who are dyslexic) may have greater access to other ways of learning than text-based knowledge. With these Socratic admonitions as the backdrop, I will move to a more recent, historical context for the ongoing work represented in this book.

Some years ago, Gerald Holton described what he called "paradigm shifts" or discernible changes in emphases that mark the history of science. The field of dyslexia research mirrors this development, with each new paradigm's explanation for dyslexia supplanting the preceding one (see Wolf and Ashby in press). In the last 25 years, dyslexia research has been largely characterized by a psycholinguistic approach; this approach replaced all previous perceptual-based explanations with a new emphasis on the linguistic basis of developmental dyslexia (Vellutino, 1979). Based largely on the long, systematic investigations by Don Shankweiler and Isabelle Liberman and their colleagues (Shankweiler and Liberman 1972), this work rests on the assumption (and the evidence) that learning to read requires a knowledge of the letter-sound or grapheme-phoneme correspondence rules of the language. This knowledge, in turn, is based on a tacit awareness by the child of the sounds or phonemes in language. Such a view resulted in what has been called the phonological-core deficit (Stanovich 1988) paradigm, and there is large consensus that a primary source of reading failure is the lack of development of phoneme-awareness skills.

What may be unique about the present moment in dyslexia research history is that there is not so much a shift away from the phonological paradigm, but rather, an attempt to integrate that knowledge base, both with new findings about a second core-deficit in time- and fluency-related processes, and also with new approaches from the neurosciences.

The recent attention to time- and fluency-related deficits in reading breakdown is the result of a convergence of three factors. First, the systematic research on the role of phonological processes in dyslexia and intervention has proven both successful and yet insufficient in dealing with the heterogeneity of reading disabilities and the complexity of reading breakdown— especially in the area of fluency. (For a recent comprehensive review, see Meyer and Felton 1999; also see Breznitz and Share 1992; Torgesen, Rashotte, and Wagner 1997; Torgesen et al. 1999; Rashotte and Torgesen 1985; Young and Bowers 1995.) The wish to address the needs of children who do not completely respond to phonological-based treatment is a motivating impulse in turning to additional explanatory principles like fluency (Lyons and Moats 1997; Torgesen et al. 1999).

The second factor is an increased awareness of the multiple, underlying sources that can contribute to or impede fluency development. An example is the concerted effort to understand the predictive ability of naming speed in reading failure, as indexed through "rapid, automatized naming" or RAN tasks (Denckla and Rudel 1976; see reviews in Wolf and Bowers 1999; 2000). So also are extensive studies that explore a range of time-related deficits in reading-disabled children in various perceptual and motor areas (see reviews in Farmer and Klein 1995; Nicolson and Fawcett 1994; Wolf, Bowers, and Biddle 2000; Wolff in press).

The third factor is related to naming-speed research and involves cumulative evidence from subtype research in developmental dyslexia. There is a growing body of work demonstrating that there are discrete groups of reading-impaired children who can be characterized by single deficits in either naming speed or phonological processes or combined deficits in both areas (Badian 1996; Lovett, Steinbach, and Frijters 2000; Manis, Doi, and Bhada 2000; Wolf et al. 2000). Known as the Double-Deficit Hypothesis, this conceptualization has several fluency-related implications (Wolf and Bowers 1999; 2000). For example, children with single naming-speed deficits are frequently difficult to diagnose in early primary years, but go on to develop fluency and comprehension problems by the end of grade 3. Further, children with both phonological and naming-speed deficits are consistently found to possess the most severe problems in reading and reading fluency. The most important implication of this conceptualization is that it provides a theoretical rationale and foundation for intervention that specifically addresses issues of speed of processing and fluency. Until very recently intervention was largely directed to treatment for phonologically based decoding problems. Children with either single processing-speed deficits or combined deficits would be only partially served by such a focus, thus fueling the ranks of children who do not respond to treatment.

This book, and the conference that preceded it, were organized to confront critical unanswered questions about time, fluency, and intervention in dyslexia. The most persistent and difficult questions have defied every effort within a phonological paradigm to answer them and are the questions that underlie this conference.

What are the nature and extent of rate-of-processing, time-, and fluency-related deficits in developmental dyslexia?

What are the hypothesized source(s) of these deficits?

Are time- and fluency-related deficits amenable to change? If so, what theoretical principles should guide intervention in these areas?

This book is organized into sections around these three, related questions, followed by a chapter by Ginger Berninger than spans all three topics.

The framework for the book has been constructed to bring several levels of evidence and types of research to bear on the questions. In the first section, evidence is presented on timing deficits in dyslexia at the behavioral level by cognitive, clinical, and experimental psychologists. The second section contains evidence, largely by neuroscientists, at three levels: neuronal, brain structure, and genetic. The third section contains research on the emerging intervention in reading fluency.

SECTION 1. THE NATURE AND EXTENT OF TIME-RELATED DEFICITS IN DEVELOPMENTAL DYSLEXIA

The papers in the first section frame the above question along behavioral, developmental, and cross-linguistic axis. There is considerable evidence and consensus that at least one type of time-related problem—naming-speed deficits (NSD)—represents a very strong predictor of reading disabilities across every language tested to date. Heinz Wimmer demonstrates that in languages like German whose orthography is relatively regular, that naming-speed deficits are even stronger predictors than in English. He uses this information to question the primacy of phonological deficits in other languages. (In a later section, Ginger Berninger states that NSD are the single most prevalent deficit among her severely impaired subjects.)

A central unresolved question explored by many in this volume is: Why would this be so? What is the underlying relationship between naming speed and reading? More specifically, are there particular relationships between processes underlying naming speed and particular forms of reading? One compelling hypothesis, first raised in work by Patricia Bowers during the nineties, is the relationship between NSD and orthographic skills. In their separate chapters Patricia Bowers and Frank Manis explore and find different forms of support for this working hypothesis. Manis' long history of research on different aspects of orthographic skills has enabled his new work to become more specific about this line of investigation. In a different section, however, Don Compton and Dick Olson do not find naming speed clearly connected to orthography, as measured in their battery's orthographic tasks. There is consensus among this book's participants that we need to continue to examine these questions in ever more differentiated ways.

In her chapter, Deborah Waber uses her extremely large database of children with multiple forms of learning disabilities to pose questions about whether NSD primarily predicts reading disabilities or also broader forms of learning disabilities (LD). In the first database exploring this same question, Denckla and Rudel (1976) found that only reading disabled children were classified by NSD, and other learning disabled children were not. Waber's data show the converse pattern. There is a critical need for this question to be pursued with careful attention to the classification of both LD and dyslexic sub-groups, potentially the putative Double-Deficit subgroups.

John Stein moves arguments about time-related deficits outside naming speed to other domains. In his essay chapter, he presents evidence showing both visual and auditory speed-of-processing differences among dyslexic children; that is, well beyond language-based deficits. This broader range of time-related deficits is supported and extended by work from the lab of Angela Fawcett and Rod Nicolson, who present, in their first chapter in this volume, an overview of the multiple time-related deficits (including auditory, visual, and motoric) found in their subjects over the last decade. A theme that occurred first in Peter Wolff's (see review, in press) early work and now in Fawcett and Nicolson's work is the finding that at the lowest level of processing (like the detection of a flash or tone), there are no speed differences; rather, when tasks require the first hint of choice, there are differences in time. John Stein speculates in his chapter that the wide range of time-related findings in dyslexia might be parsimoniously explained by a magnocellular deficit, a hypothesis strongly supported by work reported by Glen Rosen and his colleagues, Al Galaburda, and Gordon Sherman in the second section.

The upshot of the first section is that there is a convergence of evidence across several perceptual, motor, and linguistic areas and several orthographies that many dyslexic children have rate of processing differences, particularly in naming speed tasks, but also on tasks well beyond the linguistic domain. Less consensual and less resolved are questions about how these differences interfere with reading and whether they are found in children with more general learning disabilities.

2. THE HYPOTHESIZED SOURCES OF TIME-RELATED DEFICITS: NEURONAL, STRUCTURAL, AND GENETIC LEVELS

Glen Rosen colorfully describes in his essay, current work at the neuronal level from the extensive work of the Beth Israel Hospital lab where he, Al Galaburda, and Gordon Sherman have worked over the last decade and a half. Rosen and his colleagues have used an animal model to study how specific neuronal anomalies (similar to those found in autopsied brains of dyslexic individuals) can result in slower auditory processing.

Guinevere Eden and Tom Zeffiro were participants of the conference and presented evidence there at the structural level that summarized much of the cumulative fMRI imaging evidence on brain structures involved in reading and reading failure, and most recently, in naming speed. A surprising finding in their conference presentation that receives support from several authors in the second section concerns the possible role that the right cerebellum might play in dyslexia and time-related deficits. Indeed questions about the cerebellum represent an unexpected subtheme in this section.

Rod Nicolson and Angela Fawcett in their second chapter discuss evidence from dyslexic subjects on a new battery of cerebellar tasks. They hypothesize that the cerebellum should be considered as one potential source of time-related disruption in dyslexia.

Rich Ivry provided the conference participants with their most startling discovery: upon close examination, he concluded that the famous, to-date undeciphered, Disk of Phaistos in Crete is actually the first RAN! His chapter takes a decidedly more serious note. He and his colleagues, Timothy Justus, and Christina Middleton, present an important overview for dyslexia researchers on the role of the cerebellum in regulating precise timing in the brain; they argue for a slow, cautious perspective on hypotheses linking dyslexia to cerebellar dysfunction at this time.

Frank Wood's chapter throws caution to the winds, as he provides an avowedly unconventional neuroanatomical description of brain structures used in reading and fluency. An important contribution in his chapter is a new emphasis on the concept of "anticipatory facilitation" in timed processes like the RAN and reading.

Zvia Breznitz has written an equally surprise-filled chapter that discusses an unusual method of using evoked potentials for looking at the gap or discrepancy between visual and auditory rates of processing. She sees this gap as an index of the dysynchrony between visual and auditory systems in dyslexia, and a future predictor of dyslexia. Russ Poldrack uses another conceptually exciting and promising new imaging method—diffusion tensor imaging—to examine in dyslexic adults the level of white matter (essential for speed of information processing) in areas used in reading. Results involving the angular gyrus region, long hypothesized by Norman Geschwind to be implicated in dyslexia, are particularly noteworthy.

Mentioned earlier, Don Compton and Richard Olson extend our explanations of possible sources of dyslexia to the genetic level. Of considerable importance to researchers who continue to conceptualize naming speed as a phonological process, they provide compelling genetic evidence on 500 twins that there are independent relationships of both naming speed and phonological processes to reading.

3. THE QUESTION OF INTERVENTION

The third section of the book concerns fluency and intervention. Fittingly, the first two chapters stress the importance of early detection and prevention of fluency problems. Ed Kameenui and his colleagues Deborah Simmons, Roland Good, and Beth Harn, stress a new conceptualization of fluency: that is, that fluency is not simply an outcome of reading, but rather a developmental continuum of processes that need to be addressed before reading ever begins, along with phoneme awareness work. This developmental view of fluency with its implicit emphasis on fluency prevention programs is a major sub-theme in this volume.

Similarly, based on his extensive history of intervention research with Rick Wagner, Carol Rashotte, and their colleagues, Joe Torgesen makes an equally strong case for fluency prevention programs. Highlighted in this chapter are some of the most important principles of fluency instruction, including the role of anticipatory facilitation, repetition, practice, and outside reading.

The role of repeated practice is amplified in Betty Ann Levy's overview of her important, experimental fluency-intervention studies. She emphasizes in her chapter a new factor, orthographic visibility, and its importance for facilitating processing speed in children with dyslexia. Such an emphasis echoes earlier questions raised in the first section concerning the potential relationship between naming speed and specific orthographic processes in reading.

The final chapter by Ginger Berninger and her colleagues Robert Abbott, Felix Billingsley, and William Nagy, is a broad-sweeping account of several topics: naming speed and its puzzle; the "morphological fluency hypothesis" within Berninger et al's connectionist framework; and a new view of fluency. This wide-ranging paper and the questions it raises provides an ideal coda for the book.

Plato wrote that once begun, there is no real end to a "dialogue." That is what I have come to think about the Crete Dialogues that make up this book. It is my hope that the questions about time, fluency, and intervention raised first at the Crete conference and now in this book will elicit for the reader new thoughts about dyslexia and ancient questions about the role of time in human language. There is no end to such thoughts.

Maryanne Wolf
Cambridge, Massachusetts
January 11, 2001

Badian, N. 1996, November. Dyslexia: Does it exist? Dyslexia, garden-variety poor reading, and the double-deficit hypothesis. Paper presented at The Orton Dyslexia Society, Boston.

Breznitz, Z., and Share. 1992. Effects of accelerated reading rate on memory for text among dyslexic readers. *Journal of Educational Psychology* 89(2):289–97.

Coe, M. D. 1999. *Breaking the Maya Code*. New York, NY: Thames & Hudson Inc.

Daniels, P. and Bright, W. 1996. *The world's writing systems*. New York/Oxford: Oxford University Press.

Denckla, M. B., and Rudel, R. G. 1976. Naming of objects by dyslexic and other learning-disabled children. Brain and Language 3:1–15.

Farmer, M. E., and Klein, R. M. 1995. The evidence for a temporal processing deficit linked to dyslexia: A review. *Psychonomic Society* 2(4):460–93.

Havelock, E. 1976. *Origins of Western Literacy*. Toronto, Ontario: The Ontario Institute for Studies in Education.

Klein, J. 1965. *A Commentary on Plato's Meno*. Chapel Hill, North Carolina: The University of North Carolina Press.

Lovett, M. W. 1987. A developmental approach to reading disability: Accuracy and speed criteria of normal and deficient reading skill. *Child Development* 58:234–60.

Lovett, M. W., Steinbach, K. A., and Frijters, J. C. 2000. Remediating the core deficits of developmental reading disability: A double-deficit perspective. *Journal of Learning Disabilities* 33(4):334–58.

Lyons, G. R. and Moats, L. 1997. Critical conceptual and methodological considerations and reading intervention research. *Journal of Learning Disabilities* 30:579–88.

Manis, F. R., Doi, L. M., and Bhada, B. 2000. Naming speed, phonological awareness, and orthographic knowledge in second graders. *Journal of Learning Disabilities* 33:325–33.

Meyer, M. S., and Felton, R. H. 1999. Evolution of fluency training: Old approaches and new directions. *Annals of Dyslexia* 49:283–306.

Nicolson, R. I., and Fawcett, A. J. 1994. Reaction times and dyslexia. Quarterly Journal of Experimental Psychology 47:29–48.

Nussbaum, M. 1997. *Cultivating Humanity*. Cambridge, MA: Harvard Press.

Plato. Phaedrus. In *The Collected Dialogues*, eds. E. Hamilton and H. Cairns. 1961. Princeton: Princeton University Press.

Rashotte, C., and Torgesen, J. 1985. Repeated reading and reading fluency in learning disabled children. *Reading Research Quarterly* 20:180–88.

Shankweiler, D., and Liberman, I. Y. 1972. Misreading: A Search for Causes. In, *Language by Ear and by Eye*, eds .J. J. Kavanagh and I. G. Mattingly. Cambridge, MA: MIT Press.

Stanovich, K. 1988. The dyslexic and the garden-variety poor reader: The phonological core variable-difference model. *Journal of Learning Disabilities* 21:590–604.

Swiggers, P. 1996. Transmission of the Phoenician script to the West. In *The World's Writing Systems*, eds. P. Daniels and W. Bright. New York: Oxford Press.

Threatte, L. 1996. The Greek alphabet. In *The world's writing systems*, eds. P. Daniels & W. Bright. New York: Oxford Press

Torgesen, J., Rashotte, C., and Wagner, R. 1997, November. Research on instructional interventions for children with reading disabilities. Paper presented at The International Dyslexia Association conference, Chicago.

Torgesen, J., Rashotte, C., Lindamood, P., Rose, E., Conway, T., and Garven, C. 1999. Preventing reading failure in young children with phonological processing disabilities: Group and individual responses to instruction. *Journal of Educational Psychology* 91:579–93.

Vellutino, F. 1979. Dyslexia: Research and Theory. Cambridge, MA: MIT Press.

Wolf, M., and Ashby, J. In press. A brief history of time, phonology, and other explanations of developmental dyslexia. In *Brain Bases of Learning Disabilities: The Case of Reading Disabilities*, eds. K. Fisher, J. Bernstein, F. Benes, D. Waber, and M. Wolf.

Wolf, M., and Bowers, P. 1999. The "double-deficit hypothesis" for the developmental dyslexias. *Journal of Educational Psychology* 91:1–24.

Wolf, M, and Bowers, P. 2000. The question of naming-speed deficits in developmental reading disabilities: An introduction to the Double-Deficit Hypothesis. *Journal of Learning Disabilities* 33:322–24. (Special Issue on the Double-Deficit Hypothesis; Special Issue Editors: M. Wolf and P. Bowers).

Wolf, M., Bowers, P., and Biddle, K. 2000. Naming-speed processes, timing, and reading: A conceptual review. *Journal of Learning Disabilities* 33:387–407. (Special Issue on the Double-Deficit Hypothesis; Special Issue Editors: M. Wolf and P. Bowers).

Wolff, P. in press. Timing precision and rhythm in developmental dyslexia. Special Issue on Fluency in Reading and Writing. Boston, MA.

Young, A., and Bowers, P. 1995. Individual difference and text difficulty determinants of reading fluency and expressiveness. *Journal of Experimental Child Psychology* 60:428–54.

Acknowledgments

The present book is the result of a conference sponsored by the National Dyslexia Research Foundation. Set in Crete, the meetings were an extraordinary, path breaking intellectual exploration. It was a privilege to have organized the conference along with Will Baker, the Director of the Foundation. I am deeply grateful to Will Baker and the entire Foundation for their sustained vision about creative ways to encourage the cross-fertilization and dissemination of new ideas about dyslexia research. I wish to underscore my utmost thanks to the members of the Center for Reading and Language Research at Tufts for helping me organize a conference in Crete, from my sabbatical in California, through Boston! Specifically, I wish to thank Wendy Galante, Julie Jeffery, Alyssa Goldberg, and Tami Katzir-Cohen for their multiple, seemingly endless efforts, and former center member Maya Alivisatos for her help in selecting the unique Crete site. We thank Joyce Boulifant from NDRF and Colleen Osborne for their much-appreciated efforts in site-organization.

I find it very hard to find the right words to convey my thanks to each of the participants at the Conference—the outstanding conference researchers, the reflective former organizers, the young scholars, and the gracious audience members—whose shared efforts produced the most memorable scientific meeting I have ever attended. I am very grateful to you each. I especially wish to thank the three discussants, Benita Blachman, Paula Tallal (both former organizers of NDRF conferences), and Tom Zeffiro for their thoughtful and generative remarks throughout the conference. I also wish to thank the representatives of several other Foundations who by their participation and support of conferences like these are leading the way to a new level of alliances between researchers and foundations: specifically, Ron and Cindy Haan of the Haan Foundation for Children; John Chany Trust; and Helen U. Baker.

I thank Elinor Hartwig at York Press with a bit of awe for her ability to publish this book within a year of the conference. The timeliness of the topic makes this feat particularly helpful. Finally, I wish to thank my husband, Gil Noam, for his intellectual kinship, along with our sons, Ben and David, for their collective spunk, spirit, and support over time.

Contributors

Robert D. Abbott, Ph.D.
312 Miller Hall
Box 353600
University of Washington
Seattle, Washington 98195-3600
E-mail: abbottr@u.washington. edu

Ann W. Alexander, M.D.
The Morris Child Development
  Center
2035 W. 75th Street
Gainesville, Florida 32607
E-mail: awalexander@mindspring.com

Virginia W. Berninger, Ph.D.
322 Miller Hall
Box 353600
University of Washington
Seattle, Washington 98195-3600
E-mail: vwb@u.washington.edu

Felix Billingsley, Ph.D.
102 Miller Hall
Box 353600
University of Washington
Seattle, Washington 98195-3600
E-mail: felixb@u.washington.edu

Patricia Greig Bowers, Ph.D.
Department of Psychology
University of Waterloo
Waterloo, Ontario
Canada
E-mail: pbowers@watarts.uwaterloo.ca

Zvia Breznitz, Ph.D.
Laboratory for Neurocognitive
  Research
Faculty of Education
University of Haifa, Mt. Carmel
Haifa, Israel 31905
E-mail: zviab@construct. haifa.ac.il

Matthew G. Clark, Ph.D.
Center for Molecular and
  Biobehavioral Sciences
University of New Jersey at Newark
Newark, New Jersey

Donald L. Compton, Ph.D.
Special Education Department
Vanderbilt University
Box 328 Peabody College
Nashville, TN 37203 - 5701
E-mail: donald.l.compton@vander-
  bilt.edu

Chayna J. Davis, M.A.
Institute for Behavioral Genetics
University of Colorado
Campus Box 447
Boulder, Colorado 80309
E-mail: davisc@alpha.colorado. edu

John C. DeFries, Ph.D.
Institute for Behavioral Genetics
University of Colorado
Campus Box 447
Boulder, Colorado 80309
E-mail: john.defries@colorado.edu

Angela J. Fawcett, Ph.D.
Department of Psychology
University of Sheffield
Sheffield, United Kingdom
E-mail: a.fawcett@sheffield.ac.uk

R. Holly Fitch, Ph.D.
Program in Biobehavioral Science
University of Connecticut
Storrs, Connecticut

Lynn Flowers, Ph.D.
Wake Forest University School of
  Medicine
Winston-Salem, North Carolina
  27157-1043
E-mail: lflowers@wfubmc.edu

Laurie Freedman, Ph.D.
Psychology Department
University of Southern California
Los Angeles, California 90089-1061
E-mail: LFreedman@ChannelOne.com

Albert M. Galaburda, M.D.
Dyslexia Research Laboratory and
    Charles A. Dana Research Institute
Beth Israel Deaconess Medical Center
    and Harvard Medical School
Boston, Massachusetts 02215

Javier Gayan, Ph.D
Institute for Behavioral Genetics
University of Colorado
Campus Box 447
Boulder, Colorado 80309
E-mail: javier.gayan@ colorado.edu

Roland H. Good, III, Ph.D.
University of Oregon
Eugene, Oregon 97405-5208
E-mail: rhgood@darkwing.uoregon.
    edu

Elena Grigorenko, Ph.D.
Yale University Child Study Center
Yale University
New Haven, Connecticut and
Moscow State University
Moscow, Russia
E-mail: elena.grigorenko@yale. edu

Beth A. Harn, Ph.D.
IDEA
College of Education
University of Oregon
Eugene, Oregon 97403-1211
E-mail: bharn@darkwing.uoregon.
    edu

Richard B. Ivry, Ph.D.
Department of Psychology
University of California, Berkeley
Berkeley, California 94720-1650
E-mail: ivry@socrates.berkeley.edu

Timothy C. Justus, Ph.D.
Department of Psychology
University of California
Berkeley, California 94720
tjustus@socrates.berkeley.edu

Edward J. Kame'enui, Ph.D.
IDEA
College of Education
University of Oregon
Eugene, Oregon 97403-1211
E-mail: eakmee@oregon.uoregon.edu

Betty Ann Levy, Ph.D.
Department of Psychology
McMaster University
Hamilton, Ontario
Canada LP5 4K1
E-mail: levy@mcmaster.ca

J.J. Lo Turco, Ph.D.
Department of Physiology and
    Neurobiology
University of Connecticut
Storrs, Connecticut

Frank R. Manis, Ph.D.
Psychology Department
University of Southern California
Los Angeles, California 90089-1061
E-mail: manis@usc.edu

Heinz Mayringer, Ph.D.
Hellbrunnerstrasse 34
A-5020 Salzburg
Austria

Christina Middleton, Ph.D.
Department of Psychology
University of California, Berkeley
Berkeley, California 94720-1650

William Nagy, Ph.D.
Seattle Pacific University
School of Education
3307 3rd Avenue, West
Seattle, Washington 98119-1997
E-mail: wnagy@spu.edu

Professor Roderick I. Nicolson
Department of Psychology,
University of Sheffield
Sheffield, United Kingdom
E-mail: rnicolson@shef.ac.uk

Richard K. Olson, Ph.D
  Department of Psychology.
  University of Colorado
  Campus Box 345
  Boulder, Colorado 80309
  E-mail: rolson@psych.colorado.edu

Russell A. Poldrack, Ph.D.
  MGH-NMR Center and Harvard
    Medical School
  Building 149, 13th street
  Charlestown, Massachusetts 02129
  E-mail: poldrack@nmr.mgh.har-
    vard.edu

Carol A. Rashotte, Ph.D.
  Department of Psychology
  Florida State University
  Tallahassee, Florida 32306-1270
  crashott@psy.fsu.edu

Glenn D. Rosen, Ph.D.
  Dyslexia Research Laboratory
  and Charles A. Dana Research
    Institute
  Beth Israel Deaconess Medical
    Center and Harvard Medical
    School
  Boston, Massachusetts

Gordon F. Sherman, Ph.D.
  The Newgrange School and
    Educational Outreach Center
  Princeton, New Jersey

Deborah C. Simmons, Ph.D.
  IDEA
  College of Education
  University of Oregon
  Eugene, Oregon 97403-1211
  E-mail: dsimmons@oregon.uore-
    gon.edu

John Stein, F.R.E.P.
  University Laboratory of Physiology
  Oxford 0X1 3PT
  United Kingdom
  E-mail: JohnStein@physiol.ox.ac.uk

Joseph K. Torgesen, Ph.D.
  Department of Psychology
  Florida State University
  Tallahassee. Florida 32306-1270
  torgesen@psy.fsu.edu

Deborah P. Waber, Ph.D.
  Department of Psychiatry
  Children's Hospital Boston
  300 Longwood Ave.
  Boston, MA 02115
  E-mail: waber@1.tch.harvard.edu

Heinz Wimmer, Ph.D.
  Hellbrunnerstrasse 34
  A-5020 Salzburg
  Austria
  E-mail: heinz.wimmer@sbg.ac.at.

Maryanne Wolf, Ph.D.
  Center for Reading & Language
    Research
  Tufts University
  Miller Hall
  Medford, Massachusetts 02155-7019
  E-mail: maryanne.wolf@tufts.edu

Frank Balch Wood, Ph.D.
  Wake Forest University School of
    Medicine
  Winston-Salem, NC 27157-1043
  E-mail: fwood@wfubmc.edu

Section • **I**

The Nature and Extent of Time-Related Deficits in Developmental Dyslexia

Chapter • 1

The Neurobiology of Reading Difficulties

John Stein

It is really not surprising that so many children experience such difficulty with learning to read because reading is the most skilled activity that most of us ever have to undertake, and 200 years ago it was not expected that the uneducated majority would be able to read at all. However it is noteworthy that, unlike speaking, most children have to be taught to read. They do not pick it up simply by copying their parents. This is because reading and writing involve a set of highly complex, multimodal, sensorimotor interactions. Nowadays the Chomsky/Fodor view that language functions are to a large extent independent of basic sensory processing, but instead are carried out by an independent linguistic processing module, is preeminent. This linguistic school holds that reading depends entirely on the quality of the linguistic processor that a person inherits. Nevertheless the commonsense idea that more basic sensory processing skills are also important for learning to read is gaining ground. According to this view literacy problems may be caused, to some extent, by fundamental differences in sensory processing between the brains of good and bad readers. The analysis and ordering of visual inputs from print and the auditory inputs from speech may be slower and more prone to error in poor readers. But because the development of the whole brain is unusual we can see many more sensory, motor, and cognitive differences in poor readers than just their literacy problems. For the last 30 years I have been investigating the neurophysiological basis of visuomotor control: the way in which visual inputs are transformed, in particular by the posterior parietal cortex and cerebellum, to control eye and limb movements. When I heard that many children with reading problems complained that letters appear to move around, I was reminded of patients I had seen with cerebellar lesions. I started, therefore, to consider the visuo-motor basis of reading; and fast became convinced that some reading problems derive from visuomotor deficiences.

In this chapter therefore, I aim to show how reading depends on the quality of the brain's processing of visual and auditory input; and how it absolutely requires a highly sensitive visual magnocellular system to acquire good orthographic skills, and a sensitive auditory transient system to parse the phonological structure of words. These low level visual and auditory processes enable letters and their order in words to be identified visually and matched with their corresponding sounds. Then I will speculate about the genetic and immunological mechanisms that may be responsible for the wide variety of abnormalities that are seen in people with developmental dyslexia. My overall conclusion will be that reading difficulties are neither specific to reading nor exclusively linguistically based, but a consequence of mildly impaired development of a particular kind of neuron in the brain, the magnocellular neuron, so that dyslexia has widespread manifestations, which are not at all confined to reading (Stein and Walsh 1997; Stein and Talcott 1999). But poor reading is not a "disease"; it results from individual differences between different brains that would not have mattered "in the wild" before reading was invented. Recent functional imaging studies have shown that reading involves both hemispheres of the brain; but the importance of the left is enhanced as the phonological or orthographic demands of the task are made harder, while the right is more important for detecting the rhythms and intonation of speech (Demonet et al. 1993). Silent reading engages mainly the posterior part of the left hemisphere focusing on the left angular and supramarginal gyri. Reading out loud shifts activity further forward toward Broca's area in the frontal cortex, so that the whole of the temporo-frontal articulatory loop is engaged. Homologous areas in the right hemisphere are also activated to a lesser extent; but their role is enhanced only when the intonation or emotional content of speech is emphasized. Activation of posterior more than anterior areas during silent reading emphasizes the importance of the visual input to reading. That you need to see the print clearly is self evident; hence Morgan (1896) first described developmental dyslexia as "word blindness." Yet the role of vision in learning to read is consistently neglected nowadays. Following the linguistic revolution wrought by Chomsky in the 1960s, most researchers now believe that poor readers' main problem is lack of the key phonological skills required for language rather than anything to do with vision (Liberman et al. 1974; Snowling 1981). But in fact, familiar words are recognized entirely visually without any requirement for phonological mediation. Likewise irregular words cannot be successfully sounded out; hence they must be read by the visual route. Slow visual recognition of words is the greatest handicap that people with dyslexia face.

On the other hand, there is no doubt that phonological analysis is important as well. Unfamiliar words (and all words are unfamiliar to beginning readers) have to be sounded out using the letter sound correspondences that have to be learned. This sounding out engages more anterior parts of the articulatory loop. Even if the letters are sounded out entirely mentally, using "inner speech," the whole articulatory loop is engaged.

Thus, there are two reading mechanisms that, although strongly interconnected (Seidenburg 1993), are at least conceptually separable: the faster whole word semantic route, which draws heavily on the visual system, and the slower phonological route, which probably depends more on auditory mediation (Ellis 1992; Castles and Coltheart 1993). These two routes therefore depend, to some extent separately, on the processing powers of the visual and auditory systems; and it is these that I shall now deal with.

THE VISUAL MAGNOCELLULAR SYSTEM

The ganglion cells whose axons carry visual signals from the retina to the rest of the brain can be divided into two main types: 90% are known as parvo cells from their small cell bodies and restricted dendritic spread (Enroth, Cugel, and Robson 1966; Shapley and Perry 1986). These are responsible for signaling the color and fine, high spatial frequency, detail of objects. The remaining 10% are large magno cells. The dendrites of these neurons cover a retinal area up to 500 times that of parvo cells. They are not only larger, but they are more heavily myelinated, which means that their conduction velocities and membrane dynamics are much more rapid. Hence, although their spatial resolution is coarser and they do not support color vision, they respond fast and their signals arrive at the brain 10 to 20 msecs. earlier than that of parvo cells. Thus, they are important for timing events in the visual world and for detecting changes with time, such as those caused by visual motion; but they do not signal color or fine detail (Merrigan and Maunsell 1993).

On arrival at the main visual relay nucleus in the thalamus, the lateral geniculate nucleus (LGN), magno axons are separate from parvo and pass into the separate magnocellular layers of the LGN. The magnocellular LGN cells then project to layer IV C alpha of the primary visual cortex, whereas the parvocellular layers project to layer IV C beta. From there parvo and magno streams intermingle. Nevertheless the output of the visual cortex can be divided into two main streams, the "what" and "where" pathways (Ungerleider and Mishkin 1982). The ventrolateral stream projects toward the inferotemporal cortex and receives roughly equal inputs from magno and parvo pathways. It is often called the "what" pathway because it is specialized for identifying the shape, pattern, and color of objects, and therefore for identifying what they are.

In contrast, the dorsomedial pathway passes towards the visual motion area (V5/MT) in the superior temporal gyrus, and thence to the posterior parietal cortex (Stein 1992). It has been called the "where" pathway because it is specialized for detecting the current position and motion of targets, and for directing attention and movements toward them (Milner and Goodale 1995). It is dominated by input from the visual magnocellular system. As befits its function in helping the visual guidance of movements, this system projects onward to all the areas involved in the guidance of eye movements: in particular to the frontal eye fields, superior colliculus and the cerebellum.

Dyslexics' Visual Magnocellular Deficits

One advantage of the separation of the visual magno- and parvocellular systems is that their sensitivity can be assessed psychophysically in intact subjects using stimuli that selectively activate one or the other system. Spatial contrast and temporal flicker sensitivity are limited mainly by the performance of the peripheral visual system up to the level of the visual cortex. Lovegrove therefore went to Cambridge in the 1970s to learn the techniques of spatial frequency analysis from Fergus Campbell. He then returned to Tasmania and employed Campbell's sinusoidal gratings to show that the contrast sensitivity of many people with dyslexia is impaired compared with controls, particularly at low spatial and high temporal frequencies (Lovegrove et al. 1980). Thus, it was he who first suggested that people with dyslexia may have a selective impairment of the magnocellular system. With stationary gratings, he found that dyslexics' contrast sensitivity at the high spatial frequencies that are mediated by the parvocellular system was actually higher than in controls, and we have been able to confirm his results in English subjects (Mason et al. 1993). Likewise Martin and Lovegrove (1987) showed that flicker sensitivity in subjects with dyslexia tends to be lower than controls, and we have confirmed this also (Mason et al. 1993; Talcott et al. 1998). Again this suggests that people with dyslexia may have a specific magnocellular impairment.

However these results have been hotly disputed (Skottun 2000; but see Stein, Talcott, and Walsh 2000). The failures to find differences consistent with a peripheral magnocellular impairment probably result from the mildness of the impairment, and the fact that it is not found in perhaps $1/3$ of subjects with dyslexia. Most of the studies that have failed to replicate Lovegrove's results have involved only small numbers so that they have lacked the statistical power required to detect the small differences. Larger numbers are needed, and also it is sensible to screen the subjects with dyslexia for visual symptoms since these subjects are most likely to have a significant magnocellular deficit.

Testing sensitivity to visual motion has proved much more reliable, however, because motion engages not only the peripheral visual system but also central processing stages up to at least area V5/MT. In monkeys, it has been found that detecting coherent motion in a display of dots moving about randomly (random dot kinematograms—RDK) is a sensitive test for probing magnocellular function (Newsome et al. 1989). We have therefore developed a RDK test of motion sensitivity to measure the magnocellular sensitivity of adults and children quickly and conveniently. We present two panels of randomly moving dots side by side. In one of the panels, selected at random, a proportion of the dots is moved together "coherently," so that they look like a cloud of snowflakes blown in the wind. In the other, all the dots are moved randomly and the subject is asked in which panel the cloud appears to be moving. The proportion of dots that is moved together is then reduced until the subject can no longer tell on which side the dots are moving together. His threshold is then defined as the proportion of dots that have to be moved all together for him to see the coherent motion correctly on 75% of occasions. Using this test, we have found that in children and adults with dyslexia, defined as those whose reading is more than two standard deviations behind that expected from their age and similarities or matrices subtests of the British ability scales (BAS) IQ, about 75% have worse motion sensitivity than controls matched for age and IQ (Cornelissen et al. 1994; Talcott et al. 1998, 2000a, b). Like Lovegrove, our conclusion from these psychophysical studies is that $2/3$ of people with dyslexia have poor motion sensitivity, i.e., slightly impaired magnocellular function. This result has been confirmed by several other laboratories both psychophysically and by measuring evoked potentials (Livingstone et al. 1991; Maddock et al. 1992; Lehmkuhle et al. 1992), and more recently a succession of functional imaging studies have come to the same conclusion (Eden et al. 1996; Demb et al. 1997, 1998).

LGN Abnormality in Dyslexia

Lest anyone is still in doubt that many people with dyslexia do have impaired development of the visual magnocellular system, the most direct evidence would be provided by examining the magnocellular layers of the relay nucleus of the peripheral visual system, the lateral geniculate nucleus (LGN) in the thalamus. Samuel Orton, a pioneer in the study of developmental dyslexia in the 1930s, persuaded some of his patients to donate their brains to medical science. Norman Geschwind and now Albert Galaburda and colleagues have taken over this brain bank and the detailed structure of some dyslexic brains has now been studied histologically. This has demonstrated that the magnocellular layers of the LGN are indeed disordered and the neurons some 30% smaller in area than in control brains (Livingstone et al. 1991; Galaburda and Livingstone 1993). Such differences are known to arise during the early development of the brain, during the phase of rapid neuronal growth and migration at the fourth or fifth month of foetal development. One could not wish for stronger evidence that the visual magnocellular system fails to develop quite normally in some people with dyslexia.

Magnocellular Function Predicts Orthographic Skill

Since our hypothesis is that impaired visual magnocellular function impedes reading, it is incumbent on us to show an association between subjects' motion sensitivity and their reading. Therefore we have been correlating RDK thresholds with reading ability. We have been able to show that visual motion sensitivity does indeed correlate strongly with reading ability (Witton et al. 1998; Talcott et al. 2000b). This is true not only in people with dyslexia, but over the whole range of reading ability. In both unselected primary school children and adults, whether dyslexic, poor readers, or good readers, the relationship holds, so that overall visual motion sensitivity accounts for about 25% of the variance in subjects' reading ability.

As we expected, motion sensitivity predicts visual orthographic skill best. We measure this using Olson's pseudo-homophone test (Olson et al. 1989). In this test we present on a computer screen two words side by side that sound the same but have different spellings, i.e., "rain" beside "rane." The subject is asked which is the correct spelling. Because the words sound the same, this task cannot be solved phonologically by sounding out the letters. The visual form or orthography of the word must be recalled correctly. Hence Talcott found that the correlation between visual motion sensitivity and performance in this pseudo-homophone test is very strong (Talcott et al. 2000b). Again this was true not only in people with dyslexia but across the whole range of reading abilities. Good spellers in this test had high motion sensitivity, whereas poor performers had low motion sensitivity. Likewise, we found that the correlation between subjects' motion sensitivity and their performance in Castle and Coltheart's (1993) test of the spelling of irregular words was very high, because spelling irregular words also depends on a good visual memory of their orthography.

In contrast, the correlation between subjects' visual motion sensitivity and tests of phonological skill, such as the ability to read nonsense words or to form Spoonerisms was lower. Of course orthographic and phonological skills are highly correlated. But, when we controlled statistically for their correlation we found that motion sensitivity continued to account for a high proportion of the variance in orthography, but now of course independently of phonology (Talcott et al. 2000b). In other words, motion sensitivity seems to account for children's orthographic skill independently of its relationship with their phonological skill, as you would expect if this basic visual function helps to determine how well the visual component of reading develops.

Binocular Control of Subjects with Dyslexia

However one problem that constantly bedevils the hypothesis that people with dyslexia have impaired magnocellular function, is that people find it very difficult to understand how a system devoted to detecting visual motion could possibly be relevant to reading (Hulme 1988). After all we don't have to track moving targets when reading; the page is usually stationary. In fact, however, the retinal images of print are very far from being stationary when you read; even during fixation the eyes are never perfectly stationary and so visual images are always moving over the retina. Good readers can compensate for this and the print remains stationary. But many dyslexic children complain that letters seem to move around when they are trying to read, i.e., their visual world is highly unstable (Fowler and Stein 1979).

The eyes remain fixated on individual words for only about 300 msecs. before saccading to the next. Even during the fixations however they are not absolutely stationary but move around by up to one degree of visual angle-equivalent to four or five letters' worth. In normal readers, the visual magnocellular system detects such unintended motion of the letters over the retina, "retinal slip," and this signal is used to help stabilize the eyes. For movements of less than one degree the magnocellular system further sharpens the image by computationally discounting the motion, "morphing" succeeding images that have moved on to each other. But it seems that many subjects with dyslexia fail to be able to stabilize their vision in these ways when reading, so that they tend to misidentify and transpose letters when attempting to read (Cornelissen et al. 1997).

Binocular Instability of Subjects with Dyslexia

I thought that the unstable visual perceptions that many children with dyslexia experience might result from the insensitivity of their visual magnocellular systems. To test this hypothesis we measured how accurately subjects with dyslexia and controls can fixate small targets the size of letters at the normal reading distance of about 30 cms. We found that the amplitude of the unintended eye movements made during attempts to fixate for three seconds was indeed much greater in the subjects with dyslexia than in the controls (Eden et al. 1994). Furthermore these movements were different in the two eyes so that the degree of binocular convergence varied randomly from moment to moment. This helped to explain why so many children with dyslexia complain not only that the letters move from side to side but also slide over each other and in and out of the plane of the page (Cornelissen et al. 1991, 1994). We found that the unstable binocular control of these children with dyslexia was also reflected in slower and less smooth vergence pursuit tracking of a target moving in depth, with a much greater tendency for vergence to break down to conjugate gaze, hence diplopia (Stein et al. 1988; Riddell et al. 1988, 1990). The high incidence of binocular instability in subjects with dyslexia has also been confirmed by Evans et al. (1994).

Thus, it seems that an important way in which the impaired magnocellular function of people with dyslexia might interfere with their reading may be by causing binocular instability. Because the eye movements of people with dyslexia are unintended and uncontrolled, they may be misinterpreted as movements of the letters. Because this instability often causes the two eyes' lines of sight to cross over each other, the letters may seem to move around, slide over each other, and to appear to change places.

Eye Patching

We reasoned that if this is so, then simply blanking out the vision of one eye might simplify the visual confusion and help these children to see the letters properly. This is exactly what we have found in four different trials (Stein and Fowler 1981, 1985; Cornelissen et al. 1992; Stein, Richardson, and Fowler 2000). In children with binocular instability, occluding the left eye for reading and close work helped them to permanently stabilize their fixation and thereby relieve their binocular perceptual confusions (Cornelissen et al. 1992). It also helped them to learn to read; their improvements were often dramatic. In our most recent double blind controlled trial of monocular occlusion in dyslexic children with binocular instability those who received the occlusion actually caught up with the reading age of their peers. In contrast those who did not receive occlusion and who did not gain binocular stability remained lagging 1.5 years behind their chronological age. Thus, our simple treatment achieved as much progress as far more costly phonological remediation techniques ever do.

After three months occlusion, not only had the children's reading improved to this great extent, but also they could now fixate stably with their two eyes, so that they no longer needed to wear the patch. We believe that this gain of binocular stability results from the magnocellular signals from the seeing eye now successfully routing themselves to control the muscles of that eye. This is called utrocular control (Ogle 1962) and it is crucial for the final stages of precise vergence control because it enables each eye to home in accurately on a target so that both can fixate properly on it.

So now we think we can explain how magnocellular function impacts on reading, and in particular how it helps children to develop orthographic skill. Poor readers have slightly impaired development of their magnocellular neurons. As a consequence, the dense magnocellular input that visuomotor centers in the PPC, superior colliculus, and cerebellum receive is both delayed and smeared in time. In consequence, utrocular control over the muscles controlling the eye that supplied the magnocellular input is less sharply focused in time and therefore less able to stabilize the eyes during each convergent fixation. Therefore, the eyes' lines of sight may cross over each other, hence the letters can appear to do so also. This is why these people with dyslexia tend to reverse the order of neighboring letters and to reverse the order of letter features, thus confusing ds with bs and ps with qs. These are precisely the kinds of error that we find in dyslexic people with unstable binocular control.

Auditory Transient System

Only about $2/3$ of subjects with dyslexia have significant visual problems, however. The remaining $1/3$ together with about half of those with visual symptoms, have, in addition, another major cause of reading difficulties, namely deficient ability to retrieve the sounds that letters stand for; hence their phonological analysis of words is slow and prone to errors. As described earlier, unfamiliar regular words have to be read by producing the sounds that each letter stands for, "sounding out" the letters, and then blending them to identify the word. Acquisition of this phonological skill is perhaps the most important and most difficult component of learning to read (Bradley and Bryant 1983; Snowling 1987; Liberman et al. 1974).

Sound Frequency Modulation

The cues that distinguish the different letter sounds are changes in the frequency and amplitude of speech sounds. Thus, the difference between /d/ and /b/ is that in /d /the 2nd and 3rd formants rise in frequency in the first 40 ms., but in /b/ they go down. Everything else is identical in the two sounds (Tallal 1980). Thus, phonological analysis draws very heavily on the ability of the auditory system to track frequency and amplitude changes, acoustic transients, accurately. As in the visual system, such processing can be assessed, using much simpler transients than those found in speech, for example by measuring subjects' sensitivity to sinusoidal frequency or amplitude modulations of a single sinusoidal tone. Therefore, we have been measuring people's sensitivity to frequency and amplitude modulations of simple tones to see whether this relates to their phonological abilities.

McAnally, Witton, and I (McAnally and Stein 1996; Stein and McAnally 1996; Witton et al. 1998) measured subjects' sensitivity to frequency modulations by asking subjects to listen to frequency modulated (warbling) tones and then adjusting the amount of warble, the modulation depth, until they could no longer distinguish this from a pure tone. Using 2, 20 and 40 Hz frequency modulations of a 500 Hz or 1000 Hz carrier stimulus we were able to show that groups of adults and children with dyslexia were significantly worse than matched controls at hearing these changes in frequency, i.e., they required significantly greater modulation depths. Again, however, there were some children with dyslexia who were just as good as controls at this task.

Phonological Skill is Predicted by FM Sensitivity

Because we expected this stimulus to mimic to some extent the phonological cues that enable people to distinguish letter sounds, we wished to correlate their FM sensitivity with their phonological ability. A convenient test of phonological skill for reading is to get subjects to read nonsense words, non-words, such as "tegwop." Such words have never been seen before and mean nothing, so their pronunciation cannot be obtained from their visual/orthographic form; they can only be read by applying letter/sound correspondence (phonological) rules properly. Performing this task thus depends mainly on rapid and accurate application of letter/ sound conversions.

We therefore measured the number of errors and the time our subjects' took to read a list of non-words and correlated this with their FM sensitivity. As expected this showed a very strong relationship in both children and adults, so that in a class of 30 normal 10-year olds, 2 Hz FM sensitivity accounted for over 50% of their variance in non-word reading (Talcott et al. 1999, 2000b). When we controlled for the variance shared with orthographic ability to allow for the fact that the subjects had to visualize the non-words in order to read them, FM sensitivity still accounted for a substantial proportion of non-word reading variance independently of orthography. Thus, high auditory FM sensitivity seems to enable children to develop strong phonological skills, whereas poor FM sensitivity prevents this, in the same way as high visual motion sensitivity promoted orthographic skill and low sensitivity prevented it.

Amplitude Modulation (AM)

In our lab, Peter Menell (Menell et al. 1999) and Caroline Witton (Witton et al. 2001) have also demonstrated that sensitivity to amplitude modulations is also important for developing phonological skill. Witton measured sensitivity to 20 Hz amplitude modulations and found not only that subjects with dyslexia are significantly less sensitive to these than controls, but also, as for FM sensitivity, she was able to show in both subjects with dyslexia and normal readers covering the whole range of reading ability, that AM sensitivity correlates with their phonological skill as measured by non-word reading. The auditory system processes 2 Hz FM and 20 Hz AM stimuli rather differently; so what is particularly interesting is that the subjects performed differently in the two tests; their scores did not correlate with each other. Thus, performance in the 2 Hz FM and 20 Hz AM tests accounted for independent components of the subjects' variance in phonological ability. In other words our FM and AM tests probably relate to the development of different aspects of phonological skill. Two Hz FM is quite slow and represents the frequency of syllable production and intonation rather than individual phonemes, whereas 20 Hz is clearly in the range of the transients that enable us to distinguish between phonemes.

Whereas the magnocells in the visual system form a clearly separate entity responsible for processing visual transients, there is no such anatomically defined magnocellular division in the auditory system. We cannot attribute so easily the FM and AM deficits that we have found in poor readers to impaired development of an auditory magnocellular system. Nevertheless there are large celled magnocellular divisions of all the auditory relay nuclei; and there is evidence that these large neurons are specially responsible for following changes in frequency or amplitude of acoustic signals with time (Trussel 1998). There probably is an auditory magnocellular system whose function is to process auditory transients such as those important for phonological analysis, but it is not such an anatomically separate system as is the case for the peripheral part of the visual magnocellular system.

This auditory analogy with the visual magnocellular system received an additional boost from further neuropathological studies by Galaburda and colleagues (1994) in dyslexic brains post mortem. They found that, as in the LGN, the magnocellular division of the medial geniculate nucleus (MGN) which is the auditory relay nucleus of the thalamus, is disordered in the dyslexic brains, particularly on the left, i.e., the side that projects to the language hemisphere.

Etiology of People with Dyslexia's Low Sensitivity to Sensory Transients

In summary, people with dyslexia seem to have impaired processing of both visual and auditory transients, because they tend to have impaired development of magnocellular neurons in both the visual and auditory systems. These impairments help to explain their failure to develop adequate orthographic and phonological skills, respectively. Of course the question arises why they fail to develop properly the sensitivity to these sensory transients that is required for learning to read. Those who argue that dyslexia is a specifically linguistic problem suggest that the low level auditory and visual deficits are purely epiphenomena, not on the main causal chain leading to reading problems (Studdert-Kennedy and Mody 1995).

But, this argument seems implausible given the striking correlations that we have found between these sensory deficits and the cognitive skills required for reading. Also, our finding that setting right the binocular instability associated with the visual magnocellular deficit very greatly improves dyslexics' reading again strongly suggests a causal connection (Stein, Richardson, and Fowler 2000), as does Merzenich and Tallal's (1996) finding that auditory training using artificially slowed frequency transients can improve children's ability to hear them, and that this improves their ability to make phonological discriminations, hence their reading. It is much more likely that there are significant differences in the development of the magnocellular systems in brains of people with dyslexia that blunt their transient sensitivity, hence compromising their ability to develop orthographic and phonological skills. There is now a great deal of evidence for this view; and a plausible mechanism for the development of these differences can even be sketched out. The evidence is genetic, immunological, and neurological.

Genetic Linkage

It is well known that dyslexia tends to run in families, and comparison of dizygotic and monozygotic twins' reading abilities has shown that it has a heritability of c. 60%, i.e., 60% of the variance in reading abilities can be attributed to the alleles they inherit (Pennington 1991). This is a high value that is similar to the heritability of height and cognitive abilities such as verbal ability or general intelligence, but much higher than the heritability of conditions that tend to be seen as much more familial, such as diabetes or heart attacks. We have taken advantage of the large number of people with dyslexia we have seen over the years to collect, so far, over 100 families in which two or more children have severe reading problems. We retest the children in standardized orthographic and phonological tests and take blood for DNA analysis from the children and their parents. In collaboration with Professors Tony Monaco and Simon Fisher, we then look for linkage of the reading scores treated as quantitative traits (QTLs) to chromosomal markers. We are currently in the process of carrying out a screen of the whole human genome to find which sites link to reading ability; but we have already confirmed (Fisher et al. 1999) the findings of Cardon et al. (1994) and Grigorenko et al. (1997) from smaller studies carried out in Colorado and Connecticut respectively, that both phonological and orthographic impairments link to a site on the short arm of chromosome 6 near the Tumour Necrosis Factor and Major Histocompatibility Complex (MHC) immunological sites. Linkage to this region may turn out to be very significant as there is accumulating evidence that an immunological mechanism may contribute to the impaired development of magnocells in subjects with dyslexia.

Magno Surface Markers

Visual magnocells express specific surface antigens that are recognized by antibodies such as Cat 301, and these same antigens are found on large cells all over the nervous system (Hockfield and Sur 1990). For example they are also expressed in the magnocellular nuclei of the auditory system, on the large cells in the dorsal column somaesthetic nuclei, the hippocampus, and on other magno cells throughout the brain. One site of special interest is the cerebellum. This structure is the brain's main timing device, the brain's autopilot, and it receives dense input from all the magno systems throughout the brain (Stein and Glickstein 1992). Thus magnocells probably represent a distinct cerebral system with a separate developmental lineage, common surface antigens and the heavy myelination and rapid membrane dynamics that confer upon them their enhanced sensitivity to temporal transients. But their common surface antigens make them all vulnerable to antibody attack in autoimmune individuals.

Generalized Magnocellular System

Therefore, we were not surprised to find that there is a strong tendency, especially in normal readers, for auditory and visual transient sensitivity to covary in individuals (Witton et al. 1998). This again suggests that the development of auditory and visual magnocells may be under some sort of common control. Recently Corriveau and Shatz (1998) have found that Class 1 MHC molecules play an important part in the development of visual magnocellular neurons in the cat LGN and also in the hippocampus. Because Hockfield's work suggests that all magnocells throughout the brain derive from a common developmental lineage, it is reasonable to speculate that the development of all of them is regulated by the MHC system. Hence our finding that reading disability is genetically linked to a site close to the MHC complex on chromosome 6 takes on added significance, as does the evidence that people with dyslexia and their families very often demonstrate mildly abnormal immunological responses. They have a higher incidence of asthma, eczema, hay fever, and other immune conditions than controls, and families with serious autoimmune conditions such as systemic lupus erythematosus (SLE) often have dyslexic relatives as well (Hughdahl and Satz 1990).

Thus, as Miles (1983, 1993) first emphasized, dyslexics' literacy problems should really be considered just part of a much more generalized neurodevelopmental syndrome; and we now believe that all its manifestations may result from impaired development of magnocells throughout the brain. We speculate that it results from genetically mediated, disordered immunological regulation of their development in utero. This would explain not only the auditory and visual transient deficits that directly undermine the development of phonological and orthographic skills, but also the plethora of other problems that beset people with dyslexia. Their legendary clumsiness, impaired coordination and balance may be attributed to abnormal cerebellar function. The cerebellum as the brain's main timing device, receives dense inputs from all the magnocellular systems. There is now a great deal of evidence that it is deficient in dyslexia (Fawcett et al. 1996; Rae et al. 1998; Nicolson et al. 1999) together with other conditions such as autism (Courchesne et al. 1994; Dennis et al. 1999). Therefore the reduced sequencing and timing ability of dyslexics may be attributed partly to impaired cerebellar function, particularly on the right side which connects with the left (language) hemisphere. In addition there is probably reduced magnocellular input to the left hemisphere (Rae et al. 1998; Klingberg et al. 2000), which should receive more magno input than the right in order to mediate the precise timing of auditory and visual transients required for literacy. Deficient magno input to the left hemisphere may in turn lead to impaired hemispheric specialization; and thus altered magnocellular neuronal development may help to explain people with dyslexia's relative failure to establish fixed hemispheric dominance. This may underlie their tendency to problems with telling left from right, their mixed handedness, their unfixed eye dominance and many other cognitive symptoms. In short, genetically determined, immunologically mediated, mild magnocellular deficiency might explain all the wide variety of problems that people with dyslexia face.

REFERENCES

Bradley, L., and Bryant, P. 1983. Categorizing sounds and learning to read—A causal connection. *Nature* 301:419–21.

Cardon L. R., Smith S. D., Fulker D. W., Kimberling W. J., Pennington B. F., and Defries J. C. 1994. Quantitative trait locus for reading disability on Chromosome 6. *Science* 266:76.

Castles, A., and Coltheart, M. 1993. Varieties of developmental dyslexia. *Cognition* 47:149–80.

Cornelissen, P., Bradley, L., Fowler, M. S., and Stein, J. F. 1991. What children see affects how they read. *Developmental Medicine and Child Neurology* 33:755–62.

Cornelissen, P., Bradley, L., Fowler, M. S., and Stein, J. F. 1992. Covering one eye affects how some children read. *Developmental Medicine and Child Neurology* 34:296–304.

Cornelissen, P. L., Hansen, P. C., Hutton, J. L., Evangelinou, V., and Stein, J. F. 1997. Magnocellular visual function and children's single word reading. *Vision Research* 38:471–82.

Cornelissen, P. L., Richardson, A. R., Mason, A., Fowler, M. S., and Stein, J. F. 1994. Contrast sensitivity and coherent motion detection measured at photopic luminance levels in dyslexics and controls. *Vision Research* 35:1483–94.

Corriveau, R., and Shatz, C. 1998. Regulation of Class 1 MHC gene expression in the developing and mature CNS by neural activity. *Neuron* 21:505–20.

Courchesne, E., Townsend, J., and Akshoomoff, N. A. 1994. Impaired attention in autistic and cerebellar patients. *Behavioral Neuroscience* 108:848–65.

Demb, J. B., Boynton, G. M., Best, M., and Heeger, D. J. 1998. Psychophysical evidence for a magnocellular deficit in dyslexics. *Vision Research* 38:1555–59.

Demb, J. B., Boynton, G. M., and Heeger, D. J. 1997. Brain activation in visual cortex predicts individual differences in reading performance. *Proceedings of the New York Academy of Sciences* 94:13363–6.

Demonet, J. F. R., Wise, R., and Frackowiack, R. S. J. 1993. Language function explored by poistron emission tomography. *Human Brain Mapping* 1:39–45.

Dennis, M., Hetherington, C. R., Spiegler B. J., and Barnes, M. A. 1999. Functional consequences of cerebellar lesions in childhood. In *The Changing Nervous System*, ed. S. H. Broman. Oxford: Oxford University Press.

Eden, G. F., Stein, J. F., Wood, H. M., and Wood, F. B. 1994. Differences in eye movements and reading problems in dyslexic and normal children. *Vision Research* 34(10):1345–58.

Eden, G. F., VanMeter, J. W., Rumsey, J. W., Maisog, J., and Zeffiro, T. A. 1996. Functional MRI reveals differences in visual motion processing in individuals with dyslexia. *Nature* 382:66–69.

Ellis, A. W. 1992. *Reading, Writing and Dyslexia*. Erlbaum: London.

Enroth Kugel, C., and Robson, J. G. 1966. The contrast sensitivity of retinal ganglion cells in the cat. *Journal of Physiology* 187:517–52.

Evans, B. J. W., Drasdo, N., and Richards, I. L. 1994. Investigation of accommodative and binocular function in dyslexia. *Ophthalmic and Physiological Optics* 145:5–20.

Fawcett, A., Nicolson, R. I., and Dean, P. 1996. Impaired performance of children with dyslexia on a range of cerebellar tasks. *Annnals of Dyslexia* 46:259–83.

Fisher, S., Marlowe, A., Lamb, J., Maestrinin, E., Williams, D., Richardson, A., Weeks, D., Stein, J. F., and Monaco, A. 1999. A quantitative trait locus on chromosome 6p influences different aspects of developmental dyslexia. *American Journal of Human Genetics* 64:146–56.

Fowler, S., and Stein, J. F. 1979 New evidence for ambilaterality in visual dyslexia. *Neuroscience Letters* 3:214.

Galaburda, A. M., and Livingstone, M. 1993. Evidence for a magnocellular defect in developmental dyslexia. In Temporal Information Processing in the Nervous System, eds. P. Tallal, A. M. Galaburda, R. R. Llinas, and C. von Euler. *Annals of the New York Academy of Sciences* 682:70–82.

Galaburda, A. M., Menard, M. T., and Rosen, G. D. 1994 Evidence for aberrant auditory anatomy in developmental dyslexia. *Proceeding of the National Academy of Sciences* (USA). 91:8010–13.

Grigorenko et al. 1997 Susceptibility loci for distinct components of developmental dyslexia on chromosomes 6 and 15. *American Journal of Human Genetics* 60:27–39.

Hockfield, S., and Sur, M. 1990. Monoclonal CAT 301 identifies Y cells in cat LGN. *Journal of Clinical Neurology* 300:320–30.

Hugdahl, K., Synnevag, B., and Satz, P. 1990. Immune and autoimmune disorders in dyslexic children. *Neuropsychologia* 28:673–9.

Hulme, C. 1988. The implausibility of low level visual deficits as a cause of reading disability. *Cognitive Neuropsychology* 5:369–74.

Klingberg, T., Hedehus, M., Temple, E., Salz, T., Gabrieli, J. D. E., Moseley, M. E., and Poldrack, R. A. 2000. Microstructure of temporo-parietal white matter as a basis of reading ability: Evidence from diffusion tensor magnetic resonance imaging. *Neuron* 25:493–500.

Lehmkuhle, S., Garzia, R. P., Turner, L., Hash, T., and Baro, J. A. 1992. The effects of uniform-field flicker on visual evoked potentials in children with reading disability. *Invest Ophthalmology and Vision Science* 33(4): 718–24.

Liberman, I. Y., Shankweiler, D., Fischer, F. W., and Carter, B. 1974. Explicit syllable and phoneme segmentation in the young child. *Journal of Exceptional Child Psychology* 18:201–12.

Livingstone, M. S., Rosen, G. D., Drislane, F. W., and Galaburda, A. M. 1991. Physiological and anatomical evidence for a magnocellular defect in developmental dyslexia. *Proceedings of the National Academy of Sciences* (USA) 88:7943–7.

Lovegrove, W. J., Martin, F., Blackwood, M., and Badcock, D. 1980. Specific reading difficulty: Differences in contrast sensitivity as a function of spatial frequency. *Science* 210:439–40.

McAnally K. I., and Stein J. F. 1996. Abnormal auditory transient brainstem function in dyslexia. *Proceedings of the Royal Society of B.* 263: 961–5.

Maddock, H., Richardson, A., and Stein, J. F. 1992. Reduced and delayed visual evoked potentials in dyslexics. *Journal of Physiology* 459:130P.

Martin, F., and Lovegrove, W. 1987. Flicker contrast sensitivity in normal and specifically disabled readers. *Perception* 16:215–21.

Mason, A., Cornelissen, P., Fowler, M. S., and Stein, J. F. 1993. Contrast sensitivity, ocular dominance and reading disability. *Clinical Visual Science* 8(4):345–53.

Menell P, McAnall, K. I., and Stein J. F. 1999. Psychophysical and physiological responses to amplitude modulations in dyslexia. *Journal of Speech and Hearing Research* 42:797–803.

Merrigan, W. H., and Maunsell, J. R. 1993. How parallel are the primate visual pathways? Annals of Rev. *Neuroscience* 16:369–402.

Merzenich, M. M., Jenkins, W. M., Johnston, P., Schreiner, C., Miller, S., and Tallal, P. 1996. Temporal processing deficits of language-learning impaired children ameliorated by stretching speech. *Science* 271:77–81.

Miles T. 1983. *Dyslexia, the Pattern of Difficulties.* (Second ed.) Ed. Granada 1993. Whurr Wyke: London.

Milner, A. D., and Goodale, M. A. 1995. *The Visual Brain in Action.* Oxford: Oxford University Press.

Morgan, W. P. 1896 Word blindness. *British Medical Journal* 2:1378.

Newsome, W. T., Britten, K. H., and Movshon, J. A. 1989. Neuronal correlates of a perceptual decision. *Nature* 341:52–4.

Nicolson, R. I, Fawcett, A. J, Berry, E. L., Jenkins, I. H., Dean, P., and Brooks, D. J. 1999. Motor learning difficulties and abnormal cerebellar activation in dyslexic adults. *Lancet* 353:43–47.

Ogle, K. 1962. The Optical Space Sense. In *The Eye*, ed. H. Davson, Vol.IV. New York and London: Academic Press.

Olson, R. K., Wise, B., Connors, F., Rack, J., and Fulker, D. 1989. Specific deficits in component reading and language skills. *Journal of Learning Disabilities* 22:339–48.

Pennington, B. F., ed. 1991. *Reading Disabilities: Genetic and Neurological Influences.* Dordrecht, The Netherlands: Kluwer.

Rae, C., Martin, A. L., Dixon, R. M., Blamire, A. M., Thompson, C. H., Styles, P., Talcott, J., Richardson, A. J., and Stein, J. F. 1998. Metabolic abnormalities in developmental dyslexia detected by 1H magnetic resonance spectroscopy. *Lancet* 351:1849–52.

Riddell, P., Fowler, M. S., and Stein, J. F. 1988. Vergence eye movements and dyslexia. *Dyslexia Contact* 7(2):5–6.

Riddell, P., Fowler, M. S., and Stein, J. F. 1990. Spatial discrimination in children with poor vergence control. *Perceptual and Motor Skills* 70:707–18.

Seidenburg, M. S. 1993. A connectionist modelling approach to word recognition and dyslexia. *Psychological Science* 4:299–304.

Shapley, R., and Perry, V. H. 1986. Cat and monkey retinal ganglion cells and their functional roles. *TINS* 9:229–35.

Skottun, B. C. 2000. The magnocellular deficit theory of dyslexia; The evidence from contrast sensitivity. *Vision Research* 40:111–27.

Snowling, M. 1981. Phonemic deficits in developmental dyslexia. *Psychological Research* 43:219–34.

Snowling, M. 1987. *Dyslexia: A Cognitive Developmental Perspective.* Oxford: Blackwells.

Stein, J. F., and Fowler, S. 1981. Visual dyslexia. *Trends in Neuroscience* 4:77–80.

Stein, J. F., and Fowler, M. S. 1985. Effect of monocular occlusion on visuomotor perception and reading in dyslexic children. *The Lancet* 13 July, 69–73.

Stein, J. F. 1992. The representation of egocentric space in the posterior parietal cortex. *Behavioral Brain Science* 15:691–700.

Stein, J. F., and Glickstein, M. 1992. The role of the cerebellum in the visual guidance of movement. *Physiological Reviews* 72:967–1018.

Stein, J. F., and McAnally, K. I. 1996. Impaired auditory temporal processing in dyslexics. *Irish Journal of Psychology* 16:220–8.

Stein, J. F., and Talcott, J. B. 1999. The magnocellular theory of dyslexia. *Dyslexia* 5: 59–78.

Stein, J. F., and Walsh, V. 1997. To see but not to read; The magnocellular theory of dyslexia. *TINS* 20:147–52.

Stein, J. F., Riddell, P., and Fowler, M. S. 1988. Disordered vergence eye movement control in dyslexic children. *British Journal of Ophthalmology* 72:162–6.

Stein, J. F., Richardson, A. J., and Fowler, M. S. 2000. Monocular occlusion can improve binocular control and reading in dyslexic children. *Brain* 123.

Stein, J. F., Talcott, J. B., and Walsh, V. 2000. Controversy about the visual magnocellular deficit in developmental dyslexics. *Trends in Cognitive Science* 4:209–11.

Studdert-Kennedy, M., and Mody, M. 1995. Auditory temporal perception deficits in the reading-impaired: A critical review of the evidence. *Psychonomic Bulletin and Review* 2: 508–14.

Talcott, J. B., Hansen, P. C., Willis-Owen, C., McKinnell, I. W., Richardson, A. J., and Stein, J. F. 1998. Visual magnocellular impairment in adult developmental dyslexics. *Neuro-ophthalmology* 20:187–201.

Talcott, J. B., Witton, C., McClean, M., Hansen, P. C., Rees, A., Green, G. G. R., and Stein, J. F. 1999. Can sensitivity to auditory frequency modulation predict children's phonological and reading skills? *Neuroreport* 10:2045–50.

Talcott, J. B., Hansen, P. C., Elikem, L. A., and Stein, J. F. 2000a. Visual motion sensitivity in dyslexia: evidence for temporal and motion energy integration deficits. *Neuropsychologia* 38:935–43.

Talcott, J. B., Witton, C., McClean, M., Hansen, P. C., Rees, A., Green, G. G. R., and Stein, J. F. 2000b. Visual and auditory transient sensitivity determines word decoding skills. *Proceedings of the National Academy of Sciences* 97:2952

Tallal, P. 1980. Auditory temporal perception, phonics and reading disabilities in children. *Brain and Language* 9:182–98.

Trussell, L. O. 1998. Cellular mechanisms for preservation of timing in central auditory pathways. *Current Opinion in Neurobiology* 7:487–492.

Ungerleider, L. G., and Mishkin, M. 1982. Two cortical visual systems. In *The Analysis of Visual Behavior*, eds. D. J. Ingle, M. A. Goodale, and R. J. W. Mansfield. Cambridge, MA: MIT Press.

Witton, C., Talcott, J. B., Hansen, P. C., Richardson, A. J., Griffiths, T. D., Rees, A., Stein, J. F., and Green, G. G. R. 1998. Sensitivity to dynamic auditory and visual stimuli predicts nonword reading ability in both dyslexic and normal readers. *Current Biology* 8: 791–7.

Witton, C., Talcott, J. B., Staskley, C. J., Sissnet, C. J., and Stein, J. F. 2000. A complex relationship between auditory temporal processing and phonological skill. Submitted.

Chapter • **2**

Speed and Temporal Processing in Dyslexia

Angela J. Fawcett and
Roderick I. Nicolson

There is now extensive evidence that children who are dyslexic process many kinds of information more slowly than children who are not dyslexic and are of equivalent age and ability—see the chapter by Wolf and Bowers in this book for an excellent summary of much of the literature. An earlier summary is given in Fawcett and Nicolson (1994). In this chapter, we address two key questions. First, where is the "bottleneck" in information processing that leads to this loss of speed? Is there a single bottleneck, such as in sensory input, as advocated by proponents of sensory processing deficits (Lovegrove, Garzia, and Nicholson 1990; Stein and Walsh 1997; Tallal, Miller, and Fitch 1993)? Does the problem arise primarily via the need for motor output (Rudel 1985; Wolff et al. 1990)? Is there some "central" processing deficit, and if so, is it limited to speech-related tasks or is it endemic to any tasks involving skill automatization (Nicolson and Fawcett 1990)? Second, given the bottlenecks found, what are the theoretical implications for the cause(s) of dyslexia, and for the design of remediation programs?

In order to attempt to maintain coherence in this chapter, and to avoid unnecessary duplication with other chapters in this volume, we attempt to "tell the story" of the research we have undertaken on this issue over the past decade in our laboratory in Sheffield, rather than providing a comprehensive review of the area. It is important to note from the outset that this research was completed with very limited resources, in the United Kingdom. Consequently, we elected from the outset to work only with children with "pure" dyslexia (and appropriate controls) uncontaminated by factors such as low IQ, economic disadvantage, or ADHD. We used the standard exclusionary criterion of "children of normal or above normal IQ (operationalized as IQ of 90 or more on the Wechsler Intelligence Scale for Children), without known primary emotional or behavioral or socioeconomic problems, whose reading age (RA) was at least 18 months behind their chronological age (CA)." None of the subjects showed evidence of ADHD as measured on the DSM-IIIR scales (1987).[1] We considered it likely that our results would be more clear cut than those of larger studies that have chosen to use "epidemiological" samples more representative of the prevalence of dyslexia throughout the population, which include a high proportion of children, not only with dyslexia, but also with other comorbid disabilities. This should be more valuable for identifying the underlying cause(s) of dyslexia, but perhaps less valuable for identifying appropriate intervention and support procedures (Nicolson 1996).

SPEED OF PROCESSING AND DYSLEXIA

Although lack of fluency in reading is certainly a key characteristic of dyslexia, for many years there has also been extensive evidence of difficulties in speed of processing for almost all stimuli, including those for which sensory delay is unlikely to be involved. The earliest evidence came from the "Rapid Automatized Naming" technique (Denckla and Rudel 1976), in which the child has to say the names of items or colors on a page of simple pictures. Children with dyslexia show robust speed deficits on these tasks. Recently, a synthesis of phonological and speed problems (Wolf and Bowers 1999) has been proposed. This hypothesis holds that phonological deficits and naming-speed deficits represent two separate sources of reading disability, and that developmental dyslexia is characterized by both phonological and naming speed "core" deficits. Naturally, the most severe impairments are found in those children who show both of these deficits. This is the framework within which this book is written.

It may be seen from the summary above that one of the more striking features of the performance profile for children with dyslexia is an impairment in speed in almost any skill. Anecdotal

---

[1]The DSM-IIIR assessment for ADHD involves 14 simple yes/no questions with a "yes" on at least 8 being the minimal criterion for diagnosis of weak ADHD.

reports suggest this lack of fluency may characterize dyslexic performance across a range of skills (see e.g., Miles 1983). This impairment may be clearly seen in analysis of scores on the Wechsler Intelligence Scale for Children tests (Wechsler 1976, 1992) widely used in the diagnosis of dyslexia. The performance of children with dyslexia on the individual components typically shows an abnormally spiky profile, reflecting a distinctive pattern of strengths and weaknesses, with impairments in Arithmetic, Coding, Information, and Digit Span (Newton, Thomson, and Richards 1976). Digit Span and Coding are both linked to speed of processing. It is recognized that, in addition to phonological effects, developmental improvements in digit span co-vary with those in processing speed (Nicolson 1981), possibly via the mechanism of articulation rate (Baddeley, Thomson, and Buchanan 1975; Hulme et. al. 1984). Furthermore there is evidence that the reduced memory span of children with dyslexia is accompanied by an equivalent slowness of articulation rate (Avons and Hanna 1995; Nicolson, Fawcett, and Baddeley 1991). The Coding sub-test requires the user to copy examples of a particular (non-alphabetic) symbol in a list of such symbols. It clearly implicates speed of processing, and indeed Coding is a major component (50%) of the WISC-III "speed of processing" index—an index that is characteristically impaired in dyslexia.

STUDY 1: "MENTAL CHRONOMETRY" FOR DYSLEXIA

Given the established deficits in rapid naming (see above), it was established by 1990 that subjects with dyslexia will demonstrate deficiencies in speed of information processing on any task that demands continuous speeded access to lexical information. In view of the central role of information processing speed in cognitive skills, we were surprised that there appeared to be no reports of direct investigations of speed in the literature on dyslexia. One of the major achievements of cognitive psychology over the past 20 years was the development of a systematic procedure for administering a systematic sequence of reaction time tests, taking simpler and simpler materials, and looking for the stage at which anomalies first disappeared (Posner 1978). Consequently, we designed a series of experiments (Nicolson and Fawcett 1994a) using this strategy in the hope that at some point we would find a cutoff point where tasks of lesser complexity would show no deficit, whereas more complex tasks would result in a deficit—that is, the point at which performance first became abnormal. If this point lay where lexical material first appeared, this would provide further strong converging evidence for the phonological deficit hypothesis, whereas a continuing deficit with non-lexical material would indicate that the underlying cause lay deeper. Indeed, if deficits occurred right down to a simple reaction to a tone, this would suggest an underlying sensory processing problem.

We established in pilot studies that children with dyslexia showed the expected speed deficit in linguistically based tasks. Consequently, in an attempt to find normal performance, we administered increasingly simple tasks—lexical decision, choice reaction, and finally simple reaction to a tone. First, in the lexical decision task, subjects were presented auditorily with a word (or, equally probably, a morphologically valid non-word created by altering the first consonant) and had to say, as quickly as possible, "Yes" (if it was a word, such as "shop") or "No" (if it was a non-word, such as "thop"). We were interested in the speed of their response. In both reaction time experiments, the children sat with a single button in their preferred hand, and their task was to press it as quickly as possible whenever they heard a low tone. In the simple reaction task (SRT), no other tone was ever presented, but in the selective choice reaction (SCRT) task, there was an equal probability of a high tone being presented. If the high tone was presented, the subject simply had to do nothing. These are established experimental tasks introduced by Donders well over a century ago. His rationale was that the only difference between the tasks was the need to classify the stimulus before responding in the SCRT trials, and he argued that subtracting the simple reaction time from the SCRT time gave an estimate of "stimulus classification" time. Most subsequent research has preferred the choice reaction (for a two-choice reaction, the subject has two buttons, and presses the left button for the low tone and the right button for the high tone, say). Unfortunately, children with dyslexia have problems distinguishing left and right, and so any deficit in a choice reaction might plausibly be attributed to left/right confusions. The comparison between SCRT and SRT is not subject to this type of problem since only one hand is used.

Like other researchers in the area, we have found that one of the major problems of working with children with dyslexia is the heterogeneity of their performance. These differences are compounded by qualitative differences in the overlay of learned skills, and the maturation process itself. In order to control for these factors, we monitored longitudinal changes by using two age groups of children with dyslexia (mean ages 15 and 11 years), together with both reading age match and chronological age match control groups (mean ages 15, 11, and 8 years). We shall refer to the dyslexic and control groups as Dys 15 and Dys 11, Cont 15, Cont 11, and Cont 8, respectively. Note that the Cont 11 group served as the chronological age match for the Dys 11 group and also as the reading age match for the Dys 15 group. The Cont 8 group served as reading age controls for Dys 11. The results for simple reaction, selective choice reaction, and lexical access are shown in figure 1, plotted on the same graph to allow easy comparison.

On the simple reactions, the older children, whether dyslexic or control, were significantly faster than the 11-year-old children, who were faster than the 8-year-old children. There was a significant effect of age but not of dyslexia. When we compared the two dyslexic groups with their reading age controls, we found an effect of both age and dyslexia. In this case, however, the dyslexic groups were *faster* than their reading age controls. This pattern of results shows the well-known improvement in reaction time with age, but demonstrates no effect of dyslexia whatsoever.

On the selective choice reactions, by contrast, there were highly significant differences between the groups. The children with dyslexia performed significantly more slowly and less accurately than their age-matched controls, and at the level of their reading age-matched controls.

For lexical decisions, the children with dyslexia again performed significantly slower than their age-matched controls, and at the level of their reading age-matched controls, with no difference in accuracy. However, a further series of analyses on the lexical decision data was needed to check that the effect we had found did not derive from a subset of the items presented. Accordingly, we collapsed the data across the subjects in the groups, to perform

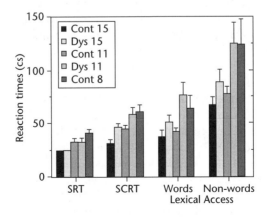

Figure 1. Reaction times for simple reactions, selective choice reactions, and lexical access.

a "by item" analysis. This showed a similar pattern of results to our standard analysis, but interestingly enough, a stronger pattern of results emerged, with the dyslexic groups now significantly worse than their reading age controls on the words.

The results of this study were particularly intriguing, There appeared to be a progressive relative penalty for our children with dyslexia as the tasks grew more demanding, starting with normal performance on the SRT, to performance at reading age level for SCRT to performance below RA level for lexical access.

In theoretical terms, the normal SRT suggests that not only their cognitive and metacognitive skills but also their motor responses were unimpaired. Consequently the most likely locus deficit of people with dyslexia appears to be the time needed to identify the stimulus ("perceptual decision impairment"). On the other hand, one might equally plausibly suggest that although the stimuli are classified just as quickly, the "central executive" simply takes longer to make the correct decision ("central executive impairment"). In practice, unfortunately, the two hypotheses are difficult to distinguish using the "behavioral" RT methodology. Consequently, we turned to a more direct investigation of the SCRT.

STUDY 2: P300 AUDITORY EVOKED RESPONSE AND THE SCRT

In principle, event-related potentials (ERP) offer the potential for identifying whether this slowing is attributable entirely to stimulus categorization problems, or whether there is some response selection component. In ERP research, a set of electrodes is attached to selected points on the subject's skull, and the electrical activity following some external event (presentation of a stimulus) is then monitored. SCRTs have been extensively studied using ERPs, and there is a robust finding that in these types of task the ERP trace shows a broad, positive component, peaking around 300 ms, and this peak is known as the P300 (or alternatively as P3). Both the origin and the functional role of the P300 remain active research frontiers (Jolicoeur 1999; Woodward et. al. 1991). Although the P300 amplitude has been most researched, the P300 latency is of more direct relevance here, in that the latency is thought to provide an index of stimulus classification speed uncontaminated by response selection factors (Coles, Gratton, and Fabiani 1990).

In the study (Fawcett et. al. 1993), eleven subjects, 6 dyslexic and 5 control, were selected from our older panels of dyslexic and control 16-year-old children, and participated in the experiment with fully informed consent. They were paid for participation. All children had an IQ of 90 or above, and had no known emotional or neurological problems. The children with dyslexia had been clinically diagnosed as dyslexic several years previously and all had a reading age at least 18 months lower than their chronological age, whereas the controls were all reading at or around their age. Furthermore, availability of their SRT and SCRT allowed us to match the groups on SRT.

The experiments were conducted using a Nicolet Pathfinder II system that was programmed to deliver binaural pure tone stimuli in an "oddball" SCRT paradigm. Subjects were requested to respond only to the rare tone (4000 Hz) and not to the frequent tone (1000 Hz). Potentials recorded within 750 ms after stimulation were averaged separately for the frequent and rare tones. Samples contaminated by excessive artifact were automatically rejected. To ensure reproducibility, two consecutive series comprising 20% rare and 80% frequent tones, presented in a pseudorandom sequence, were averaged until 100 artifact-free samples had been collected. In one subject with dyslexia, it was impossible to generate artifact-free data and the results were excluded from the analysis. Recordings were made using Ag/AgCl electrodes. Skin-electrode impedances were less than 5 Kohms. Potentials were recorded from Cz (10-20 system) referred to linked mastoids. An earth was located at Fpz. Subjects reclined in a comfortable chair with their eyes closed. They were asked to tap with their forefinger on hearing the rare tone. Recording and analysis were carried out by clinicians who were unaware of the subjects' diagnosis. An experimenter who knew the children was present in a support role.

Latencies to the N1 and P2 peaks were measured for the frequent tones, and to the N2 and P3 (P300) peaks for the rare tones. The amplitude differences between these peaks were also measured, namely N1-P2 and N2-P3. Figure 2 shows representative traces for a subject with dyslexia and a control subject. The clinicians attempted to separate the groups, blind to their status, on the basis of the individual data. By ranking the P3 (rare) latencies, all ten subjects were correctly assigned between the two categories. Ranking of amplitudes did not provide a separation between the groups. Mann-Whitney statistical analysis revealed two significant differences between the groups, namely that the dyslexic group had significantly longer N2 (rare) and P3 (rare) latencies [$z = 2.19$, $p <. 05$ and $z = 2.61$, $p <. 01$ respectively].

In summary, the group of children with dyslexia showed a temporal processing speed deficit compared with same age controls in P300 latency in selective choice reaction to auditory tones. The

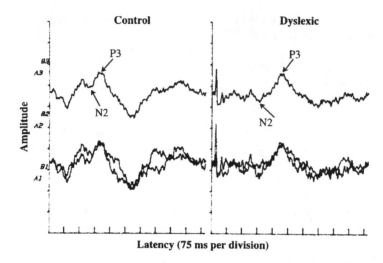

Figure 2. Auditory ERP Traces for a control child and a dyslexic child.

differences between the groups were sufficient to allow a differential diagnosis purely on the basis of the ERP data. Furthermore, the latencies correlated highly with selective choice reaction latencies obtained in earlier experimentation. The data provide convergent evidence that the deficit is not attributable to motor response selection or execution, and appears to be linked to the need to make a discrimination between stimuli. This is particularly significant in that it provides further evidence that children with dyslexia have a deficit in response categorization even for non-linguistic stimuli.

Since this experiment was completed, ERP's using the oddball paradigm have become more widely used in dyslexia research (Leppanen and Lyytinen 1997), with similar findings to the above study. Interestingly, it has been claimed that it is possible to identify differences in response to speech syllables even for infants from families with a history of dyslexia (e.g., Leppanen et al. 1999). However, the majority of ERP research in dyslexia has been with literacy-related tasks (e.g., Taylor and Keenan 1999), and so is more difficult to interpret in terms of fundamental rapid processing mechanisms.

Ongoing visual research in our laboratory (Shankardass et. al. 1999) has attempted to dissociate the sensory processing aspects of ERP latency (the N1 wave) from the central processing component (the P3 wave). An analogous visual procedure to the auditory oddball above has indicated that the N1 wave is not slowed (either for the rare or the common stimulus) but that the P3 wave is slowed (for the common stimulus) for the children with dyslexia. This suggests that the locus of the latency increase is in terms of central processing, a finding consistent with a recent MEG study (Helenius et. al. 1999) which concluded that "early visual processing is intact for dyslexic readers," showing that this pattern of results obtains in a different modality. Clearly the ERP and MEG approaches provide a fruitful source of data on the latency of processing stages in dyslexia, but a great deal more careful research needs to be undertaken before the theoretical implications are fully established. It may be, for instance, that sensory processing subtypes may be identified that show a specific impairment in sensory processing latency. Nonetheless, the evidence to date is consistent with the generalization that the speed deficit in dyslexia lies in the classification, not the perception, of stimuli.

STUDY 3: BLENDING OF PRIMITIVE SUBSKILLS INTO A TEMPORAL SKILL

The above studies led to the intriguing finding that children with dyslexia have normal sensory processing speed and normal speed of simple reaction. However, when a choice needs to be made, the children with dyslexia are affected differentially by the increase in task complexity. In an attempt to identify why this was so, we subsequently undertook a further, theoretically motivated, long-term training study investigating the time course of the blending of two separate simple reactions into a choice reaction—one of two long-term training studies reported in Nicolson and Fawcett (2000 but undertaken in 1993).

In order to avoid any problems of left right confusions or of stimulus discriminability, we used two stimuli of different modalities (tone and flash) and different effectors (hand and foot) for the two stimuli. Twenty-two subjects participated, 11 dyslexic and 11 control matched for age and IQ. In brief, following baseline performance monitoring on simple reaction to each stimulus separately (counterbalanced so that half the subjects had the hand-button paired with the tone, and the foot-button paired with the flash, and the other half vice versa), the two simple reaction tasks were combined into a choice reaction task in which half the stimuli were tones and half flashes, and the subject had to press the corresponding button, using the mapping established in the simple reactions. Each session comprised three runs, each of 100 stimuli, and subjects kept returning every fortnight or so until their performance stopped improving (in terms of speed and accuracy). The results are shown in figure 3.

Analysis of the simple reaction performance indicated that there were no significant differences between the groups either for

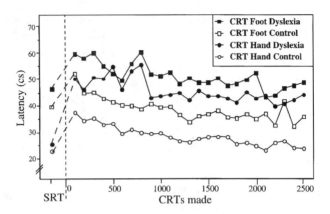

Figure 3. Median latencies over the period of CRT training.

foot or hand or for tone or flash. By contrast, initial performance on the choice reaction was significantly slower, and final performance was both significantly slower and less accurate for the children with dyslexia. Initially the dyslexic group made slightly (but not significantly) more errors (13.8% vs. 10.6%), indicating that the initial deficit cannot be attributable to some speed-accuracy trade-off by one group of children. However, by the final session, the dyslexic group made around twice as many errors on average (9.1% vs. 4.6%). Average learning rate for latency and accuracy was lower, but not significantly so, for the dyslexic group. Final choice reaction performance was very significantly both slower and less accurate than that of the controls both for hand and foot responses. Comparison of final hand and foot latency with the initial baseline SRT performance led to a dissociation, with both groups having significantly shorter final CRT latency than SRT latency for the foot responses, whereas for the hand responses, the control group had equivalent latencies and the dyslexic group had significantly longer final CRT than SRT latencies

In order to obtain more accurate estimates of the learning rates for completion times and errors, the group data were fitted using a parametric technique that has been established as the most appropriate for fitting human data on practice (Newell and Rosenbloom 1981). In brief, the curve fitted is the "power law" $P(n) = A + Bn^{-\alpha}$ where $P(n)$ refers to performance on trial n, A is the asymptotic performance as n tends to infinity, B is a scaling parameter linked directly to initial performance, and α is the learning rate. A parametric learning rate analysis was then performed using the power law equation outlined above. The best fit curves for hand response CRT were $t = 53.9\ n^{-0.073}$ for the children with dyslexia and $t = 39.4\ n^{-0.141}$ for the controls. For the foot responses the corresponding best fit curves were t = 62.3 $n^{-0.086}$; t = 50.4 $n^{-0.116}$ respectively. The parameter B was higher for the children with dyslexia than the controls (around 30% on average), reflecting the slower initial performance on the CRT. Even more interesting, however, is the difference in learning rate, which was about 1.5 times faster for the controls than the children with dyslexia (0.141 vs. 0.073; 0.116 vs. 0.086 for the hand and foot responses, respectively). This is a huge difference. Bearing in mind that the learning varies as a function of the time to the power α, if a skill takes a normal child 100 hours to master, it would take a child with dyslexia $100^{1.5}$, i.e., 1,000 hours (10 times as long) to learn the skill to the same criterion!

In summary, the children with dyslexia appeared to have greater difficulty in blending existing skills into a new skill, and their performance after extensive practice (such that the skill was no longer improving noticeably) was slower and more error-prone. In other words, they were simply less skilled, their "quality" of automatized performance was lower. It seems reasonable, therefore, to argue that this group of children with dyslexia have difficulties with the initial proceduralization of skill, and with the "quality" of skill post-training. If the CRT training results apply to children with dyslexia generally, and apply to tasks other than choice reactions, we are led to a radically new prediction for dyslexic performance, namely that rather than being at the level of children of their own age, or even, as is often considered the appropriate control group, children of the same reading age, the performance of children with dyslexia on any task will be comparable with that of much younger children, with the amount of impairment increasing as the square root of the necessary learning time.

Before considering possible interpretations of this set of differences in processing speed, we considered it valuable to report one further study designed to investigate the question of attention switching.

STUDY 4: ATTENTION SHIFTING DEFICITS IN DYSLEXIA

Attentional difficulty has often been linked to dyslexia, but few studies have investigated directly the nature of the supposed attentional disorder. One intriguing possibility is that the rapid processing problems in dyslexia are associated with attentional difficulties and in particular impaired ability to switch attention rapidly. There is considerable anecdotal evidence that children with dyslexia have difficulty "keeping on track" (Augur 1985). Around 15% of children with dyslexia also have attention deficit hyperactivity disorder

(ADHD) and around 36% of children with ADHD have dyslexia (Shaywitz, Fletcher, and Shaywitz 1994). However, despite these intriguing links, there is little experimental evidence on attention and dyslexia, or on whether children with dyslexia, but without ADHD, show evidence of attention difficulties.

There are three key aspects of attention; sustained, selective, and shifting attention (Posner and Raichle 1994). We report here an investigation of attention in children with dyslexia (Moores, Nicolson, and Fawcett 2000) using a paradigm developed by Akshoomoff and Courchesne (1994), using adolescent children with dyslexia and age- and IQ-matched controls. In the focus condition, children were asked to respond to a target shape presented singly in the center of a computer screen, ignoring any distractors. In the shift condition the target shape switched following each correct response. The study allowed us to check the following parameters in dyslexia: is there (a) a selective attention/focus attention deficit; (b) a shift attention deficit; (c) a rapid shift deficit; or (d) a sustained attention deficit?

The children with dyslexia were significantly less accurate than the controls, specifically in the "switch attention" condition. However, this was not caused by difficulties in switching attention *rapidly*, but rather in maintaining the rapid responding several seconds after switching (see figure 4). A further study was designed, presenting shapes in an intact or degraded version, to investigate this issue further, contrasting the hypothesis that children with dyslexia have reduced cognitive resources with the established hy-

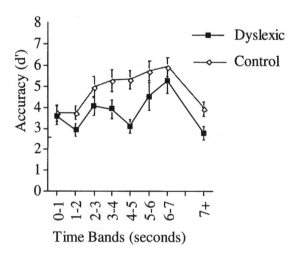

Figure 4. Accuracy as a function of time since the last correct hit in the shift condition.

pothesis that children with dyslexia suffer from a general impairment in the ability to automatize skills (Nicolson and Fawcett 1990). The children with dyslexia were less affected by the degradation, as predicted by the automatization deficit account, and in contradiction to the "reduced attentional resources" account.

OVERALL DISCUSSION

In this chapter we have covered a good deal of ground, presenting studies on speed of processing, attention, and skill acquisition. Study 1 indicated that children with dyslexia have difficulties with rapid responding, even with non-linguistic material with negligible memory load, so long as the child needed to make a choice between alternative responses. The P300 data in study 2 suggested that the impairment lay in the central executive decision time, rather than in early sensory processing. The CRT training study (study 3) showed that even after extended practice, the CRT performance of the children with dyslexia was worse than the controls (in terms of speed and accuracy), and, furthermore, their learning rate appeared to be markedly lower, to the extent that they were predicted to take ten times as long to learn to perform at normal levels on a task normally taking 100 hours to master. A key finding was the very poor initial performance and the continuing difficulty in eliminating errors. This seems to be a good characterization of all the skills we have sampled in children with dyslexia. Study 4 addressed the role of attention, in particular the ability to switch attention rapidly. In contrast to our earlier findings, the results of this experiment suggested that impairments should not be attributed to slowness in switching attention, but rather to problems in automatic performance and associated decrements in sustained performance over the course of the experiment.

We are finally in position to address the issues raised in the introduction. First, where do the bottlenecks in speeded processing for children with dyslexia arise? Second, what are the theoretical implications for the cause(s) of dyslexia, and for the design of remediation programs?

It is likely that bottlenecks arise at many stages in central processing, and in particular, difficulties appear to be exacerbated by task difficulty. Nonetheless, we can say with some confidence that the bottlenecks arise even in fundamental processing speed and in the absence of significant memory load or verbal material. By contrast, there is no evidence in the children with dyslexia reported here that there are any difficulties in sensory processing speed (though it is quite possible that the sensory input is in some sense less complete than for normal processes). We consider it most likely that there are inefficiencies in the "central executive" processing system. Unfortunately, the nature and processes of central cognitive processing remain elusive. Established models that mirror computer architectures (Barnard and Teasdale 1991; Schneider and Detweiler 1987) suggest that stimuli need to be identified via sensory processes, and then the product has to be placed on a central "bus," conveyed to the executive area—probably in the frontal lobes (Posner and Raichle 1994)—compared with the stored target {is it the high tone?}, a decision made {yes /no}, then the response loaded {motor cortex} and released {basal ganglia}; and finally the motor response made. Clearly this is a complex set of processes, and one that increases in efficiency and sophistication through maturation and experience. Our data suggest that the sensory processing and motor execution phases in themselves are not intrinsically slow, and therefore that it is the complex central processing stages that introduce delay. These findings are fully consistent with our previously espoused learning framework that suggests that children with dyslexia have difficulty with any skill that requires extensive practice (and in particular the square root heuristic noted above). Our current view (see the chapter on the cerebellum) is that these difficulties are manifested as incomplete automatization, and are attributable to abnormal cerebellar function that leads to abnormal learning (Nicolson and Fawcett 1990; 1999). It should be noted, however, that a variety of mechanisms (for instance, increased "neural noise" arising from slightly sub-optimal brain connectivity) would lead to very similar predictions for processing speed. A series of investigations, including functional imaging work, is required to provide the converging data needed to test such hypotheses.

Turning to the applied implications of the work, we consider that the use of double deficits (speed and phonology) as positive indicators of dyslexia provides a valuable extension of the existing literacy-based methods of identifying dyslexia. Indeed, we have used these findings, in addition to extant work on limitations on magnocellular function, memory, and motor skill to develop simple, effective and enjoyable 30 minute screening tests for dyslexia, from pre-school to retirement (Fawcett and Nicolson 1996, 1998; Nicolson and Fawcett 1996).

Turning to the implications for remediation, the automatization deficit account (which was substantially supported by these studies) holds that for many children with dyslexia many skills do not become automatized as quickly as normal, even though their general resource ceiling is normal. Therefore, problems arise primarily for those skills that are not automatic. Consequently (according to the automatization deficit account), if one wishes to minimize the literacy problems of children with dyslexia, it is necessary to give specialized teaching designed to automatize the subskills involved through carefully designed, carefully monitored, and long-term training programs. This is directly consistent with established good practice guidelines for supporting children with dyslexia (Gillingham and Stillman 1960; Hickey 1992; Miles 1989) which stress that an exceptionally structured, explicit, systematic, and comprehensive approach is needed, progressing in a series of small steps, with each step mastered before the next one is introduced. More interestingly, the automatization deficit account provides an underlying rationale for existing support practice, thereby allowing the full power of the cognitive theories of learning, automatization and their optimization (e.g., Anderson 1982; Ericsson, Krampe, and Heizmann 1993; Shiffrin and Schenider 1977) to be applied to the design of more cost-effective learning procedures for children with dyslexia. It is our hope that it will be possible in the future to optimize dyslexia support procedures so as not only to foster the development of automaticity but also to avoid the undoubted tedium that is the drawback of many mastery approaches (Nicolson and Fawcett 1994b).

Before concluding, it is important to note the limitations of the work presented here. First, the research is based on small numbers of children with "pure" dyslexia and small numbers of matched control children. Larger scale studies are needed to check whether our results are indeed representative of "pure" dyslexia specifically, and "epidemiological" dyslexia more generally. Second, in the studies presented here, we have not discussed the performance of children with disabilities other than dyslexia. It is very likely that children with ADHD, children with specific language impairment, and even "garden variety" poor readers, will show at least a subset of the impairments established here. Consequently it is by no means established that these impairments in speeded processing are specific to children with dyslexia. Further research is needed. We hope and expect that subsequent larger scale research will be able to illuminate these issues.

In this chapter we have presented four studies investigating aspects of speed, attention, and learning in dyslexia. Our proposal that children with dyslexia suffer from deficits in skill automatization gives an excellent general account of the range of deficits shown. However, it should be stressed that labeling the deficit as one of automatization does not explain which aspect(s) of the automatization process are impaired or why. There remains suggestive evidence (echoing suggestions made by many of the contributors to this volume) that deficits in speeded processing may be rather less tractable than others. The search for the mechanism underlying these deficits has driven our further research, and we address these issues further in our chapter on the cerebellum and learning.

REFERENCES

Akshoomoff, N. A., and Courchesne, E. 1994. ERP evidence for a shifting attention deficit in patients with damage to the cerebellum. *Journal of Cognitive Neuroscience* 6:388–99.

American Psychiatric Association 1987. *Diagnostic and statistical manual of mental disorders*, 3rd ed, revised. Washington, DC: American Psychiatric Association.

Anderson, J. R. 1982. Acquisition of cognitive skill. *Psychological Review* 89:369–406.

Augur, J. 1985. Guidelines for Teachers, Parents and Learners. In *Children's Written Language Difficulties*, ed. M. J. Snowling NFER-NELSON.

Avons, S. E. and Hanna, C. 1995. The memory-span deficit in children with specific reading-disability—is speech rate responsible? *British Journal of Developmental Psychology* 13:303–11.

Baddeley, A. D., Thomson, N., and Buchanan, M. 1975. Word length and the structure of short term memory. *Journal of Verbal Learning and Verbal Behaviour* 14:575–89.

Barnard, P. J., and Teasdale, J. D. 1991. Interacting cognitive subsystems—a systemic approach to cognitive-affective interaction and change. *Cognition and Emotion* 5(1):1–39.

Coles, M. G. H., Gratton, G., and Fabiani, M. 1990. Event-related brain potentials. In *Principles of Psychophysiology: Physical, Social and Inferential Elements*, ed. J. T. Cacioppo and L. G. Tassinary. Cambridge: Cambridge University Press.

Denckla, M. B. and Rudel, R. G. 1976. Rapid "Automatized" naming (R.A.N.). Dyslexia differentiated from other learning disabilities. *Neuropsychologia* 14:471–79.

Ericsson, K. A., Krampe, R. T., and Heizmann, S. 1993. The role of deliberate practice in the acquisition of expert performance. *Psychological Review* 100:363–406.

Fawcett, A. J., Chattopadhyay, A. K., Kandler, R. H., Jarratt, J. A., Nicolson, R. I., and Proctor, M. 1993. Event-related potentials and dyslexia. *Annals of the New York Academy of Sciences* 682: 342–45.

Fawcett, A. J., and Nicolson, R. I. 1994. Speed of processing, automaticity and dyslexia. In *Dyslexia in Children: Multidisciplinary Perspectives*, ed. A. J. Fawcett and R. I. Nicolson. Hemel Hempstead, UK: Harvester Wheatsheaf.

Fawcett, A. J., and Nicolson, R. I. 1996. *The Dyslexia Screening Test*. London: The Psychological Corporation.

Fawcett, A. J., and Nicolson, R. I. 1998. *The Dyslexia Adult Screening Test*. London: The Psychological Corporation.

Gillingham, A., and Stillman, B. 1960. *Remedial Training for Children with Specific Difficulties in Reading, Writing and Penmanship*. Cambridge MA: Educators Publishing.

Helenius, P., Tarkiainen, A., Cornelissen, P., Hansen, P. C., and Salmelin, R. 1999. Dissociation of normal feature analysis and deficient processing of letter-strings in dyslexic adults. *Cerebral Cortex* 9:476–83.

Hickey, K. 1992. *The Hickey Multisensory Language Course*, 2nd edition. Ed. J. Augur and S. Briggs. London: Whurr.

Hulme, C., Thomson, N., Muir, C., and Lawrence, A. 1984. Speech rate and the development of short term memory span. *Journal of Experimental Child Psychology* 38: 247–50.

Jolicoeur, P. 1999. Restricted attentional capacity between sensory modalities. *Psychonomic Bulletin Review* 6:87–92.

Leppanen, P. H. T. and Lyytinen, H. 1997. Auditory event-related potentials in the study of developmental language-related disorders. *Audiology and Neuro-Otology* 2:308–40.

Leppanen, P. H. T., Pihko, E., Eklund, K. M., and Lyytinen, H. 1999. Cortical responses of infants with and without a genetic risk for dyslexia: II. Group effects. *Neuroreport* 10:969–73.

Lovegrove, W. J., Garzia, R. P., and Nicholson, S. B. 1990. Experimental evidence of a transient system deficit in specific reading disability. *Journal of the American Optometric Association* 61:137–46.

Miles, E. 1989. *The Bangor Dyslexia Teaching System.* London: Whurr.

Miles, T. R. 1983. *Dyslexia: The Pattern of Difficulties.* Oxford: Blackwell.

Moores, E., Nicolson, R. I., and Fawcett, A. J. 2000. Attentional Deficits in Dyslexia: Evidence for an Automatisation Deficit? Submitted.

Newell, A., and Rosenbloom, P. S. 1981. Mechanisms of skill acquisition and the law of practice. In *Cognitive Skills and Their Acquisition*, ed. J. R. Anderson. Hillsdale, NJ: Lawrence Erlbaum Associates.

Newton, M. J., Thomson, M. E., and Richards, I. L. 1976. *The Aston Index as a Predictor of Written Language Difficulties—A Longitudinal Study.* Birmingham, UK: Aston University.

Nicolson, R. I. 1981. The relationship between memory span and processing speed. In *Intelligence and Learning*, ed. M. Friedman, J. P. Das, and N. O'Connor. London: UK.

Nicolson, R. I. 1996. Developmental dyslexia; Past, present and future. *Dyslexia: An International Journal of Research and Practice* 2:190–207.

Nicolson, R. I., and Fawcett, A. J. 1990. Automaticity: A new framework for dyslexia research? *Cognition* 35(2):159–82.

Nicolson, R. I., and Fawcett, A. J. 1994a. Reaction Times and Dyslexia. *Quarterly Journal of Experimental Psychology* 47A:29–48.

Nicolson, R. I., and Fawcett, A. J. 1994b. Spelling Remediation for Dyslexic Children: A Skills Approach. In *Handbook of Spelling: Theory, Process and Intervention*, ed. G. D. A. Brown and N. C. Ellis. Chichester: Wiley.

Nicolson, R. I., and Fawcett, A. J. 1996. *The Dyslexia Early Screening Test.* London: The Psychological Corporation.

Nicolson, R. I., and Fawcett, A. J. 1999. Developmental dyslexia: The role of the cerebellum. *Dyslexia: An International Journal of Research and Practice* 5:155–77.

Nicolson, R. I., and Fawcett, A. J. 2000. Long-term learning in dyslexic children. *European Journal of Cognitive Psychology* 12:357–93.

Nicolson, R. I., Fawcett, A. J., and Baddeley, A. D. 1991. *Working Memory and Dyslexia* (LRG 3/91). Sheffield: University of Sheffield.

Posner, M. I. 1978. *Chronometric Explorations of Mind.* Oxford: Oxford University Press.

Posner, M. I., and Raichle, M. 1994. *Images of Mind.* New York: Freeman.

Rudel, R. G. 1985. The definition of dyslexia: language and motor deficits. In *Dyslexia: A Neuroscientific Approach to Clinical Evaluation,* ed. F. H. Duffy and N. Geschwind. Boston, MA: Little Brown.

Schneider, W., and Detweiler, M. 1987. A connectionist/control architecture for working memory. In *The Psychology of Learning and Motivation* (Vol. 21), ed. G. H. Bower. New York: Academic Press.

Shankardass, A., Nicolson, R. I., Fawcett, A. J., and Pascalis, O. 1999. Event-related brain potentials in dyslexia. *Society for Neuroscience Abstracts* 25: 490.

Shaywitz, B. A., M. F. J., and Shaywitz, S. E. 1994. Interrelationships between reading disability and attention deficit-hyperactivity disorder. In *The Learning Disabilities Spectrum: ADD, ADHD and LD,* ed. A. J. Capute, P. J. Accardo, and B. K. Shapiro. Baltimore, MD: York Press.

Shiffrin, R. M., and Schenider, W. 1977. Controlled and automatic human information processing II: Perceptual learning, automatic attending and general theory. *Psychological Review* 84:127–90.

Stein, J., and Walsh, V. 1997. To see but not to read; The magnocellular theory of dyslexia. *Trends in Neurosciences* 20:147–52.

Tallal. 1993. Neurobiological basis of speech A case for the pre-eminence of temporal processing. *Annals of the New York Academy of Sciences* 682:27–47.

Tallal, P., Miller, S., and Fitch, R. H. 1993. Neurobiological basis of speech: A case for the pre-eminence of temporal processing. *Annals of the New York Academy of Sciences* 682: 27–47.

Taylor, M. J., and Keenan, N. K. 1999. ERPs to orthographic, phonological, and semantic tasks in dyslexic children with auditory processing impairment. *Developmental Neuropsychology* 15:307–26.

Wechsler, D. 1976. *Wechsler Intelligence Scale for Children Revised* (WISC-R). Slough, UK: NFER.

Wechsler, D. 1992. *Wechsler Intelligence Scale for Children,* 3rd edition. Sidcup, Kent: The Psychological Corporation.

Wolf, M., and Bowers, P. G. 1999. The double-deficit hypothesis for the developmental dyslexias. *Journal of Educational Psychology* 91:415–38.

Wolff, P. H., Michel, G. F., Ovrut, M., and Drake, C. 1990. Rate and timing precision of motor coordination in developmental dyslexia. *Developmental Psychology* 26(3):349–59.

Woodward, S. H., Brown, W. S., Marsh, J. T., and Dawson, M. E. 1991. Probing the time-course of the auditory oddball P3 with secondary reaction time. *Psychophysiology* 28:609–18.

Chapter • 3

Exploration of the Basis for Rapid Naming's Relationship to Reading

Patricia Greig Bowers

The last decade of research into developmental dyslexia has supported the view that in addition to the large amount of variance contributed to reading difficulties by deficits in phonological processing, slower naming speed for simple symbols marks a second contributor to the disorder (see Wolf and Bowers 1999 for a review). What is not well understood is the reason for the association between symbol naming speed (as typically indexed by Rapid Automatized Naming tasks devised by Denckla and Rudel 1974) and reading. Previous attempts to address this question have focused upon the relationship of RAN to orthographic knowledge. Growing out of this association has been an hypothesis that whatever the cause of slow naming (which may be several, see Wolf 1999; Denckla and Cutting 1999), its effects may be due at least partly to slow symbol recognition disrupting the easy building of links between letters that often co-occur. If the time between the recognition of several letters is longer than optimal for learning to chunk them, the processes underlying RAN may contribute directly to delays in forming orthographic codes for lexical and sublexical letter patterns. However, data from several recent studies challenge the idea that RAN-related processes affect orthographic knowledge so directly. This paper presents a modified hypothesis taking account of both earlier and newer data. I suggest that RAN may index processes that are reflected in baseline measures of identification of letter strings with low orthographic structure. It is upon this baseline that additive effects of knowledge of orthographic constraints may build. In addition, the baseline may also affect the growth of orthographic knowledge in a modest fashion.

Evidence concerning differential relationships between rapid naming and types of reading skill, including both correlational data and differential effects of various interventions, is reviewed in the first section of the paper. In the next section, research on the impact of brief exposure times on accuracy of identification of letter strings that vary in orthographic structure is reported, and the revised hypothesis concerning the RAN-reading relationship presented.

Several observations must be kept in mind as evidence is reviewed. The type of sample has been shown to affect results of studies of rapid naming's relationship to reading. The effects of rapid naming are more evident in samples of readers with lower skills, either because they are relatively new readers (e.g., grades 1, 2, and 3) or because they are poor readers whose skills are comparable to those of children in those grades (McBride-Chang and Manis 1996; Meyer et al. 1998). Relationships are not exclusive to these groups since adults with dyslexia are also characterized by slow naming speed (Felton, Naylor, and Wood 1990). McBride-Chang and Manis suggest that when reading fluency is high, naming speed may be minimally related to reading. Perhaps when children read as fluently as a good reader in grade 3 or 4, the cognitive underpinnings of that fluency, including rapid naming, are sufficient to support normal rates of future reading progress.

DIFFERENTIAL RELATIONSHIPS BETWEEN RAN AND VARIOUS MEASURES OF READING SKILL

Distinctive patterns of associations between naming speed and phoneme awareness on types of reading skills have been summarized elsewhere (e.g., Wolf and Bowers 1999; Bowers and Newby-Clark in press). Therefore this review will not be exhaustive. The pattern of findings is typically similar to that reported in an earlier study (Bowers 1995). I examined a sample of 38 children chosen to represent poor and average readers in grade 2 and followed until grade 4, when many of the children originally designated poor readers had improved their standing and could now be considered moderately poor or average readers. Particularly good readers were under-represented in this grade 4 sample. Strong relationships between digit naming speed and word and text reading speed were found, ranging from .6 to .7 in grade 4. Hierarchical regressions, controlling for WISC-R (Wechsler 1974) Vocabulary, showed that the unique variance contributed by grade

2 phonemic awareness versus naming speed differed according to the type of grade 4 reading skill assessed. Phonemic awareness had a greater independent relationship to decoding accuracy, and naming speed had a far greater relationship with latency for correct identification of both easy and harder words. It also contributed variance to comprehension measures through its relationship to quicker word identification.

Young and Bowers (1995) studied the reading of text of varying difficulty levels by poor and average readers in grade 5. Both digit naming speed and phonemic awareness were strongly associated with Word Identification scores on the Woodcock Reading Mastery Test-Revised (Woodcock 1987), but only naming speed had unique variance contributing to text speed and ratings of fluency independently of Word Identification for all levels of text difficulty. Poor readers' fluency was more affected by difficulty level of stories read than was average readers' fluency. However, on the easiest (grade 2 level) story, whose words were practiced to a criterion of accuracy before text reading, poor readers were less fluent than average readers were on the most difficult text. Errors reading the passages were more often related to phonemic awareness or, on the two easier passages, to the interaction of naming speed and phonemic awareness. The interaction term indicated that, controlling for Word Identification skill, ". . . the word accuracy [on experimental texts] of children with poor phonological skill but relatively fast naming scores was roughly equivalent to [that of] children with high phonological scores. Thus, when reading relatively easy text, competence in the ability indexed by naming speed appeared to compensate for weakness in phonological skill" (Young and Bowers 1995).

Although measures of orthographic skill were not administered in the studies cited above, the relationship between reading speed and orthographic skill has been demonstrated in other studies. For example, Barker, Torgesen, and Wagner (1992) report that reading speed and orthographic skill accuracy are related to each other independent of age, IQ, and phonological skill. This observation is relevant to the results of several subsequent studies in our lab (Bowers, Sunseth, and Golden 1999; Bowers and Newby-Clark in press; Sunseth 2000) which selected subjects representative of children with single deficits in either phonemic awareness or rapid naming and with deficits in both areas. Table 1 summarizes the results of these studies. Grade 3 children, chosen for their relative strength in phonemic awareness but weakness in rapid naming, are indeed more accurate decoders on average than children with the opposite pattern of skill (single phonemic deficit children).

Table 1.   Pattern of skills of deficit groups assessed in Grade 3 (2 studies of Sunseth 2000).

Naming Speed Deficit	Phoneme Aware Deficit	Double Deficit
Word Ident and Attack OK but less than No deficit	Word Ident and Attack relatively poor	Word Ident and Attack very poor
Slower reading	Faster reading	Slow reading
Poor spelling, especially Spelling recognition	Poor spelling, both Dictation and recognition	Very Poor spelling, both Dictation and recognition
Poor orthographic skill	Better or similarly poor Orthographic skill	Poor orthographic skill
% below 90 on Word Identification: 20% to 30%	% below 90 on Word Identification: 20% to 30%	% below 90 on Word Identification: 90%

However, these single naming speed deficit children are slower to read text and have spelling difficulties, especially in spelling recognition. On tests of orthographic accuracy, they score either worse than or equal to children with poor phonemic awareness and good naming speed, again a contrast to their relatively better standing on word identification and word attack standard scores. Additive double deficit children and interactive effects are evident, with typically more disadvantaged than either single deficit group. It is of special interest that in two samples reported by Sunseth (2000), single deficit groups did not differ in the percent of children having Word Identification scores below 90 (or the 25th percentile). From 20% to 30% of single deficit children had scores in this range, while more than 90% of double deficit children had such low scores.

Manis, Doi, and Bhadha (2000) studied grade 2 children representative of the full range of reading ability in the public schools sampled. Controlling for WISC III (Wechsler 1991) Vocabulary and either naming speed or phonemic awareness, unique contributions of the latter variables to word identification, non-word decoding, comprehension and orthographic skill were found. The familiar pattern of phonemic awareness' stronger contribution to non-word decoding and naming speed's stronger contribution to measures of orthographic skill, was evident. The pattern for digit naming and letter naming speed was similar, but stronger for letter naming speed. However, children divided into groups based upon either naming speed or phonemic awareness below or above the 25th percentile were not different from each other on the orthographic tests unless they had double deficits.

Torgesen et al. (1997) have reported results from a longitudinal study of a large representative sample of children from kindergarten through grade 5. The analyses predicting grade 2 and 3 reading in this sample showed unique contributions of both phonemic awareness and naming speed measured in kindergarten and grade 1 to reading two years later (grades 2 and 3) even controlling for reading skill at the earlier time (auto-regressive effects). However, the unique effects of naming speed controlling for auto-regressive effects were not evident in predicting reading in grades 4 and 5 from predictor measures in grades 2 and 3, whereas phonemic awareness continued to have significant if small additional effects (Torgesen et al. 1997). Without controlling for the auto-regressive effects, the pattern of results in grades 4 and 5 are of interest, because several types of reading measures were used, including reading speed and orthographic skill as well as the more usual word identification and word attack scores. In both grades, the relatively stronger effects of phonemic awareness are seen on measures of word and non-word decoding and the relatively greater effects of naming speed on reading speed and/or orthographic skill measures. When the samples are restricted to just the poorer readers (the bottom 20% of the sample), some increase is seen for the contribution of rapid naming, especially for reading speed, but in general the pattern was similar for the poor readers and the full sample. The fact that the variables still have predictive power among the restricted range represented by poor readers is noteworthy.

RELATIONSHIPS OF RAN TO READING IN LANGUAGES WITH MORE REGULAR ORTHOGRAPHIES

Cross linguistic studies are informative about the distinctive role of rapid naming in reading, and have been reviewed elsewhere (Wolf and Bowers 1999). In languages with greater orthographic regularity than English, and where phonics methods of instruction predominate, Wimmer (this volume) reports that people with dyslexia have little difficulty in accurate word recognition but do read very slowly and spell poorly. Therefore, reading achievement in orthographically regular languages is often measured by numbers of words read accurately in a certain time period, such as one minute. Rapid naming of digits emerged as the best predictor of reading differences among normal reading children and those with dyslexia in Wimmer's studies. Studying younger children, De Jong and Van der Leij (1999) report that kindergarten measures of rapid naming of objects and of phonological awareness are related to such speeded measures of reading in normal reading samples in fall and end of grade 1 and end of grade 2. (Auto-regressive analyses suggest that the effects of these variables are incorporated into the end of grade 1 scores such that no effects above that of the auto-regressor are seen in grade 2). In an older sample of Dutch children, van Daal and van der Leij (1999) found that only nonword decoding speed and rapid naming of digits and letters (not colors or objects) discriminated 12-year-old children with dyslexia from CA and RA controls. No evidence was found for children with dyslexia showing a general deficit in phonological processing, speed of processing, or working memory.

In summary, naming speed has higher unique contributions to reading speed and several measures of orthographic skill than to measures of accurate decoding. In languages with more regular orthographies, its relationship to speed of accurate reading is noteworthy, given the lower variance in reading accuracy in those languages after grade 1. However, rapid naming is also independently related to accuracy of word identification in English. Do effects of training reading skill shed light on the specific effects of rapid naming?

RAN-RELATED IMPROVEMENTS IN READING AFTER TRAINING

Many studies have demonstrated that intensive instruction in phoneme awareness and phonics improves decoding skill in poor readers. However, equally telling is the finding that these decoding skill gains are not typically accompanied by gains in fluency (e.g., Torgesen, Wagner, and Rashotte 1997; see review in Meyer and Felton 1999). The individual difference characteristic more associated with increases in fluency is rapid naming ability.

The children in the longitudinal study described above in Bowers (1995) took part each year in a study of effects of Repeated Reading (Bowers 1993). The pattern of results was generally the same each year. The speed of reading text before and after practice was related to naming speed even when word identification standard scores and errors reading passages were controlled. Phonemic awareness was unrelated to speed of reading text although it was related to errors reading text passages. Bowers (1993) reported that the effects of practice reading a passage four times was associated with naming speed, such that initially slower readers made greater gains if their naming speed was faster. And as in Bowers (1993), Young (1997) found that the effects of grade 5 poor readers' practice with text were significantly greater for the faster namers among them, even controlling for pre-practice fluency. Such a relationship was not found in either study for phonemic awareness.

Studies from other labs also find selective effects for pre-intervention naming speed on reading progress. Ring, Wise, and Olson (1998; Wise, Ring, and Olson 1999) report that after a six month period during which several remediation methods were used, poor readers' gains in time-limited word recognition, but not untimed recognition, were uniquely predicted by RAN scores. Similarly, Abbott and Berninger (1999) report that poor readers in grades 4 through 7 benefitted from different types of reading remediation over a 16-week intervention. Few measures were able to predict who would benefit more from interventions. However, progress as indicated by growth curve analyses was predicted by letter naming speed. Naming speed predicted the slope of real word efficiency (speed of reading words correctly) and the intercept for non-word reading efficiency as well as for knowledge of taught words.

Progress in accuracy of reading as well as efficiency of that reading has also been predicted by naming speed. Berninger et al. (1999) studied children designated poor readers at the end of grade 1. They showed that unique variance in the rate of growth in word and non-word reading after intervention sessions could be predicted by a RAN composite score. Levy, Bourassa, and Horn (1999) conducted a twenty-session word recognition training study. They showed that when poor readers in grade 2 were divided into faster and slower RAN groups, the slower RAN children learned training words less quickly and retained their skill less well, even controlling for the initially poorer skills of the slower RAN children. Slow RAN children found training techniques using whole words especially difficult. Levy (this volume) reports that the difficulty in whole word reading stems from a failure to note orthographic units and relate them to their pronunciation, a failure that can be remediated by making such units more visible and pronouncing them.

Relatively better RAN performance in a severely dyslexic population was associated with more improvement after intensive phonological training in the study reported by Lovett, Steinbach, and Frijters (2000). A recent report by Torgesen et al. (1999) showed strong effects of kindergarten rapid naming on accuracy measures of reading in grade 2 after a $2^{1}/_{2}$-year intervention program. This association was found in a sample chosen for their poor phonological awareness and low knowledge of letter names in kindergarten. In essence, the children who showed least progress were those with a double deficit in phonemic awareness and rapid naming; those children with better rapid naming skills benefitted most from the remediation programs.

Summing up, processes underlying rapid symbol naming (but not phonemic awareness) appear to be consistently related to training gains in sight word reading and text reading fluency; RAN-related improvement due to training over longer periods are sometimes found for accuracy measures as well. The pattern of relationships between naming speed, reading fluency, orthographic skill, and word recognition accuracy independent of phonemic awareness was reviewed above. It too found consistently large relationships of rapid naming with reading fluency, and stronger unique contributions to orthographic skill than to phonological decoding. The path from laborious and slow decoding of a word to representing that word in a fashion that supports quick and reliable reading, is more difficult if naming speed is slow.

STRATEGIES TO FIND THE REASONS FOR RAN-READING RELATIONSHIPS

The pattern of evidence reviewed above has highlighted RAN's association with sight word recognition, reading speed, and orthographic skill, without a clear understanding about the underlying reasons for this association. Indeed, such reasons are a matter of uncertainty and debate.

One strategy for addressing this question has been to decompose the RAN task itself, asking which task components are related to reading. Scarborough and Domgaard (1998), in a study of 56 grade 3 inner city children, varied the structure of the RAN task to isolate the aspect of it that affected the correlation with reading. They eliminated most possibilities, such as sustaining attention, domain-general processing speed, visual scanning, and remembering the item set. The one variable that remained necessary to the correlation with reading was the child's actual naming of letters in an array rather than making a yes/no judgment about whether the symbol was a particular letter, albeit in varying fonts. Wolf and Bowers (1999) speculate that the naming of varied items, in contrast to keeping in mind one letter and saying yes or no, requires both the relinquishing of the name of one item and the retrieval of a new name associated with a new visual symbol. Managing the inhibitory requirements of the task as well as the name retrieval aspect may be particularly difficult for the slow namer. Wolf and Obregon (1992) showed that slow and fast naming children differed not in the articulation length of their naming response but in the inter stimulus interval (ISI) between names, as if moving between items was difficult.

Such a pattern of slow retrieval and longer ISIs could mirror the typing difficulties of slow RAN children revealed in a recent study. In public schools in Waterloo Region, Ontario, children early in grade 3 are taught a touch-typing program. Seventy-four children in three classes in one of the schools were studied to determine predictors of progress in the program. The training, as well as the tests, require the child to view a sentence on a computer screen. The child types over the words in the sentence, with the child's production replacing the computer text letter by letter. The dependent typing measure combined indices of speed of typing and of number of errors such that speed of correct typing after 8 to 10 weeks of instruction was assessed. As anticipated, learning to type accurately and quickly is associated with many cognitive measures. These included phonemic awareness as tapped by the Auditory Analysis Test (Rosner and Simon 1971), working memory as measured by a modification for children of the Daneman and Carpenter sentence span test (Eastwood, Steffy, and Corning 2000), and reading accuracy (Woodcock-Johnson Word Identification subtest, Woodcock and Johnson 1989). However, the combination of just two of those measures, letter naming speed and WISC III Coding, (correlations with typing .57 and .43, respectively) accounted for 40% of the variance in later typing efficiency, with no other measure adding unique variance.[1] One hierarchical regression analysis predicting typing efficiency is shown in table 2. When order of entry was reversed, Sentence Span and Auditory Analysis Test added no unique variance. In addition to the many cognitive and motor similarities in the demands involved in WISC III Coding and in typing by copying a script, letter naming speed contributed to both error and speed components of typing efficiency measures. Recall that the child's

---

[1]Letter naming speed and Coding were associated with each other at approximately $r = .3$. A simpler measure of speed of processing, Cross Out (Woodcock-Johnson 1989), was correlated with letter naming speed ($r = .30$) and typing efficiency ($r = .29$), but uncorrelated with reading ($r = .14$). Word Identification was related to letter naming speed ($r = .66$), and typing efficiency ($r = .39$.)

Table 2. Hierarchical multiple regression analysis predicting typing efficiency at final test.

Step	Variable	R^2	R^2change	p
1	Sentence span	.11	.11	.005
2	Auditory Analysis Test	.16	.05	.041
3	Letter Naming Speed	.33	.17	.000
4	WISC III Coding	.40	.07	.005

task was to type over each of the letters in the words on the screen. Being able to quickly identify the letters in words to be typed and move smoothly from one letter identification task to the next, should aid performance in typing as well as in the RAN task itself, with long ISIs characterizing poor performance in each.

Another strategy for understanding why RAN is related to reading has been employed in my laboratory. We have formed hypotheses (on the basis of evidence reviewed above) about the nature of the association of RAN to selected components of reading, and have begun to gather data pertinent to these hypotheses. (Berninger and colleagues, this volume, have formulated other partially overlapping hypotheses based on their rich data base.)

My colleagues and I have argued that the speeded component of measures of naming speed is crucial to the unique contribution of RAN to reading. There are several ways in which speed may be relevant. Consistent with an orthographic redundancy perspective (Adams 1981; 1990), there may be a direct causal effect of slow speed of processing individual letters on ability to build both lexical and sublexical codes for orthographic patterns. These codes in turn support a sight vocabulary (Bowers et al. 1994; Wolf and Bowers 1999). Other possibilities implicate slow naming speed as reflecting a cascading system of slowed components common to naming and reading. One or many components might be involved (Wolf and Bowers 1999). A recent study by Booth et al. (2000) reports data consistent with the view that speeded visual processing is associated with orthographic knowledge in children. A task of rapid visual processing using only dots presented briefly with varying ISIs contributed unique variance to recognizing exception words, but not pseudo-words. Chase (1996) studied flicker fusion in children with dyslexia and found that RD children require substantially more time between stimuli to see two images rather than a fusion of the images. Similar results are reported in a review of the literature by Farmer and Klein (1995) and in recent work by Rose et al. (1999) and Boden and Brodeur (1999). Chase suggested that speed and quality of visual information for low spatial-frequency components is weakened in poor readers, preventing them from making sufficiently rapid visual discriminations in higher-level tasks. This need for extra time between stimuli may be reflected also in RAN performances. Stein (this volume) reports visual motion detection deficits in people with dyslexia consistent with magnocellular dysfunction in the visual system, a system associated with rapid processing. Willows (1991) reviews earlier studies and presents her own work on visual recognition tasks involving rapid stimulus presentation. She finds clear evidence that younger disabled readers make more errors and are slower at responding than normal readers of similar age and IQ. The disabled readers' difficulty seems to occur at the initial input stage rather than at a later storage stage" (p. 183).

In contrast, Manis, Seidenberg, and Doi (1999) have speculated that the orthographic difficulties of children with rapid naming deficits are associated with a deficit in learning arbitrary associations, as distinct from the impact of speed per se. Along these lines, Mayringer and Wimmer (2000) discuss their finding that grade 3 children with dyslexia and chronological age control children differed on their ability to learn new, complex pseudo-names for pictures, although they did not differ as much on ability to repeat complex pseudo-words. Furthermore, there were significant correlations between pseudo-name learning scores in grade 3 and grade 1 scores on visual naming speed for pictures as well as pseudo-word repetition. Correlations with speeded visual search scores were low. These children with dyslexia, like other German and Dutch speaking dyslexics, differ from controls in grade 3 chiefly on speed of reading and poor orthographic spelling. The authors interpret their findings as indicating there is a long-term phonological memory deficit rather than a general visual memory dysfunction associated with the orthographic deficits of the children with dyslexia. However, this interpretation may be much broader than warranted by the particular measures used in the study.

That the learning of arbitrary phonological labels for visual material might be associated with sight word learning seems consonant with the idea that memory variables might explain variance in sight word knowledge. Despite some initial speculation that naming speed and memory might be related, several labs have found that memory variables are more highly related to phonemic awareness than to naming speed (Torgesen et al. 1997; De Jong and Van der Leij 1999). Indeed, it is somewhat difficult to measure phonemic awareness apart from variance shared with working memory (Ishaik 2000). Variance on tests of either short-term memory or more complex working memory does not seem to overlap with the unique variance contributed to reading by naming speed. Whether other classes of memory variables might be associated with rapid naming and sight word knowledge remains open to question. These varied interpretations of the basis for the association of rapid naming with orthographic knowledge and reading speed require much more research attention.

Whichever theory later proves a more accurate description of the reason for naming speed-reading relationships, it is important to note that from both perspectives, a link between the visual and verbal systems is central. Should one place more emphasis on the visual recognition of a pattern that must be integrated with a verbal labeling system or instead on the role of learning the unfamiliar or arbitrary verbal labels that must be integrated with visual pattern recognition? Is it a sluggish visual system or an inflexible verbal system that acts as a bottleneck to the integration? Or is the verbal-visual connection system itself not performing at an optimal rate? Either way, the efficiency of the integration of two systems remains the core of what is being measured. Several chapters in this volume point to the need for a coordination in time of activation of orthographic and phonological information for efficient reading to occur. The chapters by Breznitz, Wimmer, Berninger et al. and Levy emphasize the importance of bringing these processes into synchrony, and the penalties incurred when slow processing impedes their integration.

TOWARD A REFINEMENT OF THE HYPOTHESIZED RELATIONSHIP

Until recently, my preferred interpretation of the naming speed reading relationship favored the link through RAN's effects on the induction of knowledge of orthographic constraints. That is, individual letter identification speed's impact upon the recognition of sublexical and lexical patterns was thought to be the route to its effects on reading. However, several recent studies in my laboratory have led me to modify and refine this interpretation, while not abandoning it. The refined hypothesis suggests that slow RAN reflects processes resulting in incomplete processing of letter strings with low orthographic structure; these same processes form the baseline for additive effects of orthographic knowledge. Such knowledge, coming from various sources, adds to the perceptibility and more complete processing of strings with higher orthographic structure. The combined effect of baseline letter string processing and orthographic knowledge results in the variability found in sight word proficiency and text reading fluency. Our typical tests of orthographic skill may also tap the combined effects of these variables. I report below the evidence supporting this position from studies that manipulated the amount of orthographic structure present in letter strings exposed briefly.

A series of studies has explored RAN's impact upon the recognition of letter strings varying in orthographic structure using the Quick Spell Test (QST). I will present this work after first reviewing the central hypotheses guiding the studies, and citing relevant work from other laboratories on contributors to sight word learning. Finally, results from my lab using two versions of the QST will be reported.

The hypothesis guiding the design of the QST argued that as a consequence of a child's slow naming speed for symbols, an ordinary amount of time looking at a word would be insufficient for the child to recognize all the letters in it. As Adams' orthographic redundancy perspective (1981; 1990) suggests, the recognition of letter patterns depends on recognizing each letter in those patterns in sufficient temporal contiguity that they become linked together and facilitate each other's perceptibility. Two related consequences of slow naming speed were anticipated: 1) delayed formation of orthographic codes for letters frequently occurring together; 2) difficulty learning the precise sequence of letters in a whole word, and thus amalgamating the full letter sequence with the word's pronunciation. Such a pattern would be consistent with Levy, Bourassa, and Horn's (1999) finding that slow-naming poor readers are especially disadvantaged by instructional methods emphasizing whole word recognition. In the relative absence of orthographic knowledge facilitating the speed of processing of common letter strings, brief presentation of strings would result in errors or omissions in identifying letters in strings with high and low orthographic structure.

One possibility for slow-naming children coping with learning to read is that they fail to fully process and remember all the letters in words they see, given the extra burden on memory imposed by failure to form orthographic codes. How fully letter strings are processed while children are learning to read particular words has been studied by several investigators. Ehri and Saltmarsh (1995), replicating and extending a study by Reitsma (1983), found that disabled readers were particularly deficient in remembering letter details in the middle of words, a deficit associated with their poor sight word learning skill. Ehri (1997) argues cogently for the place of phonological decoding skill in how fully the letter sequence is processed and amalgamated with whole word pronunciation. Share (1999) supports this view. He showed orthographic learning occurred for normal grade 2 readers of Hebrew with just four representations of novel target words in text. Share states, after reviewing the literature in this area, that ". . . relatively few exposures are sufficient for the acquisition of word-specific orthographic information among normal readers, but not disabled readers." Although he and Ehri would point to the poorer phonological skills of disabled readers as an explanation for the difference from normal readers, perhaps there is a role as well for slow speed of processing of the letter identities themselves. This role for rapid naming is supported by the results of studies reviewed above that suggest phonological training for disabled readers promotes accurate but not fluent reading, and at the same time, that rapid naming skill is associated with training-related progress in identifying words quickly and reading text fluently.

I devised the Quick Spell Test (QST) to explore these possibilities by documenting the effects of brief exposure (250 ms.) of letter strings on accuracy of identification of the letters in those strings. The type of letter string was manipulated (Bowers, Sunseth, and Golden 1999; Sunseth 2000; Rueffer 2000). Four letter words (e.g., that, went), pseudo-words (e.g., kile, meft) and illegal all-consonant non-words (e.g., dlhw, nwtl) composed the first set of stimuli used. There is a large literature on the effects of orthographic knowledge on the perceptibility of letters in words versus in isolation (the word superiority effect). This effect would suggest that children with better orthographic knowledge should show enhanced perceptual identification of letters in words and even pseudo-words compared to letters in isolation or in illegal non-words. If RAN's effects were mainly mediated through its effects on the growth of orthographic knowledge, slow RAN children should show reduced effects of orthographic structure on perceptibility of the full string. The difference between types of letter strings should be smaller for slow naming poor readers than for other children; accuracy over all strings should be lower.

In the initial study employing whole class samples (Bowers et al. 1999), we found overall effects of type of letter string such that letters in words were reported more fully than letters in pseudo-words. Letters were least accurately reported in non-words, consistent with the word superiority effect. Regression analyses found that both phonemic awareness and naming speed were related to number of accurate identifications of letters in all strings in grade 2. By grade 3, only naming speed predicted significant variance in non-words, with the effects on pseudo-words being a combination of a direct effect of naming speed and an interaction of naming speed and phonemic awareness. Another study of two groups of single deficit grade 3 children showed large effects of type of single deficit group only on the illegal (all consonant) non-word strings such that single naming speed deficit children had significantly lower identification of letters in non-words than did single phonological deficit children. The hypothesis that slow RAN rather than poor phonemic awareness would be associated with the use of orthographic knowledge in the word and pseudo-word tasks was not confirmed. Instead the most consistent result associated with the RAN deficit was the inaccurate reporting of letters in strings with very low orthographic structure.

In a subsequent study, Sunseth (2000; Sunseth and Bowers in preparation) found that low accuracy on briefly exposed non-word strings characterized grade 3 double deficit poor readers more clearly than degree of accuracy on strings with higher ortho-graphic structure. (See table 3.) Testing over 200 grade 3 children in full class samples, she defined strengths and weaknesses on naming speed and phonemic awareness as scores either above the 50th percentile or below the 30th percentile. Children were di-vided into four groups based on their patterns of deficits and strengths. The double deficit group had similar scores on phone-mic awareness as the single phonemic deficit group and had simi-lar scores on digit naming speed as the single naming speed deficit group. Both single deficit groups were impaired on recognizing let-ters in pseudo-words and especially in non-words, compared to no-deficit children. However, unlike the previous studies, they were not different from one another on the non-words. The dou-ble deficit children had significantly lower scores than other deficit groups on non-words.

Sunseth matched the double deficit children with late Grade 1 average-reading children with similar raw scores on reading mea-sures.[2] (The double deficit children had significantly lower reading scores than either single deficit group). These reading level control children were significantly better than the double deficit readers on recognizing the letters in words and pseudo-words, but equal to the double deficit poor readers on their poor performance with non-words. Their mean scores for non-words were 2.9 and 3 out of 10, respectively, while single deficit readers had scores of 4.7 and 4.8. No deficit readers identified 8.8 out of 10 strings correctly.

[2]The match was quite good for Word Attack scores, but the RA children had slightly lower Word Identification scores than the Double Deficit children.

Table 3.   Mean scores on reading and QST subtests for subgroups (Sunseth 2000).

Variable	No Deficits ($n = 17$)	Name Sp Def.($n = 18$)	Phon. Def ($n = 17$)	Double Def. ($n = 16$)	Read Lev. ($n = 15$)
Word Ident	116.9 (16)	100.3 (16.3)	92.2 (9.1)	83.1 (6.9)	101
GORT time	15.3 (4.6)	31.5 (13.8)	21.3 (4.8)	37.1 (11.1)	65.7 (28.8)
AAT	23.2 (3.2)	22.4 (2.6)	11.4 (2.4)	11.3 (2.7)	16.1 (5.4)
RAN:Digit	2.1 (.29)	1.5 (.13)	2.1 (.16)	1.4 (.18)	1.4 (.29)
QST Words	9.7 (.77)	7.3 (1.1)	8.1 (1.8)	6.4 (2.1)	9.2 (1.0)
QST Pseud	9.2 (.95)	5.8 (1.3)	6.2 (1.6)	4.7 (2.2)	6.5 (1.7)
QST Non	8.8 (1.5)	4.7 (1.2)	4.8 (1.7)	2.9 (1.4)	3.0 (2.1)

Although the pattern of results for the QST differed somewhat from sample to sample, the main finding was replicated. Accuracy on non-words was lower for all deficit reader groups, especially for double deficit readers. However, each same-age deficit group bene-fitted similarly from increasing orthographic structure if one con-siders the non-word accuracy a baseline measure. If lack of orthographic knowledge was the mediator of naming speed or phonological awareness effects on the QST, one or more of the deficit groups should have benefitted less from additional ortho-graphic structure in the letter strings. Reading-level-matched grade 1 readers were helped most in their identification of letters in strings by orthographic structure, and the same age deficit groups had similar if smaller gains.

Rueffer (2000) followed up this unexpected finding by adding a fourth condition to the QST which controlled to some extent the pronounceability of the non-word letter strings somewhat in-dependently of their orthographic structure. She devised a list of four-letter illegal non-words that contained only frequent conso-nant bigrams (e.g., blbs; chbt) in distinction to the infrequent con-sonant bigrams presented in the original non-word condition. She chose her samples based on Woodcock-Johnson Word Identifica-tion scores, with all subjects in the reading disabled (RD) group scoring below the 25th percentile on this test. There were 20 grade 4 RD children with a Mean (*SD*) Word Identification SS score = 85 (7.8) and 10 CA controls (M = 104.7, *SD* = 7.6) as well as 16 grade 2 average readers. The latter children served as reading level (RL) controls, matched to the RD group on raw scores on Word Attack.[3]

Table 4 reveals the strong effect on all groups of children of exposure to common letter patterns, whether more or less pro-nounceable. The presence of frequent bigrams in the non-words was associated with more accurate processing of these briefly ex-posed letter strings for each group of children. For example, the chronological age (CA) group identified two more high than low bigram frequency non-words (out of 10) and the RD and the RL groups identified three more high than low frequency strings. However, the low bigram frequency non-words were identified sig-nificantly more accurately by the CA children than by either the RD or RL children, who did not differ from each other. (This equiv-alence of performance for RD and RL children on this string was

---

[3]Initial selection of RL matched Grade 2 children on Word Identification was done based on fall scores; by the winter and spring when the study was conducted, the RD group had significantly better Word Identification scores than the RL con-trols, although both were much worse readers than the CA controls. However, they remained matched on Word Attack scores.

Table 4.   Mean raw (*SD*) scores on tests for Chronological Age Controls
(CA), Reading Disabled children (RD) and Reading Level
Controls (RL) (Rueffer 2000).

Variable	CA (*n* = 10)	RD (*n* = 20)	RL (*n* = 16)
Word Ident.	41.70 (2.58)[a]	34.20 (3.14)[b]	30.88 (4.16)[c]
Word Attack	18.30 (5.58)[a]	9.95 (3.10)[b]	9.38 (6.05)[b]
AAT	25.50 (2.76)[a]	18.70 (4.95)[b]	17.31 (6.60)[b]
RAN:Letters	2.22 (.50)[a]	1.87 (.33)[b]	1.71 (.25)[b]
QST:Words	10.00 (00)[a]	9.75 (.72)[a]	9.44 (1.26)[a]
QST: Pseudo	9.70 (.48)[a]	8.90 (1.29)[a]	7.62 (2.03)[b]
QST: Non-hi	8.80 (1.32)[a]	7.60 (1.98)[a]	5.69 (2.63)[b]
QST:Non-lo	6.80 (1.81)[a]	4.45 (2.96)[b]	2.56 (1.93)[b]
Ortho Accuracy	36.20 (2.44)[a]	33.10 (3.74)[a]	29.31 (4.77)[b]

Note: Groups not sharing superscripts are significantly different from each other.

also seen in the Sunseth study above.) Differences between CA and RD children did not reach significance for the pseudo-word and high bigram frequency non-words, although both groups were better at identifying these strings than the RL controls. (Low statistical power for comparisons with CA children may have influenced this result.) Nevertheless, this pattern of effects (CA = RD > RL) mirrors the pattern found on the Orthographic Choice test (Olson et al. 1985) for this sample. The more expected pattern of CA children performing better than RD children who were similar to RL children (CA > RD = RL) characterized scores not only on QST low bigram frequency illegal non-words but also on the RAN and the Auditory Analysis Test of phonemic awareness. (See table 4.)

In an exploratory effort to understand the relationships of QST and reading variables among the RD group, correlations were analyzed for these 20 children. In this sample, despite the differing mean levels of the QST subtests, RAN letters were rather uniformly correlated between .42 and .48 with each of the QST measures, most of these relationships significant at *p* < .05 level. In this study, children read texts at three levels of difficulty, and difficulty level was reflected in mean reading speed for these texts. However, letter naming speeds were correlated with speed of reading each text, again rather uniformly between –.54 to –.59. Correlations of AAT scores with QST and text speed were much lower and nonsignificant.

The samples for the QST studies reviewed above were not fully comparable, and the pattern of results not completely consistent. However, what stands out is that the poor readers and Double Deficit children differed most from other groups in the letter strings with the least orthographic structure, and each group's accuracy benefitted from each additional increase in orthographic structure. I speculate that exposure to print, decoding skill and processing speed, in varying combinations, affected orthographic knowledge. In turn, such knowledge influenced the perceptibility of QST words and pseudo-words for all children through the word superiority effect, the phenomenon that a letter in a word and even a pseudo-word is easier to identify than the same letter in isolated format. Even exposure to commonly occurring bigrams in illegal strings increased the perceptibility of letters in those strings. This enhanced perceptibility of letters due to knowledge of letter sequences does not affect the low bigram frequency strings, which are therefore reflecting the contribution of mainly lower level visual naming processes to letter string recognition. Mean levels of correct identification rise with the enhanced perceptibility due to orthographic knowledge but the base level differences in lower level visual identification skill still contribute to the performance achieved, and are reflected in the stable rank order of performances. The hypothesis that RAN reflects that part of letter string recognition associated with lower level processes might explain the similar correlations of RAN, not only with each type of letter string, but also with reading speed on texts of varying difficulty despite the differing mean levels on these variables.

The Rueffer (2000) and Sunseth (2000) studies suggest that the perceptual identification processes of poor and average grade 3 and 4 readers as well as reading level matched younger children, are able to benefit from orthographic knowledge arising from various sources, such as decoding skill and print exposure. Although enhancement of perception by higher level knowledge affects all the children, the effects of orthographic knowledge for RD and RL children starts from a much lower baseline of speed of recognition of letters in a series. Further evidence that people with dyslexia are particularly slow at processing non-words with low frequency clusters and benefit from presentation of non-words with higher frequency clusters, is presented by Van der leij and Van Daal (1999).

The idea that the baseline for letter string recognition (as indexed by low bigram frequency illegal non-words) can be separated from the effects of orthographic knowledge on that recognition, is analogous to an argument presented in Massaro et al. (1980). Their model of word perception suggests that there are two independent sources of primary recognition of words, the featural information in pre-perceptual visual storage and knowledge of orthographic structure. It is suggested here that naming speed as well as recognition of letters in low bigram frequency strings reflects (no doubt quite imperfectly) the amount of featural information about a letter string that can be processed in a brief time and still support letter recognition (lower level visual identification process). The variables may tap into the construct represented by the "abstract letter identity" component in many models of skilled reading. Perception of sight words would represent the joint effects of the lower level process enhanced by orthographic knowledge.

In short, the refined hypothesis suggests that naming speed affects sight word skill mainly through its association with a baseline for speed of visual letter string identification, upon which orthographic knowledge adds perceptual facilitation effects. Perhaps exposure to, and much practice with, common small patterns will allow orthographic knowledge to accrue for all levels of readers and all levels of naming speed, which in turn may help speed the perceptual processes involved in letter recognition in strings with high orthographic structure. Levy (this volume) shows how special efforts to highlight and practice sublexical patterns improved the word recognition of even slow RAN poor readers. Print exposure (e.g., Cunningham and Stanovich 1990), practice (e.g., Bowers and Kennedy 1993), and numerous influences on decoding accuracy (e.g., Ehri 1997) may influence the orthographic knowledge of individuals somewhat independently of their base level of speed of visual letter discrimination. This conceptualization may be more consistent with results of a study by Cutting, Carlisle, and Denckla (1998) reporting direct effects of RAN on reading not mediated through orthographic knowledge, and with Kail, Hall, and Caskey (1999) findings that processing time rather than print exposure was related to naming speed.

Studies that find that many impaired readers suffer from three deficits: phonological awareness, naming speed, and orthographic awareness, (Berninger et al. 1995; Badian 1997) may reflect the fact that all three processes can have independent (and additive) effects on reading. But it is also unsurprising that naming speed is particularly associated with the building of sight word codes, since both the amount of featural information available in a short amount of time and knowledge of orthographic constraints may affect those codes.

The perspective that processes associated with naming speed and knowledge of orthographic constraints have chiefly additive effects on sight word knowledge may inform remediation efforts. Although the baseline for perceptual identification of letter strings may change only through developmental/maturational processes, compensation for deficits in these lower level processes is possible through the additive effects of print exposure and decoding skill.

Practice with commonly occurring letter patterns may indeed need to be extraordinarily intense to overcome baseline differences. Remediation programs such as RAVE-O (Wolf, Miller, and Donnelly 2000) may provide just this type of intense exposure. Similarly, Olson, Wise and colleagues' program of text reading practice with accurate decoding support may also supply the extra exposure needed by slow naming children to gain the orthographic knowledge which will speed the perceptual processing of familiar words. By linking assessment results to remediation efforts, research informing just how and why rapid naming is related to reading progress may have practical as well as theoretical benefits.

REFERENCES

Abbott, S. P., and Berninger, V. W. 1999. It's never too late to remediate: Teaching word recognition to students with reading disabilities in Grades 4 – 7. *Annals of Dyslexia* 49:223–50.

Adams, M. J. 1981. What good is orthographic redundancy? In *Perception of Print: Reading Research in Experimental Psychology*, eds. O. J. L. Tzeng and H. Singer. Hillsdale, NJ: Lawrence Erlbaum Associates.

Adams, M. J. 1990. *Beginning to Read: Thinking and Learning about Print.* Cambridge, Massachusetts: MIT Press.

Badian, N. 1997. Dyslexia and the double-deficit hypothesis. *Annals of Dyslexia* 47:69–87.

Barker, T. A., Torgesen, J. K., and Wagner, R. K. 1992. The role of orthographic processing skills on five different reading tasks. *Reading Research Quarterly* 27:334–45.

Berninger, Abbott, Greep, Reed, Hooven, and Abbott. 1995, April. Single, double, and triple deficits in impaired readers at the end of first grade: Individual differences in learner characteristics and response to intervention. Paper presented at the annual meeting of the Society for Research in Child Development, Indianapolis, IN.

Berninger, V. W., Abbott, R. D., Zook, D., Ogier, S., Lemos-Britton, Z., and Brooksher, R. 1999. Early intervention for reading disabilities: Teaching the alphabet principle in a connectionist framework. *Journal of Learning Disabilities* 32:491–503.

Boden, C., and Brodeur, D. A. 1999. Visual processing of verbal and non-verbal stimuli in adolescents with reading disabilities. *Journal of Learning Disabilities* 32:58–71.

Booth, J. R., Perfetti, C. A., MacWhinney, B., and Hunt, S. .B. 2000. The association of rapid temporal perception with orthographic and phonological processing in children and adults with reading impairment. *Scientific Studies of Reading* 4:101–32.

Bowers, P. 1993. Text reading and rereading: Predictors of fluency beyond word recognition. *Journal of Reading Behavior* 25:133–53.

Bowers, P. G. 1995. Tracing symbol naming speed's unique contributions to reading disabilities over time. *Reading and Writing: An Interdisciplinary Journal* 7:189–216.

Bowers, P. G., Golden, J. O., Kennedy, A., and Young, A. 1994. Limits upon orthographic knowledge due to processes indexed by naming speed. In *The Varieties of Orthographic Knowledge: Theoretical and Developmental Issues*, ed. V. W. Berninger. The Netherlands: Kluwer Academic Publishers.

Bowers, P. G., and Newby-Clark, E. In press. The role of naming speed within a model of reading acquisition. *Reading and Writing: An International Journal*.

Bowers, P. G., and Kennedy, A. 1993. Effects of naming speed differences on fluency of reading after practice. *Annals of the New York Academy of Sciences* 682:318–20.

Bowers, P.G., Sunseth, K., and Golden, J. 1999. The route between rapid naming and reading progress. *Scientific Studies of Reading* 3:31–53.

Bowers, P. G., and Wolf, M. 1993. Theoretical links between naming speed, precise timing mechanisms and orthographic skill in dyslexia. *Reading and Writing: An Interdisciplinary Journal* 5:69–85.

Chase, C. 1996. A visual deficit model of developmental dyslexia. In *Developmental Dyslexia: Neural, Cognitive, and Genetic Mechanisms*, eds. C. Chase, G. Rosen, and G. Sherman. Baltimore: York Press.

Cunningham, A. E., and Stanovich, K. E. 1990. Assessing print exposure and orthographic processing skill in children: A quick measure of reading experience. *Journal of Educational Psychology* 82: 733–40.

Cutting, L., Carlisle, J., and Denckla, M. B. 1998, April. A model of the relationships among rapid automatized naming (RAN) and other predictors of word reading. Poster presented at the annual meeting of the Society for the Scientific Study of Reading, San Diego, CA.

DeJong, P. F., and Van der Leij, A. 1999. Specific contributions of phonological abilities to early reading acquisition: Results from a Dutch latent variable longitudinal study. *Journal of Educational Psychology* 91: 450–76.

Denckla, M. B., and Cutting, L. E. 1999. History and significance of rapid Automatized Naming. *Annals of Dyslexia* 49:29–42.

Denckla, M. B., and Rudel, R. G. 1974. "Rapid automatized naming" of pictured objects, colors, letters, and numbers by normal children. *Cortex* 10:186–202.

Eastwood, A. E., Steffy, R. A., and Corning, W. C. 2000, July. Children's working memory ability: Electrophysiological correlates of performance on cognitive tasks. Poster presented to the annual meeting of the Association for the Scientific Study of Consciousness, Brussels.

Ehri, L. C. 1997. Sight word learning in normal readers and dyslexics. In *Foundations of Reading Acquisition and Dyslexia: Implications for Early Intervention*, ed. B. Blachman. New Jersey: Lawrence Erlbaum Associates.

Ehri, L. C., and Saltmarsh, J. 1995. Beginning readers outperform older disabled readers in learning to read words by sight. *Reading and Writing: An Interdisciplinary Journal* 7:295–326.

Farmer, M. E., and Klein, R. M. 1995. The evidence for a temporal processing deficit linked to dyslexia: A review. *Psychonomic Society* 2:460–93.

Felton, R. H., and Brown, I. S. 1990. Phonological processes as predictors of specific reading skills in children at risk for reading failure. *Reading and Writing: An Interdisciplinary Journal* 2:39–59.

Ishaik, G. 2000, July. Working memory and phonological awareness: How unique are the two processes in predicting reading? Poster presented to annual meetings of the Society for the Scientific Study of reading, Stockholm.

Kail, R., Hall, L.K., and Caskey, B. J. 1999. Processing speed, exposure to print, and naming speed. *Applied Psycholinguistics* 20:303–14.

Levy, B. A., and Bourassa, D. C., and Horn, C. 1999. Fast and slow namers: Benefits of segmentation and whole word training. *Journal of Experimental Child Psychology* 73:115–38.

Lovett, M. W., Steinbach, K. A., and Frijters, J. C. 2000. Remediating the core deficits of developmental reading disability: A Double-Deficit perspective. *Journal of Learning Disabilities* 33:334–58.

Manis, F., Doi, L., and Bhadha, B. 2000. Naming speed, phonological awareness and orthographic knowledge in second graders. *Journal of Learning Disabilities* 33:325–33.

Manis, F. R., Seidenberg, M. S., and Doi, L. M. 1999. See Dick RAN: Rapid naming and the longitudinal prediction of reading subskills in first and second graders. *Scientific Study of Reading* 3:129–57.

Massaro, D.W., Taylor, G. A., Venezky, R.L., Jastrzembski, J. E., and Lucas, P. A. 1980. *Letter and Word Perception: Orthographic Structure and Visual Processing in Reading*. New York: North-Holland Publishing Co.

Mayringer, H., and Wimmer, H. 2000. Pseudoname learning by German-speaking children with dyslexia: Evidence for a phonological learning deficit. *Journal of Experimental Child Psychology* 75:116–33.

McBride-Chang, C., and Manis, F. 1996. Structural invariance in the associations of naming speed, phonological awareness, and verbal reasoning in good and poor readers: A test of the double-deficit hypothesis. *Reading and Writing* 8:323–39.

Meyer, M. S., and Felton, R. H. 1999. Repeated reading to enhance fluency: Old approaches and new directions. *Annals of Dyslexia* 49:283–306.

Meyer, M. S., Wood, F. B., Hart, L. A., and Felton, R. H. 1998. The selective predictive values in rapid automatized naming within poor readers. *Journal of Learning Disabilities* 31:106–17.

Olson, R. K., Kliegl, R., Davidson, B. J., and Foltz, G. 1985. Individual and developmental differences in reading disability. In *Reading Research: Advances in Theory and Practice*, Vol. 4., eds. G. E. MacKinnon and T. G. Waller. Orlando: Academic Press.

Reitsma, P. 1983. Printed word learning in beginning readers. *Journal of Experimental Child Psychology* 36:321–39.

Ring, J., Wise, B. W., and Olson, R. K. 1998, April. An investigation of the double deficit hypothesis in a computer-based remediation program. Poster presented at meetings of the Society for the Scientific Study of Reading, San Diego, CA.

Rose, S. A., Feldman, J. F., Jankowski, J. J., and Futterweit, L. R. 1999. Visual and auditory temporal processing, cross-modal transfer, and reading. *Journal of Learning Disabilities* 32:256–66.

Rosner, J., and Simon, D. P. 1971. The auditory analysis test: An initial report. *Journal of Learning Disabilities* 4:1–15.

Rueffer, K. A. 2000. An examination of the factors underlying the development of skilled reading. Unpublished M.A. thesis.

Scarborough, H. S., and Domgaard, R. M. 1998, April. An exploration of the relationship between reading and rapid serial naming. Paper presented at meeting of the Society for the Scientific Study of Reading, San Diego, CA.

Share, D. L. 1999. Phonological recoding and orthographic learning: A direct test of the self teaching hypothesis. *Journal of Experimental Child Psychology* 72:95–129.

Sunseth, K. A. 2000. The role of naming speed and phonemic awareness in reading, spelling, and orthographic knowledge. Unpublished Ph.D. dissertation, University of Waterloo.

Sunseth, K. A., and Bowers, P. G. Submitted. Rapid naming and phonemic awareness: Contribution to reading, spelling and orthographic knowledge.

Torgesen, J. K., Wagner, R. K., and Rashotte, C.A. 1997. Prevention and re- mediation of severe reading disabilities: Keeping the end in mind. *Scientific Studies of Reading* 1:217–34.

Torgesen, J. K, Wagner, R. K, Rashotte, C. A., Burgess, S., and Hecht, S. 1997. Contributions of phonological awareness and rapid automatic naming ability to the growth of word-reading skills in second- to fifth- grade children. *Scientific Studies of Reading* 1:161–85.

Torgesen, J. K., Wagner, R. K., Rashotte, C. A., Rose, E., Lindamood, P., Conway, T., and Garvan, C. 1999. *Journal of Educational Psychology* 91:579–93.

Van Daal, V., and van der Leij, A. 1999. Developmental dyslexia: Related to specific or general deficits? *Annals of Dyslexia* 49:71–104.

Van der Leij, A., and van Daal, V. H. P. 1999. Automatization aspects of dyslexia: Speed limitations in word identification, sensitivity to in- creasing task demands, and orthographic compensation. *Journal of Learning Disabilities* 32:417–28.

Wechsler, D. 1974. *Wechsler Intelligence Scale for Children - Revised* (WISC- R). New York: The Psychological Corporation.

Wechsler, D. 1991. *Wechsler Intelligence Scale for Children - Third Edition* (WISC- III). San Antonio: The Psychological Corporation.

Willows, D. M. 1991. Visual processes in Learning Disabilities. In *Learning about Learning Disabilities*, ed. B. Y. L. Wong. NY: Academic Press.

Wimmer, H.1993. Characteristics of developmental dyslexia in a regular writing system. *Applied Psycholinguistics* 14:1–34.

Wise, B. W., Ring, J., and Olson, R. K. 1999. Training phonological aware- ness with and without explicit attention to articulation. *Journal of Experimental Child Psychology* 72:271–304.

Wolf, M. 1999. What time may tell: Towards a new conceptualization of developmental dyslexia *Annals of Dyslexia* 49:3–28.

Wolf , M., and Bowers, P. G. 1999. The double-deficit hypothesis for the Developmental dyslexias. *Journal of Educational Psychology* 91:415–38.

Wolf, M., Miller, L., and Donnelly, K. 2000. Retrieval, Automaticity, Vocabulary Elaboration, Orthography (RAVE-O): A comprehensive, fluency-based reading intervention program. *Journal of Learning Dis- abilities* 33:375–86.

Wolf, M., and Obregon, M. 1992. Early naming deficits, developmental dyslexia, and a specific deficit hypothesis. *Brain and Language* 42:219–47.

Woodcock, R. 1987. *Woodcock Reading Mastery Test-Revised*. Circle Pines, MN: American Guidance Service.

Woodcock, R. W., and Johnson, M. B. 1989. *Woodcock-Johnson Psycho- Educational Battery-Revised*. Allen, Texas: DLM Teaching Resources.

Young, A. 1997, March. Relationship of phonological analysis and nam- ing speed to training effects among dyslexic readers. Paper presented to Meetings of the Society for the Scientific study of Reading, Chicago.

Young, A., and Bowers, P. G. 1995. Individual differences and text diffi- culty determinants of reading fluency and expressiveness. *Journal of Experimental Child Psychology* 60:428–54

Chapter • 4

The Relationship of Naming Speed to Multiple Reading Measures in Disabled and Normal Readers

*Franklin R. Manis and
Laurie Freedman*

A current consensus among researchers is that the central reading problem among children identified as having dyslexia is a deficit in word recognition and decoding (Rack, Snowling, and Olson 1992; Siegel and Ryan 1988; Stanovich 1988; Vellutino and Scanlon 1987). The word reading difficulties are in turn thought to be due largely to core deficits in phonological skills, as assessed by tests of phonemic awareness or nonsense word decoding (Bradley and Bryant 1985; Bruck 1992; Lyon 1995; Perfetti 1992; Rack, Snowling, and Olson 1992; Shankweiler and Liberman 1972; Stanovich and Siegel 1994; Wagner and Torgesen 1987). Some theorists argue that the phonological processing problem reduces opportunities to learn from exposure to printed words, and hence has a powerful effect on the acquisition of knowledge about printed words, including word-specific spellings and orthographic regularities (Share 1995; Stanovich 1988; 1992).

Wolf and Bowers (1993a, b; 1999) have proposed that processes related to serial naming speed form a second core deficit in reading disabled children. In this view, termed the double-deficit hypothesis, reading difficulties can result from slow symbol naming speed, independently of phonological skill. Moreover, children with both phonological coding and naming speed deficits (a double deficit) have more severe reading difficulties than children with either deficit alone. The significance of this view is that poor readers with naming speed deficits alone or in combination with phonological deficits may either be misclassified as normal readers, or given inappropriate or ineffective remediation that does not address their fundamental problems with symbol processing speed.

The present paper focuses on two central claims of the double deficit hypothesis. First, symbol naming speed and phonological processes are independent and separable contributors to variance in reading skills. Second, naming speed is linked to reading primarily by way of orthographic processes. Bowers and Wolf (1993a, b; 1999) proposed that children with slow naming times tend not to activate visual and phonological codes for printed letters and letter groups in close enough synchrony to promote the creation of high quality orthographic representations of printed words in memory. The first claim is supported by studies using the Rapid Automatized Naming (RAN) task designed by Denckla and Rudel (1976). Rapid automatized naming (using digit and letter stimuli) accounts for sizeable variance in word reading when phonological skill and IQ are partialled out (Ackerman and Dykman 1993; Badian 1993; Blachman 1984; Bowers 1995; Bowers and Swanson 1991; Cornwall 1992; Felton and Brown 1990; McBride-Chang and Manis 1996; Manis, Seidenberg, and Doi 1999; Wimmer 1993). In support of the second claim, Sunseth and Bowers (1997) reported that children with a deficit in naming speed but not in phonological awareness were impaired on measures of orthographic skill relative to readers with only a phonological awareness deficit. A subgroup with both phonological awareness and naming speed deficits (double deficit subgroup) showed about the same degree of impairment in orthographic skill as the naming speed deficit group.

Evidence that is not completely consistent with the double deficit framework has been reported by Torgesen, Wagner, and colleagues (Torgesen et al.1997; Wagner et al. 1994, 1997). In a series of longitudinal comparisons over a six-year period, they reported that the unique contribution of naming speed to later reading skills diminished between kindergarten and grade three, and in some longitudinal comparisons, was not statistically significant, whereas the contribution of phoneme awareness remained strong. Similar findings of a reduction in the magnitude of naming speed contributions to later reading have been reported by

Walsh, Price, and Gillingham (1988). Wolf and Bowers (1999) have argued that the relationship between RAN and reading ability decreases gradually as reading skill develops among normally achieving children. In contrast, naming speed remains a significant predictor of reading skill among children with dyslexia. Some evidence for the latter claim was provided for young adolescents with dyslexia by Meyer et al. (1998).

Our review of the literature led us to frame the following questions. First, which aspects of reading skill (both type of task and whether it was an accuracy or a latency measure) are most related to naming speed? Secondly, is naming speed a stronger predictor of reading sub-skills among younger or more impaired readers than among older or less impaired readers? Third, which variables might mediate the relationship between naming speed and reading speed measures? This paper discusses studies conducted in our laboratory investigating relationships among naming speed, phonological awareness, and various reading sub-skills using normal beginning readers, readers with dyslexia, and normally achieving readers of late elementary school age.

STUDY 1 (MANIS, SEIDENBERG, AND DOI 1999)

The purpose of this study was to investigate the longitudinal relationships between measures of verbal ability, phoneme awareness and RAN, and later measures of reading sub-skills, including phonological decoding, orthographic processing, and reading comprehension. The study began with a representative sample of first graders from two schools in a suburb of Los Angeles ($n = 85$). Sixty-seven of these children returned for follow-up testing in the second grade (36 boys and 31 girls). The children were representative of the full range of reading abilities present at the two schools. The only restriction was that children with limited English proficiency were excluded from the study. The children ranged in age from 7;0 to 8;11, with a mean age of 7;10. The ethnic background of the sample was 59% Caucasian, 20% Hispanic, 9% Black, 11% Asian, and 1% Native-American. Families in this community were predominantly of lower middle to middle class income levels. The distribution of reading ability in the sample, based on Woodcock Word Identification (Woodcock 1989) scores, was 13 in the first quartile (Q1), 33 in Q2, 16 in Q3 and 23 in Q4.

The battery of tests given in first grade included three standardized reading tests, the Word Identification and Word Attack sub-tests of the Woodcock Reading Mastery Tests-Revised (WRMT-R) (Woodcock 1989), and the Silveroli Classroom Reading

Inventory-Graded Oral Paragraphs (Silveroli 1984). The Word Identification and Word Attack tests assessed printed word recognition and nonsense word decoding, respectively. The Silveroli was a criterion-referenced test that yielded scores for oral paragraph reading accuracy and reading comprehension. For the Silveroli test, a comprehension score was obtained by simply counting the number of questions answered correctly by the child. The Vocabulary sub-test of the Wechsler Intelligence Scale for Children-III (WISC-III) (Wechsler 1991) was also administered. Phonemic awareness was assessed by having the children perform a sound deletion test modeled after the Auditory Analysis Test (Rosner and Simon 1971). Children listened to a word, followed by either a syllable or a single phoneme, and had to delete the sound segment from the word and pronounce the result (e.g., /staend/ without the /t/ is /saend/). Two Rapid Automatic Naming (RAN) tasks were administered using the stimuli originally administered by Denckla and Rudel (1976) and Wolf et al. (1986), a test of serial digit naming, and a test of serial letter naming.

Three tests designed to assess aspects of orthographic skill were given. *Orthographic Choice* was adapted from a similar task used by Olson et al. (1989), designed to assess knowledge of word-specific spellings. Children were given a sheet with 24 triplets containing similarly spelled words and nonsense words (e.g., *tight, tite,* and *tait*). The experimenter read a word and a sentence context aloud (e.g., "tight - His shoes were too tight"). The student was asked to circle the item that was the correct spelling of the word. Every set of items contained a correctly spelled word (*tight*), a pseudo-homophone foil that would be pronounced the same as the target word (*tite*) and an additional foil with similar spelling that did not sound the same as the target word (*tait*). The logic behind the task is that children had to utilize knowledge of the unique orthography of printed words and could not rely on phonological recoding of the stimuli. The *Word Likeness Judgement* task was adapted from a task used by Stanovich and Siegel (1994). Children were given a sheet containing twenty-four pairs of nonsense words. They were told that none of the items were actual words, but that one item always "looked more like a word." They were asked to circle the item that looked more like a word. Examples of items include beff-ffeb, nist-niir, celp-cepl, biuce- buice and nkod-knod). *Exception Word Reading* required children to read aloud words displayed on cards in groups of six. Children continued reading until six errors in a row were made. The exception words were adapted from a frequency-graded word list devised by Adams and Huggins (1986). All of the words on the list violated one or more of the common spelling-to-sound "rules" in English (e.g., *said, people, island, beauty, stomach, sword, trough, yacht*).

The main question in this study concerned whether naming speed measures in the first grade accounted for unique variance in later reading scores, and whether phoneme awareness and naming speed accounted for contrasting types of tasks (e.g., orthographic skills vs. phonological skills). Hierarchical regression analyses were conducted in which the first variable entered was Wechsler Vocabulary to control for variation in verbal ability in the sample. Following Vocabulary, either Sound Deletion, or one of the RAN variables (digits or letters) was entered, and commonality analyses were conducted to assess the independence and degree of overlap of these variables. These dependent variables were regressed on six criterion variables: Woodcock Word Identification, Woodcock Word Attack, Silveroli Reading Comprehension, Word Likeness Judgement, Orthographic Choice, and Exception Word Reading.

The results are shown in table 1 for RAN Letters and in table 2 for RAN Digits. Vocabulary accounted for small amounts of variance for three of the variables, and a moderate amount for Silveroli reading comprehension (8.2%). Sound Deletion and the two RAN tasks accounted for sizeable amounts of variance beyond that attributed to Vocabulary. The unique contribution of Sound Deletion was significant for every variable except for Orthographic Choice and Word Likeness Judgement (in combination with RAN-Letters). The unique contribution of RAN-Digits was also significant for every variable. Rapid Automatized Naming Letters tended to account for larger amounts of variance than RAN-Digits. The amount of common variance between Sound Deletion and the RAN tasks was also fairly sizeable. The RAN tasks were at their predictive best for the orthographic tasks, and comparable to Sound Deletion for Woodcock Word Identification. Both RAN tasks accounted for less independent variance than Sound Deletion for Word Attack and Silveroli Reading Comprehension.

The results replicate previous findings that RAN and phonemic awareness account for distinct variance in reading (at least for the period between first and second grade), and corroborate Bowers and Wolf's hypothesis (Bowers et al. 1994; Wolf and Bowers 1999) that symbol naming speed bears a unique relationship to orthographic skill. Phonemic awareness tended to predict Word Identification, Word Attack and Reading Comprehension skills in this young sample. The failure of RAN to account for much of the reading comprehension variance may be related to the task: children were allowed to continue on to more difficult paragraphs on the Silveroli (and hence potentially obtain a higher

Table 1.   Hierarchical regression analyses predicting reading subskills from grade 1 to grade 2 (Study 1). Total proportion of variance from vocabulary, phoneme awareness, and digit naming speed, including commonality analysis

First Grade Variables	Second Grade Variables					
	Word Ident.	Word Attack	Silv. Compr.	Orthogr. Choice	Word Likeness	Exception Words
Vocabulary: total	.028	.003	.082*	.008	.000	.01
RAN-Digits and Sound Del.: common	.131	.095	.112	.116	.162	.104
RAN-Digits: Unique	.201****	.112**	.089***	.11**	.205****	.238****
Sound Deletion: unique	.186****	.179****	.289****	.049*	.05*	.126***
Total Variance	.546****	.389****	.572****	.283****	.417****	.478****

*$p < .05$ **$p < .01$ ***$p < .001$ ****$p < .0001$

Table 2.   Hierarchical regression analyses predicting reading sub-skills from grade 1 to grade 2 (Study 1). Total proportion of variance from vocabulary, phoneme awareness, and letter naming speed, including commonality analysis

First Grade Variables	Second Grade Variables					
	Word Ident.	Word Attack	Silv. Compr.	Orthogr. Choice	Word Likeness	Exception Words
Vocabulary: total	.028	.003	.082*	.008	.000	.01
RAN-Letters and Sound Del.: common	.214	.162	.204	.085	.098	.18
RAN-Letters: Unique	.232****	.130***	.111***	.165***	.162***	.324****
Sound Deletion: unique	.103***	.179****	.197****	.02	.024	.05***
Total Variance	.577****	.474****	.594****	.278****	.284****	.564****

*$p < .05$ **$p < .01$ ***$p < .001$ ****$p < .0001$

reading comprehension raw score) if their oral reading skills were stronger. The total amount of variance accounted for was sizeable for most variables except Orthographic Choice and Word Likeness Judgement.

The reduced sample size in the second grade (*n* = 68) did not permit analyses of double deficit subgroups along the lines proposed by Wolf and Bowers (Bowers and Wolf 1993b; Wolf and Bowers 1999). Accordingly, we added subjects to the sample in the second grade and added additional tasks (Study 2).

STUDY 2: MANIS, DOI, AND BHADHA (2000)

Seventeen additional second graders were recruited and given the entire test battery discussed above. One purpose of this study was to replicate the relationships among the variables of phonemic awareness, RAN, and various reading measures obtained by Manis et al. (1999). A second purpose was to categorize children using the double deficit framework to identify particular deficits associated with single versus double deficits in phonemic awareness and naming speed. Two additional tests were added to the battery—Sound Blending, a task adapted from a measure utilized by Wagner et al. (1994), and Nonsense Word Reading. For Sound Blending, children listened to words pronounced a sound at a time, and repeated the word that they thought they heard. The Nonsense Word reading task was similar in format to the Exception Word Reading task described above, except the items were 70 nonsense words, ranging in difficulty from CVC items to two syllable non-words such as *stining* and *hoasure*.

The hierarchical regression analyses were similar to those conducted by Manis et al. (1999), except that they were conducted using concurrent measures in the second grade, rather than first to second grade predictions. The results were also similar (see table 3 for analyses involving RAN-Digits and table 4 for RAN-Letters). Analyses with Sound Deletion are in the top half of each table, and those with Sound Blending in the bottom half.

The pattern of differences in the amount of unique variance associated with either Sound Deletion or Sound Blending and the two RAN variables is consistent with the double deficit hypothesis. Rapid Automatized Naming Letters accounted for numerically larger amounts of variance than Sound Deletion for the orthographic variables of Exception Words, Letter String Choice, and Orthographic Choice, about the same as Sound Deletion for measures of reading that emphasized both orthographic knowledge and phonological decoding (Woodcock Word Identification and

Table 3.   Concurrent hierarchical regression analyses in second grade (Study 2). Total variance from vocabulary, phoneme awareness and digit naming speed, including commonality analysis

Variable	Word Ident.	Nonwords	Silv. Compr.	Orthogr. Choice	Word Likeness	Exception Words
Vocabulary: total	.136***	.081**	.234****	.016	.005	.118**
RAN-Digits and Phon. Del.: common	.115	.075	.049	.061	.051	.093
RAN-Digits: Unique	.152***	.043*	.051*	.066**	.089**	.117****
Phoneme Deletion: unique	.192****	.241****	.171****	.124***	.066*	.163****
Total Variance	.595****	.440****	.505****	.267****	.211****	.491****

$*p < .05$ $**p < .01$ $***p < .001$ $****p < .0001$

Table 4.   Concurrent hierarchical regression analyses in second grade (Study 2). Total variance from vocabulary, phoneme-awareness, and letter naming speed, including commonality analysis

Variable	Word Ident.	Nonwords	Silv. Compr.	Orthogr. Choice	Word Likeness	Exception Words
Vocabulary: total	.136***	.081**	.234****	.016	.005	.118**
RAN-Letters and Phon. Del.: common	.168	.129	.097	.16	.051	.093
RAN-Letters: Unique	.171****	.071**	.093***	.217****	.089**	.117****
Phoneme Deletion: unique	.139***	.187****	.123***	.096***	.066*	.163****
Total Variance	.614****	.468****	.547****	.489****.	.211****	.491****

$*p < .05$ $**p < .01$ $***p < .001$ $****p < .0001$

Silveroli Comprehension), and less than Sound Deletion for measures of phonological decoding (Non-word Reading and Word Attack). Rapid Automatized Naming Digits was generally a less powerful predictor than RAN-Letters, but was at its strongest for the three orthographic tasks and Woodcock Word Identification, and at its weakest for Non-word Reading and Silveroli Reading Comprehension. This pattern of results was very similar for analyses involving Sound Blending. The total amount of variance accounted for was once again sizeable for all variables except Word Likeness Judgement.

Consistent with the methods reported by Bowers (1995), children were classified into four subgroups based on their performance on digit naming and Sound Deletion. A 25th percentile cut-off score was used to form a naming speed deficit subgroup (NSD) (*n* = 14), a phonemic awareness deficit subgroup (PD) (*n* = 13), a double deficit subgroup (DD) (*n* = 8), and a no-deficit subgroup (ND) (*n* = 50). Analyses of variance were used to compare the four subgroups on all of the variables. The means and standard deviations on each variable are shown in table 5. The F-value and significance level for the univariate Anova for each measure are shown in the rightmost column of the table. Univariate Anovas for overall subgroup differences were significant for every variable except age and WISC-III Vocabulary. The pattern of subgroup differences across tasks was assessed using Tukey post-hoc tests with alpha set at 0.05 for each variable. Significant subgroup differences are symbolized by means of letter superscripts in the table. The overall picture provides partial support for the double deficit hypothesis. The two single deficit subgroups were slightly below-average readers as a group, as indicated by Woodcock Word Identification percentile scores. Both single deficit groups were also lower than the ND subgroup in Exception Words. The PD group was significantly lower than the ND subgroup on each of the phonologically related tests (Non-word Reading, Word Attack, and Sound Blending). The NSD subgroup was low on RAN-Letters and RAN-Pictures (as well as the defining measure, RAN-Digits), confirming the picture of an overall naming speed deficit. Contrary to expectations, the NSD group was comparable to the PD and ND subgroups on two of the orthographic tasks, Letter String Choice and Orthographic Choice, and comparable to the PD subgroup on the third one, Exception Words, indicating that a specific naming speed deficit was not associated with poor orthographic skill in this sample.

The double deficit hypothesis received some confirmation from the comparison of the double deficit (DD) group to the other groups. The DD group was generally the lowest performing sub-

Table 5.   Means (and standard deviations) for naming speed deficit (NSD), phonological deficit (PD), double-deficit (DD), and no deficit (ND) subgroups in a representative sample of second graders (Study 2).*

| | GROUP | | | | |
Variable	ND (n = 38)	NSD (n=18)	PD (n = 19)	DD (n = 10)	Significance Tests
RAN Digits (in secs)	28.1 (3.9)[a]	38.1 (4.6)[b]	28.9 (3.0)[a]	44.1 (10.8)[b]	$F_{(3, 84)}$ = 36.51, p < .001
RAN Letters (in secs)	26.7 (4.2)[a]	33.7 (4.9)[b]	27.9 (4.1)[a]	39.6 (8.1)[b]	$F_{(3, 84)}$ = 23.0, p < .001
RAN Pictures (in secs)	51.6 (14.7)[a]	61.0 (14.0)[b]	60.3 (20.1)[ab]	80.2 (24.2)[c]	$F_{(3, 67)}$ = 5.28, p < .01
Sound Deletion accuracy	86.3% (8.8)[a]	85.6% (8.1)[a]	58.2% (10.2)[b]	54.7% (13.0)[b]	$F_{(3, 84)}$ = 59.5, p < .001
Sound Blending acc.	68.0% (15.1)[a]	62.4% (16.1)[ab]	52.6% (18.2)[bc]	53.2% (18.3)[c]	$F_{(3, 84)}$ = 4.72, p < .01
Non-word Pron. acc.	53.3% (22.6)[a]	32.0% (18.2)[b]	19.6% (12.1)[c]	18.4% (22.8)[c]	$F_{(3, 84)}$ = 16.8, p < .001
Wdck Word Attack (% ile)	62.7 (29.6)[a]	40.1 (22.4)[b]	23.6 (15.7)[c]	15.7 (15.7)[c]	$F_{(3, 67)}$= 13.68, p < .001
Wdck Word Ident. (% ile)	70.5 (25.4)[a]	45.3 (24.2)[b]	37.0 (16.9)[b]	19.5 (18.7)[c]	$F_{(3, 84)}$ = 18.4, p < .001
Excep. Word Accuracy	56.8% (15.7)[a]	41.8% (15.0)[b]	40.4% (11.1)[b]	25.1% (15.7)[c]	$F_{(3, 84)}$ = 14.42, p < .001
Orthographic Choice Acc.	73.6% (13.3)[a]	68.0% (12.8)[ab]	64.6% (9.3)[b]	51.2% (13.3)[c]	$F_{(3, 84)}$ = 9.52, P < .001
Word Likeness Acc.	80.9% (15.8)[a]	75.9% (11.7)[a]	75.2% (12.0)[a]	61.2% (18.0)[b]	$F_{(3, 84)}$ = 4.89, p < .01
Silveroli Comp. raw score	32.7 (8.3)[a]	26.7 (12.3)[ab]	23.8 (8.3)[b]	15.9 (13.1)[b]	$F_{(3, 67)}$ = 6.7, p < .001
Age (months)	94.9 (5.1)[a]	93.8 (4.7)[a]	94.2 (3.9)[a]	91.9 (2.8)[a]	no signif. differences
Vocabulary Scaled Score	10.1 (3.3)[a]	9.4 (3.6)[a]	9.4 (2.6)[a]	9.4 (4.7)[a]	no signif. differences

*Groups with different superscripts differ significantly by planned comparisons (using the t-test) group across tasks. It was a diverse group, consisting of five children who fell below the 25th percentile on the Woodcock Word Identification test and three more "adequate" readers (Woodcock Word Identification scores ranged from the 32nd to the 48th percentile). The five lowest readers were also slower in their naming times than the three adequate readers and four of the five below-average readers had the slowest naming times in the whole sample. As a group, the DD readers performed significantly more poorly than the PD subgroup on Orthographic Choice. Many of the other differences on tasks featuring orthographic skills favored the PD subgroup (e.g., Woodcock Word Identification, Exception Words, Word Likeness Judgement) but were not statistically significant. The DD subgroup differed significantly from the NSD subgroup on Orthographic Choice, but none of the other differences were significant by Tukey post hoc test. The DD subgroup was significantly lower than the ND subgroup on almost all of the measures, supporting the hypothesis that children with both naming speed and phonological deficits are likely to have the lowest reading skills.

The data replicated the findings of Manis et al. (1999) concerning the differential patterns of predictive relationships between phonemic awareness versus RAN and reading measures, and extended them using an additional measure of phonological skill and one of phonological decoding. The results of subgroup analyses were broadly consistent with the Bowers and Wolf (1993a, b; Wolf and Bowers 1999) double deficit framework. The group with double deficits was relatively poor in reading, and differed from children with single deficits on the Orthographic Choice task. However, children with only a naming speed deficit were the least impaired across tasks in our sample and did not show the deficient orthographic skills noted by Sunseth and Bowers (1997) and Bowers (1995) using variations of the same tasks. It is possible that the relationship between RAN and orthographic deficits would emerge in a larger sample of severely impaired readers.

It is also important to point out that much of the variance in reading that is accounted for by RAN times is associated with very fast, in addition to very slow, RAN times. The top 10% of this sample on RAN-Digits (with naming times below 25 seconds for the 50 items in the array, a rate of two items per second or greater) had a mean Woodcock Word Identification percentile of 77. In contrast, the bottom 10% on RAN Digits (representing naming times over 37 seconds) had a mean Word Identification percentile of 17.

STUDY 3: NAMING SPEED AND READING IN DISABLED AND NORMAL READERS

The third study to be reported here was conducted using data from an ongoing longitudinal study following two cohorts of normal readers and readers with dyslexia beginning in the third grade (Manis et al. 1999; Joanisse et al. in press). The present analyses have not been reported elsewhere. This study addressed several additional questions, indicated below in the data analysis section.

Participants

There were 67 children with dyslexia in the fourth and fifth grades (mean age: 11 years, 3 months). Children with dyslexia scored at the 25th percentile or lower on the Woodcock Word Identification test and had a scaled score of 85 or higher on either the Peabody Picture Vocabulary Test—Revised (PPVT-R) (Dunn and Dunn 1981) or the Visual Closure Test of the Woodcock-Johnson Cognitive Abilities Test—Revised (Woodcock and Johnson 1989). The latter two tests were included to provide some assessment of general cognitive ability. The Peabody assesses receptive vocabulary and Visual Closure, the ability to generate a "visual gestalt" for an incomplete line drawing of a common object. There were 61 fifth graders who scored above the 25th percentile on Woodcock Word Identification and had a scaled score of 85 or higher on either the Peabody or the Visual Closure test. For regression analyses, all 61 were included, but for double-deficit subgroup comparisons, only children who scored above the 35th percentile were included. The latter group was termed chronologically age-matched (CA-matched) normal readers. Their mean age was 11 years, 2 months. A sample of younger normal readers (*n* = 29) equated to the children with dyslexia in Woodcock Word Identification grade level (mean age: 7 years, 9 months) was included (the reading level, or RL comparison group). Identifying test score information for the three groups is shown in table 6. It can be seen that there was a discrepancy between the children with dyslexia's Woodcock Word Identification scaled score and their Peabody and Visual Closure scaled scores. Although this is not necessarily a defining feature of dyslexia (q.v., Stanovich and Siegel 1994), it does signify that the sample is in some ways typical of dyslexic samples studied in the past.

Test Battery

In addition to the standardized tests described above, children were given the following tasks, which served as criterion variables

Table 6.   Means and standard deviations for the identification variables (Study 3).*

Variable	GROUP		
	Dyslexics ($n = 67$)	CA Group ($n = 38$)	RL Group ($n = 29$)
Age (in months)	124.5 (5.72)[a]	124.6 (5.12)[a]	93.4 (7.93)[b]
PPVT-R Standard Score	93.1 (13.1)[b]	107.5 (13.1)[c]	105.9 (11.1)[c]
Visual Closure St. Score	101.0 (13.86)[a]	102.7 (9.98)[a]	102.69 (11.2)[a]
Word Iden. St. Score	76.4 (8.27)[a]	103.1 (7.65)[b]	111.04 (8.32)[c]
Word Iden. Gr. Equiv.	3.30 (.52)[a]	5.87 (1.84)[b]	3.23 (.63)[a]

*Groups with a different superscript differ at $p < .05$ by t-test.

in the regressions below. Exception Word and Nonsense Word Reading tasks were given that were identical to the tasks described earlier (70 items read aloud until a ceiling of 6 in a row wrong was reached). The Orthographic Choice task required children to decide which of two words appearing on a computer screen was a correctly spelled word (e.g., *rane* vs. *rain*) and press a button. One item was always a pseudohomophone. Both accuracy and latency were recorded. The Semantic Categorization task prompted the child with a category name (e.g., "Is it a part of the face?") followed by one of three types of items: a target item (*eye*), a homophone foil (*knows*), or a visual foil (*note*). Children responded by pressing a button and accuracy and latency were recorded. Children saw all three types of items for a given category (there were twelve in all), but never saw the actual exemplars corresponding to the homophones (e.g., they never saw *nose*). Only the target item data were analyzed here. Accuracy and latency were also recorded for Word and Nonword Pronunciation, involving the presentation of a single word or non-word on the computer screen. There were two types of words, exception words and regular words, analyzed separately.

On the predictor side of the equation, we assessed four domains other than Peabody Vocabulary. The Recalling Sentences subtest of the Clinical Evaluation of Language Fundamentals—Revised (CELF-3) (Semel, Wiig, and Secord 1995) was given to provide a measure of verbal working memory. Children repeated verbatim sentences that they heard on a tape. A phoneme deletion task was presented as well. Children had to delete a phoneme from a spoken word (25 items) or nonsense word (15 items) and pronounce the remaining segment. The segment was always another word in the case of the word trials and always a nonsense word in the case of the nonsense word trials. Word and nonsense word scores were combined in the analyses. Children were also given the RAN-Digits and RAN-Letters tasks described earlier (50 items in 5 rows of 10 items). Finally, a letter matching task was also included to assess basic letter recognition speed under circumstances that resembled the demands of reading printed words. The task, adapted from Bigsby (1990), required children to view an array of five letters on a computer screen and decide as quickly as possible whether it contained two letters with the same name (e.g., HbntB; vBccr) or not (e.g., gLkvm). Arrays always contained a mixture of upper and lowercase letters, and the matching letters were in the same case half the time and in alternating cases the other half of the time. This task assesses the ability to recognize printed letters visually and access a stored representation of each letter's identity.

Regression Analyses

Since reading ability varied continuously in the sample, the entire sample of fourth and fifth grade normal and disabled readers ($n = 128$) was utilized for hierarchical regression analyses. These were similar to regressions discussed earlier in that verbal ability (Peabody Vocabulary score) was always entered first, followed by CELF Recalling Sentences, to assess cumulative R^2 values. These two tasks, which provided a general assessment of language skill, were followed in the regression equation by either Phoneme Deletion or one of the RAN tasks. However, there were two important differences. First, the dependent measures included both accuracy and latency measures. Second, the regressions were carried out with and without the mediating variable of Letter Matching latency, entered just before the RAN measure in the prediction of latency measures of reading.

Hierarchical regressions involving the accuracy variables are shown in tables 7 and 8 for RAN-Digits and RAN-Letters separately. Peabody Vocabulary was a good predictor of all but Orthographic Choice. CELF-3 Recalling Sentences, entered next in the equations, was also typically a significant predictor, though it accounted for little variance over and above Peabody Vocabulary.

Commonality analyses were conducted for Phoneme Deletion and the two RAN tasks. Phoneme deletion accounted for considerable unique variance in Nonsense Word reading (factoring out RAN-Digits or RAN-Letters), and somewhat less, though still considerable, variance in Woodcock Word Identification and Exception Word Reading. Phoneme deletion accounted for minimal variance in Orthographic Choice and Semantic Categorization

Table 7. Concurrent hierarchical regression analyses for 4th-5th graders ($n = 128$). Variance in accuracy measures predicted by Peabody Vocabulary, CELF-3 Recalling Sentences, Phoneme Deletion, and RAN Digits, including commonality analyses. Values through Step 2 are cumulative R-squared; subsequent values are the proportion of variance accounted for by each component.

Variable	Word Identification Accuracy	Non-word Reading Accuracy	Exception Word Reading Accuracy	Orthogr. Choice Accuracy	Sem. Cat Target trial Accuracy
Peabody Vocabulary (1st step)	.190****	.136**	.165*****	.018	.127***
CELF-3 Recalling Sentences (2nd step)	.219	.196**	.233**	.029	.161*
RAN-Digits and Phon. Del.: common	.043	.068	.064	.02	.003
RAN-Digits: Unique	.035*	.002	.032*	.022	.003
Phoneme Deletion: unique	.160****	.333****	.101***	.016	.003
Total Variance	.457****	.599****	.430****	.087*	.170****

$*p < .05$ $**p < .01$ $***p < .001$ $****p < .0001$

Table 8.   Concurrent hierarchical regression analyses for 4th-5th graders ($n = 128$). Variance in accuracy measures predicted by Peabody Vocabulary, CELF-3 Recalling Sentences, Phoneme Deletion, and RAN Letters, including commonality analyses. Values through Step 2 are cumulative R-squared; subsequent values are the proportion of variance accounted for by each component.

Variable	Word Identification Accuracy	Non-word Reading Accuracy	Excep. Word Reading Accuracy	Orthogr. Choice Accuracy	Sem. Cat. Target trial Accuracy
Peabody Vocabulary (1st step)	.190****	.136**	.165****	.018	.127***
CELF-3 Recalling Sentences (2nd step)	.219	.196**	.233**	.029	.161*
RAN-Letters and Phon. Del.: common	.064	.052	.061	.029	.005
RAN-Letters: Unique	.054**	.003	.049**	.081***	.044*
Phoneme Deletion: unique	.139***	.349****	.104***	.013	.001
Total Variance	.476****	.600****	.447 ****	.151****	.211****

*p < .05   **p < .01   ***p < .001   ****p < .0001

(target trials only) scores. In contrast to the findings for young children reported earlier, the RAN tasks did not account for much variance in Non-word Naming, Exception Word Reading, or Woodcock Word Identification. RAN-Letters, but not RAN-Digits, was a significant predictor of Orthographic Choice and Semantic Categorization scores. Phoneme deletion and RAN did not share much common variance in any of these predictions.

Analyses of the latency variables are shown in tables 9 and 10. Peabody Vocabulary was a significant predictor of the pronunciation tasks, but not the Orthographic and Semantic tasks. CELF Recalling Sentences was a generally weak predictor of these tasks (it was only significant for Non-word Pronunciation). Commonality analyses revealed that Phoneme Deletion was a weak predictor of all tasks but Exception Word Pronunciation. Rapid Automatized Naming Digits was a somewhat stronger predictor of the latency measures than it was for the accuracy measures, and RAN-Letters was even stronger. Both RAN tasks were good predictors of Orthographic Choice and Semantic Categorization latency, but they also predicted Regular Word and Nonsense Word Pronunciation latencies. They were not significant predictors of Exception Word Pronunciation latency, although Phoneme Deletion was. Phoneme Deletion and RAN tasks shared little common variance.

Letter Match latency was entered into additional regressions immediately prior to the RAN-Letters task to see if the relationship of RAN to the speeded reading measures was mediated by letter recognition speed. These results are shown in tables 11 and 12 as cumulative R-squared values (rather than the commonality analysis format used above). For convenience, the unique variance accounted for by the RAN measure is indicated in parentheses. Some evidence of mediation by Letter Matching was found to be the case for the Orthographic Choice and Semantic Categorization tasks, where Letter Matching latency reduced the unique contribution of RAN-Letters and RAN-Digits by more than half. Letter Matching did not have this effect on the relationship between the RAN tasks and Regular or Irregular Word Pronunciation latencies or Non-word Pronunciation latencies.

To summarize, we obtained several findings that are relevant to the double deficit hypothesis. First, phonological skills and rapid serial naming made differential contributions to particular aspects of word reading skill. Phoneme Deletion was related to accuracy measures of word and nonsense word pronunciation in this sample, whereas RAN was most strongly predictive of accuracy and latency measures of orthographic and semantic processing, and latency

Table 9.   Concurrent hierarchical regression analyses for 4th-5th graders ($n = 128$). Variance in latency measures predicted by Peabody Vocabulary, CELF-3 Recalling Sentences, Phoneme Deletion, and RAN Digits, including commonality analyses. Values through Step 2 are cumulative R-squared; subsequent values are the proportion of variance accounted for by each component.

Variable	Orthographic Choice	Sem. Cat. Target trial	Regular Word Pronounciation	Irregular Word Pron.	Non-word Pron
Peabody Vocabulary (1st step)	.013	.002	.122***	.119***	.08**
CELF-3 Recalling Sentences (2nd step)	.033	.033	.156	.142	.129*
RAN-Digits and Phon. Del.: common	.009	.01	.052	.041	.006
RAN-Digits: Unique	.09***	.09***	.071**	.016	.049*
Phoneme Deletion: unique	.001	.00	.026*	.07**	.001
Total Variance	.133****	.133***	.304****	.269****	.185****

*.05   **$p < .01$ ***$p < .001$ ****$p < .0001$

Table 10. Concurrent hierarchical regression analyses for 4th-5th graders (*n* = 128). Variance in latency measures predicted by Peabody Vocabulary, CELF-3 Recalling Sentences, Phoneme Deletion, and RAN Letters, including commonality analyses. Values through Step 2 are cumulative R-squared; subsequent values are the proportion of variance accounted for by each component.

Variable	Orthographic Choice Latency	Sem. Cat. Target trial Latency	Regular Word Pronunciation Latency	Irregular Word Pron. Latency	Non-word Pron. Latency
Peabody Vocabulary (1st step)	.013	.002	.122***	.119***	.08**
CELF-3 Recalling Sentences (2nd step)	.033	.033	.156	.142	.129*
RAN-Letters and Phon. Del.: common	.009	.01	.05	.034	.01
RAN-Letters: Unique	.12****	.10****	.141****	.026*	.07*
Phoneme Deletion: unique	.00	.00	.027*	.077*	.00
Total Variance	.162****	.143 ***	.374****	.279****	.209****

*.05   **$p < .01$ ***$p < .001$ ****$p < .0001$

Table 11. Concurrent hierarchical regression analyses for 4th-5th graders (*n* = 128). Variance in latency measures predicted by Peabody Vocabulary, CELF-3 Recalling Sentences, Phoneme Deletion, Letter Matching and RAN Digits (values shown are cumulative R-squared values except where unique variance is shown in parentheses).

Variable	Orthographic Choice Latency	Sem. Cat. Target trial Latency	Regular Word Pronounciation Latency	Irregular Word Pron. Latency	Non-word Pron Latency
Peabody Vocabulary (1st step)	.013	.002	.122***	.119***	.08**
CELF-3 Recalling Sentences (2nd step)	.033	.033	.156	.142	.129*
Phoneme Deletion (3rd step)	.042	.043	.233**	.253***	.136
RAN-Digits (4th step)	.133***	.133***	.304**	.269	.185*
(RAN-Digits - unique variance)	.093***	.09***	.071**	.016	.049*
Letter Matching (4th step)	.192****	.201****	.222	.279	.204*
RAN-Digits (5th step)	.218*	.228*	.282*	.312	.257*
(RAN-Digits - unique variance)	.026*	.027*	.06*	.033	.053*

*.05   **$p < .01$ ***$p < .001$ ****$p < .0001$

Table 12. Concurrent hierarchical regression analyses for 4th-5th graders (n = 128). Variance in latency measures predicted by Peabody Vocabulary, CELF-3 Recalling Sentences, Phoneme Deletion, Letter Matching and RAN Letters (values shown are cumulative R-squared values except when unique variance is shown in parentheses).

Variable	Orthographic Choice Latency	Sem. Cat. Target trial Latency	Regular Word Pronounciation Latency	Irregular Word Pron. Latency	Non-word Pron. Latency
Peabody Vocabulary (1st step)	.013	.002	.122***	.119***	.08**
CELF-3 Recalling Sentences (2nd step)	.033	.033	.156	.142	.129*
Phoneme Deletion (3rd step)	.042	.043	.233**	.253***	.136
RAN-Letters (4th step)	.162****	.143****	.374****	.279	.206*
(RAN Letters - unique variance)	.12****	.10*	.141****	.026	.07*
Letter Matching (4th step)	.192****	.201****	.222	.279	.204*
RAN-Letters (5th step)	.243**	.236*	.360****	.313	.257*
(RAN Letters - unique variance)	.051*	.035*	.138****	.034	.053*

* .05   ** p < .01   *** p < .001   **** p < .0001

measures of word and non-word reading. Further, in line with the double deficit hypothesis, the relationship between RAN and orthographic processing was mediated in part by letter recognition speed.

Double Deficit Subgroups

The remaining analyses focused on the sample with dyslexia. The 67 children with dyslexia were categorized into four subgroups with double, single, or neither deficit, based on RAN-Digits and Phoneme Awareness scores (cut-off scores at the 40th percentile for the sample with dyslexia were used for this purpose, similar to the 35th percentile cut-offs used by Bowers 1995). There were 13 subjects in each deficit subgroup, and 28 in the no-deficit group. Scores on key tasks, some of which are used in the comparisons below, are shown in table 13 for the double deficit subgroups, the CA comparison group (5th graders who scored at or above the 35th percentile), and the RL comparison group (1st and 2nd graders who scored at or above the 35th percentile and matched the overall dyslexic mean for Woodcock Word Identification).

Given the large number of tasks administered, and the small sample sizes involved in making subgroup comparisons, there is an obvious problem with power. We minimized this problem by making only certain key comparisons that were especially pertinent to the double-deficit hypothesis. These were made with the t-test, without controlling for cumulative Type I error rate. These comparisons are reported as a series of questions below. Before reporting these analyses, it is useful to summarize the descriptive data for the subgroups. As expected, the DD subgroup was most impaired in Woodcock Word Identification, followed by the PD subgroup, but all four groups were below average, based on Word Identification percentile scores (group averages ranged from the 6th to the 12th percentiles). The groups differed only slightly from one another on the PPVT-R scaled score (the PD group was lowest) and the Visual Closure scaled score (the ND group was the lowest), and all groups scored close to the normal range (90 or above) on these two tasks. The DD group had lower scores than the other groups on most of the reading tasks, in line with the double deficit hypothesis. The following specific questions were addressed.

First, are readers with dyslexia with slow serial naming (the DD subgroup and the NSD subgroup) selectively impaired in orthographic skills? If this were the case, these subgroups should be deficient on the Orthographic Choice task relative to the other two dyslexic subgroups (PD and ND). This was true only for the DD subgroup, which was less accurate than the ND subgroup ($p < .05$)

Table 13. Means (standard deviations) for naming speed deficit (NSD), phonological deficit (PD), double-deficit (DD), and no deficit (ND) subgroups of dyslexic children and other comparison groups (Study 3).

Variable	GROUP					
	ND (n = 28)	NSD (n = 13)	PD (n = 13)	DD (n = 13)	CA Group (n = 38)	RL Group (n = 29)
RAN Digits (in secs)	25.4 (2.5)	34.9 (6.5)	25.4 (3.1)	37.3 (6.4)	25.7 (6.1)	31.8(6.2)
RAN Letters (in secs)	24.7 (2.8)	30.5 (4.7)	25.2 (3.2)	31.4 (4.9)	23.6 (4.4)	27.8 (4.1)
Letter Match RT (in secs)	2.11 (.49)	2.06 (.62)	2.27 (.59)	2.12 (.43)	1.95 (.57)	2.53 (.89)
Phoneme Deletion %	63.3 (13.0)	59.0 (11.6)	31.5 (7.7)	29.8 (12.0)	74.8 (14.8)	58.62 (23.7)
Non-word Reading %	30.7 (10.3)	28.9 (10.8)	17.6 (4.4)	18.1 (10.6)	50.4 (13.8)	35.2 (12.3)
Excep. Word Reading %	45.0 (7.5)	42.8 (12.7)	37.4 (5.3)	32.3 (11.8)	57.9 (5.2)	39.4 (12.0)
Word Iden. Grade Equiv.	3.70 (.40)	3.35 (.73)	2.95 (.31)	2.73 (.77)	5.87 (1.84)	3.23 (.63)
Word Iden. Percentile	12.6 (6.4)	11.1 (9.2)	7.2 (6.9)	6.2 (10.8)	56.4 (16.7)	76.4 (13.8)
Orthographic Choice %	78.7 (7.9)	80.1 (8.9)	75.5 (10.2)	72.6 (9.6)	85.6 (5.7)	76.4 (9.0)
Orthographic Choice RT	2.27 (.76)	2.16 (.59)	1.85 (.52)	2.64 (.89)	1.71 (.45)	2.26 (.84)
Sem. Cat. Target trial %	87.9 (7.2)	88.9 (11.5)	86.5 (8.8)	84.6 (12.7)	93.8 (7.1)	91.0 (6.3)
Sem. Cat. Target trial RT	2.08 (.77)	1.97 (.48)	1.80 (.38)	2.59 (.96)	1.58 (.49)	1.95 (.50)
PPVT-R Standard Score	96.4 (13.9)	90.1 (13.8)	89.3 (12.3)	92.2 (11.7)	107.5 (13.1)	105.9 (11.1)
Visual Closure St. Score	98.6 (12.3)	103.4 (13.0)	104.2 (18.5)	100.4 (13.5)	102.7 (10.0)	102.7 (11.2)

and slower than the PD subgroup ($p < .01$). However, the NSD subgroup did not differ from the other three dyslexic subgroups in either accuracy or latency. The results indicate that only the DD subgroup appears to be deficient in orthographic skill relative to subjects with dyslexia with superior naming speeds.

Second, does the orthographic deficit in the DD group extend to the Semantic Categorization task, which requires that children discriminate printed words from homophones (e.g., *nose* vs. *knows* as a "part of the face"). It seems likely that the Orthographic Choice and Semantic Categorization tasks rely on similar mechanisms (involving recognition of the unique spellings of words), although the latter task obviously makes additional demands on semantic processes. We found that the DD subgroup differed significantly (at the 0.025 level or less) from each of the other dyslexic subgroups for Semantic Categorization latency (target trials only), but the NSD group did not. No subgroup differences in accuracy were found on this task.

Third, is there any evidence that either dyslexic subgroup with slow naming times was deficient in letter recognition speed? It is apparent from table 13 that none of the dyslexic subgroups differed from one another in Letter Matching time, nor did they differ from the CA group.

CONCLUSIONS AND THEORETICAL INTERPRETATION

What can we conclude with regard to the three overarching questions guiding this series of studies? First, which aspects of reading skill are most related to serial naming speed? The answer depends on the age level and, to some extent, reading level of the subjects. Naming speed showed strong and unique relationships with accuracy-based measures of orthographic skill among the first and second grade sample in studies 1 and 2, independently of verbal ability and phonological skill. In contrast, naming speed was a relatively poor predictor of phonological decoding skill at this age (phoneme awareness was superior at this prediction). However, for the fourth and fifth grade sample in study 3, naming speed was not related strongly to any accuracy-based measures, but instead showed relationships with timed measures of word reading. This was not due to ceiling effects for the accuracy measures, as can be seen in table 13. The relationships with reading speed were not notably stronger for orthographic processing times as opposed to other aspects of reading (e.g., word naming time). Hence, there appeared to be a shift in the types of tasks predicted by serial naming times across age. Naming speed appears to be much stronger as a predictor of word reading fluency at older ages, and the prediction of word reading accuracy declines.

Secondly, does the magnitude of predictions from naming speed to reading decrease with age? As noted above, RAN times were not strongly related to accuracy measures of component reading skills for fourth and fifth graders, whereas these relationships were quite strong for first and second graders. Although naming speeds were related to word reading speeds among fourth and fifth graders, the relationships were not as strong as the relationships of naming speed to accuracy in grades 1 and 2. A related question is whether the naming speed-reading relationship remained strong among students with dyslexia. This was investigated by dividing students with dyslexia into subgroups based on naming speed and phonological skill. The primary finding was that children with a double deficit were clearly impaired on a variety of tasks, but children with a more isolated deficit in naming speed had much less severe impairments in word reading. It is possible, of course, that deficits would be observed beyond the word level for the isolated naming speed subgroup, but this was not explored. Based on the present study, the double deficit group should be the highest priority for intervention efforts, as they may be the most resistant to instruction in reading. The greater concentration of reading deficits among double deficit children may be due to the possibility that groups with single deficits in phonological processes or naming speeds find ways to compensate for their isolated problem. For example, a group with a single deficit in phonological analysis, but not naming speed, could presumably compensate somewhat for the deficit by reading faster, thereby increasing their print exposure, which directly benefits acquisition of orthographic knowledge.

The third primary question concerned which variables might mediate the relationship between naming speed and reading speed measures. Wolf and Bowers (1999) proposed that slow letter recognition might be a source of some of the orthographic deficits noted in past studies among children with slow serial naming times. We examined letter recognition speed directly using the Letter Matching task of Bigsby (1990). In our regression analyses for the fourth and fifth graders, the RAN-reading speed relationship appeared to be partially mediated by letter recognition speed, but this effect may have been carried mostly by the normally achieving children, since none of the dyslexic subgroups, including children with double deficits, were differentially slow on the Letter Matching task. Hence, the data are equivocal with regard to the mediating role of letter recognition speed for children with dyslexia.

To sum up, there may be a developmental shift away from a specific relationship of serial naming speed to orthographic skills in the early grades, to a more general relationship between serial naming speed and fluency-based measures at the word level and perhaps beyond. This may be true even for impaired readers in the later grades, as shown here for the fourth and fifth grade students with dyslexia. This may mean that the primary practical value of serial naming speed measures might be to make fairly broad predictions about which children are at risk for fluency problems in later reading. An additional value of serial naming speed measures may be that, in combination with standard tests of phonological skill, they help identify the most impaired sub-sample of poor readers (double deficit cases). This latter group is greatly in need of early and intense remediation.

REFERENCES

Ackerman, P. T., and Dykman, R. A. 1993. Phonological processes, confrontational naming and immediate memory in dyslexia. *Journal of Learning Disabilities* 26:597–609.

Adams, M., and Huggins, A. 1986. The growth of children's sight vocabulary: A quick test with educational and theoretical implications. *Reading Research Quarterly* 20:262–81.

Badian, N. A. 1993. Phonemic awareness, naming, visual symbol processing, and reading. *Reading and Writing: An Interdisciplinary Journal* 5:87–100.

Bigsby, P. 1990. Abstract letter identities and developmental dyslexia. *British Journal of Psychology* 81:227–63.

Blachman, B. A. 1984. Relationship of rapid naming ability and language analysis skills to kindergarten and first-grade reading achievement. *Journal of Educational Psychology* 76:610–22.

Bowers, P. G. 1995. Tracing symbol naming speed's unique contributions to reading disabilities over time. *Reading and Writing: An Interdisciplinary Journal* 7:189–216.

Bowers, P. G., Golden, J., Kennedy, A., and Young, A. 1994. Limits upon orthographic knowledge due to processes indexed by naming speed. In *The Varieties of Orthographic Knowledge I: Theoretical and Developmental Issues*, ed. V. W. Berninger. Dordrecht, The Netherlands: Kluwer.

Bowers, P. G., and Swanson, L. B. 1991. Naming speed deficits in reading disability: Multiple measures of a singular process. *Journal of Experimental Child Psychology* 51:195–219.

Bowers, P. G., and Wolf, M. 1993a. A double-deficit hypothesis for developmental reading disorders. Paper presented at the biennial meetings of the Society for Research in Child Development, March, New Orleans.

Bowers, P. G., and Wolf, M. 1993b. Theoretical links among naming speed, precise timing mechanisms and orthographic skill in dyslexia. *Reading and Writing: An Interdisciplinary Journal* 5:69–85.

Bradley, L., and Bryant, P. 1985. *Rhyme and Reason in Reading and Spelling*. Ann Arbor, MI: University of Michigan Press.

Bruck, M. 1992. Persistence of dyslexics' phonological awareness deficits. *Developmental Psychology* 28:874–86.

Cornwall, A. 1992. The relationship of phonological awareness, rapid naming, and verbal memory to severe reading and spelling disability. *Journal of Learning Disabilities* 25:532–38.

Denckla, M., and Rudel, R. G. 1976. Rapid "automatized" naming (R A N): Dyslexia differentiated from other learning disabilities. *Neuropsychologia* 14:471–79.

Dunn, L. M., and Dunn, L. M. 1981. *Peabody Picture Vocabulary Test-Revised*. Circle Pines, MN: American Guidance Service.

Felton, R., and Brown, I. S. 1990. Phonological processes as predictors of specific reading skills in children at risk for reading failure. *Reading and Writing: An Interdisciplinary Journal* 2:39–59.

Joanisse, M. J., Manis, F. R., Keating, P., and Seidenberg, M. S. in press. Language deficits in dyslexic children: Speech perception, phonology and morphology. *Journal of Experimental Child Psychology*.

Levy, B. A., and Hinchley, J. 1990. Individual and developmental differences in the acquisition of reading skills. In *Reading and Its Development: Component Skills Approaches*, eds. T. H. Carr and B. A. Levy. New York: Academic Press.

Lyon, G. R. 1995. Toward a definition of dyslexia. *Annals of Dyslexia* 45:3–27.

McBride-Chang, C., and Manis, F. R. 1996. Structural invariance in the associations of naming speed, phonological awareness, and verbal reasoning in good and poor readers: A test of the double deficit hypothesis. *Reading and Writing: An Interdisciplinary Journal* 8:323–39.

Manis, F. R., Custodio, R., and Szeszulski, P. A. 1993. Development of phonological and orthographic skill: A 2-year longitudinal study of dyslexic children. *Journal of Experimental Child Psychology* 56:64–86.

Manis, F. R., Seidenberg, M. S., and Doi, L. M. 1999. See Dick RAN: Rapid naming and the longitudinal prediction of reading subskills in first and second graders. *Scientific Studies of Reading* 3:129–57.

Manis, F. R., Seidenberg, M. S., Stallings, L., Joanisse, M., Bailey, C., Freedman, L., Curtin, S. 1999. Development of dyslexic subgroups: A one-year follow-up. *Annals of Dyslexia* 49:105–34.

Manis, F. R., Doi, L. M., Bhadha, B. 2000. Naming speed, phonological awareness, and orthographic knowledge in second graders. *Journal of Learning Disabilities* 33:325–33.

Meyer, M. S., Wood, F. B., Hart, L. A., and Felton, R. H. 1998. The selective predictive values in rapid automatized naming within poor readers, *Journal of Learning Disabilities* 31:106–17.

Olson, R. K., Wise, B., Connors, F., Rack, J., and Fulker, D. 1989. Specific deficits in component reading and language skills: Genetic and environmental influences. *Journal of Learning Disabilities* 22:339–48.

Perfetti, C. A. 1992. The representation problem in reading acquisition. In *Reading Acquisition*, eds. P. B. Gough, L. C. Ehri, and R. Treiman. Hillsdale, NJ: Lawrence Erlbaum Associates.

Rack, J. P., Snowling, M. J., and Olson, R. K. 1992. The nonword reading deficit in developmental dyslexia: A review. *Reading Research Quarterly* 27:29–53.

Rosner, J., and Simon, D. 1971. The auditory analysis test: An initial report. *Journal of Learning Disabilities* 4:384–92.

Semel, E., Wiig, E., and Secord, W. 1995. *Clinical Evaluation of Language Fundamentals*, 3rd ed. San Antonio, TX: Psychological Corporation.

Shankweiler, D., and Liberman, I. Y. 1972. Misreading: A search for causes. In *Language by Ear and by Eye*, eds. J. F. Kavanagh and I. G. Mattingly. Cambridge, MA: MIT Press.

Share, D. L. 1995. Phonological recoding and self-teaching: Sine qua non of reading acquisition. *Cognition* 55:151–218.

Siegel, L. S. and Ryan, E. B. 1988. Development of grammatical sensitivity, phonological, and short-term memory skills in normally achieving and learning disabled children. *Developmental Psychology* 24:28–37.

Silveroli, N. J. 1984. *Classroom Reading Inventory.* 4th ed. Dubuque, OH: William C. Brown.

Stanovich, K. E. 1988. The dyslexic and the garden-variety poor reader: The phonological-core variable-difference model. *Journal of Learning Disabilities* 21:590–604.

Stanovich, K. E. 1992. Speculations on the causes and consequences of individual differences in early reading acquisition. In *Reading Acquisition,* eds. P. B. Gough, L. C. Ehri, and R. Treiman. Hillsdale, NJ: Lawrence Erlbaum Associates.

Stanovich, K. E., and Siegel, L. S. 1994. Phenotypic performance profile of children with reading disabilities: A regression based test of the phonological-core variable difference model. *Journal of Educational Psychology* 86:24–53.

Sunseth, K., and Bowers, P. G. 1997, March. The relationship between digit naming speed and orthography in children with and without phonological deficits. Paper presented at the annual conference of the Society for the Scientific Study of Reading, Chicago, IL.

Torgesen, J. K., Wagner, R. K., Rashotte, C. A., Burgess, S., and Hecht, S. 1997. Contributions of phonological awareness and rapid automatic naming ability to the growth of word-reading skills in second to fifth grade children. *Scientific Studies of Reading* 1:161–85.

Vellutino, F., and Scanlon, P. 1987. Phonological coding, phonological awareness, and reading ability: Evidence from a longitudinal and experimental study. *Merrill-Palmer Quarterly* 33:321–63.

Wagner, R. K., and Torgesen, J. 1987. The nature of phonological processing and its causal role in the acquisition of reading skills. *Psychological Bulletin* 101:192–212.

Wagner, R. K., Torgesen, J. K., and Rashotte, C.A. 1994. Development of reading-related phonological processing abilities: New evidence of bidirectional causality from a latent variable longitudinal study. *Developmental Psychology* 30:73–87.

Wagner, R. K., Torgesen, J. K., Rashotte, C. A. Hecht, S., Barker, T. A., Burgess, S. R., Donahue, J., and Garon, T. 1997. Changing causal relations between phonological processing abilities and word-level reading as children develop from beginning to fluent readers: A five-year longitudinal study. *Developmental Psychology* 33:468–79.

Walsh, D., Price, G., and Gillingham, M. 1988. The critical but transitory importance of letter naming. *Reading Research Quarterly* 23:108–122.

Wechsler, D.A. 1991. *Wechsler Intelligence Scale for Children Revised.* San Antonio, TX: The Psychological Corporation.

Wimmer, H. 1993. Characteristics of developmental dyslexia in a regular writing system. *Applied Psycholinguistics* 14:1–33.

Wolf, M., Bally, H., and Morris, R. 1986. Automaticity, retrieval processes and reading: A longitudinal study in average and impaired readers. *Child Development* 57:988–1000.

Wolf, M., and Bowers, P. G. 1999. The double-deficit hypothesis for the developmental dyslexias. *Journal of Educational Psychology* 91:15–438.

Woodcock, R.W. 1989. *Woodcock Reading Mastery Tests Revised.* Circle Pines, MN: American Guidance Service.

Woodcock, R. W., and Johnson, M. B. 1989. *Woodcock-Johnson Psychoeducational Battery-Revised.* Allen, TX: DLM Teaching Resources.

Chapter • **5**

Is the Reading-Rate Problem of German Dyslexic Children Caused by Slow Visual Processes?

Heinz Wimmer and
Heinz Mayringer

German children with dyslexia are interesting for questions concerned with the causation of dyslexia because they suffer mainly from a massive reading fluency problem, but less from an accuracy problem (Klicpera and Schabmann 1993; Landerl, Wimmer, and Frith 1997; Wimmer 1993; Wimmer 1996). The high reading accuracy is not astonishing because German, in contrast to English, exhibits rather regular grapheme-phoneme relations (in particular for vowel graphemes) and teaching in first grade is focused on leading children to accurate word decoding via blending. A similar manifestation of developmental dyslexia is found in other more regular orthographies such as Spanish (Rodrigo and Jimenez 1999), Italian (Zoccolotti et al., 1999), Norwegian (Lundberg and Hoien 1990) and Dutch (Yap and van der Leij 1993).

A main cognitive associate of the reading fluency impairment of German dyslexic children has been found to be a rapid naming deficit (Wimmer 1993; Wimmer, Mayringer, and Landerl 1998). In their review of the role of rapid naming deficit in reading impairments, Wolf and Bowers (1999) consider the theoretical possibility that the empirical connection between rapid naming and reading fluency deficits is caused by impedements at a low visual perceptual level. In particular, they consider the argument that, due to a dysfunctional magnocellular visual system, the processing of lower spatial frequency components will be slowed, leading to slower visual feature detection and to slower letter identifications. This, in turn, would have the consequence that associations between letters that co-occur frequently in words would not be forged easily, and this then has the consequence that a full repertoire of orthographic patterns (which contributes to reading fluency) will not accrue.

Data from a recent investigation of cognitive deficits of German children with dyslexia allow us to examine this interesting hypothesis. Our investigation included phonological tasks (short-term memory, phoneme segmentation), rapid naming tasks, and—of importance for the present hypothesis—a set of visual processing tasks. This set included purely perceptual tasks: a visual choice reaction time task and a speeded (Greek) letter identity judgment task (involving strings of two and six letters). Further tasks involved more than perceptual processes: a speeded visual continuous performance task with letter-size configurations required additional attentional control processes and a visual memory task with time-limited presentation of sequences of Greek letters required short-term memory capacity. Because the children did not know Greek letters, no phonological contributions can be assumed for the visual short-term memory task and the letter identity judgment task. If the mentioned hypothesis is valid and the problem of children with dyslexia starts with slow visual processing then we would expect poor performance of our fluency-impaired children with dyslexia on the visual tasks. In examining this prediction we followed Lovett's (1987) distinction between rate-disabled and accuracy-disabled poor readers. The expectation was that particularly the rate-disabled subgroup may exhibit slow visual processing.

METHOD

Participants

The selection of the subgroups of reading-disabled children was a two-step process. The first step was based on a classroom reading test administered in the middle of grade 3 to a large sample of about 350 children. The classroom reading test consisted of several pages of sentence lists. The content of each sentence had to be judged as being correct or not (half of the sentences were correct). An example of an incorrect sentence is "For singing you need a pocket calculator." After each sentence a yes/no response box had to be marked. The initial sentences were short and consisted of simple words, and then sentences with longer words were included. Semantic content of the sentences were kept as simple as possible so that judging the sentence as correct or incorrect should pose no difficulty. The time limit was 10 minutes and the resulting measure was correctly marked sentences within this time limit. As expected, very few errors occurred so that the score reflects solely reading rate. A practice page was used to clarify the task and the response requirements. Children were selected for further testing, when they scored below percentile 20 on the classroom reading test, but did not score below percentile 20 on a classroom arithmetics test and did not exhibit a nonverbal IQ of below 90 on Raven's Coloured Progressive Matrices. Twenty-three children fulfilled the mentioned criteria and participated in an extended assessment of reading and cognitive deficits in our department.

The subtyping into a rate-disabled and an accuracy-disabled group was based on their reading-aloud performance on the word and non-word reading subtests (two each) of an individually administered reading test (Salzburg Reading and Spelling Test, Landerl, Wimmer, and Moser 1997). We selected as rate-disabled, 10 children (9 boys) from the 23 slow readers (identified by the classroom reading test), who exhibited the slowest reading times on the individual word reading subtests, but exhibited non-word reading accuracy in the normal range (percentile 30 and higher). Their mean reading rate for words (combined for the two subtests) corresponded to a percentile rank of 12. As accuracy-disabled, we selected 10 children (8 boys) from the slow reader group (classroom test based), who exhibited the lowest accuracy scores for non-word reading among the children of the slow reader group (i.e, error rates of 22% and higher). Errors for non-words were used as criterion, because very few errors occurred for word reading. In correspondence with their slow reading on the classroom reading test, the accuracy-disabled children also showed slow reading on the individual word reading subtest, although not as slow as the rate-disabled group. Their mean reading rate for words corresponded to a percentile rank of 20 (compared to a percentile of 12 for the rate-disabled group). Because of the slow reading of the accuracy-disabled children (both on the classroom test and also on the individual word reading subtests) we refer to them as rate-accuracy-disabled in the following. Both the rate-disabled and the rate-accuracy-disabled children were poor orthographic spellers, but the large majority of the orthographically wrong spellings were phonetically acceptable. An example of such a orthographically wrong, but phonetically acceptable spelling is Medchen instead of Mädchen. The means for orthographically correct spellings corresponded to percentiles of 24 and 14 for the rate-disabled and the rate-accuracy-disabled subgroup, respectively. The 26 control children (12 boys) scored above percentile 30 on the classroom reading test and often were class-mates of one of the reading-disabled children. Their reading rate for individual word reading corresponded to a percentile of 62 and their orthographic spelling performance to a percentile of 50.

Tasks

Visual Choice Reaction Time   Children had to press, as quickly as possible, the left or right button of a response box (operated with the left and right index fingers), after a left or right pointed black arrow (about 5 cm long) appeared on the computer screen. The arrow stayed on the screen until the child had responded. One second after the response, the next stimulus was presented. Children were introduced to the task by seven training trials and encouraged to respond quickly and accurately. Then 20 test trials (half right, half left oriented arrows in unpredictable sequence) followed. Correctness of response and time between onset of the visual stimulus and response were recorded automatically. The slowest reaction times (higher than 1510 milliseconds, 1% of all reaction times) were excluded to avoid distortions of individual means. Despite these exclusions, each child had reaction times for at least 80% of the trials. For each child and each hand an average reaction time was computed for correct responses. Errors were very infrequent.

Letter Identity Judgments   On this task children had to judge the identity of Greek letters that appeared in sequences of two or six letters on the screen. The size of the letters was 2 cm. For both lengths there were six identical and six non-identical sequences. In the non-identical six letter sequences, only one letter differed from the rest, and this deviating one never appeared in initial or final position. The child was instructed to press the left button (marked with =) of the response box for identical letters and the right button (marked with ≠) for non-identical sequences. Correctness of response and time between stimulus onset and response were automatically recorded. Response errors were infrequent. Separate for the two- and the six-letter sequences, the highest response times (1%) were excluded.

Continuous Visual Performance   This was a paper-and-pencil task designed to measure attentional performance in addition to visual perception. Children were presented a page with nine lines, each line consisting of 47 Smiley and Frowney faces. The faces were circles of only 3 mm (!) diameter with two dots as eyes and with a mouth that either was upward bent for the Smiley or downward for the Frowney. The child's task was to cross out quickly the Smileys with two additional marks. The two marks could be a double quotation mark above or below the Smiley or two single quotation marks (one above, one below the Smiley). The distractors most similar to the targets were Smileys with only one mark and Frowneys with two marks. On each of the nine lines (47 faces), the child worked for 20 seconds. Because errors were less than 4% for each group, we used an item per minute score.

Visual Short-Term Memory   For the assessment of visual short-term memory, children watched the sequential build-up of a horizontal sequence of Greek letters in a presentation box in the upper section of the computer screen and had then to reproduce the sequence from memory by touching the letters in the response box in the lower section of the screen. This response mode was realized using a touch-screen. The letters of a sequence appeared from left to right, the first letter was presented for one second before the second letter was added and so on. After the letters had disappeared from the presentation box, they re-appeared simultaneously in changed order vertically arranged in the response box. The instruction to the child was to move the letters from the response box to the stimulus box by touching them in correct order. The letter touched first appeared in the first position of the stimulus box and so on. After the child has filled all positions of the stimulus box, the correct sequence appeared above the box to give feedback. Children were introduced to the task by four practice trials. Then sequences (5 items each) consisting of three, four, and five different letters were presented. Percentage of correctly reproduced sequences was used as measure.

Rapid Naming   Here we used the standard digit naming task with randomized sequences of five digits repeated ten times on a page. The two other naming tasks were of the same format, one used five one-syllable animal words (*Hund*-dog , *Fisch*-fish, *Frosch*-frog, *Pferd*-horse, *Kuh*-cow), the other used five three-syllable animal names (*Schmetterling*-butterfly, *Papagei*-parrot, *Schildkröte*-tortoise, *Krokodil*, *Elefant*). Each of the two animal naming tasks was preceded by two introductory trials. On the first trial we made sure that each child knew the names of the depicted animals, and on the second trial, consisting of three lines with three animals each, children were familiarized with the rapid naming demand. Because naming errors rarely occurred, words per minute was used as measure.

Phonological Short-Term Memory   For this assessment children had to repeat sequences of mono-syllabic pseudowords. The length of the sequences ranged from two pseudowords to four pseudowords (e.g., /rip/, /ʃoːf/, /kut/). For each length level eight items were presented. The pseudowords were pronounced by a male speaker and digitalized using sound software. Presentation was done through high-quality head-phones. All items were composed of 20 different pseudowords (all of CVC structure). The individual pseudowords were initially singly presented to check for perception or articulation problems. Afterwards items were presented blockwise with increasing sequence length. Each block was preceded by a familiarization trial. As measure for the present analysis we used the number of correctly repeated sequences combined over the three sequence lengths.

Phoneme Segmentation   Children were presented nine complex 2-syllable non-words, which started and ended with a consonant cluster (e.g., *blowisk, flamont*). Children were required to first repeat each word—to guarantee correct perception—and then had to name each of the phonemes. The instruction stressed naming of sounds instead of naming letters, but letter names were also accepted as correct responses. Because the clusters were the most difficult parts to segment, only segmentation of the onset clusters and the offset clusters (9 each) were evaluated. Two practice items familiarized the children with the task.

Results and Discussion

Table 1 shows the cognitive profiles of the two reading-disability subgroups in relation to the non-disabled control children. The indexes above the means refer to the results of test comparisons between groups. For example, the indexes 2 and 3 above the mean digit naming score of the non-disabled group (in the first data column) indicates that the mean of the rate-disabled group (referred to with 2 because of being located in the second data column) and of the rate-accuracy-disabled group (referred to with 3) are reliably lower than that of the non-disabled group. For testing the differences between the non-disabled readers and each disability subgroup we used one-sided 5% Alpha levels, because there is no theoretical reason or previous empirical result to suggest that a disability group should perform better (!) than the non-disabled

Table 1 Cognitive Profiles of Rate-Disabled and Rate-Accuracy-Disabled Children

Measure	Non-disabled $n = 26$ M (SD)	Rate-disabled $n = 10$ M (SD)	Rate-accuracy-disabled $n = 10$ M (SD)
Visual deficits			
Choice reaction (ms)	507 (102)	487 (79)	510 (69)
Letter (Greek) identity (ms)			
2 identical	887 (182)	902 (217)	926 (154)
2 non-identical	951 (155)	963 (119)	985 (154)
6 identical	899 (161)	920 (172)	924 (105)
6 non-identical	994 (197)	1027 (152)	994 (135)
Continuous performance (items/min)	53 (7)	54 (11)	56 (8)
Visual memory (% correct)	53 (19)	50 (13)	48 (16)
Rapid naming (words/min)			
Digits	127 (16)[2,3]	96 (18)	97 (23)
Animals (1-syllable words)	63 (13)[2]	53 (8)	58 (14)
Animals (3-syllable words)	51 (9)[2]	43 (7)	45 (13)
Phonological deficits			
Short-term memory (% correct)	58 (14)[3]	55 (12)	45 (17)
Segmentation (% correct)			
Onset clusters	89 (15)	94 (6)	80 (30)
Offset clusters	83 (14)[3]	88 (14)[3]	63 (22)

[2]Significant difference ($p < .05$) of rate-disabled children.
[3]Significant difference ($p < .05$) of rate-accuracy-disabled children.

group. However, for testing the differences between the two disability groups two-sided 5% Alpha levels were used.

From the means in table 1, a rather simple pattern of results is evident. The first main finding is that performance on the full set of visual processing task was essentially unimpaired for both subgroups. This is particularly remarkable for the rate-disabled subgroup. For the visual choice reaction task and for the four conditions of the letter identity task, the mean latencies of the rate-disabled group were maximally 33 milliseconds longer (in the case of six non-identical letter strings) than the means of the non-disabled group. These small non-reliable group differences have to be evaluated in relation to the large *SD*s for each group. There also were no deficits of the reading-disability subgroups, when attentional demands (continuous performance) or when short-term memory demands (visual memory) were added to visual perceptual processes. Actually, on the continuous performance task the two reading-disability subgroups tended to perform faster than the non-disabled group.

The uniformly good performance of the two reading disability subgroups on the visual processing tasks stands in contrast to the performance on the rapid naming tasks. The rate-disabled group on all three tasks performed reliably lower than the non-disabled group and the rate-accuracy-disabled group did so on the digit-naming task. On the digit-naming task, which to a higher extent than the other two tasks assesses *automatized* naming, the deficit of the two reading-disability subgroups was large. For example, the mean of the rate-disabled group was about two SDs below the mean of the non-disabled group. On the phonological processing tasks, the pattern of deficits was quite different from that of the rapid naming tasks. Phonological short-term memory and segmentation of offset clusters (at the end of two-syllable pseudo-words) was impaired only for the rate-accuracy-disabled subgroup, but not at all for the rate-disabled subgroup. Actually, the latter subgroup tended to show better segmentation performance than the non-disabled group.

In summary, the results on the rapid naming and the phonological tasks are in correspondence with our previous findings that German children with dyslexia, as a group, show a marked rapid naming deficit, but a minor difficulty with phoneme segmentation (Wimmer 1993; Wimmer et al. 1998). The subgrouping here showed that the phonological segmentation problem was limited to the rate-accuracy-disabled group, whereas the rapid-naming problem was characteristic for both subgroups. The main new finding was that both subgroups exhibited unimpaired performance on the visual processing tasks. This is particularly astonishing for the children of the rate-disabled subgroup, who exhibited very good phonological segmentation skills. For this subgroup a visual processing speed impairment would have been the perfect candidate to explain both the reading fluency problem and the rapid naming problem. More generally, the present findings speak against the possibility that a reading fluency impairment can be traced back (via poor orthographic lexicon, impaired formation of inter-letter associations, and slow letter identification) to a dysfunctional magnocellular visual system.

Our own theorizing assumes that poor visual orthographic memory build-up (underlying the fluency impairment of German children with dyslexia) is due to impaired association formation between segments of phonological word form and letters of the written word. For this associative process to occur, the phonological word representations must be segmented so that individual letters can be associated with their corresponding phonemes. This may not be a problem for our rate-disabled subgroup with close to perfect recoding accuracy. Another critical condition is that there is time overlap between activation of the phonological word representation (and the embedded phonemes) and activation of the letter recognition units. If phonological word representations are accessed too slowly from the brain areas responsible for visual letter string processing, then the visual areas may no longer be active and little association formation may occur. This speed impairment in getting from visual representations to phonological representation may be tapped by rapid naming tests. A further problem may be the long-term stability of neural visual-phonological associations underlying orthographic word representations. If such associations are only short-lived or may need many more learning-trials to become stable, then the orthographic lexicon must be impoverished. In other words, the build-up of visual-orthographic word representations may be impaired because of impaired association formation between visual and phonological representations and not because of purely visual processing impairments.

REFERENCES

Klicpera, C. and Schabmann, A. 1993. Do German-speaking children have a chance to overcome reading and spelling difficulties? A longitudinal survey from the second until the eighth grade. *European Journal of Psychology of Education* 8:307–23.

Landerl, K., Wimmer, H., and Frith, U. 1997. The impact of orthographic consistency on dyslexia: A German-English comparison. *Cognition* 63:315–34.

Landerl, K., Wimmer, H., and Moser, E. 1997. *Salzburger Lese- und Rechtschreibtest (Salzburg reading and spelling test)*. Bern: Hans Huber.

Lovett, M. W. 1987. A developmental approach to reading disability: Accuracy and speed criteria of normal and deficient reading skill. *Child Development* 58:234–60.

Lundberg, I., and Hoien, T. 1990. Patterns of information processing skills and word recognition strategies in developmental dyslexia. *Scandinavian Journal of Educational Research* 34:231–40.

Rodrigro, M., and Jiménez, J. E. 1999. An analysis of the word naming errors of normal readers and reading disabled children in Spanish. *Journal of Research in Reading* 22: 180–97.

Wimmer, H. 1993. Characteristics of developmental dyslexia in a regular writing system. *Applied Psycholinguistics* 14:1–33.

Wimmer, H. 1996. The nonword reading deficit in developmental dyslexia: Evidence from children learning to read German. *Journal of Experimental Child Psychology* 61:80–90.

Wimmer, H., Mayringer, H., and Landerl, K. 1998. Poor reading: A deficit in skill–automatization or a phonological deficit? *Scientific Studies of Reading* 2:321–40.

Wolf, M., and Bowers, P. G. 1999. The double-deficit hypothesis for the developmental dyslexias. *Journal of Educational Psychology* 91:415–38.

Yap, R., and Van-der-Leij, A. 1993. Word processing in dyslexics: An automatic decoding deficit? *Reading and Writing* 5:261–79.

Zoccolotti, P., De Luca, M., Di Pace, E., Judica, A., Orlandi, M., and Spinelli, D. 1999. Markers of developmental surface dyslexia in a language (Italian) with high grapheme-phoneme correspondence. *Applied Psycholinguistics* 20:191–216.

Chapter • 6

Aberrations in Timing in Children with Impaired Reading:
Cause, Effect, or Correlate?

Deborah P. Waber

It is now a quarter century since the appearance of a pair of groundbreaking papers by Paula Tallal and Malcolm Piercy (Tallal and Piercy 1973, 1974), in which they proposed the controversial hypothesis that language disorders may result from a low-level deficit in the processing of rapid auditory transitions. They suggested that, because of this non-linguistic deficit of temporal processing, children would not be able to perceive speech stimuli accurately and a disorder of language processing and production could evolve. In a subsequent paper, Tallal (1980) extended this hypothesis to dyslexia, suggesting that a primary disorder of auditory temporal processing results in degraded speech perception which in turn affects phonological processing and hence reading. Other investigators produced evidence indicating that dyslexia is associated with temporally related deficits in the motor (Wolff 1990, 1993) and visual systems (Lovegrove, Martin, and Slaghuis 1986; Lovegrove 1993). The significance of these intriguing associations, however, has remained uncertain.

In the past decade, stimulated in part by technological advances in cognitive neuroscience and in part by the pioneering findings cited above, interest in the role of temporal processing deficits in dyslexia has escalated. In 1993, for example, the *Annals of the New York Academy of Sciences* published a proceedings on this provocative topic (Tallal, Galaburda, Llinas, and von Euler 1993). Shortly thereafter, Farmer and Klein (1995) published a lengthy review, including invited commentaries, in *Psychonomic Bulletin and Review*, in which they summarized what had by then grown to a fairly extensive literature.

The ensuing years have witnessed a steady stream of reports in the scientific literature, too many to summarize here, which have continued to provide diverse evidence supporting (and also arguing against) the basic premise that timing deficits play a role in dyslexia. As readers of this literature can attest, the core hypothesis remains controversial and at times contentious. The conference hosted by the National Dyslexia Research Foundation and organized by Maryanne Wolf, entitled "Time, Fluency, and Developmental Dyslexia," which was the basis for the present volume, represents the most recent milestone in the effort to integrate these diverse data and provide clarity in an area that can be murky and is frequently shaped by opinion as much as by fact.

In this chapter, I will summarize research at our institution that was stimulated by the basic temporal information-processing hypothesis. In so doing, I will bring to bear data to address three fundamental questions about the relationship of timing parameters in cognitive and neural processing to reading disability: (1) Do poor readers differ from good readers in their performance on low-level measures of temporal information processing? (2) Are the deficits observed on these temporal information processing tasks specifically characteristic of children with dyslexia or are they present in children with learning problems in general? (3) What is the basis for poor performance by disabled readers on the temporal information processing tasks? Finally, I will discuss how these data may inform our appreciation of the fundamental nature of the relationship between disordered "timing" and dyslexia: cause, effect, or correlation.

CHILDREN'S HOSPITAL, BOSTON LEARNING DISABILITIES RESEARCH CENTER

Our efforts in this area began in 1996, with funding from the National Institute of Child Health and Human Development (NICHD) of a multi-disciplinary Learning Disabilities Research Center (LDRC). My colleagues and I set out to collect data on a variety of "timing" measures from a large sample of children between the ages of 7 and 11 who had been referred to a clinic for evaluation of learning problems. We also evaluated a comparison group of school children without a history of learning problems. The central organizing hypothesis that motivated the work was that "the processing of temporal information is specifically disordered in LD children." As will be apparent, we approached this hypothesis from a number of directions, sampling from different modalities and at a variety of levels of analysis.

Sample

The unusual nature of our sample was key to our investigation. In undertaking this research program, we adopted a somewhat unorthodox approach to sample selection. Rather than selecting children for the study based on specific academic performance criteria (e.g., reading test scores), as is typical, we included in our study *any child within the specified age range referred to the Children's Hospital in Boston for evaluation of learning problems.* We then excluded those children with specific co-morbidities: ADHD hyperactive type, low IQ, bilingualism, psychiatric disorder, and neurologic impairment. The remaining 203 children made up what we termed the *learning impaired* (LI) sample. We specifically did not refer to them as *learning disabled* (LD) because many would not meet conventional discrepancy-based criteria. A *non-learning impaired* (NLI) group was evaluated for comparison purposes. This group included 243 children of the same age who had not been identified as having a problem and met comparable exclusion criteria. Table 1 shows the demographic characteristics of these groups; table 2 shows cognitive ability as measured by the Kaufman Brief Intelligence Test (Kaufman and Kaufman 1990) and academic achievement as measured by sub-tests from the Wechsler Individual Achievement Test.

This research strategy reflected a theoretical position that we have outlined elsewhere (Bernstein and Waber 1990; 1997), and is based on the premise that *a learning disorder results when a child's neurodevelopmentally based complement of skills is inadequate to adapt successfully to the demands of the academic setting.* According to this approach, the disorder is defined not only by the child's deficits (e.g., reading problem), but also by the child's assets and especially by the specific demands of that child's environmental context. Within this framework, referral for evaluation is itself an indication of an adaptive failure, and therefore it constituted the primary criterion for inclusion in the clinical group.

This theoretical approach derives from the developmental systemic tradition of Luria and Vygotsky (Luria 1973) and was

Table 1.   Demographic characteristics for LI and non-LI groups

	LI Group (N = 203)		NLI Group (N = 243)		
	Mean	SD	Mean	SD	p
Parent Education (in years)					
Mother education	15.0	2.2	14.9	2.3	n.s.
Father education	15.1	2.6	14.9	3.0	n.s.
Parent Occupation					
Mother occupation	6.5	2.0	6.3	2.2	n.s.
Father occupation	6.5	2.0	6.5	2.2	n.s.
Age	9.5	1.2	9.4	1.2	n.s.
Percent Males	67%	–	44%	–	< .001
Percent Right-Handed	86%	–	91%	–	n.s.

Note: Probability levels for means based on univariate t-tests; probability levels for frequencies based on Chi-square analyses

Table 2.   Cognitive Ability and Achievement Scores for LI and non-LI groups

	LI Group (N = 203)		NLI Group (N = 243)		
	Mean	SD	Mean	SD	p-value
Kaufman Brief Intelligence Test					
Vocabulary	102.2	11.1	109.2	10.4	< .001
Matrices	102.1	10.4	109.4	14.4	< .001
Composite IQ	102.4	10.5	110.4	11.6	< .001
Wechsler Individual Achievement Test					
Basic Reading	94.7	12.6	108.6	11.8	< .001
Spelling	92.6	11.3	108.9	10.6	< .001
Numerical Operations	91.9	11.7	107.5	11.5	< .001

Note: Probability levels based on univariate t-tests.

greatly influenced by the clinical experience of Jane Holmes Bernstein and myself in the neuropsychological assessment of children with learning problems. It also finds support in the modern clinical psychology literature. Wakefield (1992a;b), for example, argues that mental disorders can be viewed ecologically within the framework of the concept of "harmful dysfunction." He defines a disorder as existing "when the failure of a person's internal mechanisms to perform their functions as designed by nature impinges harmfully on the person's well-being as defined by social values and meanings. The order that is disturbed when one has a disorder is thus simultaneously biological and social; neither alone is sufficient to justify the label *disorder*." (Wakefield 1992b, p 373).

Learning disability, and specifically dyslexia, is quintessentially suited to such an analysis. In essence, the *social expectation* of literacy contributes to the etiology of this disorder as much as any specific characteristic of brain function. At the risk of oversimplifying, if the social norm did not anticipate that all children of normal intelligence would read and meet particular, age-referenced academic performance criteria, dyslexia would not be of great concern. Historically, public education and its goal of universal literacy are recent developments. Moreover, in the absence of a specific and evolutionarily recent cultural product (phonetically based text), children would have no occasion to decipher language in its written form. From an evolutionary perspective, therefore, it should not be surprising that so many children encounter difficulty adapting to this expectation. Nor is it surprising that dyslexia emerges as a problem primarily in the developed nations where universal literacy is a shared goal of the society.

Since the children in our sample presented for evaluation primarily because they failed to adapt to socially referenced expectations and community norms, they met the Wakefield criterion for having a harmful dysfunction. Given this heterogeneous sample, we were able to select subgroups of children that conformed to more conventional definitional criteria for dyslexia or other learning disabilities. *However, our sample also provided a unique opportunity to examine to what extent behavioral characteristics of timing that have been associated with reading are, in fact, specifically associated with reading, and to what extent they may be a more general characteristic of children with neurodevelopmentally based problems that interfere with adaptation to the demands of schooling.*

The Experimental Battery

The focus of the work was a computer-based battery of tasks presented to the children in a fantasy, game-like format. Tasks were chosen either because they had been demonstrated previously to be associated with dyslexia or because of the suspicion that they would prove revealing in children with learning disabilities. All involved some aspect of timing, all were non-verbal, and all were novel to the children. The tasks, which are described in detail elsewhere (Waber, Marcus et. al. 2001; Waber, Weiler et. al. 2000; Waber, Wolff et. al. 2000; Weiler et. al. 2000), can be summarized briefly as follows:

Rapid Auditory Processing This task was modeled after the Recognition task of Tallal (1980). Children listened to pairs of brief complex tones and decided whether the tones were the same or different. Stimulus length ranged from 40 milliseconds to 250 milliseconds and the inter-stimulus intervals (ISI) ranged from 10 milliseconds to 400 milliseconds. The outcome was number correct. According to Tallal, children with dyslexia experience relatively greater difficulty than normally reading children in identifying tones accurately when the pairs are presented rapidly.

Motor Timing Control   This task was modeled after the finger tapping task of Wolff (Wolff, et. al. 1990). Children learn to tap their fingers bi-manually in time to the beat of a metronome, and are instructed to continue tapping after the metronome is turned off. In a series of studies, Wolff (Wolff et. al. 1990; Wolff 1993) demonstrated that children and adults with dyslexia have greater difficulty than normally reading controls sustaining a steady beat. The outcome of interest is the variability of the intertap intervals in the metronome-off condition.

Motor Sequence Learning   This task was introduced by Nissen and Bullemer (1987) and measures implicit learning of motor sequences, a function that is viewed by some as fundamental to language development. This seemed a promising paradigm with which to determine whether children with dyslexia and other learning difficulties had a sequencing deficit. In the paradigm, subjects press keys corresponding to the changing location of a stimulus in a visual display (figure 1). The location of the stimulus changes in a repeating sequential pattern, and with repetition the response times typically decrease, indicative of learning. A block of random trials is then interposed. If the response times then rebound, it is inferred that at least part of the decrease was due to implicit learning of the motor sequence, even though the learner may have had no explicit awareness of the sequence. The outcome measure that best discriminated our groups was number of errors.

Visual Filtering   This task measures speed of visual serial search, another rate problem that might plausibly be associated with reading and other learning problems. It requires that the child determine

Figure 1.   Sample stimulus screen for Motor Sequence Learning task. Child is to press button corresponding to brackets that contain asterisk (Waber, Marcus et al. 2001).

whether an 'X' is located on a gray shape. Line fragments are super-imposed, and their location and orientation is varied from parallel (all fragments parallel) to 100% random (all fragments displayed in random orientations) (figure 2). As the proportion of randomly oriented line fragments increases, the time to accurately report whether the 'X' is on or off the gray shape increases. The most sensitive outcome was a summary measure of speed of response.

In addition to the battery of "low level information processing" tasks, children in the NLI group completed a brief battery of measures of cognitive ability and academic achievement and children in the LI group completed an extensive clinical neuropsychological battery. We also collected neurophysiological data (quantitative EEG) using the same or analogous paradigms, which could be correlated with the behavioral data. This multi-disciplinary effort provided a comprehensive database that has allowed us to address a wide range of questions about learning disorders. Because the subject of the present volume is dyslexia, reading is the primary focus of the questions posed here. In the remainder of this chapter, I will report on data from our Center in order to address three questions concerning the relationship of timing processes to dyslexia.

QUESTION 1: DO POOR READERS DIFFER FROM GOOD READERS IN THEIR PERFORMANCE ON LOW-LEVEL TESTS OF TEMPORAL INFORMATION PROCESSING?

The most basic question we asked was whether children who are poor readers differ from those who are good readers on these non-verbal measures of temporal information processing. We selected children who obtained scores below 85 or above 115 on the WIAT Basic Reading Test (regardless of referral group), a test of single

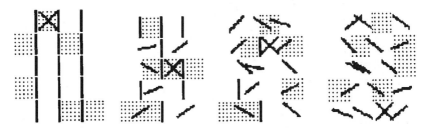

Figure 2.   Sample stimulus screens for Visual Filtering task. Stimuli with 0 %, 40%, 80% and 100% of line fragments rotated (Weiler, Harris, et al. 2000).

word identification. We then compared their performance on the four information processing measures. The answer to this question was clearly positive. As table 3 indicates, good and poor readers differed significantly on all four measures, even after adjusting for the effects of IQ. Nevertheless, the "timing" measures accounted for only a small proportion of the variance in reading scores (see, for example, Waber, Wolff et. al. 2001).

QUESTION 2: ARE THE DEFICITS OBSERVED ON THESE TEMPORAL INFORMATION PROCESSING TASKS SPECIFICALLY CHARACTERISTIC OF CHILDREN WITH DYSLEXIA?

Although we were able to demonstrate clearly that good and poor readers differed in their performance on the information processing tasks, we did not yet know whether this association was actually specific to reading, or whether these information-processing deficits might be characteristic of the LI group in general. We addressed this question from a number of perspectives.

Neuropsychological Profiles

One study, (Morgan et. al. 2000) identified 40 children referred for evaluation who scored above 90 on the four sub-tests of the Wechsler Individual Achievement Test (WIAT) that we administered to the LI group (Basic Reading, Reading Comprehension, Spelling, Numerical Operations) and compared them with 81 similarly referred children who scored below 90 on at least one of the achievement sub-tests. Neuropsychological profiles of these two groups were evaluated (figure 3). The adequate achieving LI group

Table 3.   Mean scores (expressed as z-scores) of Good (WIAT Basic Reading > 115, N = 98) and Poor (WIAT Basic Reading < 85, N = 61) Readers on the Four Low Level Information Processing Tasks

	Good Readers		Poor Readers		
Task	Mean	SD	Mean	SD	p
Rapid Auditory Processing	−.36	.91	.90	1.08	< .0001
Motor Timing Control	−.11	.98	.68	.80	< .0001
Motor Sequence Learning	−.00	.95	.68	1.58	< .002
Visual Filtering	−.00	1.11	.92	1.49	< .0001
Summary Score	−.48	2.58	3.18	2.84	< .0001

Note: Z-scores normalized to entire non-learning impaired (NLI) sample (N = 243). P-values reflect comparisons adjusted for effect of Kaufman-Brief Intelligence Test score (K-BIT). Means are unadjusted for K-BIT. Summary score is sum of z-scores for the four measures.

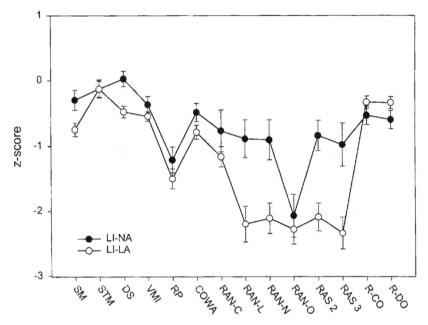

Figure 3. Mean scores adjusted for Full Scale IQ for neuropsychological measures expressed as z-scores. LI-NA = Learning Impaired-Normal Achieving; LI-LA = Learning Impaired-Low Achieving; SM = WRAML Sentence Memory; StM = WRAML Story Memory; DS = WISC-III Digit Span; RP = Repeated Patterns; COWA = Controlled Oral Word Association; RAN-C = Rapid Automatized Naming Colors; RAN-L = Rapid Automatized Naming Letters; RAN-N = Rapid Automatized Naming Numbers; RAN-O= Rapid Automatized Naming Objects; RAS-2 = Rapid Alternating Stimuli 2-Set; RAS-3 = Rapid Alternating Stimuli 3-Set; R-CO = Rey-Osterrieth Complex Figure Copy Organization; R-DO = Rey-Osterrieth Complex Figure Delayed Recall Organization (Morgan et al. 2000).

had IQ and reading scores that were significantly *above* expectation for age, but their scores were significantly *below* expectation on measures that were sensitive to rate and fluency of output. These included Controlled Oral Word Association, Repetitive Graphomotor Patterns, all Rapid Automatized Naming (RAN) sub-tests and both Rapid Alternating Stimulus (RAS) sub-tests. Nevertheless, they outperformed the low-achieving LI group on three of the RAN sub-tests (Letters, Numbers, Colors) and the RAS. Thus, both LI groups, adequate readers and poor readers, showed rate deficits, but the poor readers were especially impaired on the naming speed tasks which, like reading, required transformation of a visual symbol to a spoken word.

Information Processing

In a related study, Harris et. al. (2001) selected from our LI sample 65 children who scored in the adequate range (standard score > 90) on the four sub-tests of the WIAT. These children were compared on the low-level information processing battery with 65 children matched for age, sex, and non-verbal cognitive ability who obtained a low score on at least one of the WIAT tests. The adequate achieving LI children were also compared with 65 children from the NLI group (that is, the non-referred school sample). As a conservative comparison, we matched the adequate achieving LI children and the NLI children not only for age and sex, but also for their scores on the WIAT Basic Reading Test.

As figure 4 indicates, the adequate achieving LI group achieved scores on the information processing tasks that were generally between those of the reading-matched NLI group and those of the low achieving LI children. Statistical comparisons indicated that the adequate achieving LI children performed more poorly

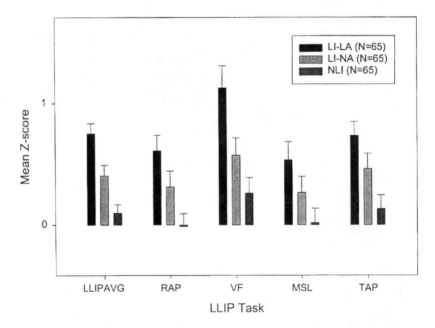

Figure 4.   Means and standard errors of scores by group on LLIP tasks. LA = Low Achieving Learning Impaired; NA = Normally Achieving Learning Impaired; NLI = Non-Learning Impaired. LLIP = Low-Level Information Processing; LLIPAVG = Average LLIP score across 4 tasks; RAP = Rapid Auditory Processing; VF = Visual Filtering; MSL = Motor Sequence Learning; PFT = Paced Finger Tapping (Harris et al. 2001).

than their NLI reading matched controls ($p < .05$) but did not differ from the low achieving referred children ($p > .5$) on a summary measure of the battery. For the individual tasks, there was similarly no difference between low achieving and adequate achieving children from the LI group on any measure; however, adequate achieving children from the LI group scored more poorly than their reading-matched NLI controls on Motor Timing Control ($p = .07$) and Rapid Auditory Processing ($p = .05$).

These findings argue against the existence of a special relationship between reading disability and performance on these information processing tasks, which have previously been associated with dyslexia: among the LI children, low achievers (mostly in reading/spelling), and adequate achievers obtained scores that were statistically comparable. Moreover, adequate achieving children from the referred group performed more poorly than NLI controls, *even though the groups were matched for single-word reading ability.*

Rapid Automatized Naming

We also evaluated the specificity of timing problems to dyslexia by examining performance on the RAN test among the LI children (Waber et. al. 2001). The RAN test (Denckla and Rudel 1976) consists of four separate cards, each of which displays five stimuli within one semantic domain (letters, numbers, colors, and objects) that are repeated in random sequence for a total of 50 stimuli per card. The task is to name the 50 stimuli on each card as quickly and accurately as possible. For this study, we defined a deficit on the RAN as a mean score for the letters and numbers sub-test that was more than one standard deviation above the mean for age, using normative data provided by Wolf and Biddle (1995).

Children were classified as having a reading disability (RD) if they met either a low achievement (score on reading test at least 1 SD below population mean) or a regression-based discrepancy (score on reading test at least 1.5 SD below score predicted by WISC-III Full Scale IQ [Reynolds 1985]) definition of impaired reading. All other children were considered adequate readers. This classification procedure was carried out twice, once using the WIAT Basic Reading subtest as the criterial reading measure and once using the Test of Word Reading Efficiency (TOWRE) Sight Word subtest (Torgeson, Wagner, and Rashotte 1999) as the criterial measure, in order to consider both reading accuracy and reading rate.

We first examined the joint distribution of naming speed deficits and RD in the referred sample. Overall, 68% of the referred sample demonstrated a naming speed deficit. By contrast, the prevalence of RD was only 32% (untimed) or 58% (timed). The prevalence of naming speed deficits was especially high among those children with RD, 85% by the untimed reading criterion for RD and 80% by the timed criterion.

Of greater interest, in terms of the specificity question, was the prevalence of naming speed deficits among the LI children who were adequate readers. When RD was classified by the un-timed reading criterion, 60% of LI children who were adequate readers showed a naming speed deficit, and 51% for the timed criterion. Thus, although the vast majority of children with RD had a naming speed deficit, such deficits were also prevalent well above the expected rate among children referred for learning problems who were adequate readers.

We next applied signal detection analysis, using a Receiver Operating Characteristic (ROC) technique, which estimates the extent to which performance on a specific test (e.g., RAN) can correctly assign individual children to a group. These analyses suggested that a one standard deviation cut-off for the RAN would yield the best discrimination between groups. When we used this criterion to discriminate the LI group from normative controls, the correct classification rate approached 80%. Further, when we compared RD children with controls, the correct classification rate approached 90%. By contrast, the classification rate for discriminating RD from non-RD LI children was only 65%, with a remarkably high false positive rate of 60% (untimed) or 51% (timed). Learning impaired children who were adequate readers were very likely to be mis-classified as poor readers by the RAN.

In sum, although most children with RD demonstrated a naming speed deficit, a substantial number of learning impaired children who were adequate readers also did so. Thus, as was the case for the information processing tasks, the extent to which slow naming speed is a specific characteristic of children with reading impairment remains open to question.

QUESTION 3: WHAT IS THE BASIS FOR POOR PERFORMANCE BY DISABLED READERS ON THE TEMPORAL INFORMATION PROCESSING TASKS?

Another question we explored was to what extent the poor performance of the dyslexic group (and of the learning impaired group as suggested above) is actually related to the temporal dimensions of the tasks. Several of our studies addressed this issue.

Low Level Information Processing Tasks

As indicated above, there was no question that the performance of good and poor readers differed on the four basic information processing tasks and also that referred children differed from non-referred children independent of their reading skill. The more difficult question was the extent to which these differences reflected temporal processing.

This problem is best illustrated by our examination of the Rapid Auditory Processing task. Table 3 leaves no doubt that good readers performed more accurately than poor readers on this task. The more important question, however, is to what extent these differences reflect differential responding to the temporal dimensions of the stimuli. In her study of dyslexic readers, Tallal (1980) predicted that individuals with dyslexia would be at a greater disadvantage compared to good readers as the stimuli were presented more rapidly (e.g., briefer interval between stimuli in a pair). Contrary to this prediction, we found that the group differences were of equal magnitude, no matter whether the stimuli were long or short or whether the ISIs were long or short (figure 5).

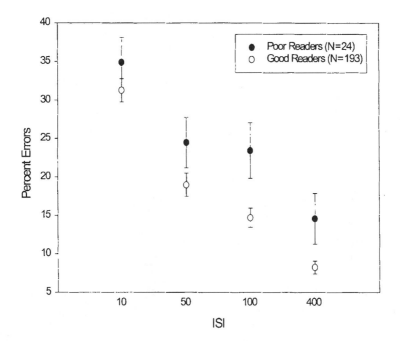

Figure 5.   Mean percent and standard errors for RAP total errors for poor and good readers by inter-stimulus interval (ISI) for 75 millisecond stimulus duration. (From Waber et al. 2001).

Paradoxically, moreover, the longest stimuli (250 milliseconds), which should have been the easiest to process if timing were the key dimension, were associated with the longest response times (figure 6). This was true for both the LI and NLI groups. We speculated that at the short ISIs, children perceived the two tones as a single stimulus, but at the longer ISIs, they needed to access auditory working memory to match the second tone to the first, and that this required more time.

A companion neurophysiological study, using quantitative electroencephalography (EEG) lent a further dimension to interpretation of the behavioral findings (Duffy, McAnulty, and Waber 1999). Auditory evoked potentials were generated to stimulus pairs consisting of 40 milliseconds complex tone stimuli with ISIs ranging from 10 to 200 milliseconds. Differences between good and poor readers were detected at both long and short ISIs, but, significantly, these emerged in different brain regions and with different latencies, depending upon the length of the ISI. For brief ISIs, the difference emerged relatively soon after the stimulus was delivered and was centered over Wernicke's area, the language area in left

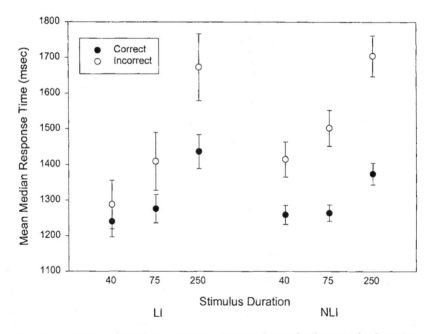

Figure 6.   Mean of median response time and standard errors for learning impaired (LI) and non-learning impaired (NLI) children by stimulus duration and response type (correct or incorrect). (From Waber et al. 2001).

posterior temporal cortex. For longer ISIs, the difference occurred much later and was more central and frontal. Thus, the processing of rapid and slower sequences of auditory stimuli may actually engage different neural mechanisms even though the behavioral response (i.e., number of errors) is superficially indistinguishable. For the rapid stimuli, performance differences could reflect primarily perceptual processing, whereas for the slower stimuli, comparable differences could reflect a cognitive process, perhaps involving auditory working memory. Relevant to the temporal hypothesis, however, the poor readers consistently processed the information less efficiently than the good readers, regardless of the length of the interval.

Quantitative EEG similarly informed our interpretation of the differences we observed on the Motor Timing Control test. As indicated above, we found that poor readers tapped with less stability than did good readers, entirely consistent with the prior work of Wolff et. al. (1990) on children with dyslexia. In order to be successful at this task, children must form an internal representation of the metronome rhythm and entrain their motor output to it. Duffy et. al. (1999) examined task-related EEG spectral coherence, which is interpreted by some as an indicator of the effectiveness of cortical connectivity, during unimanual and bimanual finger tapping maneuvers in LI and NLI children. Reliable group differences emerged, with diminished coherence in the LI children. These differences most prominently involved the left mid-temporal area and bilateral mid and posterior frontal regions, consistent with areas identified by functional magnetic resonance imaging in normal adults (Rao et al. 1997) and in good and poor readers (Rivkin et al. 2000). Duffy et al. suggested that a degraded functional connection between these areas could impede motor system access to a working memory representation of the auditory signal. An integration problem of this type could cause rhythmic tapping to be less stable, without need to posit a deficit in a central "timing" mechanism. Diminished functional integration of these areas (or other areas involving the left temporal region), moreover, could also have adverse consequences for the acquisition of fluent reading skills. Thus, both unstable rhythmic finger tapping and poor reading might reflect a common underlying process, because both depend in part on a common neural mechanism, but poor rhythmicity would not necessarily bear a *causal* relation to poor reading.

These coordinated behavioral and neurophysiological studies document differences at the neural level between children who read well or poorly in terms of their information processing. These differences, moreover, can be reflected in parameters of their responses on behavioral tasks that involve timing. The results do not, however, lend powerful support to the notion of a temporal information-processing deficit in children with dyslexia. Rather, the tasks may be better conceptualized as probes that can highlight neural regions of poor processing that can also affect reading. For example, the Rapid Auditory Processing task demonstrates poor auditory perceptual processing associated with posterior temporal cortex, an area that is generally viewed as crucially involved in reading (Horwitz, Rumsey, and Donohue 1998; Klingberg et al. 2000; Rae et al. 1998). Thus, any task that requires precise resolution of auditory stimuli may be affected, including, but not limited to, resolution of the temporal dimension. Indeed, good and poor readers differ in pitch discrimination, even when the stimuli are relatively long (Baldeweg et al. 1999; deWeirdt 1988). The extent to which diminished stimulus resolution may play a causal role in poor reading acquisition is an open question. In any event, we did not find persuasive evidence that timing per se is special.

Rapid Automatized Naming

We also approached this question in the context of the RAN test, guided by the Double Deficit Hypothesis (Wolf 1999). Wolf suggests that naming speed represents a process that is independent of phonological coding, presumably involving rate, and that these two deficits can occur independently or in combination (Double Deficit). Naming speed is thought to be most closely associated with reading rate, suggesting again that a temporal deficit may be at work.

We sought to determine not only to what extent RAN performance was associated with reading rate but more specifically *to what extent this relationship might be accounted for by a more generic processing speed component of the RAN task.* Children completed the Test of Word Reading Efficiency (TOWRE) (Torgeson, Wagner, and Rashotte 1999), which measures how many words from a graded list (words or non-words) the child can read accurately in 45 seconds. We then used hierarchical regression to determine to what extent naming speed predicted rate and, further, to what extent this association could be accounted for by a standard measure of processing speed, the Wechsler Coding sub-test (Kail and Hall 1994). In a separate study (Weiler et al. in press), we had confirmed by factor analysis that the RAN and Coding tests both loaded on the same factor, which appeared to represent processing speed.

Table 4 shows the results of these regression analyses for the Sight Word sub-test (real words). Results were entirely comparable

Table 4. **Hierarchical Regression Analysis: Models Predicting Scores on Test of Word Reading Efficiency Sight Word Sub-test**

Variable	Parameter Estimate	t	p	R2
RAN	–.27	–8.09	< .0001	.26
WIAT Basic Reading	.05	13.60	< .0001	.63
RAN	–.13	–5.18	< .0001	
Coding	.01	.59	.59	.63
WIAT Basic Reading	.05	13.59	< .0001	
RAN	–.12	–4.67	< .0001	

Note: Parameter estimates are unstandardized.

for non-words. The RAN accounted for a significant proportion of variance in reading efficiency. We next entered a measure of word reading accuracy (WIAT Basic Reading), to control for its influence on reading rate. Not surprisingly, reading accuracy accounted for a substantial amount of variance in reading efficiency, and the parameter estimate (Beta) for the RAN was somewhat reduced. Nevertheless, RAN remained a significant predictor of reading rate ($p < .0001$), even with reading accuracy included in the equation. If the contribution of RAN were essentially processing speed, we reasoned, forcing Coding into the equation before RAN should substantially reduce its influence. In fact, Coding performance was not a significant predictor of reading rate ($p > .5$), nor was the parameter estimate for RAN reduced by the addition of Coding to the equation. Thus, although the RAN reliably predicts reading rate independent of accuracy and it appears to measure processing speed, rate itself does not appear to be the determining component.

The fact that we could not document that timing was the key variable here by no means diminishes the potential significance of the remarkably robust association between performance on the RAN task and reading, which cannot be attributed to phonologic processing. Although our data indicate that slow naming speed is characteristic of children with learning impairment in general and not specific to dyslexia, the outcome measure, that is, naming speed, is likely to reflect different underlying processes in different children. Careful analysis of the relative "cost" of component processes in children with different clinical features could yield a more accurate appreciation of the significance of the RAN task for reading and other learning problems. Such specificity could inform the construction of interventions for different groups.

SUMMARY

Our studies yielded several key findings that can be integrated into the discourse on dyslexia and timing. Like most other researchers who have worked in this area, we confirmed that poor readers reliably perform more poorly than good readers on non-verbal information processing tasks that appear to have a significant temporal component.

Perhaps the most striking finding, however, is that these deficits are not unique to children with significant reading problems. Although they were somewhat more consistent and severe in LI children with documented reading deficits, they were also prevalent well above expected levels among LI children who could read. The latter group was reliably differentiated on the basis of these information-processing tasks from non-referred controls, even when the groups were matched for reading skill. The obvious question raised by these findings is the following: if timing problems play a causal role in dyslexia, why can this subgroup of learning impaired children, who also appear to have timing problems, read?

Finally, we demonstrated that the deficits that reading impaired children exhibit on these non-verbal information processing tasks do not necessarily reflect a specific response to their temporal dimensions. Rather, differences appear to arise for a variety of reasons, and there does not appear to be any single unifying mechanism.

SIGNIFICANCE

The point of departure for our studies was a set of four information processing tasks that were either selected from the published literature on dyslexia or implemented because they were plausibly associated with learning impairment. All the tasks entailed some element of timing and, as our data indicate, all effectively distinguished good from poor readers independent of IQ. The demands of these four tasks, however, differ dramatically. The temporal dimension is, in a sense, a generic feature to most performance tasks. To subsume diverse paradigms under a rubric of "timing," therefore, may not be especially meaningful. What may be most significant and remarkable about these findings is that poor readers were so consistently impaired on a collection of non-verbal tasks that bear no obvious relationship to the reading process itself. The fact of these improbable associations itself invites scrutiny.

As the title of this chapter suggests, associations between timing measures and dyslexia could, in theory, reflect three types of relationships: cause, effect, and correlation. The first is obviously the most intriguing. If the observed temporal processing deficits are low-level building blocks of higher cognitive functions, a low-level deficit could have a cascade effect, leading causally to the cardinal and defining symptom of dyslexia, disordered reading. Such a causal relationship could stimulate innovative therapeutic approaches, such as the one designed by Tallal and her colleagues to intervene in language disorders (1996).

Alternatively, the observed rate and timing differences could actually be *effects* of "poor processing." If a component neurocognitive operation is disordered, this disorder could be manifest behaviorally as either slowed output or degraded perception. This would not necessarily mean that "timing" per se was the significant factor, but rather that deficits in rate, timing, or perceptual accuracy are evidence for underlying processing problems. The same underlying problem that is manifest in aberrations of timing could also affect reading.

Our studies provided circumstantial evidence for such relationships. The qEEG study of Motor Timing Control suggests inefficient integration of component processes, with a neural substrate that may be partially shared by rhythmic finger tapping and reading. In this context, it is not necessary to posit a central timing mechanism that affects reading; rather, analysis of the finger-tapping task provided a basis for appreciating the substrate for reading. It also provided a basis for understanding the clinical observation that reading problems rarely occur in isolation, but are typically accompanied by more wide ranging difficulties involving not only language, verbal learning, and memory, but also less obviously related functions such as motor output and visuoconstructional skills. From a clinical perspective, these corollary findings are not incidental, but can have important consequences for the child's ability to adapt to the demands of schooling.

The final possibility to be considered is that some of these timing tasks, in fact, have nothing to do with reading on a functional basis, but simply tend to co-occur with reading deficits in certain individuals. One of the perplexing problems in learning disabilities research is that, as a group, learning disabled children will predictably perform less well than other children on a heterogeneous assortment of cognitive tasks (Morris et al. 1998). Generic problems of organization, efficiency, and output are prevalent, as our data once again illustrate, affecting performance across academic domains. More often than not, dyslexia resides in the context of this broad and difficult to characterize neuropsychological matrix.

The non-verbal information-processing problems associated with dyslexia may not in fact cause the reading problem, but their regular co-occurrence with cognitive features specific to dyslexia can complicate treatment. Many children with a history of early reading problems who manage to acquire literacy with intensive intervention can continue to encounter academic problems even though their mastery of reading has been substantially improved. All too often, a child who responds successfully to early intervention is graduated from special education, only to falter as the academic demands increase in the later grades. (Because the skill deficit has been remediated, the child no longer "qualifies.") Although significant advances have been achieved in our appreciation of the cognitive and neural mechanisms underlying the acquisition of reading skill, remarkably little is known about the basis for the compromises of efficiency, organization, and integration that are so widespread among children with learning problems. Efforts to parse these functions with the care and rigor that has been devoted to reading could enhance the well-being of children with co-occurring disorders of reading and other aspects of cognitive function that can compromise their adaptation to the demands of the school environment.

The explorations described here by no means resolve existing issues and controversies about temporal processing and dyslexia. Rather, they raise questions about the significance of these intriguing associations, suggest directions that may prove productive, and emphasize the importance of continuing, critical analysis of both the associations themselves and the assumptions that may accompany them.

REFERENCES

Baldeweg, T., Richardson, A., Watkins, S., Foale, C., and Gruzelier, J. 1999. Impaired auditory frequency discrimination in dyslexia detected with mismatch evoked potentials. *Annals of Neurology* 45:495–503.

Bernstein, J. H., and Waber, D. P. 1990. Developmental neuropsychological assessment: The systemic approach. In *Neuromethods*, Vol. 17, eds. A. A. Boulton, G. B. Baker, and M. Hiscock. Humana Press.

Bernstein. J. H., and Waber, D. P. 1997. Pediatric neuropsychological assessment. In *Behavioral Neurology and Neuropsychology*, eds. T. E. Feinberg and M. Farah. McGraw-Hill.

Denckla, M. B. and Rudel, R. G. 1976. Rapid Automatized Naming (RAN): Dyslexia differentiated from other learning disabilities. *Neuropsychologia* 14:471–79.

DeWeirdt, W. 1988. Speech perception and frequency discrimination in good and poor readers. *Applied Psycholinguistics* 9:163–83.

Duffy, F. H., McAnulty, G. B., and Waber, D. P. 1999. Auditory evoked responses to single tones and closely spaced tone pairs in children grouped by reading or matrices ability. *Clinical Electroencephalography* 30:84–93.

Duffy, F. H., McAnulty, G. B., Wolff, P. H., and Waber D. P. Diminished cortical connectivity during internally paced rhythmic finger tapping in children referred for diagnosis of learning problems (Unpublished manuscript).

Efron, R. 1990. *The Decline and Fall of Hemispheric Specialization.* Hillsdale, NJ: Lawrence Erlbaum Associates.

Farmer, M. E., and Klein, R. M. 1995. The evidence for a temporal processing deficit linked to dyslexia: A review. *Psychonomic Bulletin and Review* 2:460–93.

Harris, N. S., Forbes, P., Weiler, M. D., Bellinger, D., and Waber, D. P. in press. Children with adequate achievement scores referred for evaluation of school difficulties: Information processing deficiencies. *Developmental Neuropsychology.*

Hollingshead, A. B. 1975. *Two-Factor Index of Social Position.* Unpublished manuscript. Yale Station, New Haven, CT.

Horwitz, B., Rumsey, J. M., and Donohue, B. C. 1998. Functional connectivity of the angular gyrus in normal reading and dyslexia. *Proceedings of the National Academy of Science* 95:8939–44.

Kail, R. and Hall, L. K. 1994. Processing speed, naming speed, and reading. *Developmental Psychology* 30:949–54.

Kaufman, A. S., and Kaufman, N. 1990. *Kaufman-Brief Intelligence Test.* Circle Pines, MN: American Guidance Service.

Klingberg, T., Hedehus, M., Temple, E., Salz, T., Gabrieli, J. D., Moseley, M. E., and Poldrack, R. A. 2000. Microstructure of tempero-parietal white mater as a basis for reading ability: Evidence from diffusion tensor magnetic resonance imaging. *Neuron* 25:493–500.

Lovegrove, W. 1993. Weakness in the transient visual system: A causal factor in dyslexia. In Temporal information processing in the nervous system: Special reference to dyslexia and dysphasia, eds. P. Tallal and A. M. Galaburda. *Annals of the New York Academy of Sciences* 682:57–69. New York: New York Academy of Sciences.

Lovegrove, W., Martin, F., and Slaghuis, W. 1986. A theoretical and experimental case for a visual deficit in specific reading disability. *Cognitive Neuropsychology* 3:225–67.

Luria, A. R. 1973. *The Working Brain.* New York: Basic Books.

Morgan, A. M., Harris, N. S., Bernstein, J. H., and Waber, D. P. in press. Characteristics of children with adequate academic achievement scores referred for evaluation of school difficulties. *Journal of Learning Disabilities.*

Morris, R. D., Stuebing, K. K., Fletcher, J. M., Shaywitz, S. E, Lyon, G. R., Shankweiler, D. P., Katz, L., Francis, D. J., and Shaywitz, B. A. 1998. Subtypes of reading disability: Variability around a phonological core. *Journal of Educational Psychology* 90:347–73.

Nissen, M. J., and Bullemer, P. 1987. Attentional requirements of learning: Evidence from performance measures. *Cognitive Psychology* 19:1–32.

Rae, C., Lee, M. A., Dixon, R. M., Blamire, A. M., Thompson, C. H., Styles, P., Talcott, J., Richardson, A. J., and Stein, J. F. 1998. Metabolic abnormalities in developmental dyslexia detected by 1H magnetic resonance spectroscopy. *Lancet* 351:1849–52.

Rao, S. M., Harrington, D. L., Haaland, K. Y., and Bobholz, J. A. 1997. Distributed neural systems underlying the timing of movements. *Journal of Neuroscience* 17:5528–35.

Reynolds, C. R. 1985. Critical measurement issues in learning disabilities. *Journal of Special Education* 18:451–76.

Rivkin, M. J., Vajapeyam, S., Mulkern, R .V., Weiler, M. D., Hall, E. K., Yoo, S. S., Fleming, A., Hutton, C., and Waber, D. P. 2000. A fMRI study of paced finger tapping in good and poor readers. *American Academy of Neurology*. San Diego, CA.

Tallal, P. 1980. Auditory temporal perception, phonics, and reading disabilities in children. *Brain and Language* 9:182–98.

Tallal, P., Galaburda, A. M., Llinas, R., and von Euler. Temporal information processing in the nervous system: Special reference to dyslexia and dysphasia. *Annals of the New York Academy of Sciences* 682. New York, NY: New York Academy of Sciences.

Tallal, P., and Piercy, M. 1973. Defects of non-verbal auditory perception in children with developmental aphasia. *Nature* 241:468–69.

Tallal, P., and Piercy, M. 1974. Developmental aphasia: Rate of auditory processing and selective impairment of consonant perception. *Neuropsychologia* 12:83–93.

Tallal, P., Miller, S. L., Bedi, G., Wang, X., and Nagarajan, S. S. 1996. Language comprehension in language-learning impaired children improved with acoustically modified speech. *Science* 271:81–84.

Torgeson, J. K., Wagner, R. K., and Rashotte, C. 1999. *Test of Word Reading Fluency*. Austin, TX: PRO-ED, Inc.

Waber D. P., Wolff, P. H., Weiler, M. D., Bellinger, D., Marcus, D. H., Forbes, P., Wypij, D. 2001. Processing of rapid auditory stimuli in school-age children referred for evaluation of learning disorder. *Child Development* 72:37–49.

Waber D. P., Weiler, M. D., Bellinger, D., Marcus, D. H., Forbes, P., Wypij, D., and Wolff, P. H. 2000. Diminished motor timing control in children referred for diagnosis of learning problems. *Developmental Neuropsychology* 17:181–97.

Waber, D. P., Marcus, D., Forbes, P., Bellinger, D., Weiler, M. D., and Curran, T. C. in review. *Implicit Learning of Motor Sequences Is Impaired in Children with Reading Disability*.

Waber, D. P., Wolff, P. H., Forbes, P. W., and Weiler, M. D. in press. Rapid automatized naming in children referred for evaluation of heterogeneous learning problems: How specific are naming speed deficits to reading disability? *Child Neuropsychology*.

Wakefield, J. C. 1992a. Disorder as harmful dysfunction: A conceptual critique of DSM-III—R's definition of mental disorder. *Psychological Review* 99(2):232–47.

Wakefield, J. C. 1992b. The concept of mental disorder: On the boundary between biological facts and social values. *American Psychologist* 47:373–88.

Weiler, M. D., Bernstein, J. H., Bellinger, D., Waber, D. P. in press. Processing speed in children with attention deficit/hyperactivity disorder, inattentive type. *Child Neuropsychology*.

Weiler, M. D., Harris, N. S., Marcus, D. H., Bellinger, D., Kosslyn, S., and Waber D. P. 2000. Speed of information processing in children referred for learning problems as measured by a visual filtering test. *Journal of Learning Disabilities* 33:538–50.

Wolf, M. 1999. What time may tell: Towards a new conceptualization of developmental dyslexia. *Annals of Dyslexia* 49:3–28.

Wolf, M. and Biddle, K. 1995. Unpublished data.

Wolff, P. H. 1993. Impaired temporal resolution in developmental dyslexia. In Temporal information processing in the nervous system:

Special reference to dyslexia and dysphasia, eds. P. Tallal and A. M.Galaburda. *Annals of the New York Academy of Sciences* 682:87–103. New York: New York Academy of Sciences.

Wolff, P. H., Michel, G. F., Ovrut, M., and Drake, C. 1990. Rate and timing precision of motor coordination in developmental dyslexia. *Developmental Psychology* 26:349–59.

ACKNOWLEDGEMENTS

This work was supported by NICHD Learning Disabilities Research Center grant P50-HD33803 and in part by Mental Retardation Research Center grant P30-HD18655. I am grateful to the Learning Disabilities, School Function, Neuropsychology and Language and Auditory Processing Programs of the Children's Hospital, as well as to the children and families from those programs who participated and the staff and students of the public school systems of Melrose and Medford, Massachusetts for their cooperation.

I would like to express gratitude as well to my colleagues at the Children's Hospital Learning Disabilities Research Center, whose considerable efforts and critical thinking are reflected in the research reported in this chapter, David Bellinger, Jane Holmes Bernstein, Frank Duffy, Peter Forbes, Gloria McAnulty, Leonard Rappaport, Michael Rivkin, Michael Weiler, and Peter Wolff. Our LDRC Fellows, Allison Morgan, Naomi Singer-Harris, Lisa Sorensen, and Michael Kirkwood, also brought creativity and new ideas to the process. Responsibility for the ideas expressed in this chapter, however, is mine.

The Hypothesized Sources of Time-Related Deficits: Neuronal, Structural, and Genetic Levels

Chapter • 7

Animal Models of Developmental Dyslexia
Is There a Link Between Neocortical Malformations and Defects in Fast Auditory Processing?

Glenn D. Rosen, R. Holly Fitch,
Matthew G. Clark, J. J. Lo Turco,
Gordon F. Sherman, Albert M. Galaburda

On the surface, the notion that one could learn anything about language disorders from the study of animal models can, at the very least, be called into question. There are certainly many factors that would seem to work against our understanding of these complex behaviors through the use of animal models. The existence of language in non-human higher primates is not universally accepted, and there is certainly no evidence of any type of linguistic behavior in any other non-human species. Given this fact, it is difficult to imagine what an animal model of dyslexia or other language disorder might look like.

That being said, recent investigations into the anatomical, psycho-physiological, and neurophysiological substrates underlying developmental dyslexia and other language disorders has uncovered a variety of distinct attributes that characterize this disorder. Importantly, these findings have provided the foundation for their further examination using non-human subjects. In this chapter, we will review evidence of some of the biological and behavioral substrates underlying developmental dyslexia, concentrating primarily on focal malformations of the neocortex and defects in fast processing of sensory information. We will then move to a discussion of animal models that have proven useful in our understanding of how these two categories of deficits may be related.

DEVELOPMENTAL DYSLEXIA—BEHAVIORAL PHENOTYPE

The definition of developmental dyslexia has proved to be quite controversial since the disorder was first described (Hinshelwood 1917; Morgan 1896; Orton 1925). In practice, people with dyslexia are usually diagnosed by a discrepancy between their expected and actual reading level (Lyon 1995; Shaywitz, Fletcher, and Shaywitz 1994). This is not to say that developmental dyslexia is simply a disorder of reading, as there is much evidence to support the notion that people with dyslexia have difficulties with a number of other cognitive skills including phonological awareness (e.g., Brady 1991; Crain 1991; Crain et al. 1990; Liberman, Shankweiler, and Liberman 1989; Olson et al. 1989; Shankweiler et al. 1995; Torgesen 1991) and verbal working memory (e.g., Brady 1991; Crain and Shankweiler 1990; Crain et al. 1990; Liberman et al. 1989; Mann, Liberman, and Shankweiler 1980; Shankweiler and Crain 1986; Siegel and Ryan 1989; Smith et al. 1989; Swanson 1993; Swanson, Cochran, and Ewers 1989; Torgesen 1991). Not all the differences seen between people with dyslexia and controls favor those who acquire reading in a standard fashion. People with dyslexia are significantly better than normal reading controls in orthographic skills (Olson et al. 1989; Siegel, Share, and Esther 1995) and visuospatial measures, including the WISC Block Design (Gordon 1980, 1988; Harness, Epstein, and Gordon 1984).

DEVELOPMENTAL DYSLEXIA—ANATOMY AND PHYSIOLOGY

From the earliest writings on the subject, researchers believed that there was bound to be a neural substrate underlying developmental dyslexia (Orton 1925), but it was not until relatively recently that researchers began to systematically examine this issue. Drake (1968) reported a small corpus callosum as well as "excessive gyration" in the brain of a post-mortem person with dyslexia, but that work was not continued in greater depth. Galaburda and colleagues have since systematically studied the brains of post-mortem people with dyslexia, and have found three anatomical differences in their brains. These include (1) symmetry of the *planum temporale*, a language-related region of the neocortex, (2) the presence of focal malformations of the cerebral cortex, and (3) defects in primary sensory systems. Although symmetry is an important issue, and one that has been successfully modeled in animals (Galaburda et al. 1986; Rosen 1996; Rosen, Sherman, and Galaburda 1989, 1991, 1993), we will concern ourselves only with the latter two traits in this chapter as they more directly relate to the other chapters in the volume.

Minor Malformations of the Cerebral Cortex

Microscopic examination of human dyslexic brains has revealed several related forms of developmental neuropathologic malformations (Galaburda and Kemper 1979; Galaburda et al. 1985; Humphreys, Kaufmann, and Galaburda 1990). Five consecutively studied males with dyslexia and two of three females with dyslexia have foci of cerebrocortical micro-dysgenesis consisting of (1) neuronal ectopias in neocortical layer I, (2) subjacent laminar dysplasia, (3) focal microgyria, and (4) microvascular anomalies. These abnormalities range in number from 30 to 150 focal lesions per brain, tend to be located in perisylvian regions, affect the anterior vascular border-zone, and usually involve the left more than the right hemisphere (see figure 1). In female brains, ectopias are relatively uncommon. Instead, these brains have large numbers of focal, myelinated glial scars that are located in the same distribution as the ectopias (Humphreys et al. 1990). Such scarring represents the same pathogenetic mechanisms as that of the ectopias, but acts on the developing brain somewhat later, after completion of neuronal migration, when the brain is no longer able to react by producing ectopias or microgyria. By contrast, the types of pathology described above are substantially less frequent, and when present they are less severe in normative brains from comparable studies (Kaufmann and Galaburda 1989). Together, the different types of developmental neuropathology implicate a developmental window beginning early during the second half of pregnancy and terminating by the end of the second year of postnatal life.

Fast Processing Deficits

Developmentally language-impaired children (a large subset of whom are later diagnosed with dyslexia) suffer from temporal pro-

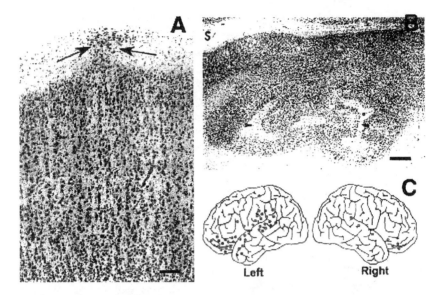

Figure 1.   Minor neocortical malformations in the dyslexic brain. A. Photomicrograph of molecular layer ectopia in layer one of a human with dyslexia (arrows). Note the paucity of cells in the outermost layer of the adjacent cortex. Bar = 400 μm. B. Region of microgyria in human dyslexic brain (arrowheads) Bar = 1 mm. C. Schematic demonstrating typical locations of molecular layer ectopias in the left and right hemispheres. Abbreviation: S = Sylvian Fissure.

cessing deficits affecting even non-linguistic sounds (Livingstone et al. 1991; Nagarajan et al. 1999; Tallal, Miller, and Fitch 1993; Tallal and Piercy 1973; Wright et al. 1997). Workers in the visual system (see Stein this volume; Chase and Jenner 1993; Cornelissen et al. 1998; Eden et al. 1996; Livingstone et al. 1991; Lovegrove, Garzia, and Nicholson 1990; Slaghuis, Lovegrove, and Davidson 1993; Stein and Walsh 1997; Williams and Lecluyse 1990; Williams et al. 1995) and somatosensory system (Grant et al. 1999) also showed deficits affecting temporal and spatial processing of stimuli in people with dyslexia, indicating that multiple sensory systems were involved. Livingstone et al. (1991), for example, found that the magnocellular component of the visual system, which is responsible for processing fast, low-contrast information, is impaired in people with dyslexia. The physiologic response of this system is slowed in comparison to controls and, in addition, the magnocellular neurons of the lateral geniculate nucleus (the primary thalamic visual nucleus) are smaller than in normals

(Livingstone et al. 1991). Moreover, examination of cell size in the medial geniculate nucleus (the primary thalamic auditory nucleus; MGN) found more small and fewer large cells in the left MGN, whereas there was no difference in cell size in controls (Galaburda, Menard, and Rosen 1994). These findings complement previous reports of anomalies in the dyslexic MGN (Galaburda and Eidelberg 1982), and are consistent with reported behavioral findings of a left hemisphere-based phonological defect in individuals with dyslexia (Ortiz Alonso et al. 1990; Schwartz and Tallal 1980).

QUESTIONS TO BE ADDRESSED

Dyslexia is a complex behavioral syndrome that includes at least disordered language processing, namely phonological deficits, and low level, perceptual deficits, namely slowed visual and auditory temporal processing of low level stimuli. One argument in the current scientific dialogue states that the cognitive problems of developmental dyslexia (linguistic and non-linguistic) are the consequence of low-level processing problems. Specifically, it is posited that language processing centers require the "correct type" of information from low level centers during development—without such information, language processing will be impaired. An alternative explanation of the data suggests that low-level processing deficits are not the cause, but rather the consequence, of high level dysfunction. Namely, if high level processing areas do not develop properly, they may not reinforce development of low level processing areas for some functions, say fast temporal processing, because they are incapable of processing those stimuli further. A third possibility, not negligible in developmental disorders, is that pathology is acquired at multiple levels at the same time. An example of the latter mechanism is a form of cerebral palsy in which circulatory deficiencies early in life lead to injury to the cortex as well as to subcortical gray masses (Friede 1975; Lyon and Robain 1967).

In considering the two types of anatomic/physiologic deficits described above, one could, on the surface, provide support for any of the arguments aforementioned. The presence of cortical malformations, located primarily in perisylvian regions, could indicate that there are fundamental structural disturbances at the cortical level that may disrupt high-level processing. The disruption of cellular architecture at the thalamic level, on the other hand, could lend support to difficulties occurring at lower levels of processing. The nature of the human material limits further investigations along these lines, and we have therefore chosen to begin to tackle some of these issues through the use of rodent models. We have developed two models of minor malformations of the cortex—one spontaneous and one induced—that we have used to explore the anatomic, physiologic, and behavioral consequences of injury to the neocortex during development. These models have suggested a strong link between neocortical malformations and fast processing systems. In the next section of this chapter, we discuss the anatomic details of these models before turning to a discussion of the behavioral and physiological consequences of these malformations.

SPONTANEOUS AND INDUCED MINOR MALFORMATIONS OF THE CORTEX

Spontaneous Malformations

Our animal model of spontaneous malformations was inspired by the reports of a link among dyslexia, left-handedness, and auto-immune disease (Geschwind and Behan 1982, 1984; Geschwind and Galaburda 1987; but see also Bryden, McManus, and Bulman-Fleming 1994; McManus and Bryden 1991). This link led us to examine the brains of immune-disordered mice where we found malformations similar in appearance to those seen in people with dyslexia. Specifically, in a series of studies, Sherman and colleagues (1985, 1987, 1990) described molecular layer ectopias appearing in a number of strains of autoimmune mice, including New Zealand Black (NZB) and BXSB. In addition to these "ectopias," these mice also have cell-free, gliotic punched-out lesions in the cortical plate (figure 2A).

Overall, about 40% to 50% of NZB and BXSB mice have ectopias. Typically, only one ectopic nest is seen in each affected brain, although up to 25% of the affected brains have multiple ectopias. Examination of the brains of fetal NZB mice showed that the earliest ectopias were present by embryonic day (E) 15, and, like the newborn (gestation is 19 days in the mouse), are associated with a disorganization of radial glial fibers and a breach (which is suspected to be caused by an injurious process) in the external glial limiting membrane (Sherman et al. 1992a). A subsequent study indicated that the small, focal breach in the external limiting membrane was created before E12 (the mechanism is unknown), and migrating neurons born during the period covering E12-18 migrate through this break (or are pushed through by later migrating neurons) leading to the formation of ectopias (Sherman et al. 1992b). The formation of ectopias is therefore due to events that occur before the end of neuronal migration in the mouse, a period corresponding to about the 4th or 5th month of gestation in the human.

In adulthood, ectopias exhibit abnormal patterns of architecture. VIP, NPY, GABA, and somatostatin-containing neurons staining are seen in a small number of neurons within the ectopias in the NZB mouse (Sherman et al. 1990). VIP and somatostatin are present in the largest numbers. Further, there was an increase in the total number of VIP neurons in the hemispheres with ectopias as opposed to those without ectopias. This difference was accounted for by more VIP neurons in the columns containing ectopias than in those in the homologous areas of the opposite hemispheres, as well as by more VIP neurons located medial to the ectopias. This indicated that the ectopias may represent not only inappropriately placed neurons, but also a problem with the regulation of their numbers. Subtle abnormalities are also seen in the hippocampus (Nowakowski and Sekiguchi 1987), and the cerebellum of the NZB was found to be unusual in a number of anatomical characteristics (Sekiguchi et al. 1991).

Several studies addressed the connection between cortical anomalies and immune status, but no relationship could be found. Specifically, embryos from BXSB mice were transplanted at the 8-cell stage into the uteruses of control mice. There were significant effects on behavior and immune status, but there was no effect on the incidence of the malformations (Denenberg et al. 1991a), suggesting the possibility of a genetic influence on the formation of the ectopias. Further research has pointed to ectopias being linked to a single gene recessive trait with incomplete penetrance (Sherman et al. 1994, 1997).

New Zealand Black mice with ectopias learn differently than those NZB mice without ectopias (Balogh et al. 1998; Denenberg et al. 1991b; Schrott et al. 1992). Thus, ectopias depress performance of black-white discrimination in a swimming T-maze, increase the time necessary to find a hidden platform in the Morris maze (Schrott et al. 1992), and interact with pawedness to affect performance on a spatial water escape task (Denenberg et al. 1991b). Importantly, post-weaning enriched environment ameliorates the decrements seen in the discrimination learning task and the Morris maze. Thus, following a relatively short period of environmental enrichment, the behavior of animals with ectopias was indistinguishable from that of controls. This suggests the possibility that early experience can compensate for early brain injury (Boehm et al. 1996; Schrott et al. 1992).

There are also tasks where ectopic mice perform in a superior manner to their non-ectopic counterparts. In the Morris maze, for

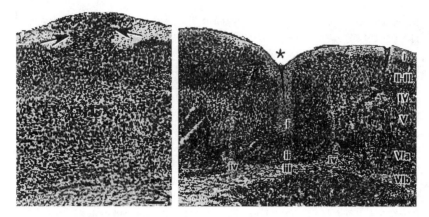

Figure 2.   Spontaneously occurring and induced minor neocortical mal-formations of mice and rats. A. Photomicrograph of a molecular layer ec-topia in an immune-disordered mouse (arrows). Bar = 400 µm. B. Photomicrograph of rat with an induced microgyria (asterisks). In com-parison with the adjacent normal six-layered cortex (right), the micro-gyria is composed of four layers. Layer i is contiguous with the adjacent molecular layer. Layer ii is composed of neurons normally found in layers II-III of normal cortex. Layer iii is a region of gliotic scarring and is the remnants of the layers IV-VIa of the normal cortex, which are destroyed by the freezing injury. Layer iv, which is often discontinuous in the micr-ogyria, is composed of subplate cells. Bar = 200 µm.

example, ectopic mice take less time to find a platform and are faster swimmers than non-ectopics (Denenberg et al. 1996). Also studied were mice that were embryo-transferred to hybrid non-autoimmune mothers. Here, too, ectopic mice were better than non-ectopics on the Morris maze, suggesting that epigenetic maternal/uterine factors do not influence the behavioral consequences of these anomalies. Ectopic mice also have superior long term reten-tion of a water escape task (Boehm et al. 1996).

Recent work by Denenberg and colleagues has pointed to some interesting parallels between the working memory deficits seen in people with dyslexia and those seen in mice with ectopias. Working memory requires an animal to disregard part of the infor-mation it has acquired on previous training trials and focus upon new information presented in the immediate trial. In a delayed matching-to-sample task (DMTS) on a water maze, non-ectopic mice took less time and swam a shorter distance to find the plat-form on trial 2 than did ectopic mice (Waters et al. 1997). In a water version of the radial arm maze, ectopic BXSB mice made significantly more working memory errors (Hyde, Sherman, and Denenberg 1996).

Summary

A number of mouse strains that were bred to develop immune disorders have shown cerebral cortical malformations similar to those seen in dyslexia. These anomalies appear to be caused by injury during the early stages of cortical development. The etiology of this injury remains unknown, although it has been shown not to be related to the autoimmune disease itself, but rather to be under genetic control. These ectopias have both positive and negative behavioral effects, and some of the latter can be ameliorated by early experience.

In the following section, a complimentary animal model is introduced which involves the induction of cortical malformations.

Induced Malformations

In order to study further the effects of neocortical malformations, we wished to develop a model where lesion location and severity could be controlled. Moreover, it was desirable to separate the other biological associations (e.g., immune-disorders) from the anatomy. Using a model developed originally by Dvorák and colleagues (Dvorák and Feit 1977; Dvorák, Feit, and Juránková 1978), we induced focal microgyria by placing a freezing probe ($\approx$ –70°C) on the skulls of newborn rats for approximately 5 seconds (Humphreys et al. 1991). The immediate effect of the freezing injury is to create a delimited region of neuronal necrosis within 24 hours. Three days post-lesion, radial glial fibers regrow, though a region of intense astrogliosis and neurons begin to migrate through that area. The beginning of the formation of a microgyria can clearly be seen by day 5, starting primarily at the periphery of the lesion, where radial glial fibers are continuing their regrowth through the damaged area. The microgyria gain their adult appearance by P15 at which time radial glial fibers can still be seen in the area of damage, although not elsewhere (see figure 2B). These results suggest that the formation of microgyria is the result of basic brain repair mechanisms occurring during the end of the period of neuronal migration (Rosen et al. 1992; Suzuki and Choi 1991).

Although occasional layer I ectopias arose following freezing injury, they were of a qualitatively different type from those seen in immune-disordered mice. The collections of neurons in ectopias always reach the pial surface and they generally have a contained, "mushroom-like" appearance, whereas the induced anomalies tend not to reach the pial surface and are more dispersed. Based on the finding of a breach in the external limiting membrane overlying areas of spontaneous ectopias (Sherman et al. 1992a), we created a small focal area of damage to the external limiting membrane by puncture wound of the neocortex. This resulted in ectopic collections of neurons in layer I of the neocortex comparable to those seen in spontaneous ectopias of humans and mice (Rosen et al. 1992).

Nonimmune-disordered mice with induced ectopias and microgyria have behavioral deficits that are, in some ways, quite similar to those seen in immune-disordered mice with spontaneous ectopias. Lesioned mice performed poorly when compared to sham-operated animals in discrimination learning, in a spatial Match-to-Sample task, and in a Lashley Type III maze. In shuttle-box avoidance conditioning, where immunological disorder compromises behavioral performance, there was no difference between lesioned and sham animals. These results reveal the similarities to the behavioral effects of spontaneous and induced neocortical malformations (Rosen et al. 1995).

Summary

In this section, two different but related models of the anatomic malformations seen in the dyslexic brain have been presented. From this work, we have been able to glean a wealth of information that would not necessarily be amenable to study in humans. We have evidence, for example, that these malformations are the result of injury occurring early in gestation and that they have a genetic component. This latter fact, combined with evidence from the human with dyslexia suggests a link with chromosomes 2, 6, and 15 which may yield more insights into the etiology of this disorder (Cardon et al. 1995; Fagerheim et al. 1999; Gilger et al. 1998; Grigorenko et al. 1997; Smith et al. 1983).

The parallels between people with dyslexia and these animal models extend to behavior as well. Thus, while it is impossible to test animals for the phonological defects exhibited by humans with dyslexia, these animals have measurable deficits in working memory—a difficulty also encountered in humans with developmental dyslexia. In the following section, we present evidence suggesting that animals with neocortical malformations also have difficulties with fast processing of auditory information.

FAST PROCESSING DEFECTS ASSOCIATED WITH SPONTANEOUS
AND INDUCED MALFORMATIONS OF THE CORTEX

Spontaneous Malformations

As described above, minor developmental cortical malformations, including microgyria, are seen in the brains of people with dyslexia and in our animal models. Concomitant studies have shown that language-impaired (LI) children, a large subset of whom have dyslexia, exhibit severe deficits in the discrimination of rapidly presented auditory stimuli, including phonological and non-verbal stimuli (i.e., sequential tones), specifically when total stimulus durations fall below 350 milliseconds (Tallal 1973). Our animal models therefore provide a natural way to test the hypothesis that neocortical malformations are associated with alterations in neurophysiological responses to auditory stimuli.

In our first experiment (Clark et al. 2000b), we tested 33 immune-disordered mice (12 ectopic and 21 non-ectopic) on a modified reflex modification paradigm. This consisted of the presentation of a pre-stimulus briefly preceding a startle-eliciting stimulus (SES)—a 105 decibels white noise burst that causes mice to exhibit an acoustic startle reflex. When the pre-stimulus is detected, the amplitude of the whole-body, acoustic startle reflex is inhibited ("pre-pulse inhibition"). The extent of pre-pulse inhibition is related to the overall detectability of the pre-stimulus.

Comparison of reflex amplitudes when a pre-stimulus is present (i.e., a cued trial) versus not present (i.e., an uncued trial) provides an objective measure of sensory detection (Wecker, Ison, and Foss 1985). For the purpose of this study, we modified the task using gap detection. Specifically, we presented a variable duration silent gap (0-100 msec) 50 milliseconds before the SES, with the gap duration on each trial randomly selected. Trials occurred every 20 seconds on average and consisted of 75 decibel continuous background white noise, the presentation of a silent gap, 50 milliseconds of additional background white noise, followed by the presentation of the SES (figure 3 inset). A complete testing session contained trials with 0 (no gap), and 9 gap intervals ranging from 2 to 100 milliseconds. For the purpose of statistical comparison, the 0 millisecond or "no gap" represented the "uncued" (baseline startle response) condition, while the "cued" conditions included gap durations of 2 to100 milliseconds.

In both non-ectopic and ectopic groups, a significant main effect of gap duration was observed—significant differences between uncued and cued responses were evident at gap durations down to 5 milliseconds, but not at 2 milliseconds. Responses were then converted to percentages, specifically representing the cued response as a percentage of baseline (uncued) response for each subject, for each condition. If no advantage was conferred by a given gap duration (i.e., no detection), the cued response should approximate the uncued one (i.e., 100%). Interestingly, here we found a significant interaction between the presence or absence of ectopia and gap durations. Ectopic mice were significantly impaired relative to non-ectopic mice at only the 5 millisecond gap condition. Ectopic and non-ectopic gap detection performance did not differ significantly at the remaining longer gap durations of 10 to100 milliseconds (figure 3).

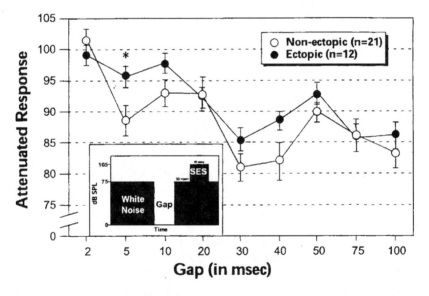

Figure 3. Gap detection in ectopic and non-ectopic mice. Inset. Schematic representing gap detection protocol. The duration of the gap varied equally and randomly between the values of 0 (no gap), 2, 5, 10, 20, 30, 40, 50, 75 and 100 milliseconds across 300 trials. SES = Startle Eliciting Stimulus. Main Figure. Results from gap detection experiment. Ectopic BXSB mice are significantly impaired relative to non-ectopic BXSB mice at only the 5 millisecond gap duration. Attenuated Response is computed by dividing the startle response to cued trials (i.e., gap durations of 2, 5, 10, 20, 30, 40, 50, 75 and 100 milliseconds) by the startle response to uncued trials (i.e., no gap condition) 100 (from Clark et al. 2000b)

Thus, ectopic and non-ectopic male BXSB mice demonstrated significant gap detection in broadband white noise down to gap durations as low as 5 milliseconds. These results approximate thresholds observed in other species including humans (Ison and Pinckney 1983) and rats (Leitner et al. 1993). At the shortest detectable gap (5 milliseconds), however, ectopic mice showed, on average, significantly less detection than non-ectopics. These results suggest that focal cortical malformations, in this case, neocortical ectopias, are related to impairments in rapid auditory processing. The current results are consistent with data obtained from children with developmental dyslexia (McCroskey and Kidder 1980; Leitner et al. 1993) wherein longer gap duration thresholds have been seen for affected individuals as compared to controls.

The experiment described above showed psychophysical differences between ectopic and non-ectopic mice. In our next experiment (Frenkel et al. 2000), we asked whether there were any neurophysiologic consequences of neocortical ectopias. We therefore implanted gold plated surface electrodes to record from primary auditory cortex on 10 immune-disordered mice (5 with and 5 without ectopias). Auditory stimuli were delivered to these anesthetized animals in order to produce an auditory event related potential (AERP). The three stimulus protocols used in this study were designed to test changes in response to differences in stimulus timing and transition. In all protocols the initial stimuli were 10.5 kHz tones, 360 milliseconds. This frequency was chosen because it is approximately at the peak of auditory sensitivity for mice. The initial 360 millisecond tone was followed at intervals of 12, 36, 72, 144, or 288 milliseconds, during which there was either silence (10-gap-10), a 0.99 kHz (10-1-10), or a 5.6 kHz tone (10-5-10). Following this interval, a second 120 millisecond 10.5 kHz stimulus was delivered. Each of the 15 trial types (three protocols, five intervals) was repeated 100 times with an intertrial interval of 600 to 700 milliseconds (figure 4A). It is important to note that data analysis of the AERP was performed without any knowledge of the histology status of mice.

The design of the study, therefore, was to determine under what conditions the second of the two stimuli would be detected (as measured by the AERPs). We found that the amplitude of AERPs to the second of the pair of 10.5 kHz stimuli, measured from peak positivity to peak negativity, increased in amplitude as a function of increasing interval between the stimuli. Responses to second stimuli were minimal at 12 milliseconds, but by 288 milliseconds, responses to second stimuli consistently approached

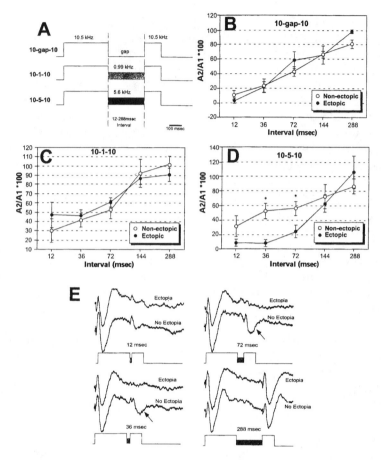

Figure 4.   Auditory Event Related Potentials (AERPs) in ectopic and non-ectopic mice. The three stimulus protocols used in a study of AERP in ectopic and non-ectopic mice. In the first two, 10.5 kHz stimuli were separated by silent gaps (10-gap-10), in another by 0.99 KHz tones (10-1-10) and in a third by 5.6 KHz tones (10-5-10). The two stimuli were separated by 12, 36, 72, 144, or 288 millisecond intervals. All tones were 84 decibels. B. Responses in the 10-gap-10 and 10-1-10 (C) protocols were nearly identical for all animals with and without ectopias. In each graph the % of the amplitude of the second to the first AERP (A2/A1 *100) is plotted against the interval between 10.5 kHz stimuli. D. The ratio of the amplitude of the second to the first AERP was significantly reduced in mice with ectopias for intervals of 36 and 72 milliseconds. E. Grand average AERPs for mice with and without ectopias. Arrows indicate the near absence of AERPs to the second stimulus after 36 and 72 milliseconds.

100% of the amplitude of the first, regardless of whether or not animals had ectopias. As shown in figures 4B and 4C, the entire response profile as a function of interval was not different between animals with or without ectopias for either the 10-gap-10 or 10-1-10 protocols.

In contrast, the amplitude of the second AERP in the 10-5-10 stimulus protocol differed significantly between mice with and without ectopias. Mice with ectopias showed small or no responses to second 10.5 kHz stimuli up to intervals of 72 milliseconds, whereas at 36 millisecond intervals animals without ectopias showed responses to second 10.5 kHz stimuli that were approximately 50% the amplitude of the response to the first stimuli. In fact, the responses to the second 10.5 kHz stimuli were diagnosed by a non-expert for the presence or absence of ectopias. The non-expert was able to categorize accurately 9 of 10 animals as having ectopias or not based solely on the amplitude of the response to the second stimulus at short intervals. The effect of the ectopia on the amplitude of the response to the second stimuli is limited to the shortest intervals, and responses are identical at longer intervals. Therefore, the attenuation in cortical response is dependent upon an interaction of stimulus timing and contrast at stimuli transitions.

Taken together, these results suggest that neocortical ectopias in mice alter auditory processing in a fashion similar to that seen in people with dyslexia. Two stimulus features that are important variables for revealing neurophysiological alterations in humans with language impairment—timing delays and rapid changes in frequency (Wright et al. 1997)—are also important variables for revealing ectopia-associated attenuation of AERPs in mice. Indeed, it appears that in animal models the presence of ectopias is associated with deficits in sensory processing when processing demands are highest. For example, in the latter study, the deficit is apparent only at short intervals when a 5.6 kHz tone precedes the second 10.5 kHz stimulus and there is no deficit when preceded by either silence or 0.99 kHz tones. Similarly, in our first study discussed above, ectopic animals show an attenuation in startle reduction only at the shortest detectable gap durations. In sum, brains with focal neocortical malformations show impairment when temporal processing demands are particularly high.

Induced Malformations

Evidence from mice with spontaneous malformations of the neocortex strongly suggests a link between the presence of cortical malformations and defects in fast processing. It seems unlikely that the immune status of these animals plays a role in these results since both ectopics and non-ectopics are equally affected. Yet, the possibility of an interaction between the cortical malformations and the immune status of the subjects cannot be ruled out. To obviate this unlikely, but potential confound, we have tested rats with induced neocortical malformations on tasks involving auditory processing using paradigms both similar and distinct from those used in testing the mice with spontaneous neocortical malformations.

As described above, children with language impairment (LI), a large subset of whom have dyslexia, exhibit severe deficits in the discrimination of rapidly presented auditory stimuli, including phonological and non-verbal stimuli (i.e., sequential tones), specifically when total stimulus durations fall below 350 milliseconds (Tallal and Piercy 1973). This two-tone sequence discrimination task, which elicited these significant differences between LI and control children, was adapted to an operant conditioning go-no go target identification paradigm for rats (Fitch et al. 1993). We sought to develop an animal model for impaired auditory temporal processing by exploiting the functional parallels between rats and humans in two-tone discrimination, and our ability to model some of the neuroanatomic anomalies seen in dyslexia. Toward that end, adult male rats with neonatally induced microgyria were tested in an operant paradigm for auditory discrimination of stimuli consisting of two sequential tones (Fitch et al. 1994). Subjects were shaped to perform a go-no go target identification using water reinforcement. Stimuli were reduced in duration from 540 to 249 milliseconds across 24 days of testing. Discrimination indices were calculated from the difference, in milliseconds, between mean latencies to respond to the target (hits) versus non-targets (false-alarms) for each subject across days. Results showed that all subjects were able to discriminate at longer stimulus durations. However, lesioned subjects showed specific impairment at stimulus durations of 332 milliseconds or fewer, and were significantly depressed in comparison to shams. These results suggest a possible link between the neuropathologic anomalies observed in some LI brains, and the auditory temporal processing deficits reported for LI subjects. More recent studies (Fitch et al. 1997) have shown that female rats, unlike males, successfully perform the auditory discrimination task at all conditions, irrespective of whether or not they have induced microgyria (figure 5). We have recently tested rats on a startle reduction paradigm that is similar to that described above for the mice. We found that rats with microgyria

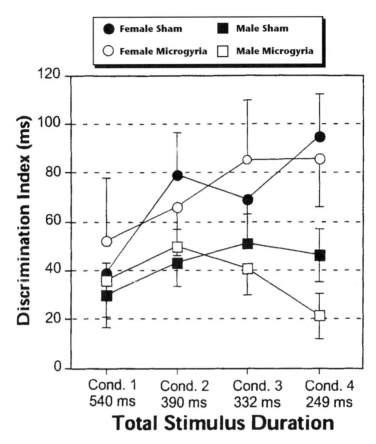

Figure 5. Fast auditory processing is disturbed in male, but not female microgyric rats. Mean discrimination index for male (square) and female (circle) lesioned (filled) and sham (open) groups at the four stimulus duration conditions. Discrimination indices are mean scores over six days of testing at each condition. The numbers under each condition are total stimulus time (pre-tone/ISI/post-tone).

showed less of a startle reduction when the time between the pre-stimulus and the SES was less than 85 milliseconds. These results lend strong support to the notion that rats with microgyria have difficulty processing fast, but not slow, auditory information (Clark et al. 2000a).

   We hypothesized that these differences in the rats' abilities to process fast auditory information might be reflected, as they are in those with dyslexia, by changes in cell sizes in the primary auditory thalamic nucleus, the MGN (Galaburda et al. 1994). We therefore measured MGN cell size, packing-density, and number in male and female rats with induced microgyria who were also tested for auditory discrimination learning. When we looked at the MGN of our male subjects, there were more small and fewer large cells in the microgyric as compared to control animals. In contrast, there were no such differences in MGN cell size distribution in the females. Moreover, MGN cell size predicted behavior in males but not females (Herman et al. 1997).

Summary

In both the case of the animals with spontaneous and those with induced malformations, there appears to be a relationship between the presence of malformations and problems with fast processing of auditory information. Furthermore, there is evidence to suggest at least one anatomic substrate for these behavioral and physiological changes in animals with malformations. These findings raise the obvious question as to the mechanism underlying this link between neocortical malformations and low-level disturbances in physiology and anatomy. We have hypothesized that after injury causes these malformations, reorganization of the cerebral cortex leads to propagation of effects throughout the brain in a top-down manner. Specifically, we posited that early injury produces malformations with normal and abnormal efferent and afferent connectivity, which could provide the conduits for the propagation of cascading effects on structures thus connected to this region. In the following section, some recent investigations of the effects of cortical malformations on cerebrocortical connectivity are discussed.

CONNECTIONAL DIFFERENCES

Spontaneous Malformations

As discussed above, immuno-histochemical studies have shown an increased density of neurofilament-immunoreactive fibers radially oriented underlying ectopias (Sherman et al. 1990). A follow-up DiI (a lipophilic tracer) study was designed to show definitively that these bundles contained afferent and efferent fibers from neurons in the ectopias. Small crystals of DiI were placed in the middle of an ectopia and the projections from the ectopia traced (Jenner, Galaburda, and Sherman 2000). In all cases there was a distinctive bundle of labeled fibers extending from the ectopic

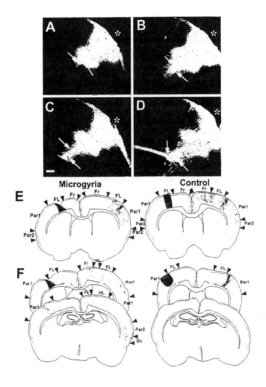

Figure 6 A-D.   Connectional changes in ectopic mice. Images illustrating a bundle of fibers from an ectopia in FL cortex of an immune-disordered mouse (arrows). The bundle is seen entering the corpus callosum in panels C and D. Bar = 200 μm. E. Connectional changes in Rats. Tracing of dark-field photomontages of injection into a microgyrus (dark gray) located in the forelimb region of the right hemisphere. Retrogradely labeled cells are represented as filled circles, and anterogradely labeled fibers are traced. Dense patches of projections are represented by light gray-filled regions. Patterns of projections to the left hemisphere are notable for an absence of the normal homotopic projections to FL as seen in the matched control. In the microgyric case, the densest projections are located in Par1 and are far less dense than those in the control. F. Heterotopic projections of Microgyric Animals. Tracing of darkfield photomontages of injection into a microgyrus located in the border between FL and Par1 of the right hemisphere of (dark gray) illustrating retrograde and anterograde connections. When compared to the matched control there is a distinct decease in density of projections to the homotopic cortical region. In addition, heterotopic projections to Fr (bottom section) and Par2 and Gu (top section) can be seen in the microgyric case but not in the control. Abbreviations: Fr = Frontal cortex (including Fr1, Fr2, and Fr3); FL = Forelimb area of parietal cortex; HL = Hindlimb region of parietal cortex; Par1 = Primary parietal cortex; Par2 = Secondary parietal cortex; Gu = Gustatory cortex.

cells through the deeper layers of the cortex. This bundle of fibers then either entered the corpus callosum, the internal capsule, or both (figures 6A-D). Depending on the location of the ectopia within the somatosensory cortex, labeling was seen in appropriate thalamic nuclei. Cortico-cortical connections were also seen between ectopias in barrel cortex and both secondary somatosensory and primary motor cortices. Rarely was there any visible connections in the contralateral cortex.

The DiI labeling from non-ectopic cortex showed a distinctly different pattern of connectivity. In no case was there labeling of fiber bundles under the injection site in the controls. In comparison to the ectopias, the non-ectopic cortex seemed to have less intense staining of the thalamic nuclei. The non-ectopic placements showed more fibers crossing the corpus callosum with distinctive patterns of connections in the contralateral cortex. These findings confirm the notion that layer I ectopias are anomalously connected by comparison to neurons in homologous cortex, which may underlie widespread dysfunction of brains containing ectopias.

Changes in Connectivity with Microgyria

Disturbed inter-hemispheric connectivity has been associated with a spontaneously occurring microgyrus in the rat. Spontaneously occurring microgyria are rare in experimental animal species. We injected *in vivo* tracers into the microgyria of adult animals. Specifically, we injected biotinylated dextran amine (BDA) into microgyric and matched control cases. In comparison to controls, animals with microgyria showed a decrease in efferent projections from the microgyric cortex to the opposite hemisphere (figure 6E). Par1 microgyria had abnormal efferent connections to secondary somatosensory cortex (Par2) of the opposite hemisphere (figure 6F). Injection of BDA into the homologous area of the undamaged hemisphere highlighted aberrant projections into frontal and Par2 cortex of the affected hemisphere (Rosen, Burstein, and Galaburda 2000). There were almost no thalamocortical or corticothalamic projections between the ventrobasal complex and the microgyrus itself. Interestingly, a dense plexus of thalamocortical fibers was often noted at the border between the malformed and normal cortex, an area shown to be important in the generation of epileptogenic discharges (Jacobs, Gutnick, and Prince 1996; Luhmann and Raabe 1996).

Summary

We had previously shown that minor malformations of the cerebral cortex were associated with defects in low-level physiologic, anatomic, and behavioral systems. What remained unexplained was how damage to high-level structures could affect these low-level substrates. We had hypothesized that after injury causes these malformations, reorganization of the cerebral cortex leads to propagation of effects throughout the brain in a top-down manner. One conduit for propagation of changes could be neuronal connections. Connections between the injured area and the thalamic target could be (1) direct, (2) developmentally transient, (3) polysynaptic, or (4) new connections produced by the injury. Our research does not speak directly to this issue, but we know from other sources that the maintenance of transient connections is one distinct possibility (Innocenti and Berbel 1991a, 1991b; Nicolelis, Chapin, and Lin 1991). Furthermore, widespread brain reorganization has been reported following a variety of developmental injuries. In hamsters, for example, neonatal lesions of the superior colliculus result in altered retinal projections (Finlay, Wilson, and Schneider 1979; Schneider 1979, 1981).

It is possible, therefore, that early injury to the cortical plate causes minor neocortical malformations with normal and abnormal efferent and afferent connectivity, which could provide the conduits for the propagation of cascading effects on structures thus connected to this region. The abnormal connectivity could theoretically be the result of the pathological maintenance of normally transient connections or the formation of novel connections. Although propagation of changes along standard connections would be easily traced, changes propagated via transient or anomalous connections require special experimental demonstration.

CONCLUSIONS

The work discussed in this chapter has pointed to a number of areas where research into the biological substrates of developmental dyslexia has been aided by the use of animal models. From examination of animals with either induced or spontaneous malformations, we have learned more about the etiology of these malformations as well as their effects on brain organization. In addition, behavioral testing has pointed to some intriguing parallels with the non-linguistic deficits seen in dyslexia and other language impairments. In the case of the spontaneous malformations, for example, there is evidence that ectopic animals have working memory deficits.

Perhaps most important for the topic at hand, however, is that the examination of these animal models has enabled us to link together the presence of minor malformations of the neocortex and defects in fast processing of auditory information. We know that the induction of a microgyria into an otherwise normal cortex profoundly disturbs the ability of that animal to process auditory information when it is presented in a fast manner. Similarly, mice with spontaneous malformations of the neocortex also have difficulties processing fast auditory information, and this difference is manifest at the physiologic level. This supports the notion that this defect in fast processing may be caused by a top-down disruption of cerebral architecture induced by the early injury. The mechanisms for this disruption are hypothesized to the result of connectional reorganization—an hypothesis that is supported by recent findings.

Although there are obvious and important limits to the types of questions that we can ask non-human animals with respect to developmental dyslexia, there are similarities in the basic biological substrates that may underlie this disorder that allow and encourage the use of animal models. It is hoped that as we learn more about the basic anatomical, behavioral, and cognitive aspects of this disorder that other similarities will become evident and allow researchers to converge on a more complete understanding of this disorder.

REFERENCES

Balogh, S. A., Sherman, G. F., Hyde, L. A., and Denenberg, V. H. 1998. Effects of neocortical ectopias upon the acquisition and retention of a non-spatial reference memory task in BXSB mice. *Brain Research* 111(2):291–3.

Boehm, G. W., Sherman, G. F., Hoplight, B. J., Hyde, L. A., Waters, N. S., Bradway, D. M., Galaburda, A. M., and Denenberg, V. H. 1996. Learning and memory in the autoimmune BXSB mouse: Effects of neocortical ectopias and environmental enrichment. *Brain Research* 726(1–2):11–22.

Brady, S. A. 1991. The role of working memory in reading disability. In *Phonological Processes in Literacy—A Tribute to Isabelle Y. Liberman*, eds. S. A. Brady and D. P. Shankweiler. Hillsdale, NJ: Lawrence Erlbaum Associates, Publishers.

Bryden, M. P., McManus, I. C., and Bulman-Fleming, M. B. 1994. Evaluating the empirical support for the Geschwind-Behan-Galaburda model of cerebral lateralization. *Brain Cognition* 26(2):103–67.

Cardon, L. R., Smith, S. D., Fulker, D. W., Kimberling, W. J., Pennington, B. F., and Defries, J. C. 1995. Reading disability, attention-deficit hyperactivity disorder, and the immune system: Response. *Science* 268(5212):787–8.

Chase, C., and Jenner, A. 1993. Magnocellular visual deficits affect temporal processing of dyslexics. In *Temporal Information Processing in the Nervous System, with Special Reference to Dyslexia and Dysphasia* Vol. 682, eds. P. Tallal, A. M. Galaburda, R. Llinas, and C. von Euler. New York: New York Academy of Sciences.

Clark, M. G., Rosen, G. D., Tallal, P., and Fitch, R. H. 2000a. Impaired processing of complex auditory stimuli in rats with induced cerebrocortical microgyria: An animal model of developmental language disabilities. *Journal of Cognitive Neuroscience* 12(5):828–39.

Clark, M. G., Sherman, G. F., Bimonte, H. A., and Fitch, R. H. 2000. Perceptual auditory gap detection deficits in male BXSB mice with cerebrocortical ectopias. *NeuroReport* 11(04):693–6.

Cornelissen, P. L., Hansen, P. C., Hutton, J. L., Evangelinou, V., and Stein, J. F. 1998. Magnocellular visual function and children's single word reading. *Vision Research* 38(3): 471–82.

Crain, S. 1991. Language acquisition in the absence of experience. *Behavioral and Brain Science* 14:597–650.

Crain, S., and Shankweiler, D. 1990. Explaining failures in spoken language comprehension by children with reading disabilities. In *Comprehension Processes in Reading*, eds. D. A. Balota, G. B. Flores d'Arcais, and K. Rayner. Hillsdale, NJ: Lawrence Erlbaum Associates.

Crain, S., Shankweiler, D., Macaruso, P., and Bar-Shalom, E. 1990. Working memory and comprehension of spoken sentences: Investigation of children with reading disorder. In *Neuropsychological Impairments of Short-term Memory*, eds. G. Vallar and T. Shallice. Cambridge: Cambridge Univeristy Press.

Denenberg, V. H., Mobraaten, L. E., Sherman, G. F., Morrison, L., Schrott, L. M., Waters, N. S., Rosen, G. D., Behan, P. O., and Galaburda, A. M. 1991a. Effects of the autoimmune uterine/maternal environment upon cortical ectopias, behavior and autoimmunity. *Brain Research* 563(1–2):114–122.

Denenberg, V. H., Sherman, G., Schrott, L. M., Waters, N. S., Boehm, G. W., Galaburda, A. M., and Mobraaten, L. E. 1996. Effects of embryo transfer and cortical ectopias upon the behavior of BXSB-Yaa and BXSB-Yaa plus mice. *Developmental Brain Research* 93(1–2): 100–8.

Denenberg, V. H., Sherman, G. F., Schrott, L. M., Rosen, G. D., and Galaburda, A. M. 1991b. Spatial learning, discrimination learning, paw preference and neocortical ectopias in two autoimmune strains of mice. *Brain Research* 562(1):98–104.

Drake, W. E. 1968. Clinical and pathological findings in a child with a developmental learning disability. *Journal of Learning Disabilities* 1:9–25.

Dvorák, K., and Feit, J. 1977. Migration of neuroblasts through partial necrosis of the cerebral cortex in newborn rats—contribution to the problems of morphological development and developmental period of cerebral microgyria. *Acta Neuropathologica* (Berlin) 38:203–12.

Dvorák, K., Feit, J., and Juránková, Z. 1978. Experimentally induced focal microgyria and status verrucosus deformis in rats—Pathogenesis and interrelation histological and autoradiographical study. *Acta Neuropathologica* (Berlin) 44:121–9.

Eden, G. F., Vanmeter, J. W., Rumsey, J. M., Maisog, J. M., Woods, R. P., and Zeffiro, T. A. 1996. Abnormal processing of visual motion in dyslexia revealed by functional brain imaging. *Nature* 382(6586):66–69.

Fagerheim, T., Raeymaekers, P., Tonnessen, F. E., Pedersen, M., Tranebjaerg, L., and Lubs, H. A. 1999. A new gene (DYX3) for dyslexia is located on chromosome 2. *Journal of Medical Genetics* 36(9):664–9.

Finlay, B. L., Wilson, K. G., and Schneider, G. E. 1979. Anomalous ipsilateral retinotectal projections in Syrian hamsters with early lesions: topography and functional capacity. *Journal of Comparative Neurology* 183: 721–40.

Fitch, R. H., Brown, C. P., O'Connor, K., and Tallal, P. 1993. Functional lateralization for auditory temporal processing in male and female rats. *Behavioral Neuroscience* 107(5): 844–850.

Fitch, R. H., Brown, C. P., Tallal, P., and Rosen, G. D. 1997. Effects of sex and MK-801 on auditory-processing deficits associated with developmental microgyric lesions in rats. *Behavioral Neuroscience* 111(2):404–12.

Fitch, R. H., Tallal, P., Brown, C., Galaburda, A. M., and Rosen, G. D. 1994. Induced microgyria and auditory temporal processing in rats: A model for language impairment? *Cerebral Cortex* 4(3):260–70.

Frenkel, M., Sherman, G. F., Bashan, K. A., Galaburda, A. M., and LoTurco, J. J. 2000. Neocortical ectopias are associated with attenuated neurophysiological responses to rapidly changing auditory stimuli. *Neuroreport* 11(3):575–9.

Friede, R. L. 1975. *Developmental Neuropathology.* New York: Springer-Verlag.

Galaburda, A. M., Aboitiz, F., Rosen, G. D., and Sherman, G. F. 1986. Histological asymmetry in the primary visual cortex of the rat: Implications for mechanisms of cerebral asymmetry. *Cerebral Cortex* 22:151–60.

Galaburda, A. M., and Eidelberg, D. 1982. Symmetry and asymmetry in the human posterior thalamus. II. Thalamic lesions in a case of developmental dyslexia. *Archives of Neurology* 39:333–6.

Galaburda, A. M., and Kemper, T. L. 1979. Cytoarchitectonic abnormalities in developmental dyslexia: A case study. *Annals of Neurology* 6:94–100.

Galaburda, A. M., Menard, M. T., and Rosen, G. D. 1994. Evidence for aberrant auditory anatomy in developmental dyslexia. *Proceedings of the National Academy of Sciences* (USA) 91(17):8010–13.

Galaburda, A. M., Sherman, G. F., Rosen, G. D., Aboitiz, F., and Geschwind, N. 1985. Developmental dyslexia: Four consecutive cases with cortical anomalies. *Annals of Neurology* 18:222–33.

Geschwind, N., and Behan, P. 1984. Laterality, hormones, and immunity. In *Cerebral Dominance: The Biological Foundations*, eds. N. Geschwind and A. M. Galaburda. Cambridge, MA: Harvard University Press.

Geschwind, N., and Behan, P. O. 1982. Left-handedness: Association with immune disease, migraine, and developmental learning disorder. *Proceedings of the National Academy of Sciences* (USA) 79:5097–100.

Geschwind, N., and Galaburda, A. M. 1987. *Cerebral Lateralization. Biological Mechanisms, Associations, and Pathology.* Cambridge, Massachusetts: MIT Press/Bradford Books.

Gilger, J. W., Pennington, B. F., Harbeck, R. J., DeFries, J. C., Kotzin, B., Green, P., and Smith, S. 1998. A twin and family study of the association between immune system dysfunction and dyslexia using blood serum immunoassay and survey data. *Brain Cognition* 36(3):310–33.

Gordon, H. W. 1980. Cognitive asymmetry in dyslexic families. *Neuropsychology* 18:645–56.

Gordon, H. W. 1988. The effect of "right brain/left brain" cognitive profiles on school achievement. In *Brain Lateralization in Children*, eds. D. L. Molfese and S. J. Segalowitz. NY: The Guilford Press.

Grant, A. C., Zangaladze, A., Thiagarajah, M. C., and Sathian, K. 1999. Tactile perception in developmental dyslexia: A psychophysical study using gratings. *Neuropsychologia* 37(10):1201–11.

Grigorenko, E. L., Wood, F. B., Meyer, M. S., Hart, L. A., Speed, W. C., Shuster, A., and Pauls, D. L. 1997. Susceptibility loci for distinct components of developmental dyslexia on chromosomes 6 and 15. *American Journal of Human Genetics* 60(1):27–39.

Harness, B. Z., Epstein, R., and Gordon, H. W. 1984. Cognitive profile of children referred to a clinic for reading disabilities. *Journal of Learning Disabilities* 17.

Herman, A. E., Galaburda, A. M., Fitch, H. R., Carter, A. R., and Rosen, G. D. 1997. Cerebral microgyria, thalamic cell size and auditory temporal processing in male and female rats. *Cerebral Cortex* 7:453 64.

Hinshelwood, J. 1917. *Congenital Word-blindness*. London: Lewis.

Humphreys, P., Kaufmann, W. E., and Galaburda, A. M. 1990. Developmental dyslexia in women: Neuropathological findings in three cases. *Annals of Neurology* 28:727–38.

Humphreys, P., Rosen, G. D., Press, D. M., Sherman, G. F., and Galaburda, A. M. 1991. Freezing lesions of the newborn rat brain: A model for cerebrocortical microgyria. *Journal of Neuropathology and Experimental Neurology* 50:145 60.

Hyde, L., Sherman, G. F., and Denenberg, V. H. 1996. Radial arm maze learning in BXSB mice: Effects of neocortical ectopias. *Society for Neuroscience Abstracts* 22:485.

Innocenti, G. M., and Berbel, P. 1991a. Analysis of an experimental cortical network: i) Architectonics of visual areas 17 and 18 after neonatal injections of ibotenic acid; similarities with human microgyria. *Journal of Neurological Transplant* 2(1):1 28.

Innocenti, G. M., and Berbel, P. 1991b. Analysis of an experimental cortical network: ii) Connections of visual areas 17 and 18 after neonatal injections of ibotenic acid. *Journal of Neurological Transplant* 2(1):29 54.

Ison, J. R., and Pinckney, L. A. 1983. Reflex inhibition in humans: Sensitivity to brief silent periods in white noise. *Perceptual Psychophys* 34(1):84–88.

Jacobs, K. M., Gutnick, M. J., and Prince, D. A. 1996. Hyperexcitability in a model of cortical maldevelopment. *Cerebral Cortex* 6:514 23.

Jenner, A. R., Galaburda, A. M., and Sherman, G. F. 2000. Connectivity of ectopic neurons in the molecular layer of the somatosensory cortex in autoimmune mice. *Cerebral Cortex* 10(10):1005–13.

Kaufmann, W. E., and Galaburda, A. M. 1989. Cerebrocortical microdysgenesis in neurologically normal subjects: A histopathologic study. *Neurology* 39(2):238–44.

Leitner, D. S., Hammond, G. R., Springer, C. P., Ingham, K. M., Mekilo, A. M., Bodison, P. R., Aranda, M. T., and Shawaryn, M. A. 1993. Parameters affecting gap detection in the rat. *Perceptual Psychophys* 54(3):395–405.

Liberman, I. Y., Shankweiler, D., and Liberman, A. M. 1989. The alphabetic principle and learning to read. In *Phonology and Reading Disability*, eds. D. Shankweiler and I. Y. Liberman. NY: Michigan Press.

Livingstone, M., Rosen, G., Drislane, F., and Galaburda, A. 1991. Physiological and anatomical evidence for a magnocellular defect in developmental dyslexia. *Proceedings of National Academy of Sciences* (USA) 88:7943–7.

Lovegrove, W., Garzia, R., and Nicholson, S. 1990. Experimental evidence for a transient system deficit in specific reading disability. *Journal of the American Optometric Association* 2(2):137–46.

Luhmann, H. J., and Raabe, K. 1996. Characterization of neuronal migration disorders in neocortical structures: Expression of epileptiform activity in an animal model. *Epilepsy Research* 26(1):67 74.

Lyon, G., and Robain, O. 1967. Etude comparative des encéphalopathies circulatoires prénatales et para-natales (hydranencéphalies, porencéphalies et encéphalomalacies kystiques de la substance blanche). *Acta Neuropathologica* (Berlin) 9(1):79–98.

Lyon, G. R. 1995. Toward a definition of dyslexia. *Annals of Dyslexia* 45:3–27.

Mann, V., Liberman, I., and Shankweiler, D. 1980. Children's memory for sentences and word strings in relation to reading ability. *Memory and Cognition* 8(8):4.

McCroskey, R. L., and Kidder, H. C. 1980. Auditory fusion among learning disabled, reading disabled, and normal children. *Journal of Learning Disabilities* 13(2):69–76.

McManus, I. C., and Bryden, M. P. 1991. Geschwind's theory of cerebral lateralization: Developing a formal, causal model. *Psychological Bulletin* 110(2):237–53.

Morgan, W. P. 1896. A case of congenital word-blindness. *Speech* 23:357–77.

Nagarajan, S., Mahncke, H., Salz, T., Tallal, P., Roberts, T., and Merzenich, M. M. 1999. Cortical auditory signal processing in poor readers. *Proceedings of the National Academy of Sciences* (USA) 96(11):6483 8.

Nicolelis, M. A. L., Chapin, J. K., and Lin, R. C. S. 1991. Thalamic plasticity induced by early whisker removal in rats. *Brain Research* 561(2):344–9.

Nowakowski, R. S., and Sekiguchi, M. 1987. Abnormalities of granule cell dendrites and axons in the dentate gyrus of the NZB/BlNJ mouse. *Society for Neuroscience Abstracts* 13:1117.

Olson, R., Wise, B., Conners, F., Rack, J., and Fulker, D. 1989. Specific deficits in component reading and language skills: Genetic and environmental influences. *Journal of Learning Disabilities* 22(6):339–348.

Ortiz Alonso, T., Navarro, M., and vila Abad, E. 1990. P300 component of the auditory event-related potentials and dyslexia. *Functional Neurology* 5(4):333–8.

Orton, S. T. 1925. "Word-blindness" in school children. *Archives of Neurology and Psychiatry* 14:581–615.

Rosen, G. D. 1996. Cellular, morphometric, ontogenetic and connectional substrates of anatomical asymmetry. *Neuroscience Biobehavior Review* 20(4):607 15.

Rosen, G. D., Burstein, D., and Galaburda, A. M. 2000. Changes in efferent and afferent connectivity in rats with cerebrocortical microgyria. *Journal of Comparative Neurology* 418(4):423–40.

Rosen, G. D., Press, D. M., Sherman, G. F., and Galaburda, A. M. 1992. The development of induced cerebrocortical microgyria in the rat. *Journal of Neuropathology and Experimental Neurology* 51(6):601 11.

Rosen, G. D., Sherman, G. F., and Galaburda, A. M. 1989. Interhemispheric connections differ between symmetrical and asymmetrical brain regions. *Neuroscience* 33:525 33.

Rosen, G. D., Sherman, G. F., and Galaburda, A. M. 1991. Ontogenesis of neocortical asymmetry: A [3H]thymidine study. *Neuroscience* 41(2–3):779–90.

Rosen, G. D., Sherman, G. F., and Galaburda, A. M. 1993. Neuronal subtypes and anatomic asymmetry: Changes in neuronal number and cell-packing density. *Neuroscience* 56(4):833–9.

Rosen, G. D., Sherman, G. F., Richman, J. M., Stone, L. V., and Galaburda, A. M. 1992. Induction of molecular layer ectopias by puncture wounds in newborn rats and mice. *Developmental Brain Research* 67(2):285–91.

Rosen, G. D., Waters, N. S., Galaburda, A. M., and Denenberg, V. H. 1995. Behavioral consequences of neonatal injury of the neocortex. *Brain Research* 681(1–2):177–89.

Schneider, G. E. 1979. Is it really better to have your brain lesion early? A revision of the "Kennard principle." *Neuropsychologia* 17:557–83.

Schneider, G. E. 1981. Early lesions and abnormal neuronal connections. *Trends in Neuroscience* 4:187–92.

Schrott, L. M., Denenberg, V. H., Sherman, G. F., Waters, N. S., Rosen, G. D., and Galaburda, A. M. 1992. Environmental enrichment, neocortical ectopias, and behavior in the autoimmune NZB mouse. *Developmental Brain Research* 67(1):85–93.

Schwartz, J., and Tallal, P. 1980. Rate of acoustic change may underlie hemispheric specialization for speech perception. *Science* 207:1380–1.

Sekiguchi, M., Shimai, K., Mariya, M., and Nowakowski, R. S. 1991. Abnormalities of foliation and neuronal position in the cerebellum of NZB/BINJ mouse. *Developmental Brain Research* 64:189–95.

Shankweiler, D., and Crain, S. 1986. Language mechanisms and reading disorder: A modular approach. *Cognition* 24:139–68.

Shankweiler, D., Crain, S., Katz, L., Fowler, A. E., Liberman, A. M., Brady, S. A., Thornton, R., Lundquist, E., Dreyer, L., Fletcher, J. M., Stuebing, K. K., Shaywitz, S. E., and Shaywitz, B. A. 1995. Cognitive profiles of reading-disabled children: Comparison of language skills in phonology, morphology, and syntax. *Psychological Science* 6(3):149–56.

Shaywitz, B., Fletcher, J., and Shaywitz, S. 1994. A conceptual framework for learning disabilities and attention-deficit/ hyperactivity disorder. *Canadian Journal of Special Education* 9(3):1–16.

Sherman, G. F., Galaburda, A. M., and Geschwind, N. 1985. Cortical anomalies in brains of New Zealand mice: A neuropathologic model of dyslexia? *Proceedings of the National Academy of Sciences* (USA) 82:8072–4.

Sherman, G. F., Jenner, A. J., and Galaburda, A. M. in press. Connectivity of ectopic neurons in the molecular layer of the somatosensory cortex in autoimmune mice. *Cerebral Cortex*.

Sherman, G. F., Morrison, L., Rosen, G. D., Behan, P. O., and Galaburda, A. M. 1990. Brain abnormalities in immune defective mice. *Brain Research* 532:25–33.

Sherman, G. F., Rosen, G. D., Stone, L. V., Press, D. M., and Galaburda, A. M. 1992a. The organization of radial glial fibers in spontaneous neocortical ectopias of newborn New-Zealand black mice. *Developmental Brain Research* 67(2):279–83.

Sherman, G. F., Stone, J. S., Press, D. M., Rosen, G. D., and Galaburda, A. M. 1990. Abnormal architecture and connections disclosed by neurofilament staining in the cerebral cortex of autoimmune mice. *Brain Research* 529:202–7.

Sherman, G. F., Stone, J. S., Rosen, G. D., and Galaburda, A. M. 1990. Neocortical VIP neurons are increased in the hemisphere containing focal cerebrocortical microdysgenesis in New Zealand Black Mice. *Brain Research* 532:232–6.

Sherman, G. F., Stone, L. V., Denenberg, V. H., and Beier, D. R. 1994. A genetic analysis of neocortical ectopias in New Zealand Black mice. *NeuroReport* 5:721–4.

Sherman, G. F., Stone, L. V., Galaburda, A. M., and Beier, D. R. 1997. Linkage analysis of neurocortical ectopias in NXSM-D mice. *Society for Neuroscience Abstracts* 23:1133.

Sherman, G. F., Stone, L. V., Walthour, N. R., Boehm, G. W., Denenberg, V. H., Rosen, G. D., and Galaburda, A. M. 1992b. Birthdates of neurons in neocortical ectopias of New Zealand Black mice. *Society for Neuroscience Abstracts* 18:1446A.

Siegel, L., Share, D., and Esther, G. 1995. Evidence for superior orthographic skills in dyslexia. *Psychological Science* 6(4):250–4.

Siegel, L. S., and Ryan, E. B. 1989. The development of working memory in normally achieving and subtypes of learning disabled children. *Child Development* 60(4):973–80.

Slaghuis, W. L., Lovegrove, W. J., and Davidson, J. A. 1993. Visual and language processing deficits are concurrent in dyslexia. *Cerebral Cortex* 29(4):601–15.

Smith, S. D., Kimberling, W. J., Pennington, B. F., and Lubs, H. A. 1983. Specific reading disability: Identification of an inherited form through linkage analysis. *Science* 219:1345–7.

Smith, S. T., Macaruso, P., Shankweiler, D., and Crain, S. 1989. Syntactic comprehension in young poor readers. *Applied Psycholinguistics* 10:429–54.

Stein, J., and Walsh, V. 1997. To see but not to read; the magnocellular theory of dyslexia. *Trends in Neuroscience* 20(4):147–52.

Suzuki, M., and Choi, B. H. 1991. Repair and reconstruction of the cortical plate following closed cryogenic injury to the neonatal rat cerebrum. *Acta Neuropathologica* (Berlin) 82(2): 93 101.

Swanson, H. L. 1993. Working memory in learning disability subgroups. *Journal of Experimental Child Psychology* 56:87–114.

Swanson, H. L., Cochran, K. F., and Ewers, C. A. 1989. Working memory in skilled and less skilled readers. *Journal of Abnormal Child Psychology* 17(2):145–56.

Tallal, P., Miller, S., and Fitch, R. H. 1993. Neurobiological basis of speech: A case for the preeminence of temporal processing. In *Temporal Information Processing in the Nervous System, with Special Reference to Dyslexia and Dysphasia*, Vol. 682, eds. P. Tallal, A. M. Galaburda, R. Llinas, and C. von Euler. New York: New York Academy of Sciences.

Tallal, P., and Piercy, M. 1973. Defects of non-verbal auditory perception in children with developmental aphasia. *Nature* 241:468–9.

Torgesen, J. K. 1991. Cross-age consistency in phonological processing. In *Phonological Processes in Literacy—A Tribute to Isabelle Y. Liberman*, eds. S. A. Brady and D. P. Shankweiler. Hillsdale, NJ: Lawrence Erlbaum Associates.

Waters, N. S., Sherman, G. F., Galaburda, A. M., and Denenberg, V. H. 1997. Effects of cortical ectopias on spatial delayed-matching-to-sample performance in BXSB mice. *Behavioral Brain Research* 84(1–2):23–29.

Wecker, J. R., Ison, J. R., and Foss, J. A. 1985. Reflex modification as a test for sensory function. *Neurobehavioral Toxicology and Teratology* 7(6):733–8.

Williams, M. C., and Lecluyse, K. 1990. Perceptual consequences of a temporal processing deficit in reading disabled children. *Journal of American Optometric Association* 61:111–21.

Williams, M. C., May, J. G., Solman, R., and Zhou, H. 1995. The effects of spatial filtering and contrast reduction on visual search times in good and poor readers. *Vision Research* 35(2):285–91.

Wright, B. A., Lombardino, L. J., King, W. M., Puranik, C. S., Leonard, C. M., and Merzenich, M. M. 1997. Deficits in auditory temporal and spectral resolution in language-impaired children. *Nature* 387(6629):176–8.

ACKNOWLEDGMENTS

This work was supported, in part, by PHS grant HD20806.

The authors wish to thank Victor H. Denenberg, Amy Herman, Christine Brown, and Paula Tallal for their contributions to the work reported here. Acknowledgments also go to Antis Zalkalns, Lisa Stone Garcia, and Heinz Windzio for technical assistance.

Chapter • **8**

Dyslexia, Learning, and the Cerebellum

Roderick I. Nicolson and
Angela J. Fawcett

In this chapter we attempt to outline the reasoning and evidence behind our hypothesis that abnormal cerebellar functioning may be at the heart of the problems suffered by people with dyslexia. We also claim that the approach provides new and provocative answers to important questions in dyslexia research. We start with a brief overview of these key questions. We then outline the new evidence that, rather than "merely" being involved in the acquisition and execution of motor skills, the human cerebellum is a central component in the acquisition and execution of cognitive skills, especially those scaffolded by spoken language. Third, we outline evidence that cerebellar function is abnormal in dyslexia. We consider three specific lines of evidence: behavioral evidence, neuroanatomical and neuroimaging evidence, and finally evidence relating to abnormalities in learning that appear to be attributable to the cerebellum. Finally, we offer a view of the origins and ontogenetic development of dyslexia in terms of cerebellar deficit from birth, and we consider the implications of this framework for the key questions in dyslexia work and for subsequent developments in the field.

KEY QUESTIONS FOR DYSLEXIA RESEARCH

Developmental dyslexia is traditionally defined as *"a disorder in children who, despite conventional classroom experience, fail to attain the language skills of reading, writing and spelling commensurate with their intellectual abilities"* (World Federation of Neurology 1968). A recent redefinition *"a specific language based disorder of constitutional origin, characterized by difficulties in single word decoding, usually reflecting insufficient phonological processing abilities"* (The Orton Dyslexia Society 1995) reflects a major achievement of dyslexia research—the identification and analysis of a phonological deficit (Bradley and Bryant 1983; Shankweiler et al. 1995; Snowling 1987; Stanovich 1988; Vellutino 1979) which became the consensus view of many dyslexia researchers.

However, one of the fascinations of dyslexia research is that, whatever one's speciality as a researcher whether it be reading, phonology, writing, spelling, education, memory, speed, creativity, hearing, vision, balance, learning, skill, genetics, brain structure, or brain function—children with dyslexia will show interesting and unusual differences in that domain. Given the need for specialization in science, many researchers have gone on to undertake incisive and insightful studies in their specific domain of expertise. This explains why, on the one hand, there is an unrivalled wealth of research on dyslexia, and why, on the other hand, the research area fails to cumulate, to build towards a "grand" theory of dyslexia. In an analogy much loved by psychologists, it is like the Hindu fable of the four blind men attempting to describe an elephant. One touches the trunk, another the leg, another the tail, another the side, leading to descriptions of "a pipe," "a tree," "a house," and "a rope" respectively. If one wants to describe the whole elephant, one needs a range of perspectives. Let us start the tour of the elephant by identifying some potent causes of confusion in the area.

Arguably the major source of confusion in dyslexia research is the different motivations of different researchers. In particular, many applied theoreticians are concerned with educational attainment, and in particular, literacy. Consequently, they analyse the different components of reading, investigate the differential effects of various interventions, and often stress (correctly) the need for support for any child who is at risk of reading failure, whether or not they are dyslexic. By contrast, "pure" theorists are interested primarily in the underlying cause(s) of dyslexia (rather than literacy per se) and so they undertake theoretically motivated tests, often in domains not directly related to literacy. In most areas of science the distinction between cause, symptoms, and treatment is clear cut—in medicine for instance, the causes, symptoms, and treatment of, say, malaria are quite different. Indeed, several diseases may have similar symptoms. Influenza and meningitis may lead to symptoms of fever, aching, and nausea similar to those of malaria, but of course the underlying causes (and treatments) are quite different. In dyslexia, this distinction is much less clear cut but it is therefore particularly important to maintain the distinctions between cause, symptom, and treatment. The starting point of our analysis is given in figure 1.

Phonological difficulties are certainly an important symptom, but only one symptom. Phonological support is clearly an important aspect of treatment, but may be only one aspect of treatment. Abnormalities around the Sylvian fissure may or may not be the underlying cause of the symptoms. There are many possible neurological substrates that could lead to the symptoms of poor reading and poor phonology. It may be that in five years it will become clear that there are, in fact, several subtypes of dyslexia, each corresponding to abnormality in a different brain region, each leading to phonological difficulties, but also to further and more distinctive symptoms (such as visual difficulties, auditory difficulties, motor difficulties, speed difficulties, etc). It is likely that these "brain-based" diagnoses will also reveal commonalities between specific types of dyslexia and other developmental disorders, including ADHD, specific language impairment, dyspraxia, and generalized learning disability. It may also be that the appropriate treatment for a given child depends critically upon the specific underlying cause(s) of the child's difficulties, rather than just the general reading symptoms displayed. In particular, if one can identify

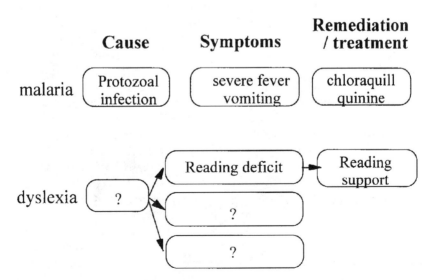

Figure 1.   Targets for a Causal Analysis

the underlying cause of a child's potential difficulties *before* they are manifested, it should be possible to give proactive support to the extent that the child will not fail to learn to read and will not suffer the concomitant emotional and educational devastation. This, then, is the big applied challenge for pure theorists—fill in the question marks in figure 1. This will facilitate early diagnosis and support for children with dyslexia (and other children with special educational needs).

Having made the case for pure theoretical research aimed at identifying the underlying cause(s) of dyslexia, we now turn to the requirements for a causal theory in general, and a causal theory of dyslexia specifically. In general terms, scientific metatheory distinguishes between descriptive theories and explanatory theories. For instance, Mendeleyev's original pattern-based hypothesis for the atomic table was an ad hoc descriptive theory, whereas the subsequent explanation of the pattern in terms of atomic weights was a truly explanatory theory. Typically scientific explanation moves from descriptive to explanatory theories. In terms of figure 1, one might argue that a good description of the symptoms was the initial stage of descriptive theory, whereas the specification of the neurological level was the explanatory stage. A related case is well made by Morton and Frith (1995), who distinguish between three levels of explanation—biological, cognitive, and behavioral, with the biological level explanation providing the deepest level of explanation. In a metatheoretical analysis, Seidenberg (1993) argues that one important requirement for an explanatory theory is that it should *"explain phenomena in terms of independently motivated principles."* A further important criterion introduced by Seidenberg is that *"an explanatory theory shows how phenomena previously thought to be unrelated actually derive from a common underlying source."* It should be noted, however, that in addition to the daunting tasks of resolving these issues, an explanatory account of a developmental disorder should explain how the symptoms (at neurological and cognitive levels) arise as a function of maturation and experience—what Thelen and Smith (1994) describe as the "ontogenetic causal chain."

Finally, turning to dyslexia, an early *a priori* analysis of the requirements for any "process deficit" theory of dyslexia was provided by Morrison and Manis (1983). These authors suggested that any viable theory must address four issues: why does the deficit affect primarily the task of reading—later described by Stanovich (1988) as the "specificity principle"; why do children with dyslexia perform adequately on other tasks; what is the mechanism by which the deficit results in the reading problems; and what is the direction of causality?

Before addressing these issues, it is important to digress somewhat and turn to the cerebellum, a crucial, but sadly neglected, brain structure.

THE CEREBELLUM

The cerebellum (figure 2) is a very densely packed and deeply folded subcortical brain structure situated at the back of the brain, sometimes known as the "hind-brain" (Holmes 1939). In humans, it accounts for 10% to 15% of brain weight, 40% of brain surface area, and 50% of the brain's neurons. There are two cerebellar hemispheres, each comprising folded cerebellar cortex, which receive massive input from all the senses, from the primary motor cortex, and from many other areas of cerebral cortex, either by "mossy fibers" from the pontine nuclei or via "climbing fibers" from the inferior olive. Output from the cerebellum is generated by Purkinje cells, goes via the deep cerebellar nuclei (dentate, interposed and fastigial nuclei), and is generally inhibitory. The cerebellar cortex comprises several phylogenetically ancient structures, including the flocculonodular node, which is situated at the caudal end and receives input from the vestibular system and projects

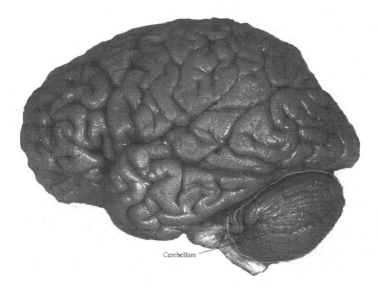

Cerebellum

Figure 2.   The Human Cerebellum. This picture was downloaded from NeuroNames and Template Atlas of the Primate Brain, http://rprcsgi.rprc.washington.edu/neuronames/ Their permission to publish is gratefully acknowledged

to the vestibular nuclei. The vermis, located on the midline, receives visual, auditory, cutaneous, and kinesthetic information from sensory nuclei and sends output to the fastigial nucleus, which connects to the vestibular nucleus and motor neurons in the reticular formation. On both sides of the vermis, the intermediate zone receives input from the motor areas of cerebral cortex through the pontine tegmental reticular nucleus. Output is via the interposed nucleus, which projects to the red nucleus, and thence the rubrospinal system for arm and hand movements, and also to the ventrothalamic nucleus. The lateral zone of the cerebellum is phylogenetically more recent, and is much larger in humans (relative to overall brain size) than in other primates (Passingham 1975) and is referred to as the neocerebellum. It is involved in the control of independent limb movements and especially in rapid, skilled movements, receiving information from frontal association cortex and from primary motor cortex via the pontine nucleus. It also receives somatosensory information about the current position and rate of movement of the limbs. Its role in skilled movement execution is generally thought to be the computation of the appropriate movement parameters for the next movement (possibly the next but one movement), and to communicate these via the dentate nucleus and the ventrolateral thalamic nucleus to the primary motor cortex. The lateral zone also sends outputs to the red nucleus, and thus the rubrospinal tract.

Damage to different parts of the cerebellum can lead to different symptoms. In humans, damage to the flocculonodular system or vermis may typically lead to disturbances in posture and balance. Damage to the intermediate zone causes problems such as limb rigidity in the rubrospinal system. Damage to the lateral zone causes weakness (loss of muscle tone) and dyscoordination or decomposition of movement (that is, previously coordinated sequences of movements, such as picking up a cup, may break down into a series of separate movements). Lesions of the lateral zone also appear to impair the timing of rapid ballistic (pre-planned, automatic) movements. However, one of the features of cerebellar damage is the great plasticity of the system. Typically normal or close to normal performance is attained again within a few months of the initial damage (Holmes 1922).

One of the fascinating aspects of the cerebellum is that the structure of the cerebellum appears to be quite different from that of the rest of the brain. In particular, the cerebellar cortex comprises a mosaic of relatively independent "microzones," comprising Purkinje cells and their associated inputs and output. These microzones, in combination with the associated pathways to and from the associated extra-cerebellar nuclei, may be thought of as a "cerebellar-cortico-nuclear microcomplex" (CCMC) able to undertake a range of tasks (Ito 1984). The complexity of the set of outputs and inputs for the CCMC allows the output from a deep cerebellar nucleus to be fed back into the system, either immediately or after further processing. This allows the cerebellum to work as a comparator, comparing the predicted input with the actual sensory input. Any difference (the "error signal") may then be used to improve the predictions the next time. It is now reasonably well established (e.g., Kawato and Gomi 1992) that some such process takes place in primitive control mechanisms such as the vestibular ocular reflex (VOR), in which the eye maintains fixation on an object despite movements of the head, and the optokinetic reflex (OKR), in which the eye tracks a moving object. Many models have been proposed, but the Marr/Albus composite model (Albus 1971; Marr 1969), in which the climbing fibers act as an error signal to the CCMC, remains a good approximation (Thach 1996). For our purposes in this chapter, a particularly interesting observation is that of Ito (1990), who noted that many skills could be construed as developing from a *feedback* model (in which a movement is made under conscious control, and the match between say hand and target is monitored continually), to a *feedforward* model (if I send these instructions to my hand it will end up at position P at time t) to an *inverse* model (in order to achieve the target, I need to execute the following [set of actions]). He makes it clear that the CCMC provides the appropriate learning and monitoring equipment to achieve these learning changes from voluntary to automatic movements, and goes on to speculate that a similar set of cerebellum-based procedures could be used to acquire more and more practised cognitive skills.

This proposed involvement of the cerebellum in cognitive skills led to considerable controversy in the field, in that the cerebellum had traditionally been considered as a motor area (Eccles, Ito and Szentagothai 1967; Holmes 1917, 1939; Stein and Glickstein 1992), and it is also claimed to be involved in the automatization of motor skill and in adaptive learning control via the cerebellar structures (Ito, 1984, 1990; Jenkins et al. 1994; Krupa, Thompson and Thompson 1993). However, as Leiner, Leiner, and Dow (1989) note, the human cerebellum (in particular, the lateral cerebellar hemispheres and ventrolateral cerebellar dentate nucleus) has evolved enormously, becoming linked not only with the frontal motor areas, but also some areas further forward in the frontal cortex, including Broca's language area (Leiner et al. 1989; Leiner, Leiner, and Dow 1991, 1993) which leads them to conclude that the cerebellum is therefore central for the acquisition of "language dexterity." In effect, then, they proposed that the cerebellum is critically involved in the automatization of any skill, whether motor or cognitive. There remains controversy over the role of the cerebellum in cognitive skills not involving speech or "inner speech" (Ackermann et al. 1998; Glickstein 1993), but there is now overwhelming evidence of the importance of the cerebellum in language (Ackermann and Hertrich 2000; Fabbro, Moretti, and Bava 2000; Silveri and Misciagna 2000), including a recent demonstration of specific cerebellar involvement in reading (Fulbright et al. 1999)

DYSLEXIA AND THE CEREBELLUM

The scene is now set for a return to dyslexia.

The Automatization Deficit Hypothesis

In our longstanding research program we attempted initially to characterize the symptoms of dyslexia from a learning perspective, leading to our "automatization deficit" hypothesis (Nicolson and Fawcett 1990) which states that children with dyslexia have difficulties becoming expert in any skill that requires "automatic" performance, and consequently will suffer problems in fluency for any skill that should become automatic through extensive practice. The hypothesis is, of course, directly consistent with the established problems in reading for children and adults with dyslexia: *"Laboratory research indicates that the most critical factor beneath fluent word reading is the ability to recognize letters, spelling patterns, and whole words effortlessly, automatically and visually. The central goal of all reading instruction—comprehension—depends critically on this ability"* (Adams 1990). The hypothesis also accounted neatly for the problems in acquiring phonological skills, which also have to be learned over a long period until they are automatic (Fawcett and Nicolson 1995). However, the distinctive strength of the hypothesis was that it was also consistent with the outcome of a series of studies in the early 1990s, in which we investigated a range of skills outside the literacy domain, and found that our panel of children with dyslexia showed severe deficits in a range of skills. These included balance (Fawcett and Nicolson 1992; Nicolson and Fawcett 1990; Yap and van der Leij 1994)[1]; motor skill (Fawcett and Nicolson 1995b; Daum

---

[1]It should be noted that, based on their study of German-speaking children with dyslexia, Wimmer, Mayringer, and Raberger (1999) claim that balance deficits occur only for children with dyslexia also suffering from attention deficit, but this is not so for the English-speaking children whom we have tested.

et al. 1993); and rapid processing (Fawcett and Nicolson 1994; Nicolson and Fawcett 1994). Furthermore, taking all the data together (Nicolson and Fawcett 1995a, b), the majority of (individual) children with dyslexia showed problems "across the board," rather than with different children showing different profiles, as would be expected if there were a range of sub-types (Boder 1973; Castles and Holmes 1996). The automatization deficit therefore provided an excellent account of the range of symptoms of dyslexia, but it did not specify an underlying neurological structure. In subsequent research we subsumed this "cognitive level" hypothesis within the "neurological level" hypothesis of cerebellar deficit, as outlined below.

The Cerebellar Deficit Hypothesis

As discussed above, deficits in motor skill and automatization point clearly to the cerebellum. Levinson (Frank and Levinson 1973; Levinson 1988), on the basis of studies of nystagmus and optokinetic fixation in children with dyslexia, has for some time argued for mild cerebellar dysfunction as a causal factor in dyslexia. However, Levinson's work had been discounted owing to shortcomings in research methodology (Silver 1987), allied, of course, to the then belief that the cerebellum was not involved in language-related skills. Furthermore, the hypothesis falls foul of the "assumption of specificity." If there are indeed problems in the cerebellum, why are the major symptoms specific to the reading domain?

In attempting to address these issues, we undertook a range of studies, using a panel of children with dyslexia whom we had tested extensively previously, and who could be described as having "pure" dyslexia, with IQ over 90, reading age at least 18 months behind their chronological age, no sign of ADHD, and no significant emotional or behavioral problems. They were compared with a control group from a similar social background, matched for age and IQ. Further information is given in our other chapter in this volume. The studies have been reported in the literature, so a relatively brief summary must suffice here.

Time Estimation

First, we undertook a theoretically motivated study. In earlier research, Ivry and Keele (1989) had suggested that the cerebellum might be centrally involved in timing functions. This hypothesis was based on a comparative study of patients with cerebellar lesions and patients with other neuropsychological disorders. The cerebellar patients showed a specific disability in estimating the duration of a short (about 1 second) tone, whereas their ability to estimate loudness was unimpaired. Given that other causal hypotheses for dyslexia made no differential predictions for these two conditions, this study gave us a good opportunity to provide a rigorous test of the cerebellar deficit hypothesis (CDH). We therefore replicated the study using our panel of children with dyslexia and control children (Nicolson, Fawcett, and Dean 1995). The results were exactly as predicted, with the children with dyslexia showing significant difficulties with the time estimation, but no such difficulties with loudness estimation. It should be stressed that this study does not in any way involve rapid processing. The task is merely to listen to tone 1 (a standard tone of 1 second in length), wait 1 second, listen to tone 2 (which will be either slightly more or less than 1 second), then say which one is the longer. Given that the memory component is exactly the same in the time estimation and loudness estimation tasks, we believe that no alternative causal explanation for dyslexia (then or now) is able to predict the dissociation between these two tasks.

Clinical Tests of Cerebellar Function

If there is indeed a cerebellar dysfunction in dyslexia, then children with dyslexia should show marked impairment on the traditional signs of cerebellar dysfunction. Clinical evidence of the range of deficits evident following gross damage to the cerebellum has been described in detail in classic works by Holmes, and by Dow and Moruzzi (1958). Traditional symptoms of cerebellar dysfunction are dystonia (problems with muscle tone) and ataxia (disturbance in posture, gait, or movements of the extremities). Apart from our own work on balance and Levinson's controversial findings (Levinson 1990), there was no evidence in the literature that children with dyslexia do suffer from this type of problem. Consequently, in another stringent test of the cerebellar impairment hypothesis, we replicated the clinical cerebellar tests described in Dow and Moruzzi, using groups of children with dyslexia and matched controls. Three groups of children with dyslexia participated, together with three groups of normally achieving children matched for age and IQ. The children had been in our research panel for some years, and at the time of testing had mean ages of 18, 14, and 10 years. This gave six groups, D18, D14, and D10; and C18, C14, and C10 for the three age groups of children with dyslexia and matched controls respectively. A fuller report is provided in Fawcett, Nicolson, and Dean (1996).

The tests in the Dow and Moruzzi (1958) battery may be divided into three types: First, two tasks assessing the ability to maintain posture and muscle tone while standing and in response to active displacement of station; second, a series of seven tests for hypotonia of the upper limbs in both a standing and sitting position, in response to active or passive displacement of the limbs; and finally, a series of five tests of the ability to initiate and maintain a complex voluntary movement.

Two factor analyses of variance were undertaken individually on the data for each test, with the factors being chronological age (10, 14, and 18 years) and dyslexia (dyslexia vs. control). The performance of the children with dyslexia was significantly worse than that of the chronological age controls on all of the 14 tasks. A further set of analyses of variance was undertaken comparing performance with that of reading age controls. In this case, the factors were reading age (10 vs. 14) and dyslexia (dyslexia vs. control). The performance of the children with dyslexia was significantly worse on 11 out of the 14 tests.

It was clear, therefore, that the between-group analyses indicated significant deficits, even compared with reading age controls, on most cerebellar tests. Further analyses were required to investigate two central issues: the relative severity of the deficits on the various tasks, and the relative individual incidence of deficit for the tasks. This was undertaken by first normalizing the data for each test for each group relative to that of the corresponding control group.[2] This procedure led to an age-appropriate "effect size" in standard deviation units (analogous to a z-score) for each test for each child (e.g., Cohen 1969). The sign was adjusted such that a negative effect size indicated below-normal performance. A child was deemed to be "at risk" on a given task if his or her effect size on that task was 1 or worse (that is, at least one standard deviation below the expected performance for that age). If data are normally distributed, one would expect 15% of the population to be at least one standard deviation below the mean, and 2% to be at least two standard deviations below.

Groups D18 and C18 were normalized relative to C18, groups D14 and C14 were normalized relative to C14, and groups C10 and D10 were normalized relative to C10. All but one task (finger to finger) produced an overall effect size for the groups with dyslexia

---

[2]For example, for the D14 group the data for postural stability for each subject were normalized by obtaining the difference of that subject's postural stability score from the mean postural stability score for group C14, and then dividing this difference by the standard deviation of the C14 group for postural stability.

of –1 or worse (at least 1 standard deviation worse than the controls). Deficits more severe than reading age (–2.26, 100%) were for finger and thumb opposition (–7.08, 79%); tremor (–4.44, 80%); arm displacement (–3.59, 100%); toe tap (–3.55, 82%); limb shake (–3.17, 83%); diadochokinesis speed of alternating tapping the table with palm and back of hand (–3.22, 69%); postural stability movement when pushed gently in the back (–2.86, 97%); and muscle tone (–2.42, 52%). The performance of the 10-year-old children with dyslexia was markedly poorer than for the older children with dyslexia on several tests of muscle tone, with effect sizes of –4 and worse.

Cerebellar Function in Further Groups of Children with Dyslexia

It should be noted, however, that even though the data reported above provided strong evidence of cerebellar impairment in the groups of children with dyslexia tested, it is possible that research with different samples of children with dyslexia and controls would lead to lower estimates of effect size and incidence rate. We investigated this issue in parallel research (Fawcett and Nicolson 1999) using a further sample of 126 children (including children with dyslexia and control children). The subjects were split into four age groups (8–9 years, 10–11 years, 12–13 years, and 14–16 years), with roughly equal numbers of control children and children with dyslexia in each group. Children with dyslexia were taken from dyslexia units at private schools, and controls were taken from the same school where possible. No selection was made on the children with dyslexia other than that they fulfilled the standard discrepancy/exclusionary criterion used in the other studies. The children with dyslexia were not matched for IQ with the controls, and in fact the control children had a higher full scale IQ overall. The control children were also reading significantly above their age level, leading to extreme effect sizes for reading and spelling for the groups with dyslexia.

A selection of experimental tasks was administered to the children, including both cerebellar tasks and other tasks known to be sensitive to dyslexia. In all the tests of cerebellar function, together with segmentation and nonsense word repetition, the performance of the groups with dyslexia was significantly worse than that of their chronological age controls. Only picture naming speed was not significantly worse. The effect size analyses also provide a similar picture to the panel study,[3] though (as one would

---

[3]Balance performance is somewhat anomalous here, in that, despite the significant effect of dyslexia, the overall effect size of the discrepancy is low. Analysis

expect for the larger and more heterogeneous set of control children) the overall effect sizes were lower. Spelling had the most extreme effect size (–4.26, 91%), with limb shake (–2.62, 86%) and postural stability (–2.88, 78%) being comparable to reading (–3.56, 92%). Segmentation was somewhat less strong[4] (–1.76, 56%), which in turn was more marked than nonsense word repetition (–1.45, 63%). In line with the earlier study, comparing children with dyslexia and controls, some of the most notable results were the exceptionally poor performance of all four groups with dyslexia on postural stability and limb shake. It is interesting to note that the balance impairment as revealed by postural stability (reaction to a push in the back) was considerably more marked than that shown by one foot balance—the number of wobbles without external disturbance (–0.51, 23%).

Direct Tests of Cerebellar Anatomy and Function

The above studies were undertaken during the mid-1990s and provide clear behavioral evidence that children with dyslexia do indeed show behavioral evidence of cerebellar abnormalities. This provides strong evidence that there is indeed some abnormality in the cerebellum or related pathways for many children with dyslexia. Nonetheless, the cerebellum is a large structure with many functions. It is important to investigate this issue further, attempting to obtain direct evidence of cerebellar problems, in the hope that more direct investigation may lead to a clearer indication of which parts of the cerebellum are not used in the normal fashion.

Neuroanatomy of the Cerebellum

In the late 1970s and 1980s, Geschwind and Galaburda, with support from The Orton Dyslexia Society, established a "brain bank" of brains of people with dyslexia, together with control brains. Painstaking analysis of this postmortem tissue by Galaburda and his colleagues has led to a number of fascinating discoveries. Early work (Galaburda and Kemper 1979; Galaburda et al. 1985) was

---

of the individual results indicated that this anomaly was attributed to high variability in the control groups, with the standard deviation almost equal to the mean. Consequently effect sizes are reduced across the board. This greater variability suggests that balance may not be a useful task for screening purposes.

[4]It is important to note that training in phonological awareness and in grapheme-phoneme translation were a central component of the teaching methods of the school for the children with dyslexia. We interpret the relatively mild deficit on phonological skills as a tribute to the quality of teaching.

confined to the cerebral cortex, and indicated differences in gross structural characteristics (decreased asymmetry of the planum temporale) together with evidence of microstructural anomalies consisting of the presence of ectopias, dysplasias, and microgyria, predominantly but not exclusively in language areas, predominantly in the left hemisphere. Structural differences may be pursued in vivo by means of magnetic resonance studies, and the research is beyond the scope of this chapter, though it is fair to say that the evidence remains unclear (Beaton 1997; Best and Demb 1999; Rumsey et al. 1997). However, currently there remains no alternative to painstaking microscopic analysis for the ectopias and dysplasias. More recently, both visual and auditory magnocellular pathways have been investigated (Galaburda, Menard, and Rosen 1994; Livingstone et al. 1991), with the authors concluding that the specimens from individuals with dyslexia had smaller magnocells in the medial and lateral geniculate nuclei. In a precise replication of the techniques used in the above studies, Finch (Finch, Nicolson, and Fawcett 2000) undertook equivalent analyses on the cerebella of the same brain specimens. Cross sectional areas and cell packing densities of Purkinje cells in the cerebellar cortex, and cells in the inferior olivary and dentate nuclei of four dyslexic and four control brains were measured using the dissector method. A significant difference in mean cell area in medial posterior cerebellar cortex was identified ($p < 0.05$), with the dyslexic cells having larger mean area. Furthermore, analysis of cell size distributions not only confirmed the significant differences in the posterior lobe ($p < 0.0001$; effect size 0.730), with an increased proportion of large neurons and fewer small neurons for the dyslexics, but also revealed significant differences in the anterior lobe ($p < 0.0001$; effect size 0.586), again with a pattern of more large and fewer small cells. Similar distributional differences were seen in the inferior olive ($p < 0.0001$; effect size 0.459). No distributional differences were found in the flocculonodular lobe or the dentate nucleus (effect sizes –0.306, –0.073 resp.). There was a mean age difference between the two groups, but the pattern of results remained unchanged when analyses accounting for the age disparity were undertaken.

While caution is necessary in generalizing from the results given the small number of specimens, together with the age difference, the pattern of abnormality—Purkinje cells in the posterior lobe and cells in the inferior olive nucleus—suggest that problems might arise on the input side (and, in particular, the error feedback loop supposedly mediated by the climbing fibers) rather than the output side to the dentate nucleus.

Biochemical Differences in Dyslexic Brains

A recent study (Rae et al. 1998) has revealed significant metabolic abnormalities in men with dyslexia. Bilateral MR spectroscopy indicated significant differences in the ratio of choline-containing compounds to N-acetylaspartate (NA) in the left temporo-parietal lobe and the right cerebellum, together with lateralization differences in the men with dyslexia but not in the controls. The authors conclude that "The cerebellum is biochemically asymmetric in men [with dyslexia], indicating altered development of this organ. These differences provide direct evidence of the involvement of the cerebellum in dyslexic dysfunction."

A PET Study of Automatic Performance and Learning Performance

The above behavioral studies suggest clearly that there must be some abnormality within the cerebellum, or perhaps in terms of the input to the cerebellum. In order to probe these findings more directly, we undertook a functional imaging study of two groups of adults with dyslexia and control adults matched for age and IQ while they undertook a behavioral task. Unlike other groups who have undertaken imaging studies while subjects were engaged in literacy-related tasks, we considered it likely to be more informative to investigate a task unrelated to reading, in that any differences obtaining could not be attributable to idiosyncratic literacy strategies. Naturally we wished to select a task that was known to involve clear cerebellar activation in control subjects. We chose to replicate a study of "motor sequence learning" (Jenkins et al. 1994), that, in addition to inducing strong cerebellar activation, had the advantage of allowing automatic (pre-learned) performance to be investigated as well as a sequence being learned.

Brain activation levels were monitored in matched groups of six adults with dyslexia and six control adults while they either performed a pre-learned sequence or learned a novel sequence of finger movements. The subjects were in fact members of our panel who had previously undertaken several of the tasks described above. They were all male and all right handed. The task involved learning a sequence of eight consecutive finger presses (with eyes closed). Each subject's four fingers of the right hand rested on a four key response pad, and every three seconds a pacing tone sounded and he had to press one of the keys. If he was right, a "correct" tone sounded, and he went on to the next response. If not, an "error" tone sounded and he tried again two seconds later. The end of the sequence was signified by three short high-pitched tones, after which the sequence restarted. In due course the sequence of eight presses was learned and then further practice led to increased automaticity. All participants learned the pre-learned sequence two hours before the scan until they could perform it without errors. They then alternated rests of two minutes and repeated trials of 3.5 minutes on the sequence ten times (55 minutes). During the last trial, subjects were given serial digit span tests to assess the automaticity of the sequence performance. Two further trials of the sequence were given while the subjects were lying on the scanner couch immediately prior to scanning, in order to ensure that they were able to perform the sequence in this context.

Analyses were undertaken using the standard UK image analysis system SPM96. (See figure 3.) Comparisons of relative levels of activation between the two groups were particularly striking. For the between-group analysis of activation increases during performance of the pre-learned sequence (compared with rest), areas of significantly greater increase ($p < .01$, corrected at $p < .05$ for

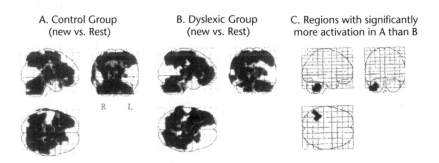

A. Control Group   B. Dyslexic Group   C. Regions with significantly
   (new vs. Rest)   (new vs. Rest)   more activation in A than B

Figure 3.   Regions of Significantly Greater Activation when learning a new sequence. Location of significant differences in activation ($p < .01$, corrected for multiple comparisons at $p < 0.05$) between subjects with dyslexia and control subjects for the comparisons of pre-learned sequence with rest (1a) and new sequence with rest (1b). The images are integrated sagittal (lengthwise, with the front of the brain at the left), coronal (from above), and transverse (from the side) projections of the statistical parametric maps (SPMs). Images produced by SPM96 (Wellcome Department of Cognitive Neurology 1996). Figures A and B give the increases in activation all over the brain when the control subjects (A) and the subjects with dyslexia (B) are learning a new sequence (compared with the rest condition). Figure C shows all regions in A that have significantly greater relative activation than in B. The only region showing on this analysis is the right hemisphere of the cerebellum.

multiple non-independent comparisons), only two regions of difference emerged: the ipsilateral (right) cerebellum, and an area of orbitofrontal cortex. No brain areas showed significantly greater increase for the dyslexic group, at the above significance level. For the between-group analysis of activation increases during performance of the new sequence learning (compared with rest), the ipsilateral cerebellum was the only area of significantly greater increase for the controls. A number of areas (right and medial prefrontal, bilateral temporal and bilateral parietal cortex) showed significantly greater increase for the dyslexic group.

It would appear, therefore, from the blood flow analyses that the control group showed relatively greater activation, compared with rest, in the right cerebellum both during performance of the pre-learned sequence and in learning the novel sequence, together with greater activation around the cingulate gyrus for the pre-learned sequence. By contrast, the dyslexic group showed greater activation in large areas of the frontal lobes when learning the novel sequence. This pattern of results confirmed the primary predictions of the CDH, namely that the dyslexic group activate their cerebellum relatively less, both in executing a pre-learned sequence and in learning a novel sequence. It also supported a secondary prediction, namely that the dyslexic group activates their frontal lobes relatively more in learning a novel sequence. The major difference between the groups was that the increase in cerebellar activation for the adults with dyslexia (compared with rest) on the two tasks was on average only 10% of that for the control group in bilateral cerebellar cortex and in vermis. This difference was highly significant ($p < .01$). The results provide direct evidence that, for this group of adults with dyslexia, the behavioral signs of cerebellar abnormality do indeed reflect underlying abnormalities in cerebellar activation.

Eye-blink Conditioning and Dyslexia

Despite the striking successes of the above research, the cerebellar deficit hypothesis is silent on many important issues. A fundamental issue is the mechanism by which such difficulties arise. One possibility (Stein and Walsh 1997) is that cerebellar performance is essentially normal, but that poor quality (in terms of timing or signal-to-noise ratio) of input to the cerebellum is in fact the true cause. A further fundamental issue is whether there is homogeneity or heterogeneity in children with dyslexia regarding the role of the cerebellum. It is evident that outside the reading domain the symptoms shown by people with dyslexia are variable, a finding that has led many theorists to posit the existence of sub-types of dyslexia (Boder 1973; Castles and Coltheart 1993). The eye-blink study (Nicolson et al. 2000) was designed to investigate both these issues directly by examining one of the fundamental processes of learning, namely classical conditioning (Pavlov 1927).

Motor learning, and classical conditioning of motor responses in particular, has been consistently linked to cerebellar function in humans. The most frequently used experimental procedure for hu-mans (Steinmetz 1999) is eye-blink conditioning which involves an acoustic conditioned stimulus (CS) which is followed by a corneal air puff unconditioned stimulus (US) after a fixed time interval. The US elicits a reflexive eye blink, and after a number of paired CS-US presentations, the eye blink occurs to the CS, before US onset and thereby constitutes a conditioned response (CR). The es-sential neuronal circuit underlying eye-blink conditioning is thought to involve the convergence of CS and US information in the cerebellum, and an efferent cerebellar projection (via the red nucleus) to the motor nuclei which control the eye-blink response (for a summary see Thompson and Krupa 1994)).

Thirteen subjects with dyslexia (12 male, 1 female, mean age 19.5 years) and 13 control subjects (11 male, 2 female) matched for age and IQ participated. The conditioning procedure used was that administered in the studies demonstrating eye-blink condi-tioning deficits in patients with selective cerebellar damage (Daum et al. 1993). In the experiment, for 60 acquisition trials an 800 millisecond auditory tone (conditioned stimulus-CS) was pre-sented. On 70% of the trials an 80 millisecond corneal air puff (unconditioned stimulus-US) was presented 720 milliseconds after the tone onset. Following the 60 acquisition trials 10 extinction trials without the air puff were presented. The cerebellar deficit hy-pothesis, uniquely of the causal hypotheses for dyslexia, predicts that the participants with dyslexia would show abnormal perfor-mance in the incidence and/or timing of the conditioned response (CR) of an eye blink in response to the tone (and before the US). Three of the group with dyslexia showed no conditioning at all. Furthermore, normally subjects show "tuning" of the CR, so that, over the course of the conditioning, it occurs closer and closer to the onset of the US. Unlike for the control group, the group with dyslexia showed no such tuning from the initial to the final acqui-sition block ($p < .05$). Furthermore, subjects initially make an ori-enting response (OR) when the CS is presented, but this normally habituates rapidly over the first few blocks. The group with dyslexia showed significantly slower OR habituation than the con-trols ($p < .05$). Individual analyses indicated that three (23%) of the group with dyslexia showed no conditioning at all; a further five (39%) showed no tuning; and a further three (23%) showed poor OR habituation (as did three of the poor tuning subjects). Rather surprisingly, four of the controls showed low conditioning, though all showed relatively normal CR tuning and all but one showed normal OR habituation. In short, although the procedure revealed inhomogeneity in the group with dyslexia, 85% of that group showed either: no conditioning; abnormally poor CR tuning; and/or abnormally low OR habituation.

We concluded that the findings provide further converging evidence of cerebellar abnormality in dyslexia, and for the first time demonstrated that there are fundamental abnormalities in the way that people with dyslexia learn.

OVERALL DISCUSSION

Following this lengthy review of our own research program, it is time to return to the questions posed at the beginning of the chapter. In particular, what are the implications for the understanding of dyslexia, for how dyslexia develops, and for future work in the area?

Summary

Let us start by summarizing the evidence to date. Behavioral studies indicated that a common symptom of performance in children with dyslexia is that it is less well automatized than normal. This occurs not only for literacy related tasks but also for all the other tasks studied. The well-established role of the cerebellum in skill learning and automatization made this a natural structure to investigate, and this line of analysis was very greatly strengthened by converging evidence from mainstream cognitive neuroscience revealing the central role of the cerebellum in language-related cognitive tasks. Direct behavioral studies indicated that our panel of children with dyslexia did in fact manifest the classic clinical symptoms of cerebellar abnormality. These symptoms were also characteristic of a much larger sample of children with dyslexia. Furthermore, we established intriguing evidence that "static" cerebellar signs such as poor postural stability and muscle tone may distinguish children with dyslexia from non-discrepant poor readers.

A neuroanatomical study of the cerebella of the specimens in the Beth Israel brain bank indicated that there were differences in Purkinje cell size and cell size distribution in posterior and anterior cerebellar cortex, and also cell size distribution in the inferior olive (source of climbing fibers), whereas no differences in the dentate (output) nucleus were found. If these findings are representative of dyslexic neuroanatomy (and given the limited number of specimens involved, this is by no means certain), this would suggest that problems arise in the error feedback loop rather than the control output loop. Given that there was insufficient time available to examine the pontine nucleus, it is not clear whether sensory input might also be abnormal. The PET study of motor sequence learning indicated that there were indeed abnormalities in cerebellar processing for subjects in our panel who had demonstrated clinical cerebellar signs. The abnormality occurred both for previously learned automatic performance, and also for ongoing learning. The majority of subjects with dyslexia showed little or no cerebellar activation in either of these tasks, and instead showed greater frontal lobe involvement in the new learning, consistent with the hypothesis that they were by-passing the automatic learning capability of the cerebellum, and instead relying more heavily on conscious strategies. These are important findings, confirming the different methods involved in sequential learning and automatic performance for the subjects with dyslexia, and, more important, confirming the behavioral indicators of cerebellar dysfunction. This in turn gives greater strength to our previously established findings that a relatively high proportion (around 80% of the larger sample investigated) of children with dyslexia show clinical signs of cerebellar abnormality.

Finally, the eye-blink conditioning study provided further converging evidence of cerebellar abnormality. It revealed a range of different problems in our group with dyslexia, including no conditioning, no habituation, and poor tuning of the conditioned response. Despite the dissociation obtained by this novel paradigm, it is difficult to attribute the different findings to different regions of the cerebellum in that the processes of eye-blink conditioning in humans are less well understood than the corresponding processes of conditioning of the nictitating membrane in rabbits. Nonetheless, the eye-blink conditioning paradigm provides a method of investigating further both homogeneity and heterogeneity in the learning deficits underlying dyslexia and other developmental disorders.

Toward a Causal Explanation

We are finally in position to attempt to fill in the blanks in figure 1.

Figure 4 (taken from Nicolson and Fawcett 1999) outlines the hypothetical ontogenetic causal chain linking cerebellar problems,

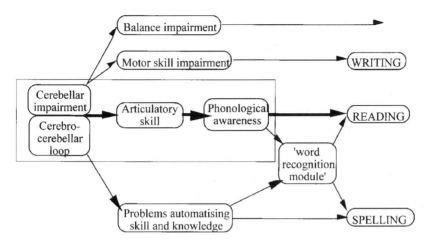

Figure 4.   Dyslexia: An ontogenetic causal chain

phonological difficulties and eventual reading problems. Note that the three criterial difficulties of writing, reading, and spelling are all accounted for in different ways. The CDH provides a natural causal explanation of the execrable quality of handwriting frequently shown by children with dyslexia (a characteristic that is but poorly addressed by most existing theories of dyslexia). Handwriting, of course, is a motor skill that requires precise timing and co-ordination of diverse muscle groups. Literacy difficulties arise from several routes. The central route is highlighted. If an infant has a cerebellar impairment, this will first show up as a mild motor difficulty—the infant may be slower to sit up and to walk, and may have greater problems with fine muscular control. Arguably our most complex motor skill, and that needing the finest control over muscular sequencing, is, in fact, that of articulation and co-articulation. Consequently, one would expect that the infant might be slower to start babbling, and, later, talking. Even after speech and walking emerge, one might expect that the skills would be less fluent, less "dextrous," in infants with cerebellar impairment. If articulation is less fluent than normal, then it takes more conscious resources, leaving fewer resources to process the ensuing sensory feedback. In particular, the processing of the auditory, phonemic structure of the words spoken may be less complete. There may, therefore, not be a natural sensitivity to onset, rime, and the phonemic structure of language—in short, one would expect early deficits in phonological awareness (see

Snowling and Hulme 1994 for a related account without the neurological underpinning). Cerebellar impairment would therefore be predicted to cause the "phonological core deficit" that has proved such a fruitful explanatory framework for many aspects of dyslexia. Given the phonological awareness difficulties, the standard explanations of reading difficulties may be applied. However, the framework here also includes a learning and automatization component, which would lead to impaired fluency and speed of reading, very much as described by the double deficit hypothesis (Wolf and Bowers 1999). We are also tempted to note that one of the key requirements in relatively skilled reading is the ability to sub-articulate rather than articulate overtly. Internalization of speech has the hallmarks of cerebellar involvement, in that a range of studies have suggested that the cerebellum is active when rehearsing actions or speech (Thach 1996). Spelling, the third criterial skill, is similar. Problems arise from a number of different routes—over-effortful reading, poor phonological awareness, difficulties in automatizing skills and eliminating errors. It may also be that the reason spelling appears particularly resistant to remediation (Thomson 1984) is that it requires the simultaneous use of both phonological skill and motor output.

The above framework therefore copes well with the task of accounting for the three criterial difficulties of dyslexia. How about Seidenberg's criteria for causal explanations? His first criterion "independently motivated principles" applies naturally, in that the CDH was motivated by the independent neuroscience work on the cognitive role of the cerebellum. The second criterion "relating apparently unrelated phenomena" is particularly appropriate. No other theory is able to handle the diverse problems in terms of problems in all primitive skills, time estimation, balance, speed, phonology, and literacy within a uniform framework.

The CDH therefore provides a novel, but intuitively plausible, causal framework for the understanding of dyslexia and its development. How does it fare with the Morrison and Manis criteria stated initially? We have already addressed their third and fourth questions—the mechanism and the direction of causality. That leaves two. First, the specificity principle. We consider that the difficulties shown appear specific to reading and spelling for two reasons. First, because these two skills represent a confluence of all that children with dyslexia find difficult—phonological skills, fluency, automatization, and multi-tasking. Second, why is performance adequate elsewhere? We suggest that one reason is that the literacy skills are critical educational attainments, and therefore these skills are put under the microscope, whereas maybe equally severe relative impairments in other skills are ignored. A more positive reason is that many skills are indeed unimpaired, and may be overcompensating. It must be stressed that skills can be acquired without much cerebellar impairment. They just require more conscious "frontal" involvement—indeed this was precisely the pattern of activation shown in the sequence learning task. The lack of automaticity is only a serious drawback if multi-tasking or extremely rapid processing is required.

Most skills, fortunately, including most "intellectual" skills typically require frontal involvement. Indeed, one might argue, following West (1991), that over-reliance on automatic patterns of thinking and behaving lead to stereotyped behavior that lacks creativity. By contrast, the need for continual thought, and perhaps the benefits deriving from continual thought, may lead in some cases to heightened levels of creativity.

Interpretations in Terms of Alternative Hypotheses

We have argued that the phonological deficit hypothesis is subsumed naturally within the CDH framework, as discussed above. It is also of interest to consider alternative causal explanations. The double deficit hypothesis (Wolf and Bowers 1999) so ably described in this book may perhaps also be accounted for in a natural manner. This is a reasonable undertaking given that Bowers and Wolf do not directly address the neural substrate underlying the speed deficit, and so the double deficit hypothesis may be considered as a cognitive level description. The key question, and one to which there is currently no clear answer, is "where does speed come from?" As children mature, their speed of processing and speed of reaction increases. This is unlikely to be a sensory phenomenon, in that the sensory pathways lengthen (albeit only slightly) as children grow. Cognitive psychologists have assumed that the overall speed increase reflects improved efficiency of the central processing mechanisms—registering information, classifying it, making decisions, accessing motor codes, executing codes, etc. It is natural to expect that the cerebellum will be centrally involved in this tuning and automatization of the central processing machinery. Indeed, we would speculate that it is inefficiencies in this central processing loop that may provide most of the difficulties for children with dyslexia, and may indeed be a more fruitful area for "brain-based learning" than the sensory processing mechanisms currently targeted by instructional regimes such as Fast Forward (e.g., Merzenich et al. 1996).

It should be noted however, that there may be alternative explanations of our findings. Stein (e.g., Stein and Walsh 1997) has argued that findings of apparent cerebellar impairment might be attributable to faulty input to the cerebellum (owing to impaired magnocellular pathways). It seems clear that there is a sub-type of dyslexia with magnocellular impairment, though the prevalence of this sub-type is not yet established. We note that the magnocellular deficit hypothesis is not wholly clear. Tallal (Tallal, Miller, and Fitch 1993) has suggested that there may be a pan-sensory impairment, including motor output as well as visual and auditory input. Stein (this volume) notes that there are magnocells in the cerebellum and in the motor output systems. Clearly it is difficult to distinguish these theories from the CDH, except insofar as the CDH suggests there need be no intrinsic problems in speed or accuracy of sensory processing—if the task is simple, there should be no problem. If one limits the magnocellular deficit hypotheses to the sensory input stage (which seems to us to be the appropriate, testable version of the hypothesis), there is considerable information that appears discrepant. The obvious point is that children with dyslexia are known to have problems in detecting rhymes, and these do not involve analysis of rapidly changing waveforms, and so should be a relative strength for children with auditory magnocellular problems. From our own work, there is no obvious explanation (on magnocellular hypotheses) of why children with dyslexia should react at normal speed for simple reactions but be slowed with the same response when a choice needs to be made (Nicolson and Fawcett 1994); no explanation of difficulties in time estimation; no explanation of why muscle tone should be lowered; no explanation of why there should be abnormal cerebellar activation in the motor sequence learning task; and no explanation of why there should be abnormal eye-link conditioning.

It may be that in due course we will find that there is a "magnocellular" sub-type (or two), a "cerebellar" sub-type, and various "mixed" sub-types of dyslexia. These are topics for further research.

CONCLUSIONS

This discussion completes the story so far. For reasons of space (and coherence) we have not been able to address the outstanding research, much of it reported in this book, that has been undertaken in other laboratories. It would be inappropriate to conclude, however, without an analysis of the weaknesses of the research to date. The key weakness is in terms of the small number of subjects participating in this research. Of necessity, given the limited funding available, we have focused on those subjects who were most likely to give clear cut results. We deliberately excluded borderline children with dyslexia, or co-morbid ADHD/children with dyslexia. We did however include all children with dyslexia who met our criteria (and were willing to participate). Nonetheless, it is clearly a priority to establish the prevalence of cerebellar symptoms in larger populations of children with dyslexia (and co-morbid groups).

In conclusion, the cerebellar deficit hypothesis is a neurological-level hypothesis that may be described at the cognitive level as an automatization deficit hypothesis. The two hypotheses between them have done a remarkable job in providing a true causal explanation of the varied findings pertaining in dyslexia research. No doubt the hypotheses are only a way station en route to a full understanding, but they do generate a number of interesting and new research avenues. Two emphases that we consider particularly significant are, first, the emphasis on how dyslexia develops, and second the renewed emphasis on learning. Consideration of how dyslexia develops in the pre-school years will surely lead to important and cost-effective methods for proactive identification and support. We consider that re-introduction of learning as the central theme in studies of learning disability has the promise to motivate a series of studies that inform theory and practice, not only in dyslexia research, but in the whole field of developmental cognitive neuroscience.

REFERENCES

Ackermann, H., and Hertrich, I. 2000. The contribution of the cerebellum to speech processing. *Journal of Neurolinguistics* 13(2–3):95–116.

Ackermann, H., Wildgruber, D., Daum, I., and Grodd, W. 1998. Does the cerebellum contribute to cognitive aspects of speech production? A functional magnetic resonance imaging (fMRI) study in humans. *Neuroscience Letters* 247:187–90.

Adams, M. J. 1990. *Beginning to Read: Thinking and Learning about Print.* Cambridge MA: MIT Press.

Albus, J. S. 1971. A theory of cerebellar function. *Math Bioscience* 10:25–61.

Beaton, A. A. 1997. The relation of planum temporale asymmetry and morphology of the corpus callosum to handedness, gender, and dyslexia: A review of the evidence. *Brain and Language* 60:255–322.

Best, M., and Demb, J. B. 1999. Normal planum temporale asymmetry in dyslexics with a magnocellular pathway deficit. *Neuroreport* 10:607–12.

Boder, E. 1973. Developmental dyslexia: A diagnostic approach based on three atypical spelling-reading patterns. *Developmental Medicine and Child Neurology* 15:663–87.

Bradley, L. and Bryant, P. E. 1983. Categorizing sounds and learning to read: A causal connection. *Nature* 301:419–21.

Castles, A., and Coltheart, M. 1993. Varieties of developmental dyslexia. *Cognition* 47:149–80.

Castles, A., and Holmes, V. M. 1996. Subtypes of developmental dyslexia and lexical acquisition. *Australian Journal of Psychology* 48:130–135.

Cohen, J. 1969. *Statistical Power Analysis for the Behavioral Sciences.* New York: Academic Press.

Daum, I., Schugens, M. M., Ackermann, H., Lutzenberger, W., Dichgans, J., and Birbaumer, N. 1993. Classical Conditioning after cerebellar lesions in humans. *Behavioral Neuroscience* 107:748–56.

Dow, R. S., and Moruzzi, G. 1958. *The Physiology and Pathology of the Cerebellum.* Minneapolis: University of Minnesota Press.

Eccles, J. C., Ito, M., and Szentagothai, J. 1967. *The Cerebellum as a Neuronal Machine.* New York: Springer-Verlag.

Fabbro, F., Moretti, R., and Bava, A. 2000. Language impairments in patients with cerebellar lesions. *Journal of Neurolinguistics* 13(2–3):173–88.

Fawcett, A. J., and Nicolson, R. I. 1994. Naming speed in children with dyslexia. *Journal of Learning Disabilities* 27:641–6.

Fawcett, A. J., and Nicolson, R. I. 1995. Persistence of phonological awareness deficits in older children with dyslexia. *Reading and Writing* 7:361–76.

Fawcett, A. J., and Nicolson, R. I. 1999. Performance of dyslexic children on cerebellar and cognitive tests. *Journal of Motor Behavior* 31:68–78.

Fawcett, A. J., Nicolson, R. I., and Dean, P. 1996. Impaired performance of children with dyslexia on a range of cerebellar tasks. *Annals of Dyslexia* 46:259–83.

Finch, A. J., Nicolson, R. I., and Fawcett, A. J. 2000. Evidence for a neuroanatomical difference within the olivo-cerebellar pathway of adults with dyslexia. *Cortex,* Submitted.

Frank, J., and Levinson, H. N. 1973. Dysmetric dyslexia and dyspraxia: Hypothesis and study. *Journal of American Academy of Child Psychiatry* 12:690–701.

Fulbright, R. K., Jenner, A. R., Mencl, W. E., Pugh, K. R., Shaywitz, B. A., Shaywitz, S. E., Frost, S. J., Skudlarski, P., Constable, R. T., Lacadie, C. M., Marchione, K. E., and Gore, J. C. 1999. The cerebellum's role in reading: A functional MR imaging study. *American Journal of Neuroradiology* 20:1925–30.

Galaburda, A. M., and Kemper, T. L. 1979. Cytoarchitectonic abnormalities in developmental dyslexia: A case study. *Annals of Neurology* 6:94–100.

Galaburda, A. M., Menard, M. T., and Rosen, G. D. 1994. Evidence for aberrant auditory anatomy in developmental dyslexia. *Proceedings of the National Academy of Sciences of the USA* 91:8010–13.

Galaburda, A. M., Sherman, G. F., Rosen, G. D., Aboitiz, F., and Geschwind, N. 1985. Developmental dyslexia—4 consecutive patients with cortical anomalies. *Annals of Neurology* 18: 222–33.

Glickstein, M. 1993. Motor skills but not cognitive tasks. *Trends in Neuroscience* 16:450–1.

Holmes, G. 1917. The symptoms of acute cerebellar injuries due to gunshot injuries. *Brain* 40:461–535.

Holmes, G. 1922. Clinical symptoms of cerebellar disease and their interpretation. *Lancet* 1:1177–1237.

Holmes, G. 1939. The cerebellum of man. *Brain* 62:1–30.

Ito, M. 1984. *The Cerebellum and Neural Control.* New York: Raven Press.

Ito, M. 1990. A new physiological concept on cerebellum. *Revue Neuro-logique* (Paris) 146:564–9.

Ivry, R. B., and Keele, S. W. 1989. Timing functions of the cerebellum. *Journal of Cognitive Neuroscience* 1:136–52.

Jenkins, I. H., Brooks, D. J., Nixon, P. D., Frackowiak, R. S. J., and Passing-ham, R. E. 1994. Motor sequence learning—a study with Positron Emission Tomography. *Journal of Neuroscience* 14:3775–90.

Kawato, M., and Gomi, H. 1992. The cerebellum and VOR/OKR learning models. *Trends in Neurosciences* 15(11):445–52.

Leiner, H. C., Leiner, A. L., and Dow, R. S. 1989. Reappraising the cerebel-lum: What does the hindbrain contribute to the forebrain. *Behavioral Neuroscience* 103:998–1008.

Leiner, H. C., Leiner, A. L., and Dow, R. S. 1991. The human cerebro-cerebellar system: Its computing, cognitive, and language skills. *Behav-ioral Brain Research* 44:113–28.

Leiner, H. C., Leiner, A. L., and Dow, R. S. 1993. Cognitive and language functions of the human cerebellum. *Trends in Neuroscience* 16:444–7.

Levinson, H. N. 1988. The cerebellar-vestibular basis of learning disabilities in children, adolescents and adults: Hypothesis and study. American Psychiatric Association Annual Meeting New Research Session (1987, Chicago, Illinois). *Perceptual and Motor Skills* 67(3):983–1006.

Levinson, H. N. 1990. The diagnostic value of cerebellar-vestibular tests in detecting learning disabilities, dyslexia, and attention deficit disorder. *Perceptual and Motor Skills* 71(1):67–82.

Livingstone, M. S., Rosen, G. D., Drislane, F. W., and Galaburda, A. M. 1991. Physiological and anatomical evidence for a magnocellular de-fect in developmental dyslexia. *Proceedings of the National Academy of Sciences of the United States of America* 88:7943–7.

Marr, D. 1969. A theory of cerebellar cortex. *Journal of Physiology* (London) 202:437–70.

Merzenich, M. M., Jenkins, W. M., Johnston, P., Schreiner, C., Miller, S. L., and Tallal, P. 1996. Temporal processing deficits of language-learning impaired children ameliorated by training. *Science* 271:77–81.

Morrison, F. J. and Manis, F. R. 1983. Cognitive processes in reading dis-ability: A critique and proposal. In *Progress in Cognitive Development Research*, ed. C. J. Brainerd and M. Pressley. New York: Springer-Verlag.

Morton, J. and Frith, U. 1995. Causal modelling: A structural approach to developmental psychopathology. In *Manual of Developmental Psycho-pathology*, Vol. 2, eds. D. Cicchetti and C. D.J New York: Wiley.

Nicolson, R. I., Daum, I., Schugens, M. M., Fawcett, A. J., and Schulz, A. 2000. Abnormal eyeblink conditioning for dyslexic children. *Experi-mental Brain Research*, submitted.

Nicolson, R. I., and Fawcett, A. J. 1990. Automaticity: A new framework for dyslexia research? *Cognition* 35(2):159–82.

Nicolson, R. I., and Fawcett, A. J. 1994. Reaction times and dyslexia. *Quarterly Journal of Experimental Psychology* 47A:29–48.

Nicolson, R. I., and Fawcett, A. J. 1995a. Balance, phonological skill and dyslexia: Towards the Dyslexia Early Screening Test. *Dyslexia Review* 7:8–11.

Nicolson, R. I., and Fawcett, A. J. 1995b. Dyslexia is more than a phono-logical disability. *Dyslexia: An International Journal of Research and Practice* 1:19–37.

Nicolson, R. I., and Fawcett, A. J. 1999. Developmental dyslexia: The role of the cerebellum. *Dyslexia: An International Journal of Research and Practice* 5:155–77.

Nicolson, R. I., Fawcett, A. J., and Dean, P. 1995. Time-estimation deficits in developmental dyslexia: Evidence for cerebellar involvement. *Proceedings of the Royal Society of London Series B-Biological Sciences* 259:43–47.

Orton Dyslexia Society. 1995. Definition of dyslexia; report from committee of members. *Perspectives* 21:16–17.

Passingham, R. E. 1975. Changes in the size and organization of the brain in man and his ancestors. *Brain Behavior and Evolution* 11:73–90.

Pavlov, I. P. 1927. *Conditioned Reflexes.* Oxford: Oxford University Press.

Rae, C., Lee, M. A., Dixon, R. M., Blamire, A. M., Thompson, C. H., Styles, P., Talcott, J., Richardson, A. J., and Stein, J. F. 1998. Metabolic abnormalities in developmental dyslexia detected by H-1 magnetic resonance spectroscopy. *Lancet* 351:1849–52.

Rumsey, J. M., Donohue, B. C., Brady, D. R., Nace, K., Giedd, J. N., and Andreason, P. 1997. A magnetic resonance imaging study of planum temporale asymmetry in men with developmental dyslexia. *Archives of Neurology* 54:1481–9.

Seidenberg, M. S. 1993. Connectionist models and cognitive theory. *Psychological Science* 4:228–35.

Shankweiler, D., Crain, S., Katz, L., Fowler, A. E., Liberman, A. M., Brady, S. A., Thornton, R., Lundquist, E., Dreyer, L., Fletcher, J. M., Stuebing, K. K., Shaywitz, S. E., and Shaywitz, B. A. 1995. Cognitive profiles of reading-disabled children: Comparison of language-skills in phonology, morphology, and syntax. *Psychological Science* 6:149–56.

Silver, L. B. 1987. The "magic cure": A review of the current controversial approaches for treating learning disabilities. *Journal of Learning Disabilities* 20:498–505.

Silveri, M. C., and Misciagna, S. 2000. Language, memory, and the cerebellum. *Journal of Neurolinguistics* 13(2–3):129–43.

Snowling, M. 1987. *Dyslexia: A Cognitive Developmental Perspective.* Oxford: Blackwell.

Snowling, M., and Hulme, C. 1994. The development of phonological skills. *Philosophical Transactions of the Royal Society of London Series B-Biological Sciences* 346:21–27.

Stanovich, K. E. 1988. Explaining the differences between the dyslexic and the garden-variety poor reader: The phonological-core variable-difference model. *Journal of Learning Disabilities* 21:590–612.

Stein, J., and Walsh, V. 1997. To see but not to read: The magnocellular theory of dyslexia. *Trends in Neurosciences* 20:147–s52.

Stein, J. F., and Glickstein, M. 1992. Role of the cerebellum in visual guidance of movement. *Physiological Reviews* 72:972–1017.

Steinmetz, J. E. 1999. A renewed interest in human classical eyeblink conditioning. *Psychological Science* 10(1):24–25.

Tallal, P., Miller, S., and Fitch, R. H. 1993. Neurobiological Basis of Speech: A Case for the Preeminence of Temporal Processing. *Annals of the New York Academy of Sciences* 682:27–47.

Thach, W. T. 1996. On the specific role of the cerebellum in motor learning and cognition: Clues from PET activation and lesion studies in man. *Behavioral and Brain Sciences* 19:411–31.

Thelen, E., and Smith, L. B. 1994. *A Dynamic Systems Approach to the Development of Cognition and Action.* Cambridge MA: MIT Press.

Thompson, R. F., and Krupa, D. J. 1994. Organization of memory traces in the mammalian brain. *Annual Review of Neuroscience* 17:519–49.

Vellutino, F. R. 1979. *Dyslexia: Theory and Research.* Cambridge, MA: MIT Press.

Wellcome Department of Cognitive Neurology 1996. Statistical Parametric Mapping SPM96. London: ICN.

West, T. G. 1991. *In the Mind's Eye: Visual Thinkers, Gifted People with Learning Difficulties, Computer Images, and the Ironies of Creativity.* Buffalo NY: Prometheus Books.

Wolf, M., and Bowers, P. G. 1999. The double-deficit hypothesis for the developmental dyslexias. *Journal of Educational Psychology* 91:415–38.

World Federation of Neurology 1968. Report of Research Group on Dyslexia and World Illiteracy. Dallas: WFN.

Chapter • 9

The Cerebellum, Timing, and Language:
Implications for the Study of Dyslexia

Richard B. Ivry,
Timothy C. Justus, and
Christina Middleton

The functional domain of the cerebellum has been greatly extended over the past decade. Prior to this period, discussion of the cerebellum was restricted to neuroscience and neurology literatures and focused on the role of this sub-cortical structure in the performance of skilled movements. Most psychologists would have been hard pressed to localize the cerebellum, let alone entertain the idea that it might contribute to cognition. Yet with the advent of modern neuroimaging techniques and emergence of cognitive neuroscience as a new interdisciplinary field, a paradigm shift has been launched. Positron emission tomography (PET) and functional magnetic resonance imaging (fMRI) studies consistently report cerebellar activation associated with mental operations such as memory retrieval, verbal fluency, and the control of attention (Fiez and Raichle 1997; Courchesne and Allen 1997). Neuropsychological studies have shown that patients with focal or diffuse cerebellar pathology are impaired on a wide range of cognitive tasks, especially those associated with higher executive control (e.g., Appollonio et al. 1993; but see Daum and Ackermann 1997).

A less explored but equally provocative role of the cerebellum is its potential link to a number of developmental psychiatric disorders. Most prominent among these is autism. Structural MRI studies have consistently reported abnormalities in cerebellar volume in children with autism (e.g., Courchesne et al. 1994), and post-mortem studies have confirmed a severe loss of Purkinje cells in individuals with autism (Bauman et al. 1997). More recently, MRI studies have identified cerebellar hypoplasia in other psychiatric populations including schizophrenic adults (Nopoulos et al. 1999) and children diagnosed with attention deficit and hyperactivity disorder (Mostofsky et al. 1998). This linkage is puzzling and raises a number of important questions. One might ask whether the cerebellum supports an essential cognitive function that, when impaired, can lead to very different disorders if combined with other neural insults and/or environmental contexts. On the other hand, it is possible that the cerebellum is especially vulnerable during development and thus serves as a useful marker of neuropathology, even though it may not contribute in a causal manner to the disorders. Indeed, distinct regions within the cerebellum are associated for autism, schizophrenia, and ADHD, perhaps providing hints as to the time at which prenatal development goes awry (Altman and Bayer 1985). Between these two extremes is the possibility that the relationships between the cerebellum and these disorders arise from independent factors, and correspondingly, the cerebellum may contribute in a causal manner to one disorder but not another.

Also included among the developmental disorders associated with cerebellar dysfunction is dyslexia. As with the psychiatric disorders, it is possible that cerebellar problems evidenced by the dyslexic population are independent of their language problems. In fact, the known relationship between cerebellar dysfunction and dyslexia is not as direct as those in the psychiatric studies noted above; the current evidence is based on indirect behavioral assays (Nicolson et al. 1995). Nonetheless, it is important to explore functional hypotheses that might account for a causal relationship between the cerebellum and dyslexia. To approach this problem, we will review two lines of evidence regarding the role of the cerebellum in cognition. We will begin with a discussion of the idea that the cerebellum operates as an internal clock, and will summarize the supporting evidence and show how the timing idea may be relevant to studies of language. We will then turn to the question of a more general involvement of the cerebellum in a distributed network supporting language functions, and specifically, how disruption in this network might be linked to dyslexia.

THE CEREBELLUM AS AN INTERNAL CLOCK

The integrity of the cerebellum is essential for coordinated movement. Despite the recent emphasis on cognitive functions, the hallmarks of cerebellar dysfunction are most pronounced in the motor domain. Patients with cerebellar lesions have difficulty maintaining posture, exhibit a tremor when reaching for objects, and have problems controlling both smooth and saccadic eye movements. The afferent and efferent pathways linking the cerebellum with the cerebral cortex, brainstem, and spinal cord put this structure in the center of the motor pathways. Based on neurophysiological, behavioral, and computational evidence, a number of theorists have emphasized a central role for the cerebellum in controlling the temporal aspects of movement.

Consider the difficulty patients with unilateral cerebellar lesions have in reaching for an object. Unlike patients with apraxia or optic agnosia, cerebellar patients are able to comprehend the goal of the desired action and accurately localize the object. They are even able to perform the complex computations for determining the trajectory, initially activating the selected muscles in an appropriate manner. The coordination problems, however, arise when the required muscular events must be precisely timed (Hore et al. 1991). These problems are especially apparent when the movement is made ballistically. Here, precise timing between the agonist and antagonist muscles is essential to ensure that the movement is terminated at the object. With cerebellar damage, this temporal pattern is frequently disrupted; the timing of the antagonist no longer appears programmed so that the rapid movement is terminated in a predictive manner. Rather, the onset of the antagonist is delayed and becomes reactive, setting the limb into a series of oscillations, or what is called an intentional tremor.

Our neuropsychological studies have been designed to provide more direct tests of the timing hypothesis. We have used a repetitive tapping task in which the participants are asked to produce a series of evenly timed intervals. At particular rates, the patients have little difficulty maintaining the target interval. Our focus has been on the consistency of these movements, measured by the standard deviation of the inter-tap intervals. In comparison to patients with other motor disorders of central origin, patients with cerebellar lesions show a consistent increase in variability (Ivry and Keele 1989). Moreover, using an analytic model that partitions the overall variability into two sources, one associated with the timing of the successive movements, which we call "clock" variability, and the other associated with the implementation of the responses, which we call "motor" variability, we have found that patients with lesions of the lateral cerebellum specifically exhibit an increase in "clock" variability (Ivry et al. 1988; Franz et al. 1996). These behavioral results converge with the anatomy of the cerebellar output nuclei. The output from the lateral regions of the cerebellum is part of ascending pathways that innervate premotor and motor cortex. As such, this region is positioned to be part of the system involved in motor planning and programming. Our hypothesis is that the cerebellum is critical for regulating the temporal aspects of movement, whereas other structures contribute to the establishment of other parameters such as muscle selection.

Timing, Learning, and Skill

A striking example of the importance of the cerebellum in internal timing is found in the literature on sensorimotor learning. One well-studied form of Pavlovian learning is eye blink conditioning. In this paradigm, a neutral stimulus such as a tone (CS) is repeatedly paired with an unconditioned stimulus such as an air puff (US). Over time, the animal comes to blink in response to the tone, thus attenuating the aversive effects of the air puff. Lesions of the cerebellum disrupt eye blink conditioning in humans and other species, either by abolishing the conditioned response or preventing the acquisition of the conditioned response (reviewed in Woodruff-Pak 1997). We have proposed that the cerebellum is essential for this form of learning because it is only adaptive if the timing between the CS and the US is represented (Ivry and Keele 1989). In support of this hypothesis, the precise timing of the conditioned blink is disturbed following focal lesions of the cerebellar cortex (Perrett et al. 1993) even though the response itself is still produced if the lesions leave the cerebellar nuclei intact. This suggests that an association between the CS and the US may occur at multiple levels of the system, but that the cerebellar cortex imposes the temporal delay between the onset of the CS and the conditioned response. In a related manner, Their et al. (2000) have recently argued that the population of Purkinje cell activity encodes the duration of saccadic eye movements, and recalibration of this population is the basis for motor learning.

Neurologists have long believed that the cerebellum is especially important for the performance of skilled movements. One idea is that, with practice, the requisite neural representations shift from a cortical to a sub-cortical locus. The timing hypothesis offers an alternative perspective. A hallmark of skilled behavior is that such behavior is performed in a consistent manner. When the cerebellum is damaged, a learned action can still be produced, but the movement appears fractionated into a series of poorly connected subunits. Precise timing allows the successive gestures to be integrated smoothly into a coordinated whole.

Perceptual Manifestations of the Cerebellar Timing System

The eye blink literature also emphasizes difficulties with defining the domain of cerebellar function. As argued above, the cerebellar cortex helps shape the topography of the conditioned response through its representation of the interval between the conditioned stimulus and the unconditioned stimulus. These are, of course, sensory events, which would suggest that the timing capabilities of the cerebellum are not strictly limited to motor processes. Moreover, the properties of an internal clock appear similar when investigated in either production or perception tasks (Keele et al. 1985; Ivry and Hazeltine 1995). Given these considerations, we tested the generality of the timing hypothesis with non-motor tasks that require the precise representation of temporal information. In our initial study, we compared the performance of various patient groups on two psychophysical tasks. For both tasks, the participants were presented with two pairs of tones. In one task, they had to judge whether the interval between the second pair of tones was shorter or longer than the interval between the first pair. Thus, they had to judge the duration of a temporal interval. In the second task, the participants judged whether the second pair of tones was softer or louder than the first pair. Here, the psychophysical discrimination is based on non-temporal properties of the stimulus events. As predicted, the patients with cerebellar lesions were selectively impaired on the duration discrimination task (Ivry and Keele 1989). Patients with Parkinson's disease or cortical lesions performed comparable to age-matched control participants.

Subsequent studies have found that these latter groups may also be impaired on perceptual timing tasks (Harrington et al. 1998a, b). However, successful performance on the duration discrimination task likely involves many other mental operations. When we apply a component analysis akin to that used in our tapping studies, the results suggest that, whereas the cerebellar problem is specific to timing, cortical lesions may produce impairments due to problems with working memory or attention (Casini and Ivry 1999; Mangels et al. 1998). Combined with the motor control and learning results described above, the evidence strongly suggests a specialized role for the cerebellum in representing the temporal relationship between events in the milliseconds range.

The timing hypothesis provides a general characterization of cerebellar function. Recent work has begun to address the important question of how the cerebellum operates an internal timing system, looking at the mechanisms through which temporal representations might be achieved. One way in which timing information could be represented is through an oscillatory process that provides a recurrent elemental unit of time, as in a pacemaker. However, temporal representations do not require pacemaker mechanisms. Alternatively, the cerebellar cortex might be viewed as a bank of hour glass timers with a range of intervals represented across a set of cortical ensembles (Ivry 1996). Computational studies have tended to favor the latter approach, demonstrating how relatively slow physiological processes within the cerebellar cortex could provide the mechanisms for forming precise temporal associations (Buonomano and Mauk 1994; Fiala et al. 1996). For example, in the eye blink paradigm, the representation of the conditioned stimulus must be sustained until the onset of the unconditioned stimulus or following learning, until the onset of the conditioned response. One would expect that such real-time representations are limited in duration, or at a minimum, need to be linked with memory systems in order to represent longer intervals. Thus, the range of the cerebellar timing system is likely on the order of hundreds of milliseconds or so, a temporal range that would seem appropriate for a system primarily involved in the control of coordinated movement. For tasks requiring longer intervals, other neural systems are engaged, perhaps in concert with the cerebellum (e.g., forming a clock-counter system).

CEREBELLAR TIMING IN SPEECH PRODUCTION AND PERCEPTION

Speech disorders are observed with many neurological disturbances. Given the role of the cerebellum in skilled movement, it is not surprising that patients with damage to this structure frequently exhibit speech disorders, or what is referred to as cerebellar dysarthria. Their speech can be irregular in rate and stress, and their phonation erratic. Some patients will tend to garble their words; others may speak with a very loud voice in which each sound is individually enunciated. This articulation is irregular, however.

The Control of Inter-articulatory Timing

Can the timing hypothesis also account for the symptoms associated with cerebellar dysarthria? One way in which this question has been addressed is to examine how well these patients can produce speech contrasts that require precise coordination among different groups of articulators. Consider the distinction between voiced and voiceless stop consonants. In terms of articulation, for voiced consonants the onset of vocal cord vibration, or voicing, is essentially synchronized with the release of airflow at the oral articulators. For example, to produce the labial /b/ sound in the initial position as in bay, the airflow commences with the parting of the lips. To produce a voiceless sound such as /p/ in the word pay, the onset of vocal cord vibration is delayed by approximately forty to sixty milliseconds. This delay is termed the voice-onset time, or VOT. Thus, precise timing is required in terms of the coordination across different sets of articulators.

For normal speakers, the distributions of VOT for voiced and voiceless stop consonants do not overlap. Ackermann and Hertrich (1997) measured VOT for a variety of initial-position stop consonants in eight patients with cerebellar dysarthria. For five of the patients, significant overlap was present in the VOT distributions; some of the voiced sounds were produced with abnormally long VOT and some of the voiceless sounds were produced with abnormally short VOT. Similarly, Ivry and Gopal (1992) reported that while the mean VOT for voiced and voiceless stop consonants was comparable between control participants and patients with cerebellar dsyarthria, the patients' productions were much more variable.

As might be expected, this increased variability has perceptual consequences. In the Ivry and Gopal study, the patients were asked to articulate four consonants, /ba/, /pa/, /da/, and /ta/. Control participants listened to a tape of the productions and labeled each sound. Interestingly, the perceptual errors were always along the voicing continuum. For example, /ba/ might be perceived as /pa/ or vice-versa. None of the errors were because the place of articulation (labial or aveolar) was misidentified, as in /ba/ versus /da/.

This dissociation suggests that cerebellar dysarthria is specific to a deficit in temporal control of the articulators. The patients are able to configure the oral articulators accurately, but lack the ability to coordinate inter-articulator actions temporally. However, this conclusion is weakened by the fact that there are no reports of the opposite pattern of deficits at present. We are unaware of any reports of patients who produce speech errors in terms of place of articulation rather than voicing.[1] Indeed, overlapping VOT

---

[1]A double dissociation is not required logically to conclude that separate processes are involved in controlling the configuration of the articulators and their timing. A process involved in configuration might also select the timing pattern, and thus damage to such a process could result in *both* VOT and place errors. However, the literature contains many examples of patients with VOT irregularities and considerably fewer examples of place irregularities.

distributions have been associated with speech disorders that do not involve the cerebellum (see Ravizza in press). Thus, it may be that the temporal measures of speech control are more sensitive to neurological disturbance.

The Use of Temporal Cues in Speech Perception

The speech production data are consistent with the hypothesis that the cerebellum is essential for controlling the precise timing involved in multi-joint actions. In this manner, the cerebellar role in speech production is another manifestation of its general contribution to coordination. A similar question can be asked in terms of speech perception. Is the cerebellum essential for extracting temporal information that might be required to distinguish one phoneme from another? As with the production data, the focus here has been on the voicing contrast. In an initial study (Ivry and Gopal 1992), we found that patients with cerebellar lesions performed similarly to control participants in categorizing syllables in which the VOT ranged from -10 ms., an example of /ba/, to +70 ms., an example of /pa/. However, there are multiple acoustic cues that can distinguish voiced from voiceless stop consonants in the initial position. For example, these sounds differ in terms of the presence or absence of energy in the region of the fundamental frequency at onset. They also differ in the duration of the formant transitions.

In contrast, for medial stop consonants, the duration of the occlusion phase may be a more essential temporal cue. Ackermann et al. (1997) tested this idea in a categorical perception task with a continuum based on two bi-syllabic German words, *boden* and *boten*. They recorded a speaker saying *boden*, a sound in which there is a brief occlusion of about ten ms. of the airflow prior to the onset of the second syllable. By extending this silent period in successive ten-ms. steps, they created a continuum of sounds between *boden* and *boten*. Patients with cerebellar dysarthria were severely impaired in categorizing these stimuli. Across the entire continuum, they were essentially unable to distinguish the two words. Thus, it appears that the cerebellum does contribute to speech perception when the critical information requires the utilization of a precise temporal cue. Note that the results of Ackermann et al. (1997) challenge the view that speech perception involves a set of dedicated modules (e.g., Liberman and Mattingly 1985). Although phonological representations have an important status for humans in terms of their importance for communication, the computational machinery for analyzing speech sounds appears to use processes similar to those involved in other types of auditory perception.

THE CEREBELLUM AND LANGUAGE

The timing hypothesis provides a parsimonious account of one way in which the cerebellum may contribute to language. Speech production is perhaps the quintessential skill exhibited by humans, and as with other motor skills, the ability to control the timing of the muscular events required for smooth articulation appears to involve the cerebellum. Similarly, certain aspects of speech perception may also involve the representation of the temporal relationships contained within the acoustic signal.

However, a broader role of the cerebellum in language has been hypothesized. The theoretical motivation for this work has come from evolutionary considerations (e.g., Leiner et al. 1993). Compared to our closest phylogenetic relatives, the neocerebellum appears to have undergone a disproportionate increase in size, especially those parts that send ascending pathways to the cerebral cortex via the dentate nucleus. Using novel polysynaptic tracing techniques, anatomists have found that these outputs not only project to traditional motor structures such as motor and premotor cortex, but are also innervate prefrontal regions thought to play an important role in higher cognitive functions.

The Cerebellum and Lexical Retrieval

Neuropsychological and neuroimaging studies have provided additional evidence of a link between the cerebellum and prefrontal cortex. Patients with cerebellar pathology, especially that resulting from bilateral atrophy, tend to perform poorly on standardized neuropsychological tasks designed to assess executive function (Appollonio et al. 1993). A high correlation between activation in lateral prefrontal cortex and the cerebellum is found in the neuroimaging literature, and many of these studies have involved linguistic tasks. Consider the seminal study of Petersen and colleagues (Petersen et al. 1989) that examined the neural bases of lexical retrieval. In the critical conditions, the participants viewed a single noun, such as "apple," and were asked either to read the word (Repeat Condition) or to generate an associated verb, such as "peel" (Generate Condition). Given that the overt motor demands were similar in the two conditions, the researchers assumed that subtracting activation observed during the Repeat condition from that observed during the Generate condition would identify the neural systems involved in semantic memory and retrieval. These regions included lateral prefrontal cortex, including Broca's area, and the right cerebellum. This pattern has been replicated in numerous other studies (see Fiez and Raichle 1997), although the areas of activation also have been found to include more posterior cortical language areas under certain conditions.

Of course, imaging studies are limited in terms of their utility for establishing function. Simply because the cerebellum is activated during verbal retrieval tasks does not mean this structure contributes in a causal manner to the retrieval process. The representation of the semantic associates as well as the executive processes required for selecting an appropriate response may be the sole province of the cerebral cortex. It may be that the cerebellar activation reflects the preparation of the various candidates, ensuring that once a response is selected it will be produced in a rapid and efficient manner (Ivry 1997).

Although subject to their own limitations, patient studies offer a more direct means for evaluating functional hypotheses. Fiez et al. (1992) presented a case study of a patient who had suffered a stroke resulting in an extensive lesion of the inferior right cerebellar hemisphere. Interestingly, the connections to left prefrontal cortex likely originate in this region. Despite the fact that his post-stroke IQ was 131, the patient was very impaired on a variety of generate tasks, showing little improvement across trials as well as producing inappropriate responses on a significant percentage of the trials. For example, he responded with "sharp" as a verb associate of "razor." Similarly, he had difficulty deciding whether a word was an adjective or verb as well as identifying synonyms.

Three hypotheses might account for these results. First, the behavioral deficits might reflect dysfunction in non-cerebellar structures secondary to the stroke (Gilman et al. 1994). Although this problem plagues all neuropsychological studies, the fact that the cerebellum is activated in an array of semantic tasks suggests that the deficits are directly related to the cerebellar pathology. Second, the deficits may reveal cerebellar involvement in lexical-semantic memory. Third, the cerebellum may be part of the executive processes involved in the retrieval and selection of information from lexical-semantic memory. In support of this hypothesis, activation within the cerebellum is reduced when the same words are used over successive sessions (Raichle et al. 1994). Under such conditions, the retrieval and selection demands are attenuated as the participants tend to report the same items.

Given that the study involved a single patient, it is also important to ask whether the deficits are typical of patients with cerebellar lesions. Working with a group of nine patients, we failed to replicate the results of Fiez et al. (1992) on the generate task (Helmuth, Ivry, and Shimuzu 1997). The patients were slower than controls on the task, but they showed a normal learning function when presented with the same list over successive trials as well as a similar increase in response time when a new list was introduced.

More recently, we have examined the role of the cerebellum in the presumed selection operation entailed by these tasks. Thompson-Schill and colleagues have argued that the left prefrontal cortex is not an essential part of lexical-semantic memory. Rather, they hypothesize that this region is part of a system required for sustaining and selecting among transient representations of candidate responses. For some words, the selection process is likely to be demanding. For example, the responses "purr," "meow," and "claw" are all actions of approximately equal association to the word "cat." For other words, the selection process is highly constrained: almost everyone will respond "cut" to the word "scissors." The left inferior frontal gyrus was sensitive to the selection demands, showing greater activation for words that had many viable responses (Thompson-Schill et al. 1997). Moreover, patients with lesions that encompassed this cortical region made more errors than control participants when responding to target words that involved high selection demands (Thompson-Schill et al. 1998). In contrast, the groups performed comparably to one another on the low selection words.

Given the similar patterns of activation within left prefrontal cortex and the cerebellum on semantic generation tasks (but see Desmond et al. 1998), we tested a group of 11 patients with focal cerebellar on the same task (Ivry, Thompson-Schill, and Middleton unpublished). The results were clear-cut: the patients rarely made any errors on the task. On almost every trial, the patients were able to generate an appropriate verb associate. They were slower to respond to the high selection items, but this increase was comparable to that seen in the controls. Thus, our results challenge the idea that the cerebellum is part of a distributed network involved in the selection of items from lexical-semantic memory.

The Cerebellum and Verbal Rehearsal

The preceding discussion addressed one hypothesized role for the cerebellum in executive functions that are essential for fluent linguistic competence. A different functional hypothesis concerning cerebello-cortical interactions can be developed by consideration of other components of the executive operations involved in language tasks. Again, the starting point is in the neuroimaging literature.

Cerebellar activation is not only prominent in verbal generation tasks, but it is also frequently observed in two tasks that place heavy demands on verbal working memory. First, during delayed response tasks, verbal information must be held in working memory for subsequent retrieval (Paulesu et al. 1993; Fiez et al. 1996; Awh et al. 1996; Desmond et al. 1997; Jonides et al. 1998). Secondly, during N-back tasks, the current contents of working memory must be constantly modified (Awh et al. 1996; Schumacher et al. 1996). These experiments also have shown that Broca's area, the supplementary motor area, and portions of the parietal lobe are associated with verbal working memory tasks.

This distributed network of activation has been considered within the framework of the working memory model proposed by Baddeley (Baddeley and Hitch 1974; Baddeley 1986). In this model, working memory is divided into three components: a central executive that coordinates information processing in all modalities and two specialized systems, a visuospatial sketchpad and a phonological loop. The specialized systems maintain domain-specific representations. The phonological loop is further divided into two subsystems: a phonological short-term store (STS) and an articulatory rehearsal mechanism (figure 1). The phonological STS is the locus of the

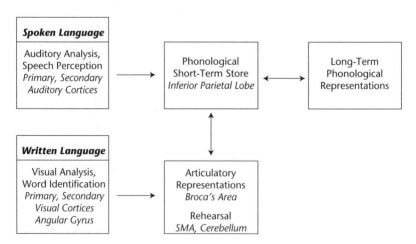

Figure 1.   Spoken and written language processed in verbal working memory, as suggested by the Baddeley phonological loop model and neuroimaging evidence. Each box represents a stage in the working memory algorithm along with the hypothesized locus of neural implementation (Adapted from Baddeley, Gathercole, and Papagno 1998).

phonological representations whereas the rehearsal process is required to refresh information in the store. In attempts to link this model to the neuroimaging data, the parietal lobe activation has been thought to correspond to the phonological STS (e.g., Awh et al. 1996; Jonides et al. 1998; but see Fiez et al. 1996; Becker et al. 1999). Similarly, processing in Broca's area, SMA, and the cerebellum are thought to correspond to the articulatory rehearsal mechanism (e.g., Paulesu et al. 1993; Fiez et al. 1996; Awh et al. 1996; Desmond et al. 1997).

The psychological evidence for separable components associated with phonological short-term memory and articulatory rehearsal comes from studies that have manipulated phonological similarity and word length (Baddeley et al. 1984). When no additional articulatory task is required, phonologically similar words are more difficult to remember than phonologically dissimilar words (the phonological similarity effect). Additionally, words with many syllables are more difficult to remember than words with fewer syllables (the word length effect). However, when articulatory suppression is added, as for example when the participant must count repeatedly from one to three while also perceiving and rehearsing the verbal stimuli, the word length effect disappears regardless of whether or not the words are read or heard. In contrast, the phonological similarity effect disappears only when the words are read.

To account for this dissociation, it is proposed that *spoken* words are automatically represented in the phonological STS. In this representation, they are susceptible to interference from words that are phonologically similar. To maintain the fidelity of the phonological representations, an articulatory rehearsal process is engaged. Because of the motor demands associated with rehearsal, the articulatory mechanism is time dependent and errors will be more pronounced for longer words. The rehearsal process is disrupted when the articulatory mechanism is occupied by the additional task of counting and therefore the advantage for short words over long words diminishes. The processing of *written* words is similar to that of spoken words, with the exception that the articulatory rehearsal mechanism must be available to convert them from orthographic to phonological representations before the information can be processed in the phonological STS. When rehearsal is not available, as during articulatory suppression, the advantages typically found for both shorter and phonologically dissimilar words is attenuated. Neuroimaging evidence also supports the idea that orthographic representations are first translated into phonological representations before entering the verbal working memory system (Schumacher et al. 1996).

The Cerebellum and Dyslexia

With these ideas in hand, we can now turn to the central topic of this volume, dyslexia. Building on the neuroimaging literature, we assume that a cerebellar contribution to language is as part of a system involved in articulation, silent or overt. This notion is consistent with current theories of motor control that assume that covert or mental "actions" engage the same processes as those involved in overt movement (Ryding et al. 1993). Within the context of verbal working memory, articulatory rehearsal plays an important role in reading, supporting the conversion from orthographic to phonological representations. As such, the cerebellum would be seen as one part of a network required for articulatory rehearsal.

If the cerebellum is part of a covert rehearsal system, then an association between cerebellar pathology and reading problems would be predicted regardless of whether or not one advocates an input-based (acoustic) or output-based (motor) kind of phonological representation. Assuming Baddeley's model, input-based representations in the phonological STS must be preceded by the operation of the articulatory rehearsal mechanism during reading. Even with well-developed input-based phonological representations, the conversion to those representations would be handicapped with cerebellar abnormalities.

However, the motor theory of speech perception (e.g., Liberman and Mattingly 1985) would predict further developmental problems for children with cerebellar abnormalities. If speech is represented as abstract motor commands associated with articulatory gestures, then cerebellar abnormalities may not just diminish the accessibility of otherwise good phonological representations, but may also interfere with the normal development of those phonological representations in the first place. While this problem might also be expected to be manifest in auditory language, it should be especially marked with written language given the demands of mapping abstract symbols onto the articulatory-based phonological representations (Liberman 1997).

The link between the cerebellum and salient phonological representations is consistent with the argument that the primary function of the phonological loop is that of a language learning device, allowing for the long-term representation of novel phonological input (Baddeley, Gathercole, and Papagno 1998). There is strong evidence that the phonological loop mediates the long-term representation of new vocabulary in children, especially when the new words have an unfamiliar phonological structure.

Moreover, the phonological similarity effect and word length effect are more pronounced when the phonological forms are unfamiliar and cannot rely on information represented in long-term memory. Thus, the rehearsal mechanism is seen as an important way in which a short-term phonological store could modify long-term phonological representations.

Note that this hypothesized functional relationship between the cerebellum, rehearsal, and dyslexia is independent of other ways in which cerebellar dysfunction could contribute to this disorder. For example, Stein (this volume) develops the idea that, in the dyslexic population, the cerebellum may operate on noisy sensory signals, and thus lead to a variety of sensorimotor and oculomotor deficits. Given that different types of dyslexia may have very different etiologies, it is possible that the cerebellum contributes in multiple ways to variations in reading ability.

A Preliminary Study of Verbal Rehearsal and the Cerebellum

Central to the preceding discussion is the hypothesis that the cerebellum is part of an articulatory rehearsal process. This hypothesis is consistent with the neuroimaging evidence associating the cerebellum and language. However, there is little direct evidence on this issue. We have begun to evaluate these ideas by testing patients with cerebellar lesions on verbal working memory tasks, applying the manipulations developed by Baddeley and his colleagues. As noted previously, the word length effect is thought to reflect the operation of an articulatory rehearsal process. In normal individuals, this effect is attenuated by the demands of a secondary rehearsal task. Correspondingly, we would expect to find an attenuated effect of word length in patients with cerebellar damage. Such a result had been observed previously in a single cerebellar case study (Silveri et al. 1998). We wished to extend these results to a larger group of cerebellar patients, testing for the word length effect using a set of abstract low-frequency English words that were either two-syllables or four-syllables in length (Justus and Ivry 2000).

To date, we have tested one patient with a right unilateral cerebellar lesion, two patients with bilateral cerebellar degeneration, and four control participants matched in education and age. The participants were asked to listen to a list of words read aloud by the experimenter and then to recall the words immediately after the last item. The number of items per list was gradually increased until a moderate level of difficulty was achieved. Based on our criteria, we used four-item lists with the three patients and one of the controls and five-item lists with the other three controls. For the main experiment, one hundred lists were presented, fifty with two-syllable words and fifty with four-syllable words.

The results showed a significant word length effect for both the patients and controls (patients: t(2) = 6.4, p = .02; controls: t(3) = 9.7, p = .002; see figure 2a and 2b). However, the size of the effect is larger for the controls compared to the patients with cerebellar damage, in particular on the second to the last item (overall word length effect: t(5) = 1.9, p = .12, ns; analysis restricted to the second to the last item: t(5) = 4.7, p = .005). The interaction is consistent with the hypothesis that the integrity of the cerebellum is essential for normal rehearsal. However, these preliminary results must be taken with caution. First, the overall interaction is not statistically significant and we need to enlarge our sample sizes. Secondly, by using our difficulty criteria (which were successful at equating the overall performance of the two groups), a difference was created between the list lengths used for the patients and most of the controls. It is noteworthy that the control participant who was tested with four-item lists showed a larger word length effect than any of the cerebellar patients (figure 2c), suggesting that the apparent difference in word-length effect between the patients and the other controls is unlikely to result from an inherent difference between remembering four-item or five-item lists.

These preliminary results suggest that damage to the cerebellum may interfere with verbal rehearsal, complimenting the work of Silveri et al. (1998), Desmond et al. (1997), and others in suggesting a role for the cerebellum in the phonological loop. Again, given the importance of the phonological loop in creating long-term phonological representations for the native language, along with the importance for these representations for reading, this suggests a possible causal relationship between abnormalities in cerebellar development and later reading problems.

CONCLUSIONS AND FUTURE DIRECTIONS

In this chapter we have considered ways in which the cerebellum may contribute to language, and in particular, reading and dyslexia. First we reviewed the evidence for the cerebellum as a specialized structure for temporal processing in movement and perception, relating this to speech production and perception. We then reviewed some of the evidence for cerebellar involvement in two linguistic processes: lexical retrieval and verbal rehearsal. We focused on the latter process as providing a possible functional link between the cerebellum and developmental dyslexia.

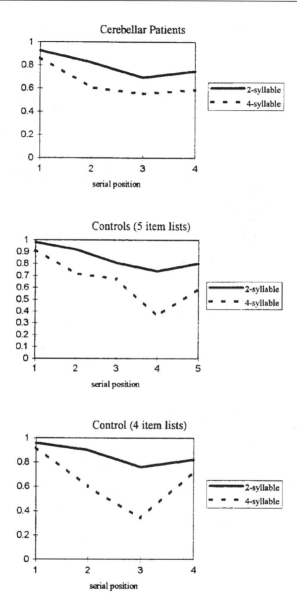

Figure 2.   Results of a verbal working memory study comparing the word length effect in cerebellar patients and controls. Each graph shows the probability of recalling an item as a function of its syllable length and serial position for (a) three patients with lesions or degeneration to the cerebellar hemisphere(s) tested with four-word lists, (b) three control subjects tested with five-word lists, and (c) one control subject tested with four-word lists (Justus and Ivry 2000).

To date, the links between cerebellar abnormalities and dyslexia remain rather indirect. The high incidence of clumsiness in dyslexia is well established, and recent evidence has indicated that cerebellar dysfunction may underlie these movement problems (Nicolson, Fawcett, and Dean 1995). However, even if we assume that cerebellar pathology and dyslexia are correlated, it is important to consider whether a causal relationship exists. With this in mind, our goal was to present one possible chain of causal relationships linking the two. In this model, we consider three relationships: the link between the cerebellum and verbal rehearsal, the link between variability in verbal rehearsal and phonological skill, and the link between phonological skill and reading ability.

The role of the cerebellum in verbal rehearsal emerged in the neuroimaging literature and this work has inspired testable predictions for neuropsychological research. Patients with localized cerebellar lesions can help clarify the parts of the cerebellum that contribute to verbal rehearsal. Manipulations involving word length, phonological similarity, articulatory suppression, and modality of presentation should help evaluate how the cerebellum fits into the Baddeley-Hitch model and alternative models. It is important to extend this work to children with developmental abnormalities in the cerebellum, rather than focus exclusively on adults with acquired lesions.

The second relationship is that between verbal rehearsal and phonological skill. Tests of working memory capacity, such as digit span and spoken text comprehension, are predictive of reading ability (Perfeti 1985). These correlations emphasize possible connections between specific working memory components and reading. In terms of phonological skill, the relationship has been considered from the reverse perspective, with impaired verbal rehearsal being one consequence of poor reading skills (e.g., Brady 1997). We are suggesting the reverse causal relationship, namely, that variation in verbal rehearsal ability will contribute to variation in the quality of phonological representation, and therefore phonological skills.

Of the three connections hypothesized in our model, that between phonological skill and reading ability is the most substantiated. Phonological skill typically has been measured using two different kinds of speech tasks, categorical perception tasks and pseudo-word repetition tasks, and the literature supports a relationship between both of these indices of phonological skill and reading ability (see Brady 1997, for review). The primary unresolved issue here is the degree to which what we are calling phonological processing is specifically phonological and not part of a greater temporal processing ability (see Farmer and Klein 1995, for review; Studdert-Kennedy and Mody 1995; Merzenich et al. 1996).

In suggesting this connection between the cerebellum, verbal rehearsal, phonological representation, and reading, we do not mean to suggest this particular etiology as *the* potential explanation for dyslexia. Given the large set of mental processes involved in comprehending written language, it is likely that there are numerous causes for dyslexia involving developmental differences in any of these various systems. Some people with dyslexia may have primarily an auditory problem and others a visual problem. Some may have a specific deficit in phonological processing and others a more general auditory or temporal impairment. Not only do we caution against a single explanation for dyslexia, but we also suggest that the role of any given brain structure such as the cerebellum could contribute in multiple ways to reading. The cerebellum may not only play a role in verbal rehearsal, but is likely to participate in multiple ways through its contributions to motor control and temporal processing.

REFERENCES

Ackermann, H., Graber, S., Hertrich, I., and Daum, I. 1997. Categorical speech perception in cerebellar disorders. *Brain and Language* 60:323–31.

Ackermann, H., and Hertrich, I. 1997. Voice onset time in ataxic dysarthria. *Brain and Language* 56:321–33.

Altman, J., and Bayer, S.A. 1985. Embryonic development of the rat cerebellum. III. Regional differences in the time of origin, migration, and settling of Purkinje cells. *Journal of Comparative Neurology* 231:42–65.

Appollonio, I. M., Grafman, J., Schwartz, V., Massaquoi, S., and Hallet, M. 1993. Memory in patients with cerebellar degeneration. *Neurology* 43: 1536–44.

Awh, E., Jonides, J., Smith, E.E., Schumacher, E.H., Koeppe, R.A., and Katz, S. 1996. Dissociation of storage and rehearsal in verbal working memory: Evidence from positron emission tomography. *Psychological Science* 7:25–31.

Baddeley, A. 1986. *Working Memory*. Oxford: Oxford University Press.

Baddeley, A. and Hitch, G. 1974. Working memory. In *The Psychology of Learning and Motivation*, ed. G. H. Bower. San Diego, CA: Academic Press.

Baddeley, A., Gathercole, S., and Papagno, C. 1998. The phonological loop as a language learning device. *Psychological Review* 105:158–73.

Baddeley, A., Lewis, V., and Vallar, G. 1984. Exploring the articulatory loop. *Quarterly Journal of Experimental Psychology* 36A:233–52.

Bauman, M. L., Filipek, P. A., and Kemper, T. L. 1997. Early infantile autism. *International Review of Neurobiology* 41:367–86.

Becker, J. T., MacAndrew, D. K., and Fiez, J. A. 1999. A comment on the functional localization of the phonological storage subsystem of working memory. *Brain and Cognition* 41:27–38.

Brady, S. A. 1997. Ability to encode phonological representations: An underlying difficulty of poor readers. In *Foundations of Reading Acquisition and Dyslexia: Implications for Early Intervention*, ed. B. Blachman. Mahwah, NJ: Lawrence Erlbaum Associates.

Buonomano, D. V., and Mauk, M. 1994. Neural network model of the cerebellum: Temporal discrimination and the timing of motor responses. *Neural Computation* 6:38–55.

Casini, L. and Ivry, R. B. 1999. Effects of divided attention on temporal processing in patients with lesions of the cerebellum or frontal lobe. *Neuropsychology* 13:10–21.

Courchesne, E., and Allen, G. 1997. Prediction and preparation, fundamental functions of the cerebellum. *Learning and Memory* 4:1–35.

Courchesne, E., Saitoh, O., Yeung-Courchesne, R., Press, G. A., Lincoln, A. J., Haas, R. H., and Schreibman, L. 1994. Abnormality of cerebellar vermian lobules VI and VII in patients with infantile autism: Identification of hypoplastic and hyperplastic subgroups with MR imaging. *American Journal of Roentgenology* 162:123–30.

Daum, I. and Ackerman, H. 1997. Neuropsychological abnormalities in cerebellar syndromes fact or fiction? *International Review of Neurobiology* 41: 455–71.

Desmond, J. E., Gabrieli, J. D., and Glover, G. H. 1998. Dissociation of frontal and cerebellar activity in a cognitive task: Evidence for a distinction between selection and search. *Neuroimage* 7:368–76.

Desmond, J. E., Gabrielli, J. D. E., Wagner, A. D., Ginier, B. L. and Glover, G. H. 1997. Lobular patterns of cerebellar activation in verbal working-memory and finger-tapping tasks as revealed by functional MRI. *Journal of Neuroscience* 17:9675–85.

Farmer, M. E. and Klein, R. M. 1995. The evidence for a temporal processing deficit linked to dyslexia: A review. *Psychonomic Bulletin and Review* 2:460–93.

Fiala, J. C., Grossberg, S., and Bullock, D. 1996. Metabotropic glutamate receptor activation in cerebellar purkinje cells as substrate for adaptive timing of the classically conditioned eye-blink response. *Journal of Neuroscience* 16:3760–74.

Fiez, J. A., Petersen, S. E., Cheney, M. K., and Raichle, M. E. 1992. Impaired nonmotor learning and error detection associated with cerebellar damage: A single case study. *Brain* 115: 155–78.

Fiez, J. A., and Raichle, M. E. 1997. Linguistic processing. *International Review of Neurobiology* 41:233–54.

Fiez, J. A., Raife, E. A., Balota, D. A., Schwarz, J. P., Raichle, M. E, and Petersen, S. E. 1996. A positron emission tomography study of the short-term maintenance of verbal information. *Journal of Neuroscience* 16:808–22.

Franz, E. A., Ivry, R. B., and Helmuth, L. L. 1996. Reduced timing variability in patients with unilateral cerebellar lesions during bimanual movements. *Journal of Cognitive Neuroscience* 8:107–18.

Gilman, S., Koeppe, R. A., Junck, L., Kluin, K. J., Lohman, M., and St. Laurent, R. T. 1994. Patterns of cerebral glucose metabolism detected with positron emission tomography differ in multiple system atrophy and olivopontocerebellar atrophy. *Annals of Neurology* 36:166–75.

Harrington, D. L., Haaland, K. Y., and Hermanowicz, N. Temporal processing in the basal ganglia. *Neuropsychology* 12:3–12.

Harrington, D. L., Haaland, K. Y., and Knight, R. T. 1998. Cortical networks underlying mechanisms of time perception. *Journal of Neuroscience* 18:1085–95.

Helmuth, L., Ivry, R., and Shimizu, N. 1997. Preserved performance by cerebellar patients on tests of word generation, discrimination learning, and attention. *Learning and Memory* 3: 456–74.

Hore, J., Wild, B., and Diener, H. C. 1991. Cerebellar dysmetria at the elbow, wrist, and fingers. *Journal of Neurophysiology* 65:563–71.

Ivry, R. B. 1996. The representation of temporal information in perception and motor control. *Current Opinion in Neurobiology* 6:851–57.

Ivry, R. B. 1997. Cerebellar timing systems. *International Review of Neurobiology* 41:555–73.

Ivry, R. and Gopal, H. 1992. Speech perception and production in patients with cerebellar lesions. In *Attention and Performance Vol. XIV: Synergies in Experimental Psychology, Artificial Intelligence, and Cognitive Neuroscience*, ed. D. E. Meyer and S. Kornblum. Cambridge: MIT Press.

Ivry, R. B. and Hazeltine, R. E. 1995. The perception and production of temporal intervals across a range of durations: Evidence for a common timing mechanism. *Journal of Experimental Psychology: Human Perception and Performance* 21:1–12.

Ivry, R. B., and Keele, S. 1989. Timing functions of the cerebellum. *Journal of Cognitive Neuroscience* 1:136–52.

Ivry, R. B., Keele, S., and Diener, H. 1988. Dissociation of the lateral and medial cerebellum in movement timing and movement execution. *Experimental Brain Research* 73:167–80.

Ivry, R., Thompson-Schill, S. L., and Middleton unpublished data.

Jonides, J., Schumacher, E. H., Smith, E. E., Koeppe, R. A., Awh, E., Reuter-Lorenz, P. A., Marshuetz, C., and Willis, C. R. 1998. The role of parietal cortex in verbal working memory. *Journal of Neuroscience* 18:5026–34.

Justus, T. C. and Ivry, R. B. 2000. Cerebellar contributions to the phonological loop. Poster presented at the annual meeting of the Cognitive Neuroscience Society, San Francisco.

Keele, S., Pokorny, R., Corcos, D., and Ivry, R. B. l985. Do perception and motor production share common timing mechanisms? *Acta Psychologia* 60:173–93.

Leiner, H. C., Leiner, A. L., and Dow, R. S. 1993. Cognitive and language functions of the human cerebellum. *Trends in Neurosciences* 16:444–7.

Liberman, A. M. 1997. How theories of speech affect research in reading and writing. In *Foundations of Reading Acquisition and Dyslexia: Implications for Early Intervention*, ed. B. Blachman. Mahwah, NJ: Lawrence Erlbaum Associates.

Liberman, A. M., and Mattingly, I. G. 1985. The motor theory of speech perception revised. *Cognition* 21:1–36.

Mangels, J. A., Ivry, R. B., and Shimizu, N. 1998. Dissociable contributions of the prefrontal and neocerebellar cortex to time perception. *Cognitive Brain Research* 7:15–39.

Merzenich, M., Jenkins, W., Johnston, P. S., Schreiner, C., Miller, S. L., and Tallal, P. 1996. Temporal processing deficits of language-learning impaired children ameliorated by training. *Science* 271:77–80.

Mostofsky, S. H., Reiss, A. L., Lockhart, P., and Denckla, M. B. 1998. Evaluation of cerebellar size in attention-deficit hyperactivity disorder. *Journal of Child Neurology* 13:434–9.

Nicolson, R. I., Fawcett, A. J., and Dean, P. 1995. Time estimation deficits in developmental dyslexia: Evidence of cerebellar involvement. *Proceedings of the Royal Society of London. Series B: Biological Sciences* 259:43–47.

Nopoulos, P. C., Ceilley, J. W., Gailis, E. A., and Andreasen, N. C. 1999. An MRI study of cerebellar vermis morphology in patients with schizophrenia: Evidence in support of the cognitive dysmetria concept. *Biological Psychiatry* 46:703–11.

Paulesu, E., Frith, C. D., and Frackowiak, R. S. J. 1993. The neural correlates of the verbal component of working memory. *Nature* 362:342–5.

Perfetti. C. A. 1985. *Reading Ability.* Oxford: Oxford University Press.

Perrett, S. P., Ruiz, B. P., and Mauk, M. D. 1993. Cerebellar cortex lesions disrupt learning-dependent timing of conditioned eyelid responses. *Journal of Neuroscience* 13:1708–18.

Petersen, S. E., Fox, P. T., Posner, M. I., Mintun, M., and Raichle, M. E. 1989. Positron emission tomographic studies of the processing of single words. *Journal of Cognitive Neuroscience* 1:153–70.

Raichle, M. E., Fiez, J. A., Videen, T. O., MacLeod, A. M., Pardo, J. V., Fox, P. T., and Petersen, S. E. 1994. Practice-related changes in human brain functional anatomy during nonmotor learning. *Cerebral Cortex* 4:8–26.

Ravizza, S. 2001. Relating selective brain damage to impairments with voicing contrasts. *Brain and Language* 77:95–118.

Ryding, E., Decety, J., Sjoholm, H., Stenberg, G., and Ingvar, D. H. 1993. Motor imagery activates the cerebellum regionally. A SPECT rCBF study with 99mTc-HMPAO. *Cognitive Brain Research* 1:94–99.

Schumacher, E. H., Lauber, E., Awh, E., Jonides, J., Smith, E. E., and Koeppe, R. A. 1996. PET evidence for an amodal verbal working memory system. *Neuroimage* 3:79–88.

Silveri, M. C., Di Betta, A. M., Filippini, V., Leggio, M. G., and Molinari, M.1998. Verbal short-term store-rehearsal system and the cerebellum: Evidence from a patient with a right cerebellar lesion. *Brain* 121:2175–87.

Studdert-Kennedy, M. and Mody, M. 1995. Auditory temporal perception deficits in the reading-impaired: A critical review of the evidence. *Psychonomic Bulletin and Review* 2:508–14.

Their, P., Dicke, P. W., Haas, R., and Barash, S. Encoding of movement time by populations of cerebellar Purkinje cells. *Nature* 405:72–76.

Thompson-Schill, S. L., D'Esposito, M., Aguirre, G. K., and Farah, M. J. 1997. Role of left inferior prefrontal cortex in retrieval of semantic knowledge: A reevaluation. *Proceedings of the National Academy of Sciences of the United States of America* 94:14792–97.

Thompson-Schill, S. L., Swick, D., Farah, M. J., D'Esposito, M., Kan, I. P., and Knight, R. T. 1998. Verb generation in patients with focal frontal lesions: A neuropsychological test of neuroimaging findings. *Proceedings of the National Academy of Sciences of the United States of America* 95:15855–60.

Woodruff-Pak, D. S. 1997. Classical conditioning. *International Review of Neurobiology* 41:341–66.

ACKNOWLEDGMENTS

This paper is dedicated to Alvin Liberman, who provided inspiring discussions over the years on many topics, and in particular, helped develop the ideas described in this paper on the possible relationship between covert rehearsal and phonological knowledge. This work was supported by grants from the National Institute of Health (NS30256) and the National Science Foundation (ECS-9873474). The authors are grateful to Susan Ravizza and Brent Stansfield for their comments on this work.

Chapter • **10**

A Structural Basis for Developmental Dyslexia
Evidence from Diffusion Tensor Imaging

Russell A. Poldrack

Studies of developmental dyslexia using functional imaging techniques have found disrupted activation of the left angular gyrus, and functional connectivity analyses have demonstrated functional disconnection of this region in dyslexia. I review evidence suggesting that this disconnection may reflect disruption of white-matter tracts in the brain, which subserve communication between disparate regions of the cerebral cortex. A novel magnetic resonance imaging (MRI) technique known as diffusion tensor imaging has been used to demonstrate a correlation between white matter structure and reading ability in both adults with dyslexia and normal adults. These results could reflect either epigenetically determined differences in white-matter structure or experience-dependent plasicity of white matter structure. The relation of white matter structure and reading ability may be mediated by the role of myelinated white matter in the rapid transmission of neural signals.

Reading is a complex skill that requires coordination of visual, phonetic, and lexical codes (Adams 1990). Consistent with the multimodal cognitive demands of reading, neuroimaging and lesion studies have demonstrated that reading involves a widespread network of regions in the cerebral cortex (for review, see Demb, Poldrack, and Gabrieli 1999; Fiez and Petersen 1998). Studies of the neurobiology of developmental dyslexia have attempted to understand the role of these different cortical regions, but there is much that remains to be understood about the functional bases of reading disorders. In this chapter, I will present results using a novel magnetic resonance (MR) imaging technique, which suggest that some aspects of reading ability may be determined by the structure of the white matter tracts that connect different cortical regions. After reviewing the evidence for dysfunction and functional disconnection of the left angular gyrus, I will review evidence for white matter dysfunction in dyslexia. I will conclude with some speculative remarks about the possible sources and importance of such white matter dysfunction.

CORTICAL STRUCTURES IN DEVELOPMENTAL DYSLEXIA

From the first studies of the neurology of reading, it has been suggested that the left angular gyrus is a critical structure for reading skill. Starr (1889) noted that lesions to the angular gyrus resulted in alexia (inability to name words, also called "word blindness") and agraphia (inability to write). The well-known studies of Dejerine (1891; 1892) provided further evidence about the role of the angular gyrus. In particular, he reported a patient who was first stricken with "pure alexia"—the inability to read words but preserved ability to write—following a stroke. Two weeks before the patient's death, a second stroke rendered him unable to write as well. Postmortem evaluation revealed that the initial stroke had affected the left occipital cortex and the splenium of the corpus callosum. The second stroke had affected the left inferior parietal cortex including the angular gyrus. This finding, which has been subsequently confirmed many times over, suggested to Dejerine that the role of the left angular gyrus was to connect visual word processes (based in the occipital cortex) with auditory language processes (based in the superior temporal cortex). This view of the left angular gyrus as a multimodal convergence zone for auditory and visual information was championed more recently by Geschwind (1965). Because of the important role of the left angular gyrus in the neurology of acquired reading disorders, it has been proposed by a number of researchers that dysfunction of this region was also implicated in developmental dyslexia. Early workers such as Morgan (1896) and Hinshelwood (1900) attributed developmental reading problems to defects in the angular gyrus (see ch. 27 of Finger 1994), and this idea was also affirmed by Geschwind (1965).

However, despite this longstanding idea, there was, until recently, very little direct evidence regarding the status of the angular gyrus in developmental dyslexia. This dearth of evidence has recently been remedied by studies using neuroimaging and neuropathology techniques, which have provided a great deal of knowledge about the neural correlates of reading disability.

Baseline Physiological and Anatomical Differences

A number of studies have used positron emission tomography (PET) techniques to examine differences in resting-state cerebral blood flow between readers with dyslexia and normal readers. Several of these found no differences in resting blood flow in the angular gyrus region between readers with dyslexia and normal readers (Gross-Glenn et al. 1991; Rumsey et al. 1987, 1992). However, two studies did find decreased resting blood flow in the left inferior parietal region using H2-15O PET (Rumsey et al. 1994a and b). These positive findings are consistent with localized neuropathology in the angular gyrus, but they could also reflect functional differences in resting-state cognitive processes (e.g., Binder et al. 1999).

Postmortem studies of the brains of individuals with dyslexia by Galaburda and colleagues (1985; Humphreys, Kaufmann, and Galaburda 1990) have demonstrated cortical abnormalities extending throughout the perisylvian cortices bilaterally (though somewhat left-lateralized). The territory of cortical malformations included but was not limited to the inferior parietal cortex, suggesting that focal cortical malformations are not specific to this region. In addition, there was a decreased degree of hemispheric asymmetry in the planum temporale (the posterior aspect of the superior temporal gyrus, which lies hidden within the Sylvian fissure) in these individuals compared to normal populations. Abnormalities of the lateral and medial geniculate nuclei of the thalamus have also been observed (Galaburda, Menard, and Rosen 1994; Livingstone et al. 1991), suggesting that the neuropathology in dyslexia extends across both cortical and subcortical regions. Interpretation of these postmortem studies is difficult, though, due to the lack of sufficient data for characterizing the reading and language abilities of the subjects and the existence of other neurological problems (such as epilepsy or traumatic brain injury) in these subjects.

A large number of studies have used structural neuroimaging techniques (including computerized tomography [CT] and structural MRI) to examine noninvasively structural differences between normal readers and readers with dyslexia (reviewed by Eckert and Leonard 2000; Semrud-Clikeman 1997). Attention has focused particularly on abnormalities in the planum temporale and inferior parietal cortex, with roughly half of published studies finding evidence for decreased hemispheric asymmetry in dyslexia. However, Eckert and Leonard (2000) have argued persuasively that these positive findings are likely to have arisen due to confounding of such factors as intelligence, handedness, and socioeconomic status with reading ability.

Taken together, these structural imaging and postmortem studies provide limited support for the notion that the angular gyrus is frankly pathologic in developmental dyslexia, but they do not support the idea that this pathology is anatomically limited to the angular gyrus or inferior parietal region.

Functional Differences

Studies using functional imaging techniques including PET and functional MR imaging (fMRI) have examined differences in cortical activation between readers with dyslexia and normal readers (for a complete review, see Demb et al. 1999). Because phonological processing difficulties are prominent in dyslexia, a number of studies have examined activation on tasks requiring phonological processing (such as rhyme judgments). A consistent finding of these studies has been decreased activation of the left temporo-parietal region in individuals with dyslexia compared to normal readers. Decreased activation in the left temporo-parietal cortex of adults with dyslexia during phonological processing was first found by Rumsey et al. (1992) using PET, and has subsequently been replicated by other groups using both PET (Paulesu et al. 1996) and fMRI (Shaywitz et al. 1998). Temple et al. (2001) recently found a similar decrease in children with dyslexia performing a rhyme judgment task. Another PET study found decreased activation in this region during reading of both exception words and pseudowords, as well as during phonological and lexical decision tasks (Rumsey et al. 1997). Further analysis of this data set found that the level of blood flow in the angular gyrus region was significantly correlated with reading skill in normal subjects but inversely correlated with reading skill in readers with dyslexia (Rumsey et al. 1999). Together, these results provide strong support for functional differences in the angular gyrus in developmental dyslexia.

FUNCTIONAL CONNECTIVITY IN DYSLEXIA

The abnormal activation of temporo-parietal cortex in developmental dyslexia observed using functional imaging could reflect localized malfunction of the cortical structures in this region. Alternatively, this abnormal activation could reflect a derangement of the inputs from other cortical regions into the angular gyrus— that is, a functional disconnection of the angular gyrus. This question has been examined using techniques that measure the correlation of imaging signals between different brain regions, known as functional connectivity (Friston 1994).

Functional connectivity of the angular gyrus was first examined in adults with dyslexia by Horwitz, Rumsey, and Donohue (1998), who re-analyzed the PET data from Rumsey et al. (1997) using correlational techniques. During reading of both pseudo- words and exception words, normal readers exhibited significant correlations between cerebral blood flow in the angular gyrus and a number of other brain areas including occipital, inferior temporal, and cerebellar regions. In addition, significant correlation between blood flow in the angular gyrus and inferior frontal cortex was observed during pseudo-word reading. In readers with dyslexia, there were no significant correlations between blood flow in angular gyrus and any of the other regions observed in normal readers; in a direct comparison, the correlation between angular gyrus and a number of frontal, temporal, occipital, and cerebellar regions was significantly greater in normal readers than readers with dyslexia. These findings are consistent with the notion that the angular gyrus is functionally disconnected in dyslexia.

One question about the Horwitz et al. (1998) finding concerns the degree to which it is task-specific. The finding could reflect a general lack of functional connectivity between the angular gyrus and other cortices, perhaps reflecting some general dysfunction of the angular gyrus. Alternatively, it could reflect a deficit specific to reading or language processing. This question was examined by Pugh et al. (2000), who re-examined an fMRI data set from Shaywitz et al. (1998) using functional connectivity analysis. In that study, readers with dyslexia and normal-reading adults performed a set of tasks with varied phonological demands: line orientation, letter case, single letter rhyme, non-word rhyme, and semantic category judgments.

Correlations in fMRI activity during each of these tasks were examined between the angular gyrus and several other regions (primary visual cortex, lateral extrastriate cortex, and Wernicke's area/superior temporal gyrus). This analysis demonstrated that the deficit in functional connectivity was specific to tasks requiring processing of written words. Whereas the left angular gyrus was significantly correlated with all other regions for all tasks in normal readers, this correlation was only significant for readers with dyslexia on the letter-case and single-letter rhyme tasks. For both the non-word rhyme and semantic categorization tasks, the correlation was insignificant for the dyslexic group. This difference only occurred in the left hemisphere, consistent with previous functional imaging findings. The Pugh et al. (2000) results suggest that the breakdown in functional connectivity of the angular gyrus in developmental dyslexia is not a blanket disorder, but rather reflects cognitive demands specific to the processing of written language.

The imaging studies described heretofore have provided strong evidence in favor of functional disconnection of the inferior parietal cortex during reading in adults with dyslexia, but they cannot determine the underlying neurobiological mechanisms for this disconnection. Differences in functional connectivity could reflect deficits in the fine timing of neural responses, which is thought to be important for synchronization of neural responses across brain regions (e.g., Roelfsema et al. 1997). Given the extensive literature suggesting deficits in the processing of rapidly transient information in dyslexia (reviewed by Farmer and Klein 1995; Wright, Bowen, and Zecker 2000), it is plausible (but speculative) that deficits may occur in the fine timing of neural responses in dyslexia. The specificity of the disconnection to tasks involving reading suggests that it does not reflect a basic physiological deficit within the angular gyrus; rather, it is more plausible that task-driven decreases in functional connectivity may reflect deficits in the synchronization of neural processing between the angular gyrus and other cortical regions via white matter tracts.

IMAGING WHITE MATTER: DIFFUSION TENSOR MRI

Given the findings of functional disconnection in dyslexia, the status of white matter in dyslexia is of great interest. However, until very recently, it was not possible to image the structural integrity of white matter tracts by non-invasive means. Although standard T1-weighted and T2-weighted magnetic resonance imaging (MRI) techniques can provide some information about the myelination of white matter (e.g., Paus et al. 1999), they do not provide sufficiently specific information to make inferences about the structural integrity and directional orientation of white matter tracts. However, an MRI technique developed in the last decade now provides the ability to image the microstructure of white matter tracts. Known as diffusion tensor MR imaging (DTI), this technique allows noninvasive mapping of white matter tracts and determination of their structural integrity and coherence.

Diffusion-weighted MR imaging techniques measure the diffusion (on the order of microns) of water molecules in a particular direction (Basser 1995; Basser, Mattiello, and LeBihan 1994). Diffusion tensor imaging takes diffusion-weighted imaging a step further by imaging diffusion in a number of different directions (usually six). From these images, one can calculate the diffusion tensor at each voxel, which is a matrix describing the spatial orientation and degree of diffusion; this tensor can be visualized as an ellipsoid, which represents diffusion in a three-dimensional space (see figure 1). From the tensor are then derived the principal eigenvectors (corresponding to the principal axes of the diffusion ellipsoid) and their associated eigenvalues (corresponding to the relative strength of diffusion along each of the principal axes). These values provide a summary description of diffusion in each direction.

An essential concept in understanding the use of DTI in mapping white matter is that of *diffusion anisotropy*. In an unstructured medium (such as a large glass of water), most water molecules (except those very near the walls of the glass) will diffuse isotropically— that is, they are equally likely to move in any direction. This corresponds to a diffusion ellipsoid that is a perfect sphere (see figure 1, left panel). In a medium with directionally oriented structure, diffusion becomes anisotropic, meaning that diffusion is not equal in all directions (see figure 1, right panel). In particular, Moseley et al. (1990) showed that diffusion is anisotropic in the white matter of the brain. The white matter tracts of the brain have highly regular directional structure, with large bundles of axons running in the same direction. In addition, these axons are sheathed in myelin, which repels water and thus prevents diffusion through the walls of

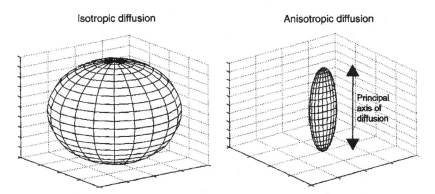

Figure 1.   Depiction of diffusion as an ellipsoid in three dimensions.

the axon. The regular orientation of axons and their myelination leads to diffusion that is much greater along the length of the axon than against the axon walls. Diffusion tensor imaging can be used to image the major direction of diffusion (corresponding to the principal eigenvector of the diffusion tensor), which provides information about the orientation of axons in each voxel. In addition, one can measure the degree of anisotropy using a measure known as fractional anisotropy (Pierpaoli and Basser 1996). This measure reflects the strength of the directional orientation of diffusion in each voxel (i.e., the degree to which diffusion occurs in one particular direction).

The use of DTI as a means to measure the orientation of white matter tracts has been validated by comparison to the classic postmortem studies of Dejerine (Makris et al. 1997). The location and extent of several major fiber tracts were predicted based upon the Dejerine map, and the DTI data were compared to these predictions based upon the orientation of the primary eigenvector in each voxel. The DTI results closely matched the predicted locations of each fiber bundle (across regions of interest, 96% of the hypothesized fiber tract orientations were consistent with the DTI findings), demonstrating the validity of DTI in determining the orientation of white matter tracts.

It is tempting to attribute differences in anisotropy to myelination, and in fact there is a strong positive relationship between myelination and diffusion anisotropy. Anisotropy is correlated with myelination as measured using histological markers (Wimberger et al. 1995). In addition, diffusion anisotropy increases with myelination in newborns (Huppi et al. 1998) and young children (Klingberg et al. 1999), and anisotropy decreases in regions of demyelination in multiple sclerosis (Werring et al. 1999). However, there are a number of other biophysical properties that can also influence the degree of anisotropy. This is evident from the fact that diffusion is anisotropic even in unmyelinated white matter (Wimberger et al. 1995), although to a lesser degree than in myelinated white matter. Other factors that may influence anisotropy include axonal packing density, axon size, axon number, integrity of the cell membrane, and the coherence of axonal orientation. These factors are poorly understood at present, and more basic research is necessary before the biophysical bases of diffusion anisotropy are fully understood.

Each voxel in a DTI study may be as large as 3 cm^3, which corresponds to many thousands of axons per voxel of white matter. Diffusion within that voxel will be determined both by microstructural features of these axons (such as myelination) as well as the coherence of axonal orientation within the voxel. Although it is not possible to directly decompose these aspects of the DTI signal, it is possible to determine the degree to which orientation is coherent between neighboring voxels, which provides an approximation to the degree of coherence within the voxel. Coherence is determined by measuring the dot product of the diffusional direction of neighboring voxels; to the degree that axons are regularly oriented across voxels, this coherence measure will be larger. Using such a measure, Klingberg et al. (1999) found that the frontal white matter in the right hemisphere exhibited more coherent axonal orientation than the left hemisphere, whereas anisotropy differed between children and adults. Although the crossing of multiple fiber tracts cannot be visualized using standard DTI techniques, recently developed methods (known as "supertensor" techniques) allow imaging of multiple fiber tracts within a single voxel, and may provide further knowledge about the relationship between coherence and diffusion anisotropy.

Diffusion Tensor Imaging in Dyslexia

If the disrupted functional connectivity of the angular gyrus in dyslexia reflects white matter disruption, then this disruption should be evident using DTI. In order to investigate this question, Klingberg et al. (2000) administered DTI to eleven adults with no history of reading or language problems and six adults with a history of developmental dyslexia. The group with dyslexia was significantly impaired on the Woodcock-Johnson Word ID task (mean 87.3 ± 4.4) compared to the normal readers (mean 111 ± 2.6), as well as on the Word Attack test (dyslexic mean 93.7 ± 5.9; normal reader mean 111 ± 4.3). The scores of the subjects with dyslexia suggest that they exhibited some degree of compensation for their reading disorders, though all reported continued difficulties in reading.

Diffusion images for each subject were normalized into a standard stereotactic space (after motion correction), and anisotropy maps created from these images were compared statistically between the readers with dyslexia and normal reading groups using SPM. This analysis found regions in the temporo-parietal white matter bilaterally that exhibited greater anisotropy for the normal readers compared to the readers with dyslexia (see figure 2). There were no corresponding differences found for T1-weighted anatomical images, suggesting that the difference was specific to the diffusion measure. In order to investigate the relationship between white matter structure and reading more directly, all subjects were

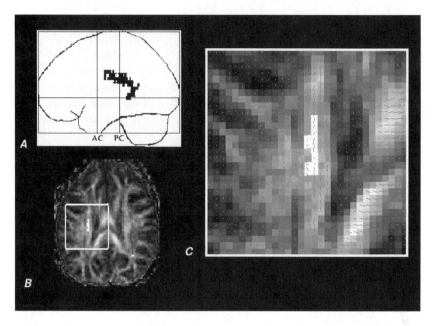

Figure 2.   (A) Sagittal projection of the left hemisphere VOI where there was a significant difference in anisotropy between the poor readers and the control group. The contour and the superimposed grid represents the standard anatomical space (Talairach and Tournoux 1988). AC = anterior commissure; PC = posterior commissure. The VOI had a volume of 960 mm3, and was located within x = (-36 to -26), y = (-50 to -10), z = (0 to 32) mm relative the to anterior commissure.

(B) Axial slices from an anisotropy image of one control subject. Left hemisphere is to the left in the image. Slice location is 24 mm above the anterior-posterior commisural line. The gray scale values in each voxel represent fractional anisotropy, with lighter grays representing higher anisotropy. Voxels highlighted in white showed both a significant group difference between dyslexic and normal readers and a significant correlation between Word ID scores and anisotropy across groups.

(C) Part of the image in figure 2B shown at higher magnification. The small lines in each voxel represent the direction of the first eigenvector (after Makris et al. 1997), which is the main direction of diffusivity and thus can be interpreted as representing the main direction of the axons within a voxel. Adapted from Klingberg et al. (2000) with permission of the authors.

entered into a whole-brain correlational analysis (without regard to group membership) that identified regions showing significant correlation between anisotropy and scores on the Woodcock-Johnson Word ID test. This analysis identified a region in the left temporoparietal white matter that overlapped with the left-hemisphere region identified by the group analysis (as shown in figure 2). The correlation between reading ability and anisotropy remained significant when effects of age and gender were removed in an analysis of covariance (ANCOVA).

One possible explanation for these findings was that they reflected general intelligence. Anisotropy in the left-hemisphere was correlated with scores on the Matrix Analogies Test (MAT: a test of nonverbal intelligence), providing some evidence for this explanation. In order to examine this issue, Klingberg et al. (2000) performed a stepwise regression on anisotropy values using both Word ID and MAT scores as regressors. This analysis found that the correlation between MAT scores and anisotropy was secondary to reading ability: When variance related to Word ID scores was removed there was no remaining correlation between MAT and anisotropy, whereas when variance related to MAT scores was removed there was still significant variance explained by Word ID scores. These findings clearly showed that the observed relationship between reading ability and white matter structure was not mediated by general intelligence.

The orientation of the white matter tracts involved in reading was investigated by classifying the direction of diffusion in each voxel in terms of one of the three main axes of the brain (anterior-posterior, inferior-superior, or left-right). The group difference in white matter structure appeared in voxels that were primarily oriented in the anterior-posterior direction. This is most consistent with a disruption of long fiber tracts connecting frontal, parietal, and occipital cortices (Makris et al. 1999). Because of the variability of the location of particular fiber tracts across individuals (e.g., Burgel et al. 1999), it is difficult to determine precisely the tract in which this disruption occurred. On the basis of previous maps (Makris et al. 1997; 1999), the disruption is likely to fall within the arcuate fasciculus, superior longitudinal fasciculus, and/or external capsule.

What is the Direction of Causality?

Because the findings of the Klingberg et al. (2000) study were purely correlational, it is not possible to establish whether the differences in white matter structure are directly causal in reading ability. The results could reflect epigenetically determined individual differences in white matter structure that lead to differences in reading ability. Such individual differences could affect any of a number of white-matter factors including the degree of myelination. One particular possibility is that immune system factors could affect the myelination of white-matter tracts. There are a number of immune factors that are known to result in myelin damage and death of oligodendrocytes (the glial cells that form myelin in the central nervous system) (Merrill and Scolding 1999). It must be noted however, that most developmental demyelinating diseases are not focal and are associated with long tract signs (such as Babinski signs and increased spasticity); these signs are not generally observed in dyslexia (A. Galaburda, personal communication).

An association between immune system dysfunction (including autoimmune disorders) and dyslexia was first proposed by Geschwind and Behan (1982), but subsequent studies have found mostly negative results (e.g., Gilger et al. 1992; Gilger et al., 1998; Pennington et al. 1987). At the same time, it bears noting that the most prominent genetic linkage for developmental dyslexia has been localized to the human leukocyte antigen (HLA) region on chromosome 6 (Cardon et al. 1994; Gayan et al. 1999). Genes in this region code for a number of histocompatibility factors, which mediate the immune system's recognition of cells as self or other, and a number of autoimmune disorders (including lupus, rheumatoid arthritis, and type 1 diabetes) have been linked to HLA in humans. The possibility of immune system mediation of white-matter dysfunction is further suggested by the fact that a protein found on the surface of oligodendrocytes and myelin sheaths (myelin/oligodendroctye glycoprotein) is coded within the same HLA region that has been linked to dyslexia (Pham-Dinh et al. 1993); however, this is a very large region of the genome and this link remains highly speculative. Thus, it is possible that differences in white matter structure between individuals are related to genetic polymorphisms in HLA that have been found by linkage studies, but confirmation of this finding will require a combination of diffusion tensor imaging with genetic linkage studies.

Another possibility is that the disruption of white matter structure is a consequence of cortical malformations. Rosen, Galaburda, and colleagues (see Rosen this volume) have examined the effects of induced cortical malformations in rats, which have similar neuropathological features to the cortical malformations observed in postmortem studies of individuals with dyslexia. These malformations result in impairments of the processing of rapidly changing acoustic information (Fitch et al. 1994; Herman et al. 1997), similar to those observed in humans with specific language impairment (Tallal and Piercy 1973) and dyslexia (Tallal 1980). Recent work has demonstrated that these cortical malformations result in abnormal connectivity with the thalamus and contralateral hemisphere (Rosen, Burstein, and Galaburda 2000), suggesting that localized cortical abnormalities could have widespread effects on connectivity. Of particular interest is the fact that similar cortical malformations and perceptual impairments occur spontaneously in autoimmune mice (Sherman, Galaburda, and Geschwind 1985), which lends plausibility to an immunological basis for the neural deficits in dyslexia.

Although there are several possible avenues to disturbance of white matter structure in dyslexia, it is equally possible that differences in white matter structure could represent the effect rather than the cause of reading ability. For example, they could reflect differential reading experience in adults, since individuals with poor reading skills spend less time reading. Functional imaging studies have demonstrated differences in neural processing of spoken language between literate and illiterate adults (Castro-Caldas et al. 1998), consistent with changes in function related to acquisition of reading skill, but no similar results have been reported for brain structure. Although there is (to my knowledge) no evidence for experience-related plasticity in white matter structure, plausible pathways exist for activity-related mediation of myelination. In particular, the phosphorylation of myelin basic protein (MBP) in oligodendrocytes (an important step in central nervous system myelination) is mediated by nonsynaptic extracellular signals (including nitric oxide and superoxide) that are released during neuronal activity (Atkins and Sweatt 1999). In the peripheral nervous system, Schwann cells (which are responsible for myelination of peripheral axons) are also sensitive to action potentials in premyelinated axons (Stevens and Fields 2000). These findings provide indirect support for the possibility that activity-dependent mechanisms could lead to learning-related changes in myelination, but much more knowledge about the molecular neurobiology of myelination is necessary before such a relation can be established.

WHITE MATTER AND DYNAMIC SENSORY PROCESSING IN DYSLEXIA

A large body of research suggests that individuals with dyslexia exhibit difficulties with the processing of dynamic sensory information in addition to their problems with phonological processing (see Stein et al. this volume). Recent work has shown that these impairments of dynamic sensory processing (both auditory and visual) are correlated with reading ability and correlated across modalities (Witton et al. 1998), and it appears that dynamic sensory processing in auditory and visual modalities are correlated with different aspects of reading ability (Booth et al. 2000; Talcott et al. 2000). A number of imaging studies have examined neural processing of such signals in dyslexia. Eden et al. (1996) first examined visual motion processing in dyslexia using fMRI. They found that whereas moving visual stimuli resulted in activation of area MT in normal readers, readers with dyslexia did not exhibit such activation. This result was extended by Demb, Boynton, and Heeger (1998), who examined performance on a speed discrimination task in readers with dyslexia and normal readers using fMRI. Activation in and around area MT differed between readers with dyslexia and normal readers, and was significantly correlated with reading speed. These results are consistent with anatomical evidence for deficits in the magnocellular visual pathway (Livingstone et al. 1991). In the context of white matter disorders, it is of particular interest that area MT is highly myelinated (Tootell and Taylor 1995) and consistent with the need for rapid transmission of neural signals.

Processing of dynamic acoustic stimuli has been examined using fMRI by Temple et al. (2000). Adults with and without dyslexia were presented with non-speech sounds containing either fast or slow frequency transitions (modeled after the formant transitions that distinguish some speech sounds). Normal readers exhibited activation of the left dorsolateral prefrontal cortex for fast versus slow transitions, whereas readers with dyslexia failed to exhibit such activation. In addition, training that resulted in improved dynamic acoustic processing resulted in increased activation in the left prefrontal cortex. Another study using magnetoencephalography (MEG) found that the response of auditory cortex to brief successive acoustic events was impaired in individuals with dyslexia (Nagarajan et al. 1999). Together with the findings of the visual motion studies, these results confirm the existence of deficits in transient sensory signal processing across multiple sensory modalities.

It is possible that the disruption of white matter found by Klingberg et al. (2000) could relate directly to the disruption of dynamic sensory processing that has been observed in dyslexia. In particular, dysmyelination or reduction of axon size of white matter tracts connecting sensory cortices to higher-level cortex would result in selective disruption of rapid signal transmission. Because Klingberg et al. (2000) did not collect measures of dynamic sensory processing, it is not possible to determine whether white matter structure was directly related to rapid processing. However, it is unlikely that the white matter disruption found by Klingberg et al. (2000) can provide a complete explanation for deficits in dynamic sensory signal processing in dyslexia, since such difficulties have been found on tasks that are likely to rely upon brainstem mechanisms (Dougherty et al. 1998; McAnally and Stein 1996). Differences in neural structure have also been found in both the magnocellular components of both medial geniculate and lateral geniculate (Galaburda et al., 1994) nuclei in the thalamus, consistent with disruption at a subcortical level. These findings suggest that deficits in dynamic sensory processing may reflect more systematic pathology of neural pathways for rapid processing that extends beyond the cerebral cortex and white matter (see Stein et al. this volume). Further work is necessary to determine how white matter structure is related to dynamic sensory processing.

DISCRETE VERSUS CONTINUOUS PATHOLOGY IN DYSLEXIA

One interesting implication of the present results concerns the epidemiological nature of developmental dyslexia. In a longitudinal study of a group of 414 children, Shaywitz et al. (1992) found that the reading skills of children with dyslexia fell within a single normal distribution of reading performance, rather than making up a separate distribution at the tail of the normal reading distribution. In particular, Shaywitz et al. found that discrepancy scores (measuring the difference between reading ability and general intelligence) followed a normal distribution, and that the variability of these discrepancy scores over time equaled that predicted by a normal distribution model. On the basis of these data, Shaywitz et al. argued that dyslexia represents the far end on a continuum of reading skill, just as hypertension reflects one tail of a continuous distribution of blood pressure. The DTI results of Klingberg et al. (2000) are consistent with this notion, and may provide a structural explanation for some of the variability in reading skill across individuals. In particular, the finding of a significant correlation between reading skill and white matter structure in both normal readers and readers with dyslexia suggests that some continuously variable factor affects both white matter structure and reading ability.

The continuous nature of the white-matter/reading relationship seems on its face to be at odds with the findings of discrete neuropathology in postmortem studies of subjects with dyslexia (Galaburda et al. 1985; Humphreys, Kaufmann, and Galaburda 1990). However, there are a number of ways to resolve this apparent discrepancy. First, it is possible that both cortical malformations and white matter disturbance are driven by a common continuously varying factor, but that white matter and gray matter respond differently to this factor. For example, an autoimmune process could result in discrete pathology in the cerebral cortex (Sherman et al. 1985) while resulting in more graded effects on white matter myelination. It is also possible that the patients examined at postmortem by Galaburda and colleagues suffered from language-learning impairments in addition to dyslexia, and that the observed cortical malformations reflect the compound neuropathology related to these disorders in combination. Because there is limited neuropsychological information available about these patients, it is not possible to address this issue on the basis of existing data. Further work is necessary to understand the relationship between cortical and white matter pathologies in dyslexia.

CONCLUSIONS

Results using diffusion tensor MR imaging have demonstrated a relationship between white matter structure and reading ability in both normal readers and readers with dyslexia. This finding provides a structural substrate for the findings of functional disconnection that have been found by a number of functional imaging studies. Further understanding of these findings will require DTI imaging of preliterate children and examination of changes in white matter structure that accompany reading acquisition, and studies combining DTI with genetic linkage studies to understand the possible genetic bases of white matter dysfunction.

REFERENCES

Adams, M. J. 1990. *Beginning to Read: Thinking and Learning about Print.* Cambridge, MA: MIT Press.

Atkins, C. M., and Sweatt, J. D. 1999. Reactive oxygen species mediate activity-dependent neuron-glia signaling in output fibers of the hippocampus. *Journal of Neuroscience* 19(17):7241–8.

Basser, P. J. 1995. Inferring microstructural features and the physiological state of tissues from diffusion-weighted images. *NMR Biomed* 8(7–8): 333–44.

Basser, P. J., Mattiello, J., and LeBihan, D. 1994. Estimation of the self-diffusion tensor from the NMR spin echo. *Journal of Magn Reson B* 103(3): 247–54.

Binder, J. R., Frost, J. A., Hammeke, T. A., Bellgowan, P. S., Rao, S. M., and Cox, R. W. 1999. Conceptual processing during the conscious reading state: A functional MRI study. *Journal of Cognitive Neuroscience* 11(1):80–95.

Booth, J. A., Perfetti, C. A., MacWhinney, B., and Hunt, S. B. 2000. The association of rapid temporal perception with orthographic and phonological processing in children and adults with reading impairment. *Scientific Studies of Reading* 4:101–32.

Burgel, U., Schormann, T., Schleicher, A., and Zilles, K. 1999. Mapping of histologically identified long fiber tracts in human cerebral hemispheres to the MRI volume of a reference brain: Position and spatial variability of the optic radiation. *Neuroimage* 10(5):489–99.

Cardon, L. R., Smith, S. D., Fulker, D. W., Kimberling, W. J., Pennington, B. F., and DeFries, J. C. 1994. Quantitative trait locus for reading disability on chromosome 6 [see comments]. *Science* 266(5183):276–9.

Castro-Caldas, A., Petersson, K. M., Reis, A., Stone-Elander, S., and Ingvar, M. 1998. The illiterate brain: Learning to read and write during childhood influences the functional organization of the adult brain. *Brain* 121(Pt 6):1053–63.

Dejerine, J. J. 1891. Sur un cas de cecite verbale avec agraphie, suivi d'autopsie. *Memoirs de la Societe de Biologie* 43:197–201.

Demb, J. B., Boynton, G. M., and Heeger, D. J. 1998. Functional magnetic resonance imaging of early visual pathways in dyslexia. *Journal of Neuroscience* 18(17):6939–51.

Demb, J. B., Poldrack, R. A., and Gabrieli, J. D. E. 1999. Functional neuroimaging of word processing in normal and dyslexic readers. In *Converging Methods for Understanding Reading and Dyslexia*, eds. R. Klein and P. McMullen. Cambridge, MA: MIT Press.

Dougherty, R. F., Cynader, M. S., Bjornson, B. H., Edgell, D., and Giaschi, D. E. 1998. Dichotic pitch: A new stimulus distinguishes normal and dyslexic auditory function. *NeuroReport* 14:3001–5.

Eckert, M. A., and Leonard, C. M. 2000. Structural imaging in dyslexia: The planum temporale. *Mentally Retarded Developmental Disabilities Research Review* 6(3):198–206.

Eden, G. F., VanMeter, J. W., Rumsey, J. M., Maisog, J. M., Woods, R. P., and Zeffiro, T. A. 1996. Abnormal processing of visual motion in dyslexia revealed by functional brain imaging [see comments]. *Nature* 382(6586):66–69.

Farmer, M. E., and Klein, R. M. 1995. The evidence for a temporal processing deficit linked to dyslexia: A review. *Psychonomic Bulletin and Review* 2(4):460–93.

Fiez, J. A., and Petersen, S. E. 1998. Neuroimaging studies of word reading. *Proceedings of the National Academy of Sciences* (USA) 95(3)914–21.

Finger, S. 1994. *Origins of Neuroscience*. New York: Oxford University Press.

Fitch, R. H., Tallal, P., Brown, C. P., and Galaburda, A. M. 1994. Induced microgyria and auditory temporal processing in rats: A model for language impairment? *Cerebral Cortex* 4(3):260–70.

Friston, K. J. 1994. Functional and effective connectivity in neuroimaging: A synthesis. *Human Brain Mapping* 2:56–78.

Galaburda, A. M., Menard, M. T., and Rosen, G. D. 1994. Evidence for aberrant auditory anatomy in developmental dyslexia. *Proceedings of the National Academy of Sciences* (USA) 91(17):8010–13.

Galaburda, A. M., Sherman, G. F., Rosen, G. D., Aboitiz, F., and Geschwind, N. 1985. Developmental dyslexia: Four consecutive patients with cortical anomalies. *Annals of Neurology* 18(2):222–33.

Gayan, J., Smith, S. D., Cherny, S. S., Cardon, L. R., Fulker, D. W., Brower, A. M., Olson, R. K., Pennington, B. F., and DeFries, J. C. 1999.

Quantitative-trait locus for specific language and reading deficits on chromosome 6p. *American Journal of Human Genetics*, 64(1):157–64.

Geschwind, N. 1965. Disconnection syndromes in animals and man. *Brain* 88:237–294.

Geschwind, N., and Behan, P. 1982. Left-handedness: Association with immune disease, migraine, and developmental learning disorder. *Proceedings of the National Academy of Sciences* (USA) 79(16):5097–5100.

Gilger, J. W., Pennington, B. F., Green, P., Smith, S. M., and Smith, S. D. 1992. Reading disability, immune disorders and non-right-handedness: Twin and family studies of their relations. *Neuropsychologia* 30(3): 209–27.

Gilger, J. W., Pennington, B. F., Harbeck, R. J., DeFries, J. C., Kotzin, B., Green, P., and Smith, S. 1998. A twin and family study of the association between immune system dysfunction and dyslexia using blood serum immunoassay and survey data. *Brain Cognition* 36(3):310–33.

Gross-Glen, K. Duara, R., Barker, W. W., Loewenstein, D., Chang, J. Y., Yoshii, F., Apicella, A. M., Pascal, S., Boothe, T., Sevush, S., Jallad, B. J., Novoa, L., and Lubs, H. A. 1991. Positron emission studies during serial word-reading by normal and dyslexic adults. *Journal of Clinical and Experimental Neuropsychology* 13:531–44.

Herman, A. E., Galaburda, A. M., Fitch, R. H., Carter, A. R., and Rosen, G. D. 1997. Cerebral microgyria, thalamic cell size and auditory temporal processing in male and female rats. *Cerebral Cortex* 7(5): 453–64.

Hinshelwood, J. 1900. Congenital world-blindness. *Lancet* 1:1506–8.

Horwitz, B., Rumsey, J. M., and Donohue, B. CC. 1998. Functional connectivity of the angular gyrus in normal reading and dyslexia. *Proceedings of the National Academy of Sciences* (USA) 95(15):8939–44.

Humphreys, P., Kaufmann, W. E., and Galaburda, A. M. 1990. Developmental dyslexia in women: Neuropathological findings in three patients. *Annals of Neurology* 28(6):727–38.

Huppi, P. S., Maier, S. E., Peled, S., Zientara, G. P., Barnes, P. D., Jolesz, F. A., and Volpe, J. J. 1998. Microstructural development of human newborn cerebral white matter assessed in vivo by diffusion tensor magnetic resonance imaging. *Pediatric Research* 44(4):584–90.

Klingberg, T., Hedehus, M., Temple, E., Salz, T., Gabrieli, J. D., Moseley, M. E., and Poldrack, R. A. 2000. Microstructure of temporo-parietal white matter as a basis for reading ability: Evidence from diffusion tensor magnetic resonance imaging. *Neuron* 25(2):493–500.

Klingberg, T., Vaidya, C. J., Gabrieli, J. D., Moseley, M. E., and Hedehus, M. 1999. Myelination and organization of the frontal white matter in children: A diffusion tensor MRI study. *Neuroreport* 10(13):2817–21.

Livingstone, M. S., Rosen, G. D., Drislane, F. W., and Galaburda, A. M. 1991. Physiological and anatomical evidence for a magnocellular defect in developmental dyslexia. *Proceedings of the National Academy of Sciences* (USA) 88(18):7943–7.

McAnally, K. I., and Stein, J. F. 1996. Auditory temporal coding in dyslexia. *Proceedings of the Royal Society London- B. Biological Science* 263(1373):961–5.

Makris, N., Meyer, J. W., Bates, J. F., Yeterian, E. H., Kennedy, D. N., and Caviness, V. S. 1999. MRI-Based topographic parcellation of human cerebral white matter and nuclei II. Rationale and applications with systematics of cerebral connectivity. *Neuroimage* 9(1):18–45.

Makris, N., Worth, A. J., Sorensen, A. G., Papadimitriou, G. M., Wu, O., Reese, T. G., Wedeen, V. J., Davis, T. L., Stakes, J. W., Caviness, V. S., Kaplan, E., Rosen, B. R., Pandya, D. N., and Kennedy, D. N. 1997. Morphometry of in vivo human white matter association pathways with diffusion-weighted magnetic resonance imaging. *Annals of Neurology* 42(6):951–62.

Merrill, J. E., and Scolding, N. J. 1999. Mechanisms of damage to myelin and oligodendrocytes and their relevance to disease. *Neuropathology and Applied Neurobiology* 25(6):435–58.

Morgan, W. P. 1896. A case of congenital world-blindness. *British Medical Journal* 2:1378.

Moseley, M. E., Cohen, Y., Kucharczyk, J., Mintorovitch, J., Asgari, H. S., Wendland, M. F., Tsuruda, J., and Norman, D. 1990. Diffusion-weighted MR imaging of anisotropic water diffusion in cat central nervous system. *Radiology* 176(2):439–45.

Nagarajan, S., Mahncke, H., Salz, T., Tallal, P., Roberts, T., and Merzenich, M. M. 1999. Cortical auditory signal processing in poor readers. *Proceedings of the National Academy of Sciences* (USA) 96(11):6483–8.

Paulesu, E., Frith, U., Snowling, M., Gallagher, A., Morton, J., Frackowiak, R. S., and Frith, C. D. 1996. Is developmental dyslexia a disconnection syndrome? Evidence from PET scanning. *Brain* 119(Pt 1):143–57.

Paus, T., Zijdenbos, A., Worsley, K., Collins, D. L., Blumenthal, J., Giedd, J. N., Rapoport, J. L., and Evans, A. C. 1999. Structural maturation of neural pathways in children and adolescents: In vivo study. *Science* 283(5409):1908–11.

Pennington, B. F., Smith, S. D., Kimberling, W. J., Green, P. A., and Haith, M. M. 1987. Left-handedness and immune disorders in familial dyslexics. *Archives of Neurology* 44(6):634–9.

Pham-Dinh, D., Mattei, M. G., Nussbaum, J. L., Roussel, G., Pontarotti, P., Roeckel, N., Mather, I. H., Artzt, K., Lindahl, K. F., and Dautigny, A. 1993. Myelin/oligodendrocyte glycoprotein is a member of a subset of the immunoglobulin superfamily encoded within the major histocompatibility complex [see comments]. *Proceedings of the National Academy of Sciences* (USA) 90(17):7990–4.

Pierpaoli, C., and Basser, P. J. 1996. Toward a quantitative assessment of diffusion anisotropy. *Magn Reson Med* 36(6):893–906.

Pugh, K. R., Mencl, W. E., Shaywitz, B. A., Shaywitz, S. E., Fulbright, R. K., Constable, R. T., Skuldarski, P., Marchione, K. E., Jenner, A. R., Fletcher, J. M., Liberman, A. M., Shankweiler, D. P., Katz, L., Lacadie, C., and Gore, J. C. 2000. The angular gyrus in developmental dyslexia: Task-specific differences in functional connectivity within posterior cortex. *Psychological Science* 11:51–56.

Roelfsema, P. R., Engel, A. K., Konig, P., and Singer, W. 1997. Visuomotor integration is associated with zero time-lag synchronization among cortical areas. *Nature* 385(6612):157–61.

Rosen, G. D., Burstein, D., and Galaburda, A. M. 2000. Changes in efferent and afferent connectivity in rats with induced cerebrocortical microgyria. *Journal of Comparative Neurology* 418(4):423–40.

Rumsey, J. M., Berman, K. F., Denckla, M. B., Hamburger, S. D., Kruesi, M. J., and Weinberger, D. R. 1987. Regional cerebral blood flow in severe developmental dyslexia. *Archives of Neurology* 44(11):1144–50.

Rumsey, J. M., Andreason, P., Zametkin, A. J., Aquino, T., King, A. C., Hamburger, S. D., Pikus, A., Rapoport, J. L., and Cohen, R. M. 1992. Failure to activate the left temporoparietel cortex in dyslexia: An oxygen 15 positron emission tomographic study [published erratum appears in Archives of Neurology 1994 March 51(3):243]. *Archives of Neurology* 49(5):527–34.

Rumsey, J. M., Andreason, P., Zametkin, A. J., King, A. C., Hamburger, S. D., Aquino, T., Hanahan, A. P., Pikus, A., and Cohen, R. M. 1994a. Right frontotemporal activation by tonal memory in dyslexia: An O15 PET study. *Biological Psychiatry* 36(3):171–80.

Rumsey, J. M., Zametkin, A. J., Andreaason, P., Hanahan, A. P., Hamburger, S. D., Aquino, T., King, A. C., Pikus, A., and Cohen, R. M. 1994b. Normal activation of frontotemporal language cortex in dyslexia, as measured with oxygen 15 positron emission tomography. *Archives of Neurology* 51(1):27–38.

Rumsey, J. M., Nace, K., Donohue, B., Wise, D., Maisog, J. M., and Andreason, P. 1997. A positron emission tomographic study of impaired word recognition and phonological processing in dyslexic men. *Archives of Neurology* 54(5):562–73.

Rumsey, J. M., Horwitz, B., Donohue, B. C., Nace, K. L., Maisog, J. M., and Andreason, P. 1999. A functional lesion in developmental dyslexia: Left angular gyral blood flow predicts severity. *Brain Language* 70(2): 187–204.

Semrud-Clikeman, M. 1997. Evidence from imaging on the relationship between brain structure and developmental language disorders. *Seminars in Pediatric Neurology* 4(2):117–24.

Shaywitz, S. E., Escobar, M. D., Shaywitz, B. A., Fletcher, J. M., and Makuch, R. 1992. Evidence that dyslexia may represent the lower tail of a normal distribution of reading ability [see comments]. *New England Journal of Medicine* 326(3):145–50.

Sherman, G. F., Galaburda, A. M., and Geschwind, N. 1985. Cortical anomalies in brains of New Zealand mice: A neuropathologic model of dyslexia? *Proceedings of the National Academy of Sciences* (USA) 82(23): 8072–4.

Starr, M. A. 1889. The pathology of sensory aphasia, with an analysis of fifty cases in which Broca's centre was not diseased. *Brain* 12:82–99.

Stevens, B., and Fields, R. D. 2000. Response of Schwann cells to action potentials in development. *Science* 287(5461):2267–71.

Talairach, J., and Tournoux, P. 1988. *A Co-Planar Stereotactic Atlas of the Human Brain.* Stuttgart: Thieme.

Talcott, J. B., Witton, C., McLean, M. F., Hansen, P. C., Rees, A., Green, G. G., and Stein, J. F. 2000. Dynamic sensory sensitivity and children's word decoding skills. *Proceedings of the National Academy of Sciences* (USA) 97(6):2952–7.

Tallal, P. 1980. Auditory temporal perception, phonics, and reading disabilities in children. *Brain Language* 9(2):182–98.

Tallal, P., and Piercy, M. 1973. Defects of non-verbal auditory perception in children with developmental aphasia. *Nature* 241(5390):468–9.

Temple, E., Poldrack, R. A., Protopapas, A., Nagarajan, S., Salz, T., Tallal, P., Merzenich, M. M., and Gabrieli, J. D. 2000. Disruption of the neural response to rapidly transient acoustic stimuli in dyslexia: Evidence from functional MRI. *Proceedings of the National Academy of Sciences* (USA) 97(25):13907–12.

Temple, E., Poldrack, R. A., Salidis, J., Deutsch, G., Merzenich, M. M., Tallal, P., and Gabrieli, J. D. E. 2001. Disrupted neural responses to phonological and orthographic processing in dyslexic children: An fMRI study. *Neuroreport*, in press.

Tootell, R, B. H., and Taylor, J. B. 1995. Anatomical evidence for MT and additional cortical visual areas in humans. *Cerebral Cortex* 5:39–55.

Werring, D. J., Clark, C. A., Barker, G. J., Thompson, A. J., and Miller, D. H. 1999. Diffusion tensor imaging of lesions and normal-appearing white matter in multiple sclerosis. *Neurology* 52(8):1626–32.

Wimberger, D. M., Roberts, T. P., Barkovich, A. J., Prayer, L. M., Moseley, M. E., and Kucharczyk, J. 1995. Identification of "premyelination" by diffusion-weighted MRI. *Journal of Computer Assisted Tomography* 19(1):28–33.

Witton, C., Talcott, J. B., Hansen, P. C., Richardson, A. J., Griffiths, T. D., Rees, A., Stein, J. F., and Green, G. G. 1998. Sensitivity to dynamic auditory and visual stimuli predicts nonword reading ability in both dyslexic and normal readers. *Current Biology* 8(14):791–7.

Wright, B. A., Bowen, R. W., and Zecker, S. G. 2000. Nonlinguistic perceptual deficits associated with reading and language disorders. *Current Opinions in Neurobiology* 10(4): 482–6.

ACKNOWLEDGMENTS

I would like to acknowledge the important contribution of my collaborators on the work described herein, particularly John Gabrieli, Torkel Klingberg, and Elise Temple. I would also like to thank Al Galaburda, Torkel Klingberg, and Debbie Waber for helpful comments on an earlier version of this chapter.

Chapter • 11

On the Functional Neuroanatomy of Fluency Or Why Walking Is Just As Important to Reading as Talking Is

Frank Balch Wood,
Lynn Flowers, and
Elena Grigorenko

The ideas we consider here are best understood as proposals that derive from quite simple and basic functional neuroanatomic distinctions. Thus derived, the proposals involve an application to behavior in general and to reading fluency in particular. The neurofunctional distinctions are consensual; it is their application that is arguable and hypothetical. As such, although they are not without some empirical basis in clinical and research experience, they await—and define—further focused research investigations. It is therefore their heuristic value that concerns us the most: if they provide some fresh perspectives on the topic of fluency, and particularly if they stimulate further research across the spectrum from chromosome to classroom, then they will serve their purpose regardless of the degree to which their particular implications are confirmed by subsequent experience. This set of ideas is naturally framed in a particular question about what would constitute a working understanding of the concept of fluency in reading. We wish to be concise and present these ideas in the form of simple assertions, with some subsequent elaborations and explanations, along with some indication of the empirical implications.

TWO TYPES OF FLUENCY

Fluency is a combination of many skills, two of which are especially important: (1) fast recognition reaction time to visual letters, words, or phrases, and (2) anticipatory processing of those same stimuli. One indication that fluency—or at least rapid naming skill—involves two or more separate factors is found in a recent report from our genetic studies (Grigorenko et al. in press). It shows that rapid naming has separate genetic linkages involving chromosome 1 and chromosome 6. The critical feature of the finding is that the linkage of rapid naming fluency on chromosome 1 has a high lod score, over 5, specifically when the linkage on 6 is separately statistically accounted for. In other words, rapid naming as a phenotype has separate variance accounted for by separate linkages on chromosomes 1 and 6. Granted, just how distinct or overlapping the two mechanisms are on chromosome 1 and chromosome 6 remains a subject for future clarification. It also remains for future research to delineate with precision what underlying behavioral characteristics truly define the two or more separate factors within rapid naming, if in fact they are discriminably different.

In our proposal, the first type of fluency is defined as fast reaction time. This type is also sometimes described as automaticity, which adds a connotation of familiarity or practiced responding to the more limited notion of fast response time only. As learning proceeds, response times decrease and the response become less effortful or attention demanding (hence, we say, the response becomes automatic). Fluent or "easy" sight word recognition is a typical example. The neural substrate of this process is often described as involving an increasing tuning of neurons for the particular stimuli in question, which is by definition the consequence of repeated exposure and response to the stimuli. In some situations, this tuning is accompanied by a progressive reduction in the actual number of neurons involved; in other situations the number of involved neurons actually increases. It is not yet known with certainty which of these (reduction or increase in participating neurons) is characteristic of automatized letter, word, or phrase recognition, but in either case the changes are the result of increasing practice and are manifest as decreased reaction time.

The second type of fluency we term anticipatory processing. It is central to the reading of any text, indeed any laterally displayed series of individual items, as in the Rapid Automatized Naming (RAN) test cards of Denckla and Rudel (1974). In such situations, the items that are "ahead" or "yet to come" in the sequence are also processed at least preliminarily, which processing in turn facilitates the actual response to them when attention and responding shifts to them. This facilitation includes a reduction in the reaction time, but that reduction is not related to practice; it is instead related to anticipation, i.e., some form of "pre-processing" of the coming stimuli. Thus, if the item presently eliciting a response is A, and the subsequent item to the right is B, the anticipatory processing of B facilitates responding to B when attention shifts fully to B. Perhaps we could term this "proactive" facilitation. However, it is interesting that in some cases the response to A is also directly facilitated by B, prior to any overt response to B—what might be called "retroactive" facilitation. Maryanne Wolf (1991) and colleagues have pioneered in the demonstration that this type of anticipatory processing makes rapid naming from RAN cards faster than rapid naming from individually presented stimuli, as on a computer screen.

We may illustrate this type of anticipatory fluency anecdotally from our case experience. A relatively severely traumatically brain injured 11-year-old girl, when reading out loud, will stumble on a word she knows if it is followed by a word she does not know—occasionally even if that word is not the next word to the right, but still further to the right, of the one she is currently pronouncing. She will on the other hand pronounce the word fluently, if it is followed by a familiar word or words. The automaticity of the pronunciation of a given word is thus influenced by the familiarity of a succeeding word or words.

Notably, Wolf and Bowers (1999) have also stressed the relation of rapid naming fluency to skill in reading comprehension. That relation can be understood in the present context as involving a more semantic type of proactive and retroactive facilitation, not only from one word to the next, but also from one phrase, sentence, or paragraph to the next. The derivation of meaning from text, during real time "progress" through the text, is almost by definition closely related to anticipation from one word to subsequent words. Comprehension inherently involves anticipatory fluency.

A central thesis of this presentation is that anticipatory facilitation, although not the only component of fluency, is particularly important, perhaps because it is typically overlooked. An undue preoccupation with response time itself risks neglect of what is conceptually half of the fluency domain, and as a practical matter perhaps more than half. Skilled reading may ultimately have more to do with integrative, hence anticipatory, processing than with item-for-item recognition and response. From a functional neuroanatomical perspective, neglect of this domain may also constitute neglect of the potential contribution of large regions of cerebral space that are outside the classic "reading" or "language" areas. Let us consider an important initial distinction or subdivision, as follows.

DISTINCTIONS IN CEREBRAL SPACE

One of the most global, functionally relevant distinctions within cerebral space is cytoarchitectural—between cortex that is relatively more densely pyramidal and cortex that is relatively more densely granular. Pyramidal cells are large and function to integrate numerous inputs into one or a relatively few outputs, whereas granular cells are substantially smaller and appear to be the final cortical targets of ascending sensory input, whose feature processing algorithm approaches, at least to some degree, a one-to-one or even one-to-many logic. Such granule cells, in turn, seem to converge on pyramidal cells in a many-to-one fashion, notwithstanding the multiplicity and parallelism of such convergences, and notwithstanding the extensive feedback circuits that apparently amplify or extend, in space or in time, these convergences. For almost a century, the relative proportion of pyramidal to granular cells, in a given region of cortex, has been thought to have functional significance. That is fairly routine in the case of motor (more pyramidal) versus sensory (more granular) cortex, but a subsequent common yet oversimplified division of the cortex into frontal (more pyramidal and more "output" oriented) versus posterior (more granular and "input" oriented) is unhelpful for our present purposes, notwithstanding that such a distinction could certainly be said to characterize the anterior and posterior banks of the central sulcus.

Numerous observers (see especially von Economo 1929) have recognized that the granular versus pyramidal regions of cortex are not exclusively posterior versus anterior, respectively. The dorsolateral cortical topography of this distinction includes a high frontal-parietal, relatively pyramidal, stratum and a lower frontal-parietal, relatively granular, stratum. A rough marker for this distinction parietally is the intra-parietal sulcus, dividing the angular gyrus (relatively granular) from the superior parietal lobule (more pyramidal). Analogously, in frontal cortex the mid frontal sulcus separates inferior dorsolateral prefrontal cortex (more granular, about as much so as the angular gyrus) from the superior frontal area (more pyramidal) containing, among other things, the frontal eye fields. In brief, it may be said that the cortex seen from a lateral perspective has two dimensions that roughly map on to the pyramidal-granular distinction. There is the obvious motor versus sensory distinction that is roughly anterior versus posterior, but there is also a superior versus inferior (also relatively pyramidal versus relatively granular) distinction that is to some extent orthogonal to the anterior-posterior or motor versus sensory distinction. The underlying significance of this cytoarchitectural subdivision may have to do with the cognitive processing that is differentially supported, or at least differentially facilitated, by the two architectures. The "granular" phase of cognitive processing is inherently detail-oriented, representational, and field-independent; the "pyramidal" is inherently integrative, dynamic (i.e., concerned with continuous re-representations), and goal directed (i.e., not entirely free from the surrounding environmental "field"). This cognitive distinction, when seen in the dorsal to ventral dimension of lateral cerebral space, corresponds to a major division in human anatomy. There is a dorsal medial cortical stream involving the legs and feet and the programming of lateral eye movements, that is concerned not only with walking through space but also with reaching distal goals in that space. There is also a dorsolateral stream involving the hands and fingers along with eye movement convergence, all concerned more with proximal space involving the hands.

Hands and fingers do details—they specialize in behaviors that deal with isolated features of the environment, apart from the larger context. Feet, which are dorsal in the above scheme, do travels. They specialize in behaviors that explore the larger environmental context-behaviors that are sequentially arranged so as to traverse relatively larger regions within that contextual space. These latter behaviors are then by definition more context-bound. Again, hands often adopt a tonic, fixed posture, and deal mostly either with stationary objects or with objects whose movement is being stopped or at least grasped. Legs and feet by their nature propel their owners through space in a constantly changing perceptual manifold. Taken seriously, this distinction would suggest that "going somewhere" in cognitive space might also require invoking the cognitive operations in which the feet and legs specialize.

Another case from our experience will illustrate the issue of dynamic fluency from a different perspective. Consider a ballet

dancer who sustained a significant head injury, involving prominent superior frontal-parietal components. She recovered well, and
regained the ability to adopt and hold any dance posture, however
difficult, even when it placed a major demand on the leg muscles.
On command to adopt any particular posture, she complied ex-
pertly and flawlessly. As a consequence, she acquired notable expertise in yoga after her injury. She remained, however, so
dys-fluent in the sequential expression of these postures that she
could never dance, much less resume her dancing career.

Another relevant neural distinction is within the neurochem-
ical domain, between dopaminergic and noradrenergic modulation of sensorimotor and cognitive processes. T. J. Crow (Crow
and Arbuthnott 1972) is usually credited with the original formu-
lation that stresses the anticipatory quality of dopaminergic modulation versus the consummatory quality of noradrenergic
modulation—the former having an ancient evolutionary association with olfaction which is the original distal sense modality; the
latter having an equally ancient association with gustation which
is the original proximal sense modality. The interaction of neuro-
chemical and cognitive processes implies dopaminergic facilitation
of exploratory behavior, including evidence seeking, hypothesis
confirming, and general abstraction. Goal-directedness, or the capacity to maintain a distal target in spite of local distractions, and
to relate appropriate proximal events to that distal target, is especially likely to be involved with dopaminergic modulation. Of the
several theoretical accounts describing this aspect of dopaminergic
functioning, see especially Previc (1999), who argues that it is this
dopaminergic modulation—not the cortical apparatus itself being
modulated—that is the substrate of biological intelligence.

Anthropological considerations are instructive. Humans
evolved away from their ape-like origins and their forest environment, under the pressure of drier climate and a sparser landscape,
requiring traveling longer distances on a relatively regular basis.
The adaptations supporting that development appear to include a
strong dopaminergic "boost" which has implications ranging from
improved temperature regulation and more protein consumption
to more goal directed thought processes and more tendency
toward abstract representations of reality (see again Previc 1999).

FLUENCY IN CEREBRAL SPACE

In this light, let us then consider a provisional functional neuroanatomical mapping that seeks to represent the two basic aspects
of reading fluency. The "pure" reaction time aspect of fluency, in-

volving rapid and effortless response to familiar stimuli, may be associated with more ventral systems and considered a consequence of learning within those systems. Many functional neuro-imaging investigators, including ourselves, are finding ventral posterior hypoactivity when subjects with dyslexia try to read. See Wood and Flowers (2000) for a review. The two most prominent areas appear to be area 37, at the ventrolateral temporo-occipital junction, and the lingual-fusiform gyri, on the ventromedial temporo-occipital surface. It should be noted that these areas respond to auditory as well as visual phonemic information, at least when stimulus target identification is required. Fast, automatized reaction times to stimuli are more or less classically associated with processing in these same areas. See Garrett et al. (2000), in which we point out that metabolic activation in this left area 37 region, in response to a letter versus non-letter detection task, is inversely correlated with accuracy of performance. This suggests that the fluency that accompanies accuracy and fast response time may then be signaled by reduced metabolic demand in this area, as though the tuning were finer and the cortical processing more efficient.

We are not yet in possession of converging evidence to implicate the dorsomedial processing stream involving the leg, foot, and lateral eye movement areas in our second type of fluency, that involving anticipatory fluency. That constitutes our major proposal for further empirical research, therefore. We predict that properly controlled studies of fluent reading should not only show changes in the ventral visual processing areas but also in the dorsomedial cortex, in areas that normally involve the integration of visual information with hand and foot activity. More particularly, we suggest that it is the anticipatory component of fluency that would particularly invoke the activity of these dorsomedial areas, since the cognitive operations of anticipatory fluency would require, or at least benefit from, the participation of those brain areas best specialized for the daily behaviors that involve traversing significant distances in space and maintaining goal directedness while doing so. Dys-fluent silent reading is often called "reading with the lips." In that context, we propose that fluent reading, whether silent or oral, may be termed "reading with the feet."

CLASSROOM IMPLICATIONS

The implications for remedial strategies are vast; we mention only two. First, instead of being an "add-on" only after phonemic awareness training has been accomplished, fluency training in many forms should precede and set the background for phonemic awareness training. In respect to response time fluency, we should expect that repetition, a lot more of it than we thought necessary, and a lot of it incidental as well as intentional, should be inherent in very early classroom teaching of pre-reading skills. To direct a six- year-old child's attention to individual phonemes would be an easier task if much phonemic repetition and "play" with phonemes had preceded the overt instructional attempts. Familiarity breeds fast reaction time fluency and would, in this proposal, be expected to facilitate "handling" of phonemes. In functional neuroanatomic terms, the cortex that must eventually learn to handle the phonemes as discrete items can be tuned or primed for that learning by prior familiarity, i.e., by reaction time fluency.

In the second place, however, phonemic awareness training in isolation is ecologically and neuroanatomically overly circumscribed if its only result is the simple ability to isolate phonemes. Our notion of anticipatory fluency suggests that goal directedness should be recovered in reading instruction and remediation, even to the simple extent of encouraging attention "ahead" in the text or series of words or letters. Here, too, this anticipatory aspect of fluency should precede explicit phonemic awareness training. It is not that phonemic awareness training should be delayed, however; it is rather that anticipatory training should be hastened. Walking, after all, precedes talking in development; so the analogy between walking and talking is available and can be invoked quite early, even at the beginning stages of explicit phonemic awareness training.

Readers at any stage of development can profitably be encouraged to notice and process the goal or direction of any speech or text, no matter how simple. What's coming next in this word, sentence, or discourse? Where is this speech or text going? What question is being answered? What sort of path is it leading us down? In the simplest form, these are the questions of blending, i.e., the question of what whole word is produced by these individual phonemes. We believe the question is even better stated dynamically: toward what word do these individual phonemes lead? Recursively, the same algorithm applies at successively larger scales, as follows. Toward what sentence do these words lead? Toward what meaning, or in answer to what question, do these sentences lead? Toward what insight or perspective, what "view," do these meanings lead? In brief, where are we going with this text?

Note that this emphasis on goal directedness is entirely different from saying that "reward" needs to be made more prominent. The point is not reward in itself, but the increasing cognitive satisfaction derived from continually updated viewpoints about where the activity is going next and what perspectives are thereby being gained. It is closely analogous to climbing a hill on a landscape; each series of steps gains a broader view.

We mention as an additional aside that goal oriented behavior is often socially facilitated and supported. In the classroom, therefore, group activities such as choral reading and recitation provide social support, invoking other-directedness in the sense of non-self directedness. They also provide externally objectified references about where the performance, whether reading or recitation, is going. Communal activity by definition "carries" individual activities in a common vessel, moving in a common direction, thereby assisting with goal orientation.

The classic, never to be surpassed, statement of the importance of anticipatory fluency in language and education, is due to the great American psychologist, William James, in his famous chapter on the stream of thought in volume one of his *Principles of Psychology*, originally published in 1890. Language, he said, may be analogized to what birds do. Sometimes, they perch on fence posts; just so, the "substantive" events of language, the nouns, verbs, adjectives, and adverbs have content on which the mind rests or reflects. Sometimes, however, birds fly; in such manner also do the "transitive" events of language, for example, the "if's" that let us know a "then" is coming, signal the anticipation and direction of meaning. They set thought in flight. Meaning is interesting, to be sure, just as the resting posture of a bird might be; but with birds, no one misses the greater fascination of the flight, and with language no one should miss the special quality of transitive states and other states that depict directionality more than content. These states are difficult to observe introspectively, because they are " . . . always on the wing, so to speak, and not to be glimpsed except in flight." James (1950) also derived the educational implication, "If to hold fast and observe the transitive parts of thought's stream be so hard, then the great blunder to which all schools are liable must be the failure to register them, and the undue emphasizing of the more substantive parts of the stream."

REFERENCES

Crow, T. J., and Arbuthnott, G. W. 1972. Function of catecholamine-containing neurones in mammalian central nervous system. *National New Biology* 238(86):245–6.
Denckla, M. B., and Rudel, R. G. 1974. Rapid automatized naming of pictured objects, colors, letters and numbers by normal children. *Cortex* 10:186–202.

Garrett, A. S., Flowers, D. L., Absher, J. R., Fahey, F. H., Gage, H. D., Keyes, J. W., Porrino, L. J., and Wood, F. B. 2000. Cortical activity related to accuracy of letter recognition. *NeuroImage* 11:111–23.

Grigorenko, E., Wood, F., Meyer, M., and Pauls, D. in press. Linkage studies suggest a possible locus for developmental dyslexia on chromosome 1. *American Journal of Medical Genetics (Neuropsychiatric Genetics)* 105.

James, W. 1950. The Principles of Psychology, Volume I. Dover Publications, Inc. Previc, F. H. 1999. Dopamine and the origins of human intelligence. *Brain & Cognition* 41(3):299–350.

von Economo, C. 1929. *The Cytoarchitectonic of the Human Cerebral Cortex.* Oxford University Press: London.

Wood, F. B., and Flowers, D. L. 2000. Dyslexia: Conceptual issues and psychiatric comorbidity. In *Functional Neuroimaging in Child Psychiatry*, eds. J. Rumsey and M. Ernst. Cambridge University Press: Cambridge, United Kingdom.

Wolf, M. 1991. Naming speed and reading: the contribution of the cognitive neurosciences. *Reading Research Quarterly* 26:123–40.

Wolf, M., and Bowers, P. 1999. The double deficit hypothesis for the developmental dyslexias. *Journal of Educational Psychology.*(?)

Chapter • **12**

The Determinants of Reading Fluency:
A Comparison of Dyslexic and Average Readers

Zvia Breznitz

The new working definition of dyslexia has suggested that "dyslexia is evident when accurate and fluent word reading and/or spelling develops very incompletely or with great difficulty" (British Psychological Society 1999, p.18).

For years, the study of dyslexia has mainly focused on word reading accuracy, and a phonological core deficit was held as the primary source of inaccuracy in word reading in individuals with dyslexia (see Liberman and Shankweiler 1991 for a review). As such, reading fluency was presented as an outcome of the effectiveness of phonological processing (Lyon and Moats 1997). However, recent reading intervention research demonstrates that direct intensive intervention in phonemic awareness improves decoding and word identification in poor readers, but yields only minimal gains in reading fluency (see Lyon and Moats 1997; Meyer and Felton 1999 for a review).

In different studies, it was suggested that reading rate and accuracy are both components of reading fluency (Torgesen et al. 2000; Kame'enui 2000). Researchers generally agree about the role that reading accuracy plays in fluent reading. Reading rate has been viewed in several ways. One perspective conceives of word reading rate as a dependent variable, an outcome of the effectiveness of the reading skills (Carver 1990; Gough and Tunmer 1986). According to this position, effective decoding accuracy and comprehension influences word reading rate and enhances fluency in word reading (Gough and Tunmer 1986). An alternative view, nonexclusive of the former, holds that word reading rate can function as an independent variable and influence the quality of reading skills. (Breznitz 1987a; see Breznitz 1990 for a review). By controlling and manipulating reading rate in a series of experiments, the role of reading rate as an independent factor in reading has been extensively studied and documented.

READING RATE AS AN INDEPENDENT FACTOR

In a systematic research project carried out among a wide age range of readers from second graders to college students, the effect of different reading rates on decoding accuracy and comprehension was measured. The experiments were carried out in both Hebrew and English, among normal and dyslexic readers. In each experiment the reading rate for each subject was individually controlled and manipulated using a computer-based program (Breznitz 1987a, 1987b, 1988, 1990a, 1990b, 1991, 1993,1997a, 1997b; Barnea and Breznitz 1998; Breznitz, DeMarco, and Hakerem 1993; Breznitz et al. 1994; Breznitz and Share 1992; Liken 2000). In the first set of experiments there were four reading rate conditions that each contained parallel forms of reading items presented to the subjects by computer (Breznitz 1987a, 1987b, 1988, 1990; Breznitz and Share 1992). Each block contained 12 short reading items matched for length, word frequency, and comprehension complexity. Each item contained one paragraph composed of two or three sentences followed by comprehension questions. In all conditions reading time, decoding errors, and comprehension were measured.

In the first condition (baseline: self-paced1) all subjects read aloud the test items at their own self-paced reading rate. Data indicated that regardless of accuracy, comprehension scores, reading level, and age, self-paced reading rate was not stable and varied even when reading equivalent reading items. The variance rates of each subject observed during the self-paced reading rate condition served as the basis for the subsequent reading rate manipulations. In the second reading rate condition (fast-paced) the subjects read a set of additional items matched in length and complexity to the baseline test, but were prompted to accelerate their reading rate in accordance with the average of the highest reading rates each exhibited in the self-paced baseline test. In the third condition (slow-paced) the subjects read a set of additional items and were prompted to decelerate their reading rate in accordance with the average of the lowest reading rates each exhibited in the self-paced baseline test. In the fourth condition (self-paced2) all subjects again read a series of items at their own self-paced reading rate. All the analyses reported here were based only on the items that were correctly comprehended.

Results indicated that subjects in each of the different experimental groups were able to read faster than they normally do and to maintain this rate during the experimental manipulation. When prompted to read at the fastest rate achieved during self-paced reading, decoding errors decreased and comprehension increased as compared to the baseline condition (see Breznitz 1993 for a review; Breznitz 1997a). Slowing the reading rate below the self-paced rate increased decoding accuracy but decreased comprehension (Breznitz 1987a). No significant differences were found between the two self-paced reading rate conditions in reading time, errors, or comprehension. These results demonstrated that young and adult normal readers and readers with dyslexia can read faster than their self-paced reading rate and that reading at a speeded rate can increase accuracy and comprehension. However, individuals do not routinely accelerate their own reading pace, as indicated by the similar results in reading time, number of errors, and comprehension score in both the initial and subsequent self-paced tests (self-paced1 and self-paced2). At least on the basis of a one-time experimental acceleration manipulation, there was not a self-learning transfer from the acceleration process (see Breznitz and Share 1992).

THE ACCELERATION PHENOMENON

The observed decrease in decoding errors and concomitant increase in comprehension with speeded reading has been referred to as "the acceleration phenomenon" (see Breznitz 1993 for a review). The benefits from the acceleration phenomenon have been found to be particularly strong among readers with dyslexia (Breznitz 1997a, b). We suggested previously that there might be a "reading rate discrepancy" between the ability and actual performance of each reader (see Breznitz 1997a). It is conceivable that the gain from the acceleration manipulation is based on this discrepancy. It is not clear, however, why readers do not usually read at a rate consistent with their potential ability, especially when reading performance is more effective at this rate. Based on the potential effect of reading rate on effective reading, it is important to study the underlying contributors to reading rate.

THE UNDERLYING FACTORS OF READING RATE

An in-depth investigation was designed to verify the underlying factors operating in reading rate. As a first step, an additional research project was designed to clarify the basic factors that affect self-paced, slower, and fast reading rates. Using behavioral measures such as reaction time and performance accuracy, a comprehensive line of research has demonstrated that as opposed to self-paced routine reading rate and slower reading rate, the fast-paced reading rate influences the efficiency of various cognitive processes and enhances reading performance. The acceleration manipulation extends attention span and reduces distractibility in reading (Breznitz 1988). It also helps overcome some of the limitations of short-term memory and enhances processing in working memory (Breznitz and Share 1992; Breznitz 1997b), increases word retrieval from the mental lexicon (Breznitz 1987a, 1990), and aids children with dyslexia in partially surmounting their phonological deficits (Breznitz 1997a). In addition, this process has enhanced speech prosody by shortcutting the "bad pauses" and increasing the rate of vocalization between segments of words (Breznitz 1990).

The positive effect of a fast-paced reading rate on cognitive processing and reading skills brought about a further set of experiments designed to verify the origins of reading rate (Barnea and Breznitz 1998; Breznitz in press a, b). The assumption was that word reading is based on word decoding and word identification skills. These processes are based on the lower-level processing of information in the visual and the auditory modalities and on higher-level processing that requires operation of the orthographic and the phonological systems. Here we assumed that reading rate is based on the speed at which each of the above components processes information and on the speed at which the information is transferred between the components. Rapid processing in the different components would increase reading rate and enhance reading effectiveness. Slow processing in one or more of the components would decrease reading rate and impair the entire reading process. Based on those assumptions it is conceivable that the word reading deficits of readers with dyslexia can also be conceptualized as an outcome of slow processing speed in the various components that are activated in reading. This issue needs to be clarified.

SPEED OF PROCESSING AMONG READERS WITH DYSLEXIA

A variety of studies have indicated that people with dyslexia exhibit slower reaction time in performing verbal and nonverbal tasks than normal readers (e.g., Boden and Brodeur 1999; Breznitz in press; Chase 1996; Kail 1986, 1991). Empirical findings indicate that readers with dyslexia are characterized by slow working memory processes (Breznitz 1997b; Breznitz and Share 1992), slow word retrieval and access to the internal lexicon (Breznitz 1987a; Bowers and Wolf 1993; Flowers 1995; Nicolson and Fawcett 1994; Wimmer et al. 1998), slow naming-speed (e.g., Wolf 1991; Bowers and Wolf 1993;), reduced cross-modality integration rates (e.g., Nicolson and Fawcett 1993a; Tzeng and Wang 1984; Yap and Van der Leij 1993; Rose et al. 1999), slowed temporal processing (e.g., Tallal et al. 1993; McAnally and Stein 1996), and slowed motor responses (e.g., Wolff 1993, in press). There is a common agreement that readers with dyslexia exhibit difficulties when processing high-level linguistic information, particularly in the phonological system (see Snowling 1995 for a review). In general, readers with dyslexia have been found to be slower than age-matched normal controls in processing phonological tasks (Breznitz 1997a). Recent work suggests that orthographic processing deficits may also be implicated (Barker, Torgesen, and Wagner 1992; Cunningham and Stanovich 1990; Stanovich and West 1989; Zecker 1991). Young readers with dyslexia have been found to process orthographic information slower than age-matched controls (Breznitz in press, a). However, researchers do not all agree as to whether dyslexics' difficulties in word reading also stem from lower-level deficits. Although some studies fail to find differences between people with dyslexia and normal readers in processing lower level visual and auditory information (e.g., Joniss et al. 1999; Aaron 1993; Velluntino 1987), other studies suggest that subjects with dyslexia are slower than control subjects when processing lower-level information in both the auditory and visual modalities.

The Auditory Domain

In experiments using behavioral reaction time measures, readers with dyslexia have been found to be slower than normal readers in performing various lower-level linguistic and nonlinguistic auditory tasks. In general this slowness was observed when the task required processing of two or more stimuli in sequence. When stimuli were presented rapidly, subjects with dyslexia exhibited longer choice reaction times to pure tones (De Weirdt 1988; McAnally and Stein 1996) and to frequency modulated tones (Stein and McAnally 1995; Talcott et al. 1999). They were also significantly slower in tonal-pattern discrimination (Pinheiro 1977; Tallal 1980; Watson and Miller 1988, 1993), gap detection

(Ludlow et al. 1983), auditory fusion (McCroskey and Kidder 1980; Farmer and Klein 1993), auditory rhythm discrimination (Seashore et al. 1960), and temporal processing of speech segments (Tallal, 1980; Tallal, Miller, and Fitch 1993; Tallal and Stark 1982; McCroskey and Kidder 1980; Reed 1989; Farmer and Klein 1993).

The Visual Domain

A number of researchers maintain that specific low-level visual-perceptual dysfunctions are significantly involved in the etiology of dyslexia (Hill and Lovegrove 1993; Goolkasain and King 1990; Kroening, Kosslyn, and Wolff 1991; Solman and May 1990; Stein 1991). Dyslexic readers' performance has been observed to be significantly inferior to that of normal readers on tasks involving rapid as opposed to static visual information displays. These differences have been observed on measures including visual persistence tests, flicker sensitivity, temporal order judgment, and metacontrast (Galaburda and Livingstone 1993; and reviews by Lovegrove, Martin, and Slaghuis 1986; Williams and LeCluyse 1990; Lovegrove and Williams 1993). Subjects with reading disability were also found to show prolonged temporal visual integration and longer visual persistence (DiLollo, Hansen, and McIntyre 1983; Mazer et al. 1983; Bjaalid, Hoien, and Lundberg 1993). In addition, data has indicated that subjects with dyslexia were slower than control subjects when discriminating the visual features of letters (Willows, Kruk, and Corcos 1993; Di Lollo, Hansen, and McIntyre 1983). Some of the problems people with dyslexia have with visual temporal processing apparently persist even into adulthood (Hayduk, Bruck, and Cavanagh 1993).

The Question

The above data has shown that subjects with dyslexia exhibit slowness in processing information in the primary sensory modalities and at more high-level stages of cognitive processing. It has also been established that subjects with dyslexia are slow in word reading, suggesting that there might be a connection between those factors. If indeed an association between speed of processing of the sensory modalities, the linguistic systems, and word-reading rate exists, it is not yet clear how and in which direction those components are connected and how they affect word reading fluency. These issues will need to be clarified.

As a first step to resolve those issues, more in-depth data was needed from normal readers and subjects with dyslexia concerning the speed at which the reading related modalities and systems process information. Word reading is clearly based on processing information in more than one channel, and any activation that relies on more than one process must take into consideration the manner and the speed at which each channel can process information. Thus it is vital to determine whether the speed of processing of the visual and auditory modalities and the orthographic and phonological systems is different. If speed of processing of the various components is indeed different, there are several questions that can be asked: first, how these processing differences affect (or relate to) word-reading rate; second, how they affect word reading fluency; and third, whether the pattern of speed of processing of the modalities and the systems is similar for subjects with dyslexia and normal readers.

Word reading is an information processing activity characterized by speed and accuracy of performance. Speed of information processing is essentially the time that passes from the moment the external stimulus is presented to the subject's modalities until he or she responds to this stimulus. During this time the information moves through several stages of activation: input, central processing, and output (Atkinson and Shiffrin 1971). In the input stage, the information is received on a perceptual level through all the senses. In the central processing stage, a manipulation of some sort is carried out on the incoming information. Short-term memory (STM) and working memory (WM) systems are activated, followed by comparison of the incoming information with the existing representations in long-term memory (LTM) (Swanson 1987). The final (output) stage is involved in motoric activation. This stage is regarded as a response to the first two stages. Due to the fact that each stage activates a different level of processing and involves different skills, it is important to determine the manner and speed at which each stage processes information and its relationships to word reading rate. It is conceivable that subjects with dyslexia differ from normal readers in these functions.

Methodological Considerations

Current research on word reading rate focuses almost exclusively on data obtained from behavioral measures, namely, behavioral reaction time and response accuracy. These measures provide information about the cognitive processes at the conclusion of the processing sequence, which includes completion of sensory, cognitive, and motor processes (Bentin 1989). As such, these types of behavioral output measures cannot specify all the covert component operations that contribute to a particular cognitive process, nor can they determine the relative processing times required by individual stages. Furthermore, they cannot determine which processes occur serially, in parallel, or overlap in time (Brandeis and Lehmann 1994; Johnson 1995). For this reason it is difficult to determine the extent to which dysfunction or slowness at early stages of processing contributes to reading fluency deficits on the basis of behavioral measures.

Online Evaluation of Processing Speed

In an attempt to track online information about cognitive activity, various studies have employed the event related potential (ERP) technique in addition to measurement of behavioral responses. Event related potential methodology is based on electroencephalographic (EEG) data. It provides real-time imaging of the neural system's responses to sensory stimulation (Bentin 1989) and so allows us to track the timing of perceptual and cognitive activity online during word recognition. Event related potentials are extracted from raw EEG data by averaging the neural responses to a number of equivalent trials in a given experiment. This process is believed to result in all non-stimulus-related random activity averaging to zero, so that what remains is a waveform that shows effects due to the stimulus of interest. Event related potentials consist of various discrete components, or brain waves, that can be related to different stages of information processing. These components are usually designated by their polarity (P, N) and by the latency of their maximal amplitudes in milliseconds. Areas of brain specialization can be identified by observing variations of amplitude and latency in ERP components across different scalp locations (see Halgren 1990). Event related potential components reflect the time course of sensory and cognitive processes with millisecond (ms) resolution that cannot be directly inferred from behavior. Nevertheless, the data obtained from behavioral and electrophysiological measures are complementary, as each provides information about the same cognitive activity.

Event Related Potentials and Reading

Previous work has shown that ERP measurement has useful applications in reading research. Event related potential components can indicate the point at which some variable has its effect on information processing in general, and on linguistic processing in particular. Since the main interest of the present work is speed of processing of information, this paper will focus mainly on the latencies of the ERP components. The components that are most relevant to the present work are the N100-P200 complex and the P300 family of components. The N100 is a negative component evoked at about 100 ms. after stimulus onset (Hyde 1997). The N100 is assumed to reflect an exogenous response that relates to sensory activity elicited by the stimuli (Johnstone et al. 1996). In addition it is thought to index attention to the stimuli (Novak Ritter, and Vaughan 1992; Leppanen and Lyytinen 1997). The P200 is a positive component evoked at about 200 ms. It is thought to reflect both exogenous and endogenous processes (Dunn et al. 1998). The P200 has been reported in relation to feature detection (e.g., Luck and Hillyard 1994), selective attention (e.g., Hackely and Valle-Inclon 1998), and working memory function (e.g., Smith 1993). The P300 is a positive endogenous component that appears between 280 and 600 ms. after the onset of the stimulus. Various researchers have suggested that the P300 reflects the central activation of information processing (e.g., Palmer, Nasman, and Wilcox 1994). Others have suggested that the P300 reflects updating in working memory (e.g., Israel et al. 1980; Pratt in press), cognitive resource allocation (Kramer, Strayer, and Buckley 1991), and mental effort (e.g., Wilson, Swain, and Ullsperger 1998). P300 latency is believed to reflect higher-order cognitive processing such as stimulus evaluation and categorization (Polich 1987; Polich and Heine 1996). Consequently it has been suggested that P300 latency can serve as a temporal measure of neural activity underlying the speed of attention, resource allocation, and immediate memory operation (Cohen and Polich 1997; Polich and Heine 1996).

Evidence from Dyslexic Subjects

There are not many studies that have employed ERP measures for studying dyslexia. However, those that have been done provide some insight into the modalities and systems activated in reading. Several of these studies have evaluated latency differences between components produced by subjects with dyslexia and controls, but even these studies did not report them directly in relationship to speed of processing variations between the modalities or systems which might affect reading performance.

Data in the auditory-phonological domain indicates that, subjects with dyslexia exhibit later N140 (Neville et al. 1993), P200 (Taylor and Keenan 1990), and P300 (Fawcett et al. 1993) components than controls during auditory recognition tasks requiring the subjects to distinguish between two tones (1000 HZ as compared to 2000 HZ), to distinguish between two phonemes (see also Erez and Pratt 1993; Breznitz in press), or to perform several rhyming tasks at different levels of complexity (Taylor and Keenan 1990, 1999). A number of studies that used ERP measures to study visual-orthographic processing among subjects with dyslexia have reported evidence of delayed onsets of N100s and P200s among dyslexic as compared to normal readers during the processing of lower-level nonlinguistic visual stimuli (Brandeis, Vitallo, and Steinhausen 1994; Breznitz and Meyler accepted; Cohen and Bresline 1984; Harter, Deiring, and Wood 1988; Harter et al. 1988). Subjects with dyslexia also exhibited longer N200 (Taylor and Keenan 1990) and N230 (Neville et al. 1993) latencies when required to distinguish between letters and symbols presented visually. Data has also been obtained indicating that readers with dyslexia exhibit longer P300 latencies during simple, lower-level, visual linguistic tasks, i.e., grapheme identification (Johannes et al. 1994; Holcomb, Ackerman, and Dykman 1985, 1986; Breznitz in press; Harter et al. 1988, 1989).

Theoretical Considerations

As previously mentioned, it is not clear from the available data what the actual processing speed of each modality (auditory and visual) and system (phonological and orthographic) is during the processing of linguistic information, to what extent their speeds of processing differ, and to what extent subjects with dyslexia differ from normal readers in those domains. Based on the physiological and cognitive characteristics of the modalities and systems that are activated in word reading, it can be assumed that each is processing information in a different manner and speed.

At the lower level, the visual modality provides information about the visual patterns of words or parts of words. It begins by perceiving the written symbol through the visual route. Data has indicated that incoming nonlinguistic visual information reaches the visual cortex after about 70 ms. (Schmolesky et al. 1998). The auditory modality is the speech-based route and provides phonemic information about printed symbols through the articulatory loop (Baddeley 1986). Nonlinguistic auditory information arrives in the auditory cortex at about 30 ms. following stimulus onset (Heil et al. 1999). These data show that the visual-perceptual processing of symbols begins more slowly than auditory processing. Whether the same applies for lower-level linguistic information is not yet clear.

There is reason to believe that information at the level of words is processed in a different manner from nonlinguistic information. Evidence suggests that phonological processing is sequential (Rosenzweig, Leiman, and Breedlove 1996), whereas orthographic information processing is achieved in a more holistic manner (e.g., Willows, Kruk, and Corcos 1993). These results suggest that at the higher level, orthographic processing may be faster than phonological processing (Breznitz 1997a; Barnea and Breznitz 1998). Theoretically, the above arguments support the notion that during normal reading each modality and system is processing information at a different pace. Whether this argument is correct and whether similar patterns can be seen among readers with dyslexia is a separate question.

SPEED OF PROCESSING OF THE MODALITIES AND THE SYSTEMS

Evidence from Normal and Dyslexic Readers

An additional comprehensive research project was designed in an attempt to study the speed of processing of various stages of activation in the visual and auditory modalities and the orthographic and phonological systems, and their relationships to fluency in reading among normal and dyslexic readers. In these experiments, both behavioral and electrophysiological measures were used. In all the experiments, a choice reaction time procedure was used. Because word reading rate is the focus of the present chapter, the data reported here will refer to speed of processing of linguistic information at the level of words and the components that compose words (i.e., subwords: graphemes and phonemes) and pseudo-words.[1]

Method

Subjects In previous studies, data pointed to developmental differences in speed of processing (see Kail and Salthouse 1994). In order to overcome this issue, 36 adult subjects with dyslexia and 36 age-matched control university students (mean age = 24.3, s.d. 0.9) were recruited to participate in the current experiments. The decision to study speed of processing among the adult population was based on additional assumptions that inter-individual variance in

---

[1]For information on speed of processing of lower level nonlinguistic processing and higher level contextual processing see Breznitz in press; Liken and Breznitz 1999; Breznitz and Liken 2000.

reading-related cognitive abilities among this population would be reduced due to cognitive and reading skills stabilization. Furthermore, the reading deficits of adult subjects with dyslexia are presumably not due to insufficient reading experience or lack of exposure to print. Consequently, determination of the physiological and cognitive factors involved in speed of processing is facilitated.

Experimental Procedure

Basic Test Measures   All subjects were given a behavioral test battery, which included a wide range of reading and cognitive measures. The reading measures included reading time and decoding accuracy of phonemes, grapheme identification tasks, words/pseudo-words reading, reading in context, comprehension, and phonological and orthographic processing. The cognitive tests included attention span, short-term memory, working memory, speed of processing, rapid automatized naming (RAN) , rapid alternating stimulus (RAS), and verbal fluency measures.

Experimental Measures   Speed of processing of nonlinguistic and linguistic lower level and higher level information within and across each modality and system was studied. The speeds of processing measured were based on ERP latencies and behavioral reaction times, and were tested by manipulating the level of the complexity of the experimental tasks. In this chapter, we will focus on two data sets from this project that evaluated stimuli in the linguistic domain.

The first set includes lower level processing in the visual and auditory modalities. Speed of processing of the visual modality was evaluated in a task that required subjects to distinguish between different graphemes. Speed of processing of the auditory modality was studied in a task where subjects were required to distinguish between different phonemes. These visual and auditory experiments were identical in terms of stimulus exposure and ISIs (inter-stimulus intervals).

The second set of data presents analyses based on higher level processing in the orthographic and the phonological systems.[2] A lexical decision task was used to study the speed of processing of higher-level phonological and orthographic systems. The words (orthographic processing) and the pseudo-words (phonological processing) for this experiment were identical in length, exposure

---

[2]For additional data see Barnea and Breznitz 1998; Breznitz in press a, b; Liken and Breznitz 1999; Breznitz and Liken 2000; Liken in press.

time, and ISI. Speed of processing in all of the experiments was measured by behavioral reaction time and ERP latencies.

EVENT RELATED POTENTIAL AND REACTION TIME LATENCIES ANALYSIS

For all of the experimental tasks, two pronounced ERP components were identified in the two groups of subjects: an early P200 component, which is believed to be related to perception, discrimination, and evaluation of the input information, and a later P300 component, which is considered to represent higher cognitive processing at the level of memory (i.e., Halgren 1990). In addition, behavioral reaction time and accuracy data were included in each experiment to measure the output stages of activation.

Because across tasks the most prominent waveforms occurred at electrode Cz, the means and standard deviations (s.d.) of the ERP latencies in each experiment were referenced to the Cz electrode. It is important to note that the location of the CZ electrode (at the vertex of the brain) gives it a specific role in information processing.

Results

Behavioral Reaction Time and Accuracy   Significant differences between the two groups of subjects were obtained in accuracy and reaction time in most of the subtests of the basic test battery (see table 1). The subjects with dyslexia were slower and less accurate as compared to the normal controls. In the experimental tasks significant differences between the two groups were also obtained in accuracy for higher level processing (words/pseudo-words task) and in reaction time for both the lower and the higher level tasks (see table 2). The subjects with dyslexia were less accurate and slower than the controls. In the lower level processing tasks, accuracy for both groups was almost perfect.

Event Related Potential Results

Between Modalities and Systems Speed of Processing Comparisons
Among all adult readers (subjects with dyslexia and controls) the visual modality was found to process lower-level linguistic information at a slower speed than the auditory one (see table 3). In contrast the phonological system was found to process higher-level linguistic information slower than the orthographic one. This slowness appeared in delayed P200 and P300 ERP latencies

Table 1. Behavioral baseline Measures.

Tasks	Dyslexics N = 36		Controls N = 36		F
	Mean	SD	Mean	SD	
Raven	45.7	5.6	45.9	3.6	1.2
Oral comprehension (out of 6)	3.9	0.9	5.1	0.5	4.7**
Silent comprehension(out of 6)	4.5	0.8	5.9	0.3	4.9**
Oral reading time (in sec)	166	3.6	71	1.0	5.8**
Silent reading time (in sec)	127	4.6	67	0.8	5.3**
Oral reading errors	19.4	3.3	3.7	1.4	6.3**
Phonological accuracy (out of 50)	38.1	3.4	44.1	1.1	0.5
Phonological processing time (in sec)	110	2.9	76.3	0.9	4.2**
Orthographic accuracy (out of 50)	39.8	2.8	45.5	0.8	0.7
Orthographic processing time (in sec)	96	3.5	52	1.3	5.3**
Total word production fluency	14.3	2.9	19.0	1.7	4.0**
WAIS Digit Symbols	8.2	2.5	10.7	1.9	3.6**
WISC-R Symbol Search	30.4	4.5	35.6	2.1	3.1**
Digit naming, time (RAN)	25.0	17.1	18.2	3.3	2.9*
Letters naming time (RAN)	28.0	13.1	20.0	4.8	2.7**
Object naming, time (RAN)	47.7	15.1	35.9	5.1	3.2**
Colors naming, time (RAN)	34.7	14.1	25.6	3.8	3.1**
RAS naming Time	51.2	16.1	39.3	3.8	3.5**
D2 CPT test accuracy (of 40)	27.7	11.4	36.5	5.1	4.0**
Word reading accuracy (out of 50)					
Word reading time					
Pseudo-words reading accuracy					
Pseudo-words reading time					

$p > .05$* $p > .01$** $p > .001$***

and longer reaction times (see table 3). The above findings provide evidence that among normal readers as well as among subjects with dyslexia, each modality and system that is activated in word reading processes information at a different speed.

Between Groups Comparisons   The subjects with dyslexia were consistently slower than the controls at all stages of activation. They exhibited significantly delayed P200 and P300 latencies and longer

Table 2. Experimental Measures: Reaction Time (in Seconds) and Accuracy

Test	Dyslexic		Control		
Auditory linguistic, correct(of 20)	18.7	3.5	19.4	1.3	n.s.
Auditory linguistic, time	500.3	66.7	411.3	39.5	11.9***
Visual linguistic, correct (of 20)	16.5.	2.2	17.1	2.8	n.s
Visual linguistic, time	563.4	74.4	455.5	53.1	5.1*
Pseudo-words, correct (of 40)	28.1	2.2	37.1	1.8	5.0*
Pseudo-words, time	2264.6	409.9	1703.9	269.6	15.4***
Words, correct (of 40)	33.5	2.8	39.9	3.1	6.2**
Words, time	1566.7	203.8	1299.0	102.9	7.8**

$p > .05*$ $p > .01*$ $p > .001***$

Table 3. ERP latencies for Cz electrode and time gap scores between (visual-auditory) and (phonological-orthographic) processing.

Task	Dyslexic		Control	
	X	SD	X	SD
Auditory P200	216	25.1	173	11.5
Visual P200	247	27.0	198	14.6
P200 Gap Visual-Auditory	31	15.1	25	9.0
Auditory P300	367	59.6	321	24.7
Visual P300	403	44.1	353	31.2
P300 Gap Visual-Auditory	36	12.0	32	8.7
Words P200	196	33.1	156	23.0
Pseudo-words P200	298	47.6	177	28.3
P200 Gap Words-Pseudo-words	102	19.0	21	3.7
Words P300	434	33.4	367	36.8
Pseudo-words P300	524	58.9	416	22.6
P300 Gap Words-Pseudo-words	90	18.9	49	9.8

$p > .05*$ $p > .01**$ $p > .001***$

reaction times than the normal readers. The differences between the two groups appeared at the lower and higher levels of linguistic processing in the visual and auditory modalities (grapheme/phoneme identification) and in the orthographic and phonological systems (words/pseudo-words reading). The most pronounced speed-of-processing differences between the two groups appeared mainly in P200 latencies when processing phonological information (see table 3). In previous studies where young subjects with dyslexia and normal readers were employed, similar results were observed (see Breznitz in press).

Preliminary Conclusions

The visual and the auditory modalities and the orthographic and the phonological systems among both groups of subjects appear to operate on different time scales. This effect was reflected in the latencies of the ERP components and reaction times. Distinctions between the speed of activation must be based on the modality and the system that are activated specifically in the task, the stage at which the information is being processed, and the complexity of the task. In the normal course of reading among the adult population, lower level information in the visual modality at the perception stage (P200) is processed at a mean rate of about 200 ms. and information in the auditory modality is processed at about 170 ms. Information at the working memory stage (P300) in the visual modality is processed at a mean rate of 350 ms., and in the auditory modality it is processed at about 320 ms. Higher-level phonological information in the perception stage (P200) is being processed at a mean rate of about 180 ms., and higher level orthographic information is processed at a mean rate of about 150 ms. At the working memory (P300) stage, the phonological system is processing information at a mean rate of about 416 ms., and the orthographic one works at a mean rate of 360 ms. (see table 3).

Group comparisons indicated that the subjects with dyslexia were slower than normal readers in processing information in the modalities and the systems that are activated in word reading. This slowness appeared at all levels and stages of activation observed in this research. When processing lower level information in the modalities, the time gap between the subjects with dyslexia and the normal controls in P200 and P300 latencies did not exceed + 50 ms. At higher levels of processing in the phonological and the orthographic systems, the time gap between the two groups in speed of processing grew. The larger speed of processing differences between the two groups appeared at the perception stage (P200) in the pseudo-words task with a mean gap of 121ms.

Theoretical Issues

The data presented here raise a few important questions. First, because the modalities and systems required for word reading appear to work on different time scales, the speed at which information is being processed within the components and the transfer between components might be a keystone of reading rate and affect word reading fluency. Second, successful word reading requires integration between graphemes and phonemes. This process is based on making an exact match between the visual and the auditory representation of printed materials. The fact that each modality and system processes information at a different speed might suggest that for efficient word reading to take place, either the gap between the processing speed of the various components needs to be limited, or a certain degree of coordination and synchronization between the various components would need to take place. Failure at some level of this coordination process may underlie some of the reading deficits observed in subjects with dyslexia.

It has been suggested that efficient processing within and between the systems promotes the timing, coordination, and integration of information arriving from each system, thereby facilitating lexical access (see Bowers and Wolf 1993). Recent models of word recognition have emphasized the importance of the reciprocal transfer of information between the modalities and the systems for successful word recognition to occur (e.g., Harm Siedenberg 1999). It is conceivable that successful transfer of information between modalities and systems during word reading is an outcome of speed synchronization between the various components that are activated in word reading. Because of the limitations of the human information processing system, such as rapid decay and restricted capacity in short-term memory (i.e., Anderson 1994), synchronization can be achieved only if each modality and system at each stage of activation is processing information at an "appropriate speed." A wider gap between the speed of processing of the auditory and the visual modalities and/or between the orthographic and the phonological systems might interfere with synchronization between the different processes at different levels of activation. Based on this suggestion further analyses were conducted in an attempt to verify the gap differences in speed-of-processing between the modalities and between the systems among the two groups of subjects and to evaluate the effects of these processing gaps on word reading rate.

The "Gap Time Scores"

To evaluate these "gaps" between modalities and systems, several "gap time scores" were computed. These scores were based on the differences in processing time between the various components at the different stages of activation of the experimental tasks.

Analysis

Gap time scores were computed separately for P200 and P300 ERP latencies, calculated according to the peak amplitudes for P200 and P300 at the Cz electrode for each type of stimulus. Several scores were calculated for each measure. The first scores were based on lower-level linguistic skills: (1) auditory (phoneme discrimination) minus visual (grapheme discrimination). Separate scores compared P200 latency differences and P300 latency differences. The second set of scores were based on higher-level linguistic processing: (2) phonological (pseudo-word reading) minus orthographic (word reading). Again, one score was computed to compare P200 latencies and another compared P300 latencies.

Results

Results indicated significant gap time scores within each group of subjects between the modalities and between the systems. The gap scores appeared in each stage and level of processing (see table 3). Regardless of the level of processing (task and ERP latencies), the gap scores among the normal readers were steady and limited, ranging between 25 to 49 ms. However among the subjects with dyslexia, significant differences between the gap scores were obtained, with gap scores among the readers with dyslexia ranging between 31and 102 ms. As the results in table 3 indicate, the gap scores for subjects with dyslexia increased with the complexity of the tasks.

Although speed of processing all tasks at all stages was slower among the subjects with dyslexia than for the controls, no significant differences were found between the two groups of subjects in the speed of processing (SOP) gap scores for P200 and P300 latencies in the lower level visual minus the auditory tasks. Significant differences were found between the two groups in the SOP gap scores for the P200 and P300 in the phonological minus the orthographic tasks, with significantly larger gap scores among the readers with dyslexia. The most prominent differences between the two groups appeared in the P200 latency gap score of pseudowords minus words (see table 3).

Speed of Processing and Word Reading Rate

A central question of the present chapter is how speed of processing of the modalities and the systems and the time gaps between the processing speed of these components affect word reading rate and word reading fluency. Furthermore, it will be important to determine whether subjects with dyslexia and controls differ in these characteristics.

ANALYSIS

Bivariate correlation analyses were first conducted among all the variables investigated in order to determine whether it was possible to carry out stepwise multiple regressions for word reading rate prediction. The results revealed correlations (in the range of $r = .11$ to $r = .58$) between all the variables. In light of these results, stepwise multiple regressions analyses were conducted in an attempt to determine which of the independent variables best accounted for the word reading rate score computed for each subject based on the mean of reading time achieved in the baseline word reading test.

Results

The Subjects with Dyslexia   Three variables entered this equation in the following order: (1) the P200 latency in processing pseudo-words, ($R = .43$, $R^2 = .21$, $SE = .86$, $p < .001$), (2) P200 latency for words ($R = .53$, $R^2 =. 31$, $SE = .83$, $p < .001$), and (3) P200 time gap score of pseudo-words minus word ($R =. 62$, $R^2 =. 40$, $SE = .82$, $p < .001$).

The Normal Readers   Three variables entered into the regression equation in the following order: (1) P300 latency for pseudo-words, ($R = .27$ $R^2 = .5$, $SE = 2.0$, $p < .05$), (2) P300 latency for words ($R = .46$, $R^2 =. 29$, $SE = .3$, $p < .001$), and (3) performance time of the phonological baseline test ($R = .52$, $R^2 = .35.$, $SE = .1$, $p < .001$).

Group Comparisons   Among both groups of subjects, reading rate was best predicted by the speed of processing of the phonological system. Among the subjects with dyslexia, this variable explained 43% of the variance in reading rate, and among the controls, this variable accounted for 27% of the variance. Speed of processing of the orthographic system explained an additional 10% of the reading rate variance among the subjects with dyslexia and 19% among the controls. Reading rate of each group of subjects was best predicted by speed of processing at a different stage of brain activation. Among the readers with dyslexia the lower level processing (the P200 - possibly reflecting perception and stimuli evaluation) was found to be the best predictor of their word reading rate; among the controls higher cognitive processing (the P300— possibly reflecting working memory) was the best predictor of their word reading rate. Thus, our data suggest that the speed of processing of the phonological system, and to some degree the orthographic system, determines to a large extent word reading rate.

Conclusions

These results did not come as a surprise because much of the data point to phonological core deficits as the central problem of subjects with dyslexia word reading deficits (see Snowling 1999 for a review). However we suggest that one of the sources of these deficits is in the speed of processing of this system. Reading rate encompasses the speed at which each of the word reading components processes information, specifically with respect to word recognition skills (i.e., phonological and orthographic skills). Furthermore, based on our results, which indicate that at least at the word level the phonological system is slower than the orthographic one, it can be claimed that slower processing might act more to determine the reader's own self-paced word reading rate as compared to a fast processing rate. It is plausible that because the above results appeared to a large extent among the subjects with dyslexia, it is conceivable that this phenomenon is more pronounced among the impaired readers. This claim has some implications for intervention. However it is clear that this issue needs to be further investigated. Additionally, among the normal readers, word reading rate in each system is mostly determined by P300 latency, possibly reflecting the working memory stage. Among the subjects with dyslexia lower level processing speed of the systems, possibly at the perception and stimuli evaluation and discrimination (P200 latency) stage, determine the word reading rate.

Our data support the previous notion that indicates the importance of working memory in effective word reading (i.e., Swensone 1998). Based on the limitations of this system in processing information it is conceivable that in normal word reading activity, the speed at which the acoustic (phonological representation of the code) information is matched with the visual code is a causal factor in word reading rate. The fact that among the readers with dyslexia the speed of processing of the perception stage determined most of the word reading rate might point to the fact that among this population, word reading is not an automatic skill and relies constantly on perception and evaluation of the incoming information from the written materials. Support for this notion can be seen in an additional study (Breznitz and Gilore in preparation) which indicated that dyslexic readers do not have stable words patterned in their mental lexicon. At each encounter with the same word, they read it in a different way. Moreover these data also indicate that subjects with dyslexia do not have a stable pattern for mistakes. Even their mistakes are read each time in a different way. Such a process would serve to slow down the entire reading activity. As we suggested earlier, word reading rate is one of the key factors of word reading fluency and the question is to what extent speed of processing of the modalities and the systems affect word reading fluency.

THE RELATIONSHIPS BETWEEN WORD READING FLUENCY AND SPEED OF PROCESSING

By accepting the simple definition of fluency (Torgesen 2000) which suggests that fluent reading is composed of rate and accuracy, we computed a fluency score for each subject that was based on word reading rate and word reading accuracy in the word reading baseline test. In an attempt to represent the two fluency components as equally as possible in the computed score, it was important that the calculation of this score took under consideration the time per word correctly read and the total number of words each subject correctly read out of the total words he or she read in the entire test. The fluency score was computed as follows:

W + * 100 = word fluency score
W * Tw

where W + = the total test words correctly read
W = total words read in the test
Tw = time per word correctly read

In an attempt to determine which of the speed of processing measures best predicted word reading fluency among each group of subjects, stepwise multiple regression analyses were conducted. Among the readers with dyslexia two variables were entered into the regression equation in the following order: (1) P200 latency of the orthographic minus the phonological gap time score ($R = .49$, $R^2 = .23$, $SE = .46$, $p < .001$) and (2) P200 latency for pseudo-words, ($R = .64$, $R^2 =. 38$, $SE = .30$, $p < .001$). Among the normal readers, two variables were entered into the regression equation in the following order: (1) P300 latency of the orthographic minus the phonological gap time score ($R = .35$, $R^2 = .15$, $SE = 1.6$, $p < .001$) and (2) P300 latency of the phonological task ($R = .44$, $R^2 = .24$, $SE = .9$, $p < .001$).

Data indicated that the time gap score between the orthographic and the phonological systems predicted word reading fluency among both groups of subjects. Among the subjects with dyslexia, it explained 49% of the variance in this measure and among the controls, it accounted for only 35%. For both groups speed of processing of the phonological system was the second best predictor of word fluency. Among the subjects with dyslexia, it explained an additional 15% of word reading fluency and among the controls, it only explained an additional 9% of the variance.

How the "Time Gap" Affects Fluency

Based on the present results and Breznitz (in press) we suggest that these "time gaps" cause an asynchrony in speed-of-processing of the incoming information and therefore impair the effectiveness of word reading fluency. By definition asynchrony stems from a lack of coordination between the different components of the action to be processed. Thus, this "asynchrony phenomenon" can only exist if the following criteria are met: (1) more than one system and/or stage of cognitive operation is involved in the processing task, (2) there is a difference in the speed at which each component processes information, and (3) the SOP of various systems and components is not sufficiently coordinated to allow effective integration.

Word reading, by its nature, involves a number of processes. As our findings indicated, each is activated at a different speed and in a different manner. Word reading is an uncompromising process: exact correspondence and coordination between the various components are required. As our data indicated, the between modality asynchrony among adult subjects with dyslexia plays a crucial role in word reading fluency. The larger gap between the orthographic and phonological systems diminishes synchronization between the two and impairs fluency in word reading.

Moreover, as for reading rate, our data indicated that for each group of subjects word reading fluency was best predicted by a different speed of processing stage. Among the dyslexic readers the lower level processing (possibly at the perception and stimuli evaluation level, i.e., the P200) explained word fluency the best, whereas among the controls higher cognitive processing (possibly at the working memory stage, i.e., the P300) was the best predictor for word reading fluency.

The working memory system includes a visual scratch-pad, the phonological loop, and a critical central executive component (Baddely 1986) which may serve as a buffer zone. It is plausible that the synchronization between the incoming information from the visual-orthographic and the auditory-phonological routes occurs there. A buffer zone is crucial in the reading process, particularly since this activity relies on incoming information from two different channels that also operate on different time scales. In contrast, the perceptual system does not have a buffer zone. This fact might add extra difficulties for the subjects with dyslexia in synchronization of the incoming information in word reading.

Although our findings indicate that in general subjects with dyslexia are slower than the controls in reading and processing reading relevant information, no significant differences were found between the two groups of adult subjects in the gap time scores of the P200 or P300 in the grapheme and phoneme identification tasks. In a previous study (see Breznitz in press), young subjects with dyslexia were observed to exhibit the asynchrony phenomenon at all levels of processing, (Breznitz in press). Among adults with dyslexia, the between modality asynchrony occurs in the higher-level orthographic minus phonological processing condition (words minus pseudo-words). It is conceivable that the asynchrony phenomenon was found among adults with dyslexia only in higher-level processing tasks because the lower-level linguistic components (graphemes and phonemes) are limited in number. Thus over the years, adults with dyslexia have been exposed to the same alphabetic codes over and over and have stored them as patterns that they can retrieve in a better way when needed. They learn over the years to synchronize between the speed of processing of the visual and the auditory modalities at the lower level and manage to close the speed gap between the two modalities at that level to a point that will no longer impair the quality of processing and performance accuracy at this level. By contrast there are numerous words in one's language and the number of times that the reader meets the same word is limited. In addition, each time a subject with dyslexia encounters a word, there may be differences in the form, which they encode. Thus, compensation at the higher levels may be impossible.

Our data among the normal readers indicates that a "time gap" within the range of about 25 to 50 ms. might be considered as a natural time gap between channels. A gap within this framework of time does not seem to interfere with the efficiency of word reading fluency. Among the readers with dyslexia, the gap between the processing speeds of the various components is not limited and ranges between 30 to 100 ms. This wide range of time gaps affects the efficiency of word reading fluency. Based on these results it is conceivable that in order to overcome this "gap" limitation, a certain degree of speed coordination and synchronization between the various components would need to take place (see also Berninger this issue). As an outcome of our studies, we suggest that a higher degree of between channels synchronization can be achieved by using reading rate as a monitor of word reading fluency. As compared to decoding accuracy and comprehension, reading rate as a time measure spreads over a wide range of possibilities. As such, it can serve as a monitor for the entire reading

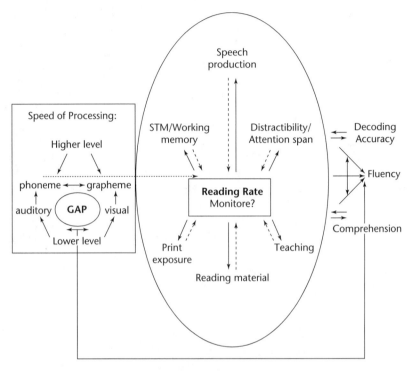

Figure 1.   Reading rate as a monitor of the reading process: flexible, ab-sorbent, sensitive, and objective

process. This "monitor" absorbs and affects the influence of lower- and higher-level physiological and cognitive processes in the modalities and the systems that are activated in reading; they enhance decoding accuracy and comprehension and bring about word reading fluency (see figure 1). The monitor can balance or regulate the input and be sensitive to SOP differences, slowing down or speeding up processes as needed. This monitor would serve to control processes flexibly to bring about reading fluency.

Our data indicated that there might be an acceptable "gap range" within which the monitor can operate. A wider time gap, however, would lead to impaired word-reading fluency. When such a result is observed there are two possible interpretations: (1) The monitor itself may be impaired or (2) the processing gaps of the relevant channels may be too disparate for any monitor to regulate. It is conceivable that beyond a certain time range external compensation strategies would need to be enlisted. We would like to suggest that one of the strategies that can be used in order to reduce the time gap between the processing routes and improve word reading fluency is to use the acceleration manipulation adapted to the reading rate of each individual subject.

There are likely gaps at other levels in the reading process that will also need to be accounted for, and future studies should address this possibility. This paper has demonstrated gaps between the visual and the auditory modalities and the orthographic and the phonological systems within a measure, but it is also possible that the various SOP measures that we have used may have different gaps in their activation patterns. For example, it would be important to determine if there is the same gap between the perception stage (P200) and working memory (P300) onset in normal readers and readers with dyslexia. Similarly, it is possible that the duration of the components (i.e., their "width") could also vary, perhaps indicating differences in the time devoted to each process. A hypothesis that is suggested by Berninger (this issue) concerning the central executive may then also need to monitor and account for these types of gaps. These within-modality gaps may tap into the various levels of activation occurring during reading. It can be argued that linguistic processing in reading activity includes several stages of verbal fluency: (1) At the lower level, fluency is based on accuracy and speed of grapheme phoneme recognition and production (subwords), (2) At the middle level, fluency is an outcome of accuracy, speed, and comprehension of single words, and (3) At the higher-level, fluency is an outcome of accuracy, speed, and comprehension of text.

It can be hypothesized that a monitoring system might also be responsible for regulating the level of activation while reading—switching between single letters, words, sentences, and a discourse level. Reading fluency relies on fluency at each of these levels. Accuracy and rate are important factors for the lowest levels of linguistic processing (i.e., grapheme and phoneme identification). At higher levels, however, comprehension processes will also be a factor. Most researchers up to now have discussed fluency in terms of higher level aspects, but it appears that mastery at each level of analysis will be important for reading acquisition and remediation of reading disabled individuals.

REFERENCES

Aaron, P. G. 1993. Is there a visual dyslexia? *Annals of Dyslexia* 43:110–24.
Ackerman, P. T., Arnhalt, J. M., and Dykman, R. A. 1986. Inferential word decoding weakness in RD children. *Learning Disability Quarterly* 9: 315–24.
Ackerman, P. T., Dykman, R. A., and Gardner, M. Y. 1990. Counting rate, naming rate, phonological sensitivity, and memory span: Major factors in severe dyslexia. *Journal of Learning Disabilities* 23:325–27.

Ackerman, P. T., Dykman, R. A., and Oglesby, D. M. 1994. Visual event-related potentials of dyslexic children to rhyming and nonrhyming stimuli. *Journal of Clinical and Experimental Neuropsychology* 16:138–54.

Adams, M. J. 1990. *Beginning to Read: Thinking and Learning about Print.* Cambridge, MA: MIT Press.

Anderson, J. R., Reder, L. M., and Lebiere, C. 1996. Working memory: Activation limitations on retrieval. *Cognitive Psychology* 30(3):221–56.

Atkinson, R. C., and Shiffrin, R. M. 1971. The control of short-term memory. *Scientific American* 225(2):82–90.

Baddely, A. 1986. Modularity, mass action, and memory. *Quarterly Journal of Experimental Psychology: Human Experimental Psychology* 38(4A): 527–33.

Barker, T. A., Torgesen, J. K., and Wagner, R. K. 1992. The role of orthographic processing skills on five different reading tasks. *Reading Research Quarterly* 27(4):334–5.

Barnea, A., and Breznitz, Z. 1998. Phonological and orthographic processing of Hebrew words: Electrophysiological aspects. *Journal of Genetic Psychology* 159:492–504.

Bentin, S. 1989. Electrophysiological studies of visual word perception, lexical organization, and semantic processing: A tutorial review. *Language and Speech* 32:205–20.

Bjaalid, I. K., Hoien, T., and Lunberg, I. 1993. Letter identification and lateral masking in Dyslexics and normal readers. *Scandinavian Journal of Educational Research* 37(2):151–61.

Boden, C., and Brodeur, D. A. 1999. Visual processing of verbal and non-verbal stimuli in adolescents with reading disabilities. *Journal of Learning Disabilities* 32(1):58–71.

Bowers, P. G., and Wolf, M. 1993. Theoretical links among naming speed, precise timing mechanisms and orthographic skill in dyslexia. *Reading and Writing* 5:69–85.

Brandeis, D., and Lehmann, D. 1994. ERP mapping: A tool for assessing language disorders. In *Cognitive Electrophysiology*, eds. H. J. Heinze, T. F. Mante, and G. R. Mangun. Boston: Birkhauser.

Brandeis, D., Vitacco, D., and Steinhausen, H. D. 1994. Mapping brain electric micro-states in dyslexic children during reading. *Acta Paedopsychiatrica* 56(3):239–47.

Breznitz, Z. 1987a. Increasing first-graders' reading accuracy and comprehension by accelerating their reading rates. *Journal of Educational Psychology* 79:236–42.

Breznitz, Z. 1987b. Reducing the gap in reading performance between Israeli lower- and middle-class first grade pupils. *Journal of Psychology* 121:491–501.

Breznitz, Z. 1988. Reading performance of first graders: The effects of pictorial distractors. *The Journal of Educational Research* 82:47–52.

Breznitz, Z. 1990. Vocalization and pauses in fast-paced reading. *Journal of General Psychology* 117:153–9.

Breznitz, Z. 1991. Anxiety and reading comprehension: A longitudinal study of Israeli pupils. *Reading Improvement* 28:89–96.

Breznitz, Z. 1997a. Enhancing the reading of dyslexics by reading acceleration and auditory masking. *Journal of Educational Psychology* 89:103–13.

Breznitz, Z. 1997b. The effect of accelerated reading rate on memory for text among dyslexic readers. *Journal of Educational Psychology* 89:287–99.

Breznitz, Z. (under revision). Speed of phonological and orthographic processing among adult dyslexic readers: Electrophysiological aspects. *Brain and Language.*

Breznitz, Z. (in press). The effect of reading rate accelerating on brain activity of adult dyslexic and normal readers: Electrophysiological evidence. *Educational Psychology Review.*

Breznitz, Z., DeMarco, T., and Hakerem, G. 1993. Topographic measures of cerebral activity during reading of text at fast-and-slow paced rates. *Brain Topography* 6(2):117–21.

Breznitz, Z., DeMarco, T., Shammi, P., and Hakerem, G. 1994. Self-paced versus fast-paced reading rates and their effect upon comprehension and event-related potentials. *The Journal of Genetic Psychology* 155:397–407.

Breznitz, Z., and Gilore (in preparation).

Breznitz, Z., and Meyler, A. (accepted). Lower-level auditory and visual processing among adult dyslexic readers: Electrophysiological evidence. *Brain and Language.*

Brexnitz, Z., and Share, D. L. 1992. The effect of accelerated reading rate on memory for text. *Journal of Educational Psychology* 84:193–200.

British Psychological Society 1999.

Carver, R. P. 1990. *Reading Rate: A Review of Research and Theory.* San Diego, CA: Academic Press.

Chase, C. H. 1996. A visual deficit model of developmental dyslexia. In *Developmental Dyslexia: Neural, Cognitive, and Genetic Mechanisms*, eds. C. H. Chase, G. D. Rosen, and G. F. Sherman. Baltimore, MD: York Press.

Ciesielski, K. J. 1989. Event related potentials in children with specific visual cognitive disability. *Neuropsychologia* 27:303–13.

Cohen, J., and Bresline, P. W. 1984. Visual evoked responses in dyslexic children. *Annals of the New York Academy of Sciences* 425:338–43.

Cohen, J., and Polich, J. 1997. On the number of trials needed for P300. *International Journal of Psychophysiology* 25(3):249–55.

Compton, D. L., and Carlislie, J. F. 1994. Speed of word recognition as a distinguishing characteristic of reading disabilities. *Educational Psychology Review* 6:115-40.

Cunningham, A. E., and Stanovich, K. E. 1990. Assessing print exposure and orthographic processing skill in children: A quick measure of reading experience. *Journal of Educational Psychology* 82:733–40.

DeWeirdt, W. 1988. Speech perception and frequency discrimination in good and poor readers. *Applied Psycholinguistics* 9(2):163–83.

Di Lollo, V., Hansen, D., and McIntyre, J. S. 1983. Initial stages of visual information processing in dyslexia. *Journal of Experimental Psychology: Human Perception and Performance* 9:923–35.

Dunn, B. R., Dunn, D. A., Linguis, M., and Andrews, D. 1998. The relation of ERP components to complex memory processing. *Brain and Cognition* 36(3):355–76.

Erez, A., and Pratt, H. 1992. Auditory event related potentials among dyslexic and normal reading children:3CLT and midline comparisons. *International Journal of Neuroscience* 63(3–4):247–64.

Farmer, M. E., and Klein, R. K. 1993. Auditory and visual temporal processing in dyslexic and normal readers. In Temporal information processing in the nervous system, eds. P. Tallal, A. M. Galaburda, R. R. Llinas, and C. von Euler. *Annals of the New York Academy of Sciences* 682:339–41.

Fawcett, A. J., Chattopadhyay, A. K., Kandler, R. H., Jarratt, J., Nicolson, R. I., and Proctor, M. 1993. Event-related potentials and dyslexia. In *Temporal Information Processing in the Nervous System: Special Reference to Dyslexia and Dysphasia*, eds. P. Tallal, A. M. Galaburda, R. R. Llinas, and C. von Euler. New York: New York Academy of Sciences.

Flowers, L. D. 1995. Neuropsychological profiles of persistent reading disability and reading improvement. In *Developmental and Acquired Dyslexia: Neuropsychological and Neurolinguistic Perspectives*, eds. C. K. Leong, and R. M. Joshi. Neuropsychology and Cognition 9. Norwell, MA: Kluwer Academic Publishers.

Galaburda, A., and Livingstone, M. 1993. Evidence for a magnocellular defect in developmental dyslexia. In *Temporal Information Processing in the Nervous System*, eds. P. Tallal, A. M. Galaburda, R. R. Llinas, and C. von Euler. Annals of the New York Academy of Sciences 682:70–82.

Goolkasian, P., and King, J. 1990. Letter identification and lateral masking in the dyslexic and average readers. *American Journal of Psychology* 103(4):519–38.

Gough, P., and Tunmer, W. 1986. Decoding and reading disability. *Remedial and Special Education* 7:6–10.

Griffiths, T. D., Rees, G., Rees, A., Green, G. G., R., Witton, C., Rowe, D., Buechel, C., Turner, R., and Frackowiak, R. S. J. 1998. Right parietal cortex is involved in the perception of sound movement in humans. *Nature Neuroscience* 1(1):74–79.

Hackley, S. A., and Valle-Inclan, F. 1998. Automatic alerting does not speed late motoric processes in a reaction-time task. *Nature* 391(6669): 786–8.

Halgren, E. 1990. Insights from evoked potentials into the neuropsychological mechanisms of reading. In *Neurobiology of Higher Cognitive Function*, eds. A. B. Scheibel and A. F. Wechsler. NY: Guilford Press.

Harm, M. W., and Seidenberg, M. S. 1999. Phonology, reading acquisition, and dyslexia: Insights from connectionist models. *Psychological Review* 106(3):491–528.

Harter, M. R., Anllo-Vento, L., Wood, F. B., and Schroeder, M. M. 1988. Separate brain potential characteristics in children with reading disability and attention deficit disorder: Color and letter-relevance effects. *Brain and Cognition* 7:115–40.

Harter, M. R., Deiring, S., and Wood, F. B. 1988. Separate brain potential characteristics in children with reading disability and attention deficit disorder: Relevance-independent effects. *Brain and Cognition* 7:54–86.

Harter, M. R., Miller, S. L., Price, N. J., and LaLonde, M. E. 1989. Neural processes involved in directing attention. *Journal of Cognitive Neuroscience* 1(3):223–7.

Hayduk, S., Bruck, M., and Cavanagh, P. 1993. Do adult dyslexics show low level visual processing deficits? In Temporal information processing in the nervous system, eds. P. Tallal, A. M. Galaburda, R. R. Llinas, and C. von Euler. *Annals of the New York Academy of Sciences* 682:351–3.

Heil, M., Rolke, B., Englekamp, J., Roesler, F., Oezcan, M., and Henninghausen, E. 1999. Event-related brain potentials during recognition of ordinary and bizarre action phrases following verbal and subject-performed encoding conditions. *European Journal of Cognitive Psychology* 11(2):261–80.

Hill, R., and Lovegrove, W. 1993. One word at a time: A solution to the visual deficit in the specific reading disabled? In *Facets of Dyslexia and its*

Remediation, eds. S. F. Wright, and R. Groner. North-Holland: Elsevier Science.

Holcomb, P. J., Ackerman, P. T., and Dykman, R. A. 1985. Cognitive event-related brain potentials in children with attention and reading deficits. *Psychophysiology* 22:656–67.

Hyde, M. 1997. The NI response and its applications. *Audiology and Neuro-otolology* 2(5):281–307.

Isreal, J. B., Wickins, C. D., Chesney, G. L., Donchin, E. 1980. The event-related brain potentials in children as an index of display-monitoring workload. *Human Factors* 22(2):211–24.

Johannes, S., Mangun, G. R., and Muente, T. F. 1994. Developmental dyslexia and cerebral lateralization: Electrophysiological findings. *Nervenarzt* 65(12):859–64.

Johnson, C. J. 1995. Effects of color on children's naming of pictures. *Perceptual and Motor Skills* 80:1091–1101.

Johnstone, S. T., and Barry, R. J., Anderson, J. W., and Coyle, S. F. 1996. Age-related changes in child and adolescent event-related potential component morphology, amplitude, and latency to standard and target stimuli in an auditory oddball task. *International Journal of Psychophysiology* 24(3):223–38.

Kail, R. 1986. Sources of age difference in speed of processing. *Child Development* 57(4):969–87.

Kail, R. 1991. Developmental changes in speed of processing during childhood and adolescence. *Psychological Bulletin* 109:490–501.

Kail, R.1992. Processing speed, speech rate, and memory. *Developmental Psychology* 28: 899–904.

Kail, R., and Salthouse, T. A. 1994. Processing speed as a mental capacity. *Acta Psychologica* 86:199–225.

Kramer, A. F., Strayer, D. L., and Buckley, J. 1991. Task versus component consistency in the development of automatic processing: A psychophysiological assessment. *Psychophysiology* 28(4):425–37.

Kroening, O., Kosslyn, S. M., and Wolff, P. 1991. Mental imagery and dyslexia: A deficit in processing multi-part visual objects? *Brain and Language* 41:381–94.

Leiken, M., and Breznitz, Z. 1999. Syntactic processing in Hebrew sentences: Electrophysiological aspects. *Genetic, Social, and General Psychology Monographs* 125(2):173–191.

Leppaenen, P. H. T., and Lyytinen, H. 1997. Auditory event-related potentials in the study of developmental language-related disorders. *Audiology and Neuro-Otology* 2(5):308–40.

Liberman, I. Y., and Shankweiler, D. 1991. Phonology and beginning reading: A tutorial. In *Learning to Read: Basic Research and its Implications*, eds. L. Rieben and C. A. perfetti. Hillsdale, NJ: Lawrence Erlbaum Associates, Inc.

Lovett, M. W. (1987). A developmental approach to reading disability: Accuracy and speed criteria of normal and deficient reading skill. *Child Development*, 58, 234–260.

Lovett, M. W. 1992. Developmental Dyslexia. In *Handbook of Neuropsychology*, eds. F. Boller and J. Grafman. Amsterdam: Elsevier.

Lovegrove, W., Martin, F., and Slaghuis, W. 1986. A theoretical and experimental case for a visual deficit in specific reading disability. *Cognitive Neuropsychology* 3:225–67.

Lovegrove, W., and Williams, M. C. 1993. Visual temporal processing deficits in specific reading disability. In *Visual Processes in Reading and Reading Disabilities*, eds. D. M. Willows, R. S. Kruk, and E. Corcos. Hillsdale, NJ: Lawrence Erlbaum.

Luck, S. J., and Hillyard, S. A. 1994. Electrophysiological correlates of features analysis during visual search. *Psychophysiology* 31(3):291–308.

Ludlow, C. L., Cudahy, E. A., Bassich, C., and Brown, G. L. 1983. Auditory processing skills of hyperactive, language-impaired, and reading-disabled boys. In *Central Auditory Processing Disorders*, eds. E. Z. Lasky, and J. Katz. Baltimore: University Park Press.

Lyon, G. R., and Moats, L. C. 1997. Critical conceptual and methodological considerations in reading intervention research. *Journal of Learning Disabilities* 30(6):578–88.

McAnally, K. I., and Stein, J. F. 1996. Auditory temporal coding in dyslexia. *Proceedings of the National Academy of Sciences: Biological Sciences* 263(1373):961–5.

McCroskey, R. L., and Kidder, H. C. 1980. Auditory fusion among learning disabled, reading disabled, and normal children. *Journal of Learning Disabilities* 13:18–25.

Mazer, S. R., McIntyre, Murray, Till, and Blackwell 1983. Visual persistence and information pick-up in learning disabled children. *Journal of Learning Disabilities* 16(4):221–5.

Meyer, M. S., and Felton, R. H. 1999. Repeated reading to enhance fluency: Old approaches and new directions. *Annals of Dyslexia* 49: 283–306.

Neville, H. J., Coffey, S. A., Holcomb, P. J., and Tallal, P. 1993. The neurobiology of sensory and language processing in language-impaired children. *Journal of Cognitive Neuroscience* 5: 235–53.

Nicolson, R. I., and Fawcett, A. J. 1993a. Toward the origin of dyslexia. In *Facets of Dyslexia and its Remediation*, eds. S. F. Wright and R. Groner. North-Holland: Elsevier Science.

Nicolson, R. I., and Fawcett, A. J. 1993b. Children with dyslexia classify pure tones slowly. In Temporal information processing in the nervous system, eds. P. Tallal, A. M. Galaburda, R. R. Llinas and C. von Eurler. *Annals of the New York Academy of Sciences* 682:387–89.

Nicolson, R. I., and Fawcett, A. J. 1994. Reaction times and dyslexia. Quarterly Journal of Experimental Psychology: *Human Experimental Psychology* 47A:29–48.

Nicolson, R. I., and Fawcett, A. J. 1995. Persistent deficits in motor skills of children with dyslexia. *Journal of Motor Behavior* 27:641–46.

Novak, G., Ritter, W., and Vaughan, H. G. 1992. Mismatch detection and the latency of temporal judgments. *Psychophysiology* 29(4):398–411.

Palmer, B., Nasman, V. T., and Wilson, G. F. 1994. Task decision difficulty: Effects on ERPs in a same-different letter classification task. *Biological Psychology* 38(2–3):199–214.

Perfetti, C. 1992. The representation problem in reading acquisition. In *Human Brain Electrophysiology*, eds. P. B. Gough and L. C.

Pinheiro, M. L. 1977. Tests of central auditory function in children with learning disabilities. In *Central Auditory Dysfunction*, ed. R. W. Keith. New York: Grune and Stratton.

Polich, J. 1987. Task difficulty, probability, and inter-stimulus interval as determinants of P300 from auditory stimuli. *Electroencephalography and Clinical Neurophysiology: Evoked Potentials* 68(4):311–20.

Polich, J., and Heine, M. R. D. 1996. P300 topography and modality effects from a single stimulus paradigm. *Psychophysiology* 33(6):747–52.

Pratt, H. (in press). Evoked potentials evidence on the mode of encoding in short-term memory. *The Educational Psychology Review.*

Reed, M. A. 1989. Speech perception and the discrimination of brief auditory cues in reading-disabled children. *Journal of Experimental Child Psychology* 48:270–92.

Regan, D. (1989). Amsterdam: Elsevier.

Rose, S. A., Feldman, J. F., Futterweit, L. R., and Jankowski, J. J. 1998. Continuity in tactual-visual cross modal transfer: Infancy to 11 years. *Developmental Psychology* 34(3):435–40.

Rosenzweig, M. R., Leiman, A. L., and Breedlove, S. M. 1996. *Biological Psychology.* Sunderland, MA: Sinauer Associates, Inc.

Schmolesky, M. T., Wang, Y., Hanes, D. P., Thompson, K. G., Lentgeb, S., Schall, J. P., and Leventhal, A. G. 1998. Signal timing across macaque visual system. *Journal of Neurophysiology* 79(6):3272–8.

Seashore, C. E., Lewis, D., et al. 1960. *Seashore Measures of Musical Talents Revised.* New York: Psychological Corporation.

Smith, M. E. 1993. Neurophysiological manifestations of recollective experience during recognition memory judgments. *Journal of Cognitive Neuroscience* 5(1):1–13.

Smith, M. E., and Halgren, E. 1989.Dissociation of recognition memory components following temporal lobe lesions. *Journal of Experimental Psychology: Learning, Memory, and Cognition* 15(1):50–60.

Snowling, M. J. 1995. Phonological processing and developmental dyslexia. *Journal of Research and Reading* 18:132–8.

Solman, R. T., and May, J. G. 1990. Spatial localization discrepancies: A visual deficiency in poor readers. *American Journal of Psychology* 103: 242–63.

Stanovich, K. E., and West, R. F. 1989. Exposure to print and orthographic processing. *Reading Research Quarterly* 24:402–33.

Stein, J. F. 1991. Vision and language. In *Dyslexia: Integrating Theory and Practice*, eds. M. Snowling, and M. Thomson. London: Whurr.

Stein, J. F., and McAnally, K. 1995. Auditory temporal processing in developmental dyslexics. *Irish Journal of Psychology* 16:220–8.

Swanson, H. L. 1987. Verbal coding deficits in the recall of pictorial information by learning disabled readers: The influence of a lexical system. *American Educational Research Journal* 24:143–70.

Swanson, H. L., and Alexander 1997. Cognitive processes as predictors of word recognition and reading comprehension in learning disabled and skilled readers: Revisiting the specificity hypothesis. *Journal of Educational Psychology* 89(1):128–58.

Talcott, J. B., Witton, C., McClean, M., Hansen, P. C., Rees, A., Green, G. G. R., and Stein, J. F. 1999. Can sensitivity to auditory frequency modulation predict phonological and reading skills? *Neuroreport* 10:2045–50.

Tallal, P. 1980. Auditory temporal perception, phonics, and reading disabilities in children. *Brain and Language* 9:182–98.

Tallal, P., Miller, S., and Fitch, R. H. 1993. Neurobiological basis of speech: A case of the preeminence of temporal processing. In Temporal information processing in the nervous system, eds. P. Tallal, A. M. Galaburda, R. R. Llinas, and C. von Eurler. *Annals of the New York Academy of Sciences* 682:421–23.

Tallal, P., and Stark, R. E. 1982. Perceptual/motor profiles of reading impaired children with or without concomitant oral language deficits. *Annals of Dyslexia* 32:163–76.

Taylor, M. T., and Keenan, N. K. 1990. Event related potentials to visual and language stimuli in normal and dyslexic children. *Psychophysiology* 27:318–27.

Taylor, M. T., and Keenan, N. K. 1999. ERPs to orthographic, phonological, and semantic tasks in dyslexic children with auditory processing impairment. *Developmental Neuropsychology* 15(2):307–26.

Torgesen, J. K. 2000. Individual differences in response to early interventions in reading: The lingering problem of treatment resisters. *Learning Disabilities Research and Practice* 15(1):55–64.

Tzeng, O., and Wang, W. S. 1984. Search for a common neurocognitive mechanism for language and movements. *American Journal of Physiology* 246:904–11.

Vellutino, F. R. 1987. Dyslexia. *Scientific American* 256(3):34–41.

Watson, B. U. 1988. Auditory temporal processing and reading disability. *Journal of the Acoustical Society of America* 84(Suppl. 1):Y21.

Watson, B. U., and Miller, T. K. 1993. Auditory perception, phonological processing and reading ability/disability. *Journal of Speech and Hearing Research* 36:850–63.

Williams, M. C., and LeCluyse, K. 1990. Perceptual consequences of a temporal processing deficit in reading disabled children. *Journal of American Optometric Association* 61(2):111–21.

Willows, D. M., Kruk, R., and Corcos, E. 1993. Are there differences between disabled and normal readers in their processing of visual information? In *Visual Processes in Reading and Reading Disabilities*, eds., D. M. Willows, R. S. Kruk, and E. Corcos. Hillsdale, NJ: Lawrence Erlbaum.

Wilson, G. F., Swain, C. R., and Ullsperger, P. 1998. ERP components elicited in response to warning stimuli: The influence of task difficulty. *Biological Psychology* 47(2):137–58.

Wimmer, H., Mayringer, H., and Landerl, K. 1998. Poor reading: A deficit in skill automatization or a phonological deficit? *Scientific Studies of Reading* 2:321–40.

Wolf, M. 1991. Naming speed and reading: The contribution of the cognitive neurosciences. *Reading Research Quarterly* 26:123–41.

Wolff, P. H., Michel, G. F., and Ovrut, M. 1990. The timing of syllable repetitions in developmental dyslexia. *Journal of Speech and Hearing Research* 33:281–89.

Wolff, P. H. 1993. Impaired temporal resolution in developmental dyslexia. *Annals of the New York Academy of Science* 682:87–103.

Yap, R., and van der Leij, A. 1993. Word processing in dyslexics. *Reading and Writing* 5:261–79.

Zecker, S. G. 1991. The orthographic code: Developmental trends in reading disabled and normally achieving children. *Annals of Dyslexia* 41:178–92.

Chapter • 13

Genetic and Environmental Influences on Reading and RAN:
An Overview of Results from the Colorado Twin Study

*Donald L. Compton, Chayna J. Davis,
John C. DeFries, Javier Gayçn, and
Richard K. Olson*

There is now overwhelming evidence that phonological processing abilities are central to the acquisition of early word-reading skills (e.g., Adams 1990; Brady and Shankweiler 1991). Additionally, there is mounting evidence to suggest that severe disruptions in phonological processes are a primary cause of early reading failure (Bradley and Bryant 1983; Felton and Brown 1990; Olson et al. 1989; Shankweiler and Liberman 1989; Share 1995; Siegel and Ryan 1988; Snowling 1991; Stanovich 1988, 1992; Torgesen, Wagner, and Rashotte 1994; Velluntino and Scanlon 1987; Wagner and Torgesen 1987). Specifically, children who encounter problems learning to read often experience significant difficulties in the use of spelling-sound correspondences when reading words, which has been linked to phonological processing difficulties (e.g., Rack, Snowling, and Olson 1992; Share 1995; Stanovich and Siegel 1994; Vellutino et al. 1996). This convergence of findings has led to the phonological-core deficit hypothesis, which postulates that deficits in phonological processing are the primary cause of word reading problems in reading disabled (RD) children (Bradley and Bryant 1983, 1985; Liberman and Shankweiler 1979; Olson et al. 1990; Snowling 1987; Stanovich and Siegel 1994; Stanovich 1988; Vellutino et al. 1996).

Although the phonological-core deficit hypothesis is widely accepted, Wolf and Bowers (1991, 1993, 1999) have proposed that processes related to serial naming speed represent a second core deficit in children with RD. This alternative model, known as the double-deficit hypothesis, presumes that phonological deficits and problems with rapid automatized naming (RAN) are separable sources of reading dysfunction, and that the presence of deficits in both processes leads to severe reading problems. Furthermore, Wolf and Bowers (1999) contend that the current practice of including naming speed deficits under the phonological rubric may lead to mis-classification and the possibility of inappropriate remediation of RD children whose reading problems are associated with naming speed deficits (see also Lovett, Steinbach, and Frijters 2000). In support of the double-deficit hypothesis, Wolf and Bowers make several broad claims regarding the relationships between phonological processing ability, rapid naming speed, and reading skill in RD and normally achieving children.

Their first claim is that the basic processes underlying serial naming speed and phonological processing ability are substantially different, allowing each skill to contribute variance to different reading skills independently. The second is that RAN performance is differentially related to reading ability in RD and normally achieving individuals. Namely, in normally achieving children the correlation between RAN and reading ability decreases steadily as reading skill develops, whereas naming speed remains a significant predictor of both concurrent and future reading skill in RD children. The third claim is that phonological skills and rapid naming speed differentially predict variance in reading ability depending on the characteristics of the reading skill assessed. For instance, Wolf and Bowers (1999) argue that naming speed is most strongly related to word- and text-reading fluency, whereas phonemic awareness skill is uniquely associated with word attack ability. In addition, Bowers and Wolf (1993) have previously offered a specific mechanism whereby naming speed is related to the rate at which children can induce orthographic patterns from exposure to print. Specifically, children with slow naming speed activate the visual and phonological codes for printed letters too slowly to allow efficient encoding of the letter combinations found in words, thus limiting the development of orthographic representations in the lexicon.

Empirical studies have generally confirmed many of the relationships that form the basis of the double-deficit hypothesis. For example, it has consistently been reported that RAN correlates moderately with other phonological tasks in both normally achieving and at-risk readers (Blachman 1984; Cornwall 1992; Felton and

Brown 1990; Mann 1984), suggesting that there is partial independence between the two skills. In addition, both cross-sectional and
longitudinal studies have shown that RAN and phonemic awareness
are partly independent in their prediction of both concurrent and
future reading achievement in normally achieving and RD readers
(Ackerman and Dykman 1993; Blachman 1984; Bowers 1995;
Felton and Brown 1990; Manis, Doi, and Bhadha 2000; Manis,
Seidenberg, and Doi 1999; Scarborough 1998; Vellutino et al. 1996).
In normally achieving children the correlation between RAN and
word recognition ability decreases as reading skill develops (Walsh,
Price, and Gillingham 1988; Wolf 1991), whereas in RD children
RAN performance remains a significant predictor of concurrent and
future word reading skill (McBride-Chang and Manis 1996; Meyer et
al. 1998). Finally, there is emerging evidence to suggest that phonological skills and rapid naming speed differentially predict variance
in reading ability depending on the characteristics of the reading
skill assessed. Recently, Manis et al. (1999) summarized the literature on the RAN-reading relationship and concluded that RAN performance accounts for unique variance in both word reading
accuracy and speed, with the relationships being strongest for speed
measures. Furthermore, Manis et al. reviewed results from various
studies indicating that RAN was a better predictor of orthographic
coding ability compared to non-word reading skill.

In sum, the phenotypic relations between phonological processing ability, rapid naming speed, and reading skill in normally
achieving and RD children appear to be consistent with the
double-deficit hypothesis. The purpose of this chapter is to extend
the phenotypic performance profile of RD children through the
use of multi-variate genetic analyses. Specifically, these analyses
were designed to examine the genetic and environmental relationships between phonemic awareness skill, rapid naming speed, and
various word reading skills. Results from the genetic analyses will
be discussed in relationship to the phenotypic performance profile
specified by the double-deficit hypothesis.

The behavioral-genetic analyses presented in this chapter
compare correlation and covariance matrices for monozygotic
(MZ) twins and dizygotic (DZ) twins in order to partition phenotypic variance into that attributable to genetic factors (h^2 and a^2),
shared environment (c^2), and nonshared environment (e^2). For a
detailed description of this methodolgy see Neale and Cardon
(1992). Identical (MZ) twins share the same genes while fraternal
(DZ) twins share only half their segregating genes on average
(Plomin, DeFries, and McClearn 1990). With the assumption of
equal shared environment for the MZ and DZ twin pairs, contrasts

between within-pair similarities for MZ and same-sex DZ pairs provide evidence regarding the relative influence of genetic factors and shared environmental factors, while within-pair differences for MZ twins provide evidence for the influence of nonshared environment, including test error. In this chapter, comparisons of correlations or covariance matrices for MZ and DZ twins were used to estimate individual variation due to genetic factors (h^2 or a^2), shared environment (c^2), and non-shared environment (e^2) in twin pairs thought to represent the general population, and in a group of twins in which at least one of the pair has a school history of reading problems. This allowed genetic and environmental influences to be compared across the different twin groups. We also present evidence for the genetic and environmental etiology for deviant groups of twins that are selected from the extreme low end of the normal distribution on a particular variable.

Results from four different sets of analyses are presented in this chapter. The first employed is the DeFries and Fulker (1985) regression procedure to derive estimates of genetic and environmental influences in twin groups in which at least one of the twins within a pair was selected from the extreme low end of the normal distribution on various variables (RAN, word recognition, non-word reading, and orthographic coding). Furthermore, the regression procedure was extended to examine bivariate genetic and environmental relationships between RAN and various word-level reading skills in the RAN-deviant twin pairs. The second set of analyses used a multi-variate ACE (Additive genetic, Common environment, and random Environment effects) model to explore the genetic and environmental correlations between RAN and general reading skill in groups of twins with and without school histories of reading problems. The third set of analyses employed a Cholesky decomposition procedure to examine the independent and shared genetic and environment influences between phonemic awareness skill, rapid naming speed, and various word reading skills in groups of twins with and without school histories of reading problems. The final set of analyses presents results from quantitative-trait locus (QTL) analysis of RAN performance by means of a multipoint mapping method and eight informative DNA markers on the short arm of chromosome 6.

THE COLORADO LEARNING DISABILITIES RESEARCH CENTER TWIN SAMPLE AND TEST BATTERY

Data on samples of twins have been collected since 1982 from 27 school districts across the state of Colorado as part of the Colorado

Learning Disabilities Research Center (CLDRC; DeFries et al. 1997). Subjects in the CLDRC include identical and fraternal twin pairs, ranging in age from 8 to 18, who are identified based on evidence from school records that at least one twin member has experienced some sort of problem learning to read. In addition, twin pairs without a school history of reading problems have been tested to form a control group. Exclusionary criteria prescribed that all subjects in the sample used here have verbal or performance IQ on the Wechsler Intelligence Scale (Wechsler 1974) of above 85, that they have no obvious neurological or severe emotional problems, no uncorrected sensory deficits, and that English is the first language spoken in the home. The total sample currently consists of more than 800 twin pairs in which one or both members of the pair has a school history of reading problems (affected group) and more than 450 twin pairs with no school history of reading problems (control group).

A diverse battery of tests that included measures of phonological awareness, RAN, word recognition, phonological decoding, orthographic coding, and reading comprehension was administered to each subject. All tests were administered individually by trained examiners in a quiet laboratory setting. The tests were presented in a fixed order as part of a larger test battery during two 2.5 hour sessions. A portion of the test battery was administered in one session in John DeFries' laboratory at the Institute for Behavioral Genetics with the remainder being administered in a different session on the same day in Richard Olson's laboratory at the Department of Psychology. Performance by the affected group on the experimental tasks was standardized against the control group and then age and age-squared were regressed out of the variables.

The tests used in the present set of analyses consisted of two different measures of phonological awareness, eight different RAN measures divided equally between two different formats, two measures of isolated word recognition skill, two measures of non-word reading skill, three measures of orthographic coding, and one reading comprehension test (for details see Olson et al. 1989, 1994). The phonological awareness measures included a phoneme segmentation and transposition task in which subjects take the first sound from the front of a word, put it at the end, and add the sound /ay/ (e.g., rope would become ope-ray) and a phonemic deletion task in which subjects are asked to remove a specified phoneme from the non-word and if done correctly, the result is a word (e.g., "say prot, now say prot without the /r/ sound" - pot). Rapid naming speed was assessed using four different measures of RAN (letters, numbers, colors, pictures). Subjects were asked to name as quickly as possible a set of randomly ordered stimuli distributed across a card. The number of items for each category that are named correctly in 15 seconds is the subject's score. In several of the analyses, performance on the letter and number RAN tasks were combined (using z scores) to form an alphanumeric RAN score, and colors and pictures were similarly combined to form a non-alphanumeric RAN score. In addition, four different measures of RAN (letters, numbers, colors, objects) designed by Denckla and Rudel (1976) were administered to a subset of the sample. Subjects' scores for each category being the amount of time to name 50 items. The measures of word recognition were the Peabody Individual Achievement Test (PIAT) word recognition sub-test (Dunn and Markwardt 1970), and an experimental Time-Limited Word Recognition Test (Olson et al. 1989;1994). The Time-Limited Word Recognition Test was designed to assess isolated word recognition accuracy and latency. The response to a word was counted correct only if the correct response was initiated and detected by a voice key within two seconds. The first non-word reading test included 45 one-syllable non-words, ranging from CVC to CC-CVCV (e.g., ter and strale), while the second test contained 40 two-syllable non-words (e.g., hodfen, lobsel, strempick). Accuracy and median correct reaction times were combined into a single score for each of the two non-word reading tests. Orthographic coding was estimated using measures requiring subjects to recognize the correct spelling of a target word with phonologically similar background foils. Measures included the word-pseudohomophone choice task that required a speeded forced-choice between a word and a phonologically identical pseudohomophonic non-word (e.g., rain and rane), the homophone choice task in which subjects heard a sentence such as "Which is a fruit?" and then asked to choose the correct spelling (pair and pear), and the Peabody Individual Achievement Test (PIAT) spelling sub-test (Dunn and Markwardt 1970) where the subject is asked to identify the correct spelling of a word among four orthographically and often phonologically similar alternatives printed on a card (e.g., clowdy, cloady, cloudey, or cloudy). Accuracy and median correct reaction times were combined into a single score for the word-pseudohomophone choice and the homophone choice tasks. Finally, subjects were given the Peabody Individual Achievement Test (PIAT) reading comprehension sub-test (Dunn and Markwardt 1970).

A Comparison of RAN Formats

Prior to presenting results from the various genetic analyses, one issue related to the RAN tasks used in the CLDRC battery must be addressed. The format of the RAN tasks that has been used since the inception of the CLDRC is somewhat different from the traditional RAN task designed by Denckla and Rudel (1976). The traditional RAN task assesses the time taken by a subject to name 50 items, whereas the alternative RAN task used in the CLDRC asks subjects to name as many items as possible in 15 seconds. To test whether these two formats of RAN were equivalent, both formats of serial RAN (traditional and alternative) were administered to a subset of the CLDRC twin sample (307 subjects), and the relationship between these measures and various word reading skills were examined using commonality analysis (Compton et al. 2000). Results of commonality analyses indicate that a considerable amount of explained difference in various word reading skills was common to the two different RAN formats. However, the alternative RAN measure explained more unique variance in word reading skills than the traditional RAN task. Results indicate that the alternative RAN task is at least as good as the traditional RAN task in capturing word-level reading variance, and therefore all the subsequent analyses will use this alternative format of the RAN task.

Univariate and Bivariate Analyses of Shared and Independent Genetic Influences in Deviant Groups

In the first set of analyses presented in this section the proportion of deviant groups (g) membership due to genetic factors (h^2_g), and shared environment (c^2_g) were estimated from twins who were selected from the extreme low end of the normal distribution on different variables (RAN, word recognition, non-word reading, and orthographic coding). Twins in the deviant group are called "probands." The average genetic and environmental etiology for proband-group membership is determined by the status of the second member of the pair, called the "co-twin," who may also be a "proband" if he or she also falls below the criterion for deviance on the selection variable. For example, if group membership in the low tail for RAN were entirely due to genetic influence, then both members of an MZ twin pair would be probands in the deviant group, whereas the co-twins of DZ twin probands would regress half way toward the population mean, on average, because they share approximately half of their segregated genes. In contrast, if shared family environment were the only cause of deviant group membership, then all DZ and MZ co-twins of probands would also be probands, regardless of their genetic similarity status. Actual results fall between these extremes, reflecting the balance of genetic and shared environment influence on deviant group membership (for details see, DeFries and Fulker 1985).

In this set of analyses, the various deviant twin groups were formed by selecting probands of same-sex twin pairs from the entire sample (pairs with and without a history of reading problems). A proband was defined as the twin of a pair who was at least –1.5 SD below age peers on the criterion variable. If both members of a twin pair met the classification criterion for deficit-group membership, they were entered twice in the analysis, with twin members exchanging proband and co-twin status (known as "double entry"). The standard errors for the estimates are based on the actual number of twin pairs in the analysis. Table 1 presents univariate estimates of genetic (h^2_g) and shared environment (c^2_g) influences in deviant groups of twins selected on word recognition, non-word reading, orthographic coding, alphanumeric RAN, and non-alphanumeric RAN. Results indicate that significant genetic and shared environmental influences existed for group deficits in each of the variables. Selecting for a group deficit in word recognition skill resulted in approximately equal estimates of genetic and shared environmental influences. For group deficits in

Table 1.   Genetic (h^2_g) and Shared-Environmental (c^2_g) Influences on Group Deficits in Word Recognition, Non-word Reading, Orthographic Coding, Alphanumeric RAN, and Non-alphanumeric RAN

Task	MZ Prob- and	MZ Cot- win	DZ Prob- and	DZ Cot- win	h^2_g (SE)	c^2_g (SE)
Word Recognition (MZ = 252, DZ = 180)	–2.58	–2.43	–2.52	–1.80	.46 (.08)*	.49 (.09)*
Non-word Reading (MZ = 213, DZ = 149)	–2.58	–2.21	–2.59	–1.45	.59 (.10)*	.26 (.10)*
Orthographic Coding (MZ = 190, DZ = 143)	–2.60	–2.16	–2.51	–1.52	.44 (.11)*	.38 (.10)*
Alphanumeric RAN (MZ = 139, DZ = 88)	–2.14	–1.43	–2.15	–1.04	.37 (.13)*	.30 (.12)*
Non-alphanumeric RAN (MZ = 123, DZ = 91)	–2.06	–1.42	–2.06	–0.96	.45 (.13)*	.24 (.12)*

Note. The numbers of MZ and DZ twin pairs for each of the measures are presented in parentheses. SE = adjusted standard error; Word Recognition = Composite of the PIAT Word Recognition sub-test and the Timed-Limited Word Recognition Test; Non-word Reading = Composite of the combined accuracy and median correct reaction times variables for the One-Syllable and Two-Syllable Non-word Reading Tests; Orthographic Coding = Accuracy and median correct reaction times variable for the Word-Pseudohomophone Choice test.

Non-shared Environmental Influences (e^2_g) = 1 – ($h^2_g + c^2_g$).

*$p < .05$ for estimates significantly greater than 0.

non-word reading and non-alphanumeric RAN, the genetic influence appears somewhat stronger than the influence of shared environment, with results showing an opposite trend for group
deficits in orthographic coding and alphanumeric RAN. However,
none of the contrasts between the genetic and shared environmental influences within the different variables were significant.
In general, results of the univariate analyses indicate that both alphanumeric and non-alphanumeric RAN performance are moderately heritable in the RAN deviant groups.

Even though the group deficits in the different variables all
show significant genetic influence, it cannot be assumed that the
same genes are operating to produce these deficits. The degree of
common genetic influence across different variables can be assessed by a bivariate extension of the DeFries and Fulker (1985)
univariate regression procedure. In the bivariate extension, the
proband is selected for a deficit on one variable and the co-twin
regression to the population mean assessed for the second variable
(Stevenson et al. 1993). The resulting bivariate estimate of h^2_g is a
function of the group heritabilites for the two variables and the
degree to which these group heritabilites are influenced by the
same genes. In the first set of bivariate analyses, deficit groups in
both alphanumeric and non-alphanumeric RAN (proband performance below –1.5 SD) were formed and the bivariate heritabilities
between the deviant RAN groups and word recognition, non-word
reading, and orthographic coding estimated. Results of these
analyses are shown in figure 1. The bivariate heritabilities between
alphanumeric RAN performance and word reading, non-word
reading, and orthographic coding ranged from .38 to .48 and were
all statistically significant ($p < .05$). In contrast, the bivariate heritabilities between non-alphanumeric RAN and the various word-
level reading skills were somewhat lower, ranging from .26 to .35,
and were not statistically significant. However, it is important to
note that with the present sample size and standard error estimates, contrasts in bivariate heritability across word reading
tasks in the two RAN deficit groups were not significant. In addition, interactions between bivariate heritability in the various
word-level reading skills and RAN format (alphanumeric vs. non-
alphanumeric) were also insignificant.

In sum, results indicate common genetic influence between
alphanumeric RAN and word-level reading skills in a group of subjects selected for poor alphanumeric RAN performance. In other
words, subjects with deficits in alphanumeric RAN skill tend
to also have deficits in word reading skills that are influenced,
in part, by a common set of genes. In addition, results tend to

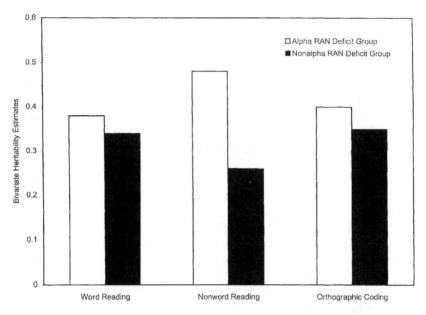

Figure 1. Bivariate heritability estimates between alphanumeric and non-alphanumeric RAN deficit groups and various word-level reading measures.

suggest slightly greater genetic overlap between alphanumeric RAN and word reading skills compared to non-alphanumeric RAN and word reading skills. This trend mirrors the general phenotypic profile in which differences between good and poor readers are greater for alphanumeric stimuli than for non-alphanumeric stimuli (Bowers, Steffy, and Tate 1988; Felton and Brown 1990; Murphy, Pollatsek, and Well 1988; Wolf 1999; Wolf, Bally, and Morris 1986). Taken together these results imply the existence of a unique association, both behaviorally and genetically, between serial naming speed of alphanumeric symbols and word reading skill.

A second set of bivariate analyses was completed to examine whether the degree of common genetic influence between RAN performance and reading skill was similar when deficit groups were selected using the various word-level reading skills. Deficit groups in word recognition, non-word reading, and orthographic coding (proband performance below –1.5 SD) were formed and the bivariate heritabilities between alphanumeric and non-alphanumeric RAN estimated. Results of these analyses are shown in figure 2. Estimates of bivariate heritability between alphanumeric RAN and the word-level reading skills were somewhat lower when reading skill was used to select deviant group members, ranging from .18 to

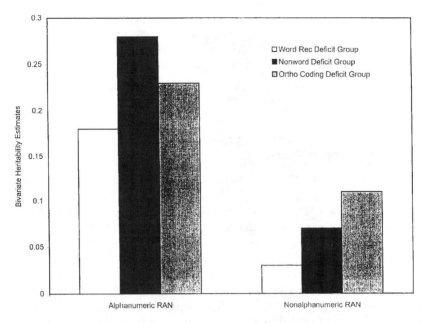

Figure 2.   Bivariate heritability estimates between word recognition, non-word reading, and orthographic coding deficit groups and alphanumeric and non-alphanumeric RAN.

.28 (all were statistically significant, $p < .05$). Similarly, bivariate heritability estimates between non-alphanumeric RAN and the word-level reading skills were lower when selecting deviant groups based on word reading skill, ranging from .04 to .11 (all were statistically insignificant). Again, due to constraints on sample size and relatively large standard error estimates, contrasts in bivariate heritability across RAN formats in the various deviant reading groups were not significant. Likewise, interactions between bivariate heritability in the two RAN formats and word reading skill were statistically insignificant. The overall trend in bivariate heritabilities suggests relatively equal common genetic influence between RAN and the various word reading measures. This result does not support the hypothesis of a specific link between RAN and orthographic coding as proposed by Bowers and Wolf (1993).

In sum, selecting deviant groups based on word-level reading performance tended to result in greater genetic overlap between alphanumeric RAN and word reading skills compared to non-alphanumeric RAN and word reading skills. In addition, results also imply that selecting deviant groups based on word-level reading skill tended to result in lower common genetic influence between RAN and word reading skill. However, caution must be exercised when making comparisons across the two different bivariate analyses. Estimates of bivariate heritability from the first analysis (RAN deficit groups) may be biased upwards because the positive school history group had already been selected for low performance on reading measures.

Genetic and Environmental Correlations Between RAN and General Reading Skill in Affected and Control Twin Groups

In this set of analyses, the genetic and environmental influences on general reading skill and RAN were examined using a bivariate latent trait ACE model (Davis et al. submitted; Neale and Cardon 1992). Because the various RAN and reading measures were normally distributed within the combined proband and co-twin sample (with lower mean performance compared to the control sample with no school history of reading problems), it was possible to use the classic genetic model employing MZ and DZ covariance matrices to assess a^2, c^2, and e^2 for individual differences across the sample range, rather than for the proband group deficits as done in the previous analyses. A naming speed latent variable (RAN) was formed using the four different observable measures of serial naming speed, namely letters (LET), numbers (NUM), colors (COL), and pictures (PIC). Similarly, a latent variable representing reading skill (READ) was formed using word reading (REC), spelling (SPELL), and reading comprehension (COMP) sub-tests from the PIAT. Comparisons were made between same sex twin pairs in the affected group (MZ = 324, DZ = 263) and control group (MZ = 221, DZ = 139). Of particular interest was the possibility that differential relationships between genetic and environmental influences on general reading skill and RAN exist in the two twin groups.

As depicted in figure 3, the bivariate ACE model partitions the phenotypic variances and covariances for each variable (READ and RAN) into additive genetic (AREAD and ARAN), shared environment (CREAD and CRAN), and non-shared environment (EREAD and ERAN) effects. The path coefficients for additive genetic, shared environmental, and non-shared environmental influences on the READ variable are labeled as a, c, and e, respectively. The corresponding coefficients for the RAN variable are a′, c′, and e′, respectively. The cross-trait genetic (rA), shared environment (rC), and non-shared environment (rE) correlations are also depicted in figure 3. In each variable twin pairs are treated as a case (labeled as T^1 and T^2 in figure 3), and the MZ pairs are analyzed in

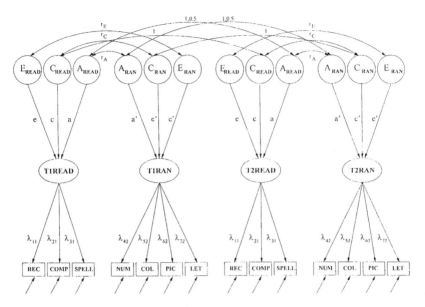

Figure 3. Path diagram for the bivariate twin genetic model.

a separate group from DZ pairs. In addition, the affected and control twin groups were modeled separately to allow comparisons across groups. In the structural equation model, effects of additive genes are set at 1.0 for MZ twins (sharing identical genes) and .5 in DZ twins (sharing half their segmenting genes) and shared environment effects are set to 1.0 in both MZ and DZ twins, indicating similar shared environments for twins. Genetic and environmental effects were estimated by fitting models using the Mx statistical modeling package (Mx: Statistical Modeling, Neale et al. 1999).

Before presenting results from the genetic ACE analysis, results from the phenotypic model, with two correlated factors, fitted simultaneously for the affected (path estimates shown outside the parentheses) and control (path estimates shown inside the parentheses) groups are presented. The model, depicted in figure 4, includes the phenotypic correlations between the two latent variables (READ and RAN) as well as loadings for each of the measures on the latent variables. While the chi-square test of the model, (χ^2 (82) = 292.63, $p < .001$), was significant, the various fit indices that are less sensitive to large sample sizes (χ^2/df = 3.57; rmsea = .011) indicate an adequate fit of the data (Hayduk 1987). For both the affected and control groups, the factor loadings of the alphanumeric RAN variables (NUM and LET) on the RAN latent trait were larger than for the non-alphanumeric RAN variables

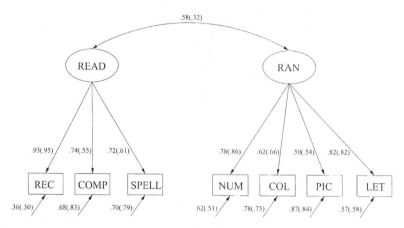

Figure 4.   Parameter estimates for the full bivariate phenotypic model for the affected and control groups. Estimates for the control group are shown in parentheses (after Davis et al. in preparation).

(COL and PIC). Similarly, the REC variable had the greatest factor loading on the READ latent variable in both groups, suggesting disproportionate influence of word recognition skill in estimating the READ latent variable. Finally, the RAN-READ correlation was almost twice as large in the affected group compared to the control group (.58 compared to .32).

In order to test for homogeneity of variances and covariances between groups, various parameter estimates for the affected and control groups were equated and the resulting fit estimate compared to that of the full model. Table 2 presents results from the full model (model 1) and various model contrasts. In model 2, all path coefficients were equated between the two groups resulting in a significant decrease in model fit, (χ^2 (15) = 91.36, $p < .001$). This result indicates that the factor structure in affected and control groups cannot be collapsed into a single group model without seriously affecting the model fit. One further model contrast was used to test parameter differences across groups. In model 3, the correlation between the READ and RAN latent variables were equated across groups, resulting in a significant decrease in model fit, (χ^2 (1) = 24.30, $p < .001$). This result suggests a differential relationship between RAN and READ in the affected and control groups.

A similar result has previously been reported in groups of good and poor reading third and fourth grade children by McBride-Change and Manis (1996). One criticism of the McBride-Change and Manis study was that the good and poor readers differed significantly in reading skill, which may have contributed to

Table 2. Model Comparisons of the Phenotypic Relationships Between Affected and Control Groups

Model	χ^2	df	p	χ^2/df	rmsea	vs	$\Delta\chi^2$	Δdf	$p\,\Delta\chi^2$
1. Full	292.63	82	< .001	3.57	.011				
2. Affected = Control	383.99	97	< .001	3.96	.034	1	91.36	15	< .001
3. Equal $r_{\text{READ-RAN}}$	316.93	83	< .001	3.82	.018	1	34.30	1	< .001

group differences in the RAN-reading correlation. A similar criticism could also be made of the phenotypic model presented here. To address the possible effects of unequal reading level on group differences in RAN-READ correlations, an additional phenotypic model was fitted using a reading-level match design. To accomplish this, older affected twins were matched with younger control twins, resulting in a mean reading level of approximately the sixth grade (as estimated by the PIAT) in both groups. Results of the reading-level match model were similar to the previous model using the entire sample of affected and control groups. As in the previous analysis, model comparisons indicated that the affected and control groups could not be collapsed into a single group without significantly decreasing model fit. Furthermore, model comparisons also indicate differences in the RAN-READ correlation in the affected (.55) and control (.27) groups. Thus, differences in the RAN-READ correlation do not appear to be the result of unequivalent reading skill across the affected and control groups.

Results from the full genetic model are displayed in figure 5. For simplicity, only the latent variables are shown and the genetic, shared environment, and non-shared environment coefficients have been squared to provide direct estimates of a^2, c^2, and e^2 for the READ and RAN variables in the affected (estimates shown outside the parentheses) and control (estimates shown inside the parentheses) groups. In the full genetic model, the chi-square test of the model, (χ^2 (182) = 725.39, $p < .001$), was significant, whereas the various fit indices that are less sensitive to large sample sizes (χ^2/df = 3.99; rmsea = .051) suggest an adequate fit of the data. Results indicate substantial and relatively equal heritability estimates of reading skill in the affected (.85) and control (.76) groups. In contrast, shared environmental influences on reading skill accounted for virtually no variance in either group. Heritability estimates for RAN were also substantial and relatively equal in the affected (.58) and control (.62) groups. However, in the case of RAN, shared environmental influences accounted for a sizable

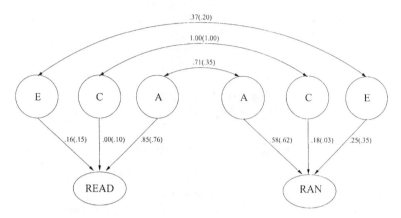

Figure 5.   Parameter estimates for the full bivariate ACE genetic model (displaying only one twin) for the affected and control groups. Estimates for the control group are shown in parentheses (after Davis et al. in preparation). The shared environment correlations of 1.0 between the READ and RAN variables were due to the extremely small estimates of c^2 for the control group on the RAN variable and the affected group on the READ variable.

portion of RAN variance. Finally, the genetic correlation between RAN and READ was considerably larger in the affected group (.71) compared to the control group (.35). This result suggests greater genetic overlap between RAN and word reading skills in the affected group compared to the control group.

To explore whether the RAN-READ genetic correlations are actually different in the two groups, a series of model comparisons were carried out. Table 3 presents results from the full genetic model (model 1) and various model contrasts. In model 2 all path coefficients were equated between the two groups resulting in a significant decrease in model fit, (χ^2 (23) = 106.39, $p < .001$). This result indicates that affected and control groups cannot be collapsed into a single group genetic model without seriously affecting the model fit. In model 3, the genetic paths for RAN and READ, along with the genetic correlation path between READ and RAN were equated across groups, resulting in a marginally significant decrease in model fit, (χ^2 (3) = 8.08, $p < .05$). Equating only the RAN-READ genetic correlation between groups (model 4) significantly affected the model fit, (χ^2 (1) = 7.53, $p < .005$). In contrast, equating the genetic paths for the RAN and READ variables across groups (model 5) did not significantly affect the model fit, (χ^2 (2) = .34, $p = .84$). Results suggest the existence of a differential genetic relationship between RAN and READ in the affected and control group.

Table 3. Model Comparisons of the Genetic Relationships Between Affected and Control Groups

Model	χ^2	df	p	χ^2/df	rmsea	vs	$\Delta\chi^2$	Δdf	$p\,\Delta\chi^2$
1. Full	725.39	182	< .001	3.99	.051				
2. Affected = Control	831.78	205	< .001	4.06	.060	1	106.39	23	< .001
3. Equal r_A, and $a_{READ} = a_{RAN}$	733.47	185	< .001	3.96	.052	1	8.08	3	< .05
4. Equal r_A	732.92	183	< .001	3.99	.052	1	7.53	1	< .005
5. $a_{READ} = a_{RAN}$	725.73	184	< .001	3.94	.051	1	.34	2	.84

In sum, results from the phenotypic and genetic models converge to suggest the existence of a unique association between serial naming speed and reading development within the affected group. However, the results from the bivariate ACE model ignore the possibility that the significant genetic correlation between RAN and reading skill is somehow mediated by phonological awareness skill. Now we will present a test of this possibility.

Genetic and Environmental Correlations Between Phonemic Awareness, RAN, and Word Reading Skill in Affected and Control Twin Groups

In this set of analyses, the genetic and environmental influences on word reading skill (WR) and RAN were examined after first removing the genetic and environmental effects of phonological awareness (PA) skill. In order to accomplish this, a multivariate adaptation of the ACE model known as the Cholesky decomposition was employed (Neale and Cardon 1992). In this procedure, illustrated in figure 6 (upper model) for the three variable model, the first latent variable, F1, has effects on all three variables, PA, RAN, WR; the second factor, F2, is uncorrelated with the first and has effects on the remaining variables RAN and WR; and the last factor, F3, is specific to WR. Adapting the Cholesky procedure to behavioral-genetic applications requires each of the latent variables (in this case F1–F3) be decomposed into genetic and environmental components as shown in figure 6 (lower model). Thus, F1 (A1, C1, E1) is assigned to estimate genetic and environmental influences of phonological awareness skill and as much of the genetic and environmental influences related to RAN and WR as possible. Then F2, (A2, C2, E2) explains the genetic and environ-

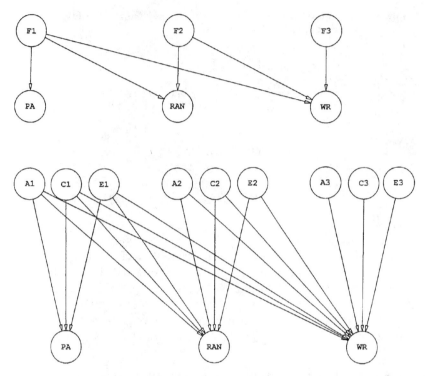

Figure 6.   Path diagrams for the general three variable Cholesky decomposition (upper figure) and the three variable genetic Cholesky decomposition (lower figure).

mental influences related to RAN remaining after the effects of F1 are removed and as much of the genetic and environmental influences as it can related to WR. Finally, F3 (A3, C3, E3) explains the remaining genetic and environmental influences on WR after that related to F1 and F2 are removed. The underlying mechanism of the decomposition is essentially that of hierarchical regression.

Latent variables were used to estimate PA skill (phoneme deletion and phoneme segmentation and transposition tests), RAN (alphanumeric RAN and non-alphanumeric RAN), and WR ability (PIAT WR and Time-Limited WR) in the analysis. Cholesky factors were estimated by fitting models using the Mx statistical modeling package (Mx: Statistical Modeling, Neale et al. 1999). Estimates of the genetic (A), shared environment (C), and non-shared environment (E) factor covariance matrices in the affected and control groups are presented in table 4. In the full Cholesky genetic model the chi-square test was significant, (χ^2 (114) = 265.45, $p < .001$); however the various fit indices that are less sensitive to large sam-

Table 4. Genetic (A), Shared Environment (C), and Non-Shared Environment (E) Factor Loadings on Phonological Awareness (PA), RAN, and Word Reading (WR) in the Affected and Control Groups Computed From a Full ACE Cholesky Model

Variables	Genetic			Shared Environment			Non-Shared		
	A1	A2	A3	C1	C2	C3	E1	E2	E3
	Affected Group								
1. PA	.92	–	–	.21	–	–	.34	–	–
2. RAN	.50	.73	–	–.15	.24	–	.21	.30	–
3. WR	.76	.22	.51	–.14	.10	.00	.22	–.02	.20
	Control Group								
1. PA	.83	–	–	.50	–	–	.24	–	–
2. RAN	.31	.62	–	.00	.36	–	.16	.60	–
3. WR	.58	.07	.55	.19	.42	.00	.37	–.04	.00

ple sizes (χ^2/df = 2.32; rmsea = .016; TLI = .96) indicate an acceptable model fit. The parameter estimates for the affected and control groups were equated and the resulting fit estimate compared to that of the full model, (χ^2 (27) = 99.94, p < .001). This significant result indicates that the Cholesky factor structure in the affected and control groups cannot be collapsed into a single group model without seriously affecting the model fit. Due to the complexity of the overall model and limitations in space, no further model comparisons are reported.

Considering results from the affected group first, it can be seen that PA skill was highly heritable ($.92^2$ = .84) with very little influence of shared ($.21^2$ = .04) or non-shared ($.34^2$ = .12) environment. In addition, the PA genetic factor (A1) loading on the RAN (.50) and WR (.76) variables was relatively high, indicating a significant amount of common genetic influence between PA and both RAN and WR. This was not true in the case of shared and non-shared environmental influences. The second factor, RAN, was also highly heritable ($.50^2$ + $.73^2$ = .78) with very little influence of shared ($-.15^2$ + $.24^2$ = .08) or non-shared ($.21^2$ + $.30^2$ = .13) environment. The relatively large A2 loading on RAN (.73) indicates significant independent genetic variance in RAN after removing the genetic effects of PA. Furthermore, the moderate A2 loading on the WR variable (.22) suggests the possibility of significant genetic covariance between RAN and WR even after the genetic effects of PA have been removed. Finally, WR skill was highly heritable ($.76^2$ + $.22^2$ + $.51^2$ = .89) with very little influence of shared environment ($-.14^2$ + $.01^2$ + $.00^2$ = .03) in the affected group. In addition, the high A3 factor loading (.51) indicates that there is considerable independent genetic variance associated with word reading beyond that associated with both PA and RAN, much of which is associated with general verbal ability. These results suggest a considerable amount of genetic independence between RAN and PA skills, and furthermore that the genetic covariance between RAN and WR in the affected group is somewhat independent of PA skill.

Turning to the control group, results suggest several minor differences in the factor covariance matrices between the two groups. In the control group, the heritability of PA was somewhat lower ($.83^2 = .69$) and the influence of shared environment ($.50^2 = .25$) moderately higher than in the affected group. In addition, the somewhat lower loadings of the PA genetic factor (A1) on RAN (.31) and WR (.58) suggests less common genetic influence between PA and both RAN and WR in this group. Rapid automatized naming was also less heritable ($.31^2 + .62^2 = .48$) in the control group with very little influence of shared environment ($.00^2 + .36^2 = .13$), but a relatively high estimate of non-shared environment ($.16^2 + .60^2 = .39$). The relatively large A2 loading on RAN (.62) again indicates significant independent genetic variance in RAN after removing the genetic effects of PA. However, the very modest A2 loading on the WR variable (.07) in the control group indicates little genetic covariance between RAN and WR after the genetic effects of PA have been removed. In contrast, the relative large C2 loading on WR suggests there may be some shared environment covariance between RAN and WR. Finally, WR skill in the control group was less heritable ($.58^2 + .07^2 + .55^2 = .64$) with a larger estimate of shared environment influence ($.19^2 + .42^2 + .00^2 = .22$) compared to the affected group. In addition, the relatively high A3 factor loading (.55) also indicates that there is considerable independent genetic variance related to word reading skill beyond that associated with both PA and RAN in the control; again much of this independent variance was associated with individual differences in verbal ability. Results in the control group indicate that RAN and PA are more independent skills, but unlike the affected group there was limited genetic covariance between RAN and WR independent of PA skill. These results support the proposed phenotypic profile (based on the double-deficit hypothesis) of a unique association between serial naming speed and reading development in poor readers.

Finally, we tested the hypothesis that phonological skills and rapid naming speed differentially predict variance in reading ability depending on the characteristics of the reading skill assessed. To accomplish this two more Cholesky decomposition analyses were completed using the affected group. In the first, word recognition skill was replaced by a non-word reading (NWR) latent variable (formed using the one-syllable and two-syllable non-word reading tasks). In the second, word reading skill was replaced by an orthographic coding (OC) latent variable (formed using the word-pseudohomophone choice, homophone choice, and PIAT Spelling tasks). Comparing results across these two analyses should allow for the hypothesized link between RAN and orthographic coding to be assessed. Factor covariance matrices for the analyses are shown in table 5. Inspection of the covariance matrices for NWR and OC indicates a very similar pattern of factor loadings across the two latent variables. It is true that factor loadings are in the predicted direction, with the PA genetic factor (A1) loading somewhat higher on NWR (.74) than on OC (.65) and the RAN genetic factor (A2) loading slightly higher on OC (.35) than on NWR (.28). However, the magnitude of these contrasts are far too small to support a specific link between RAN and orthographic coding skill in the affected group.

Quantitative-Trait Locus for RAN Deficits on Chromosome 6p

In this final section we present results from QTL analysis of RAN performance by means of a multipoint mapping method and eight informative DNA markers on chromosome 6. For this analysis, a total of 73 sib-pairs were selected from the CLDRC sample of twin pairs with a school history of reading problems. Probands were identified as subjects with a composite RAN score (calculated using z scores from the four different RAN sub-tests) at least one *SD* below the CLDRC control sample. In addition to the Center's

Table 5. Genetic (A), Shared Environment (C), and Non-Shared Environment (E) Factor Loadings on Phonological Awareness (PA), RAN, and Non-word Reading (NWR)/Orthographic Coding (OC) in the Affected Group Computed From a Full ACE Cholesky Model

Variables	Genetic			Shared Environment			Non-Shared		
	A1	A2	A3	C1	C2	C3	E1	E2	E3
1. PA	.91	–	–	.22	–	–	.36	–	–
2. RAN	.44	.73	–	.05	.34	–	.21	.34	–
3. NWR	.74	.26	.45	–.10	.09	.00	.26	–.01	.32
1. PA	.88	–	–	.32	–	–	.34	–	–
2. RAN	.47	.72	–	.05	.34	–	.22	.30	–
3. OC	.65	.35	.55	–.21	.13	.00	.19	–.08	.24

standard battery of tests, each subject had either a blood or cheek sample collected for linkage analysis. Sibs and both parents from each family were genotyped with these markers according to methods described in Hall et al. (1996) and Idury and Cardon (1997). The multipoint model-free procedure used in this analysis was developed by Fulker, Cherny, and Cardon (1995). Results from the QTL analysis are expressed as LOD scores, which is the log-likelihood ratio for linkage. Significant LOD scores are an indication of linkage between a particular behavior and a chromosome location. Results from the QTL analysis in the RAN deficit group are presented in figure 7. As can be seen in the figure, there is evidence for linkage between markers D6S461 and D6S291. This region has previously been linked to several other word reading component skills such as phonemic awareness, phonological decoding, and orthographic coding (Cardon et al. 1994; Fisher et al. 1999; Gayán et al. 1999; Grigorenko et al. 1997). This result adds to the existing evidence linking a relatively diverse set of reading and related language skills to the 6p region.

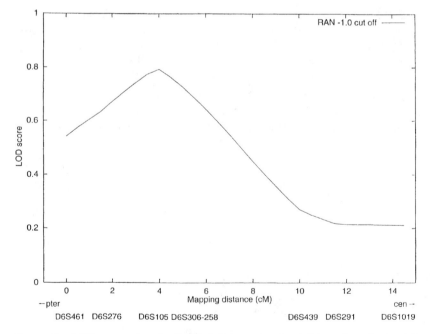

Figure 7.   LOD scores for the RAN deficit group (< −1 SD proband criteria) fitted using the DeFries and Fulker model. Chromosome location is expressed in centimorgans proximally from marker D6S461.

Summary

Results from these genetic analyses and previous behavioral studies seem to converge in a way that complements several, but not all, aspects of the basic phenotypic performance profile for reading disability proposed by Wolf and Bowers (1999). Specially, results of the univariate genetic analyses of group deficits indicate that both alphanumeric and non-alphanumeric RAN performance were moderately heritable in RAN deviant groups. Furthermore, bivariate analyses indicated common genetic influence between alphanumeric RAN and various word-level reading skills (i.e., word recognition, non-word reading, or orthographic coding), whether the proband group was selected based on RAN or word-level reading skill.

Results from the bivariate ACE model for individual differences also established the existence of a significant genetic correlation between RAN and reading skill in groups of twins with and without a school history of reading problems. Moreover, results indicated a significantly larger RAN-READ phenotypic and genetic correlation in the affected group. These results were argued to support the existence of a unique genetic association between serial naming speed and reading development within the affected group.

Cholesky analyses confirmed and extended those of the bivariate ACE model by controlling for the genetic and environmental influences of phonological awareness on RAN and word reading and then examining the genetic covariation between RAN and word reading. Results from the Cholesky analyses seem to suggest that RAN and PA have both shared and independent genetic etiologies in both affected and control groups. However, only in the affected group was there a possibility of genetic covariance between RAN and word reading independent of phonological awareness skill.

We also explored the Wolf and Bowers (1993, 1999) hypothesis that there is a stronger relationship between RAN and orthographic coding than between RAN and phonological decoding. Results from the bivariate analyses, using the DeFries and Fulker (1985) regression procedure and the Cholesky analyses contrasting factor covariance matrices for non-word reading and orthographic coding latent variables, do not support the existence of a specific link between RAN and orthographic coding measures in the affected group. Finally, results from QTL analysis suggests linkage of RAN skill to a small region on the short arm of chromosome 6 located near other word reading related skills (e.g., phoneme awareness, phonological decoding, and orthographic coding).

REFERENCES

Ackerman, P. T, and Dykman, R. A. 1993. Phonological processes, confrontation naming, and immediate memory in dyslexia. *Journal of Learning Disabilities* 26:597–609.

Adams, J. M. 1990. *Beginning to Read.* Cambridge, MA: MIT Press.

Blachman, B. A. 1984. Relationship of rapid naming ability and language analysis skills to kindergarten and first-grade reading achievement. *Journal of Educational Psychology* 76:610–22.

Bowers, P. G. 1995. Tracing symbol naming speed's unique contributions to reading disability over time. *Reading and Writing* 7:189–216.

Bowers, P. G., Steffy, R., and Tate, G. 1988. Comparison of the effects of IQ control methods on memory and naming speed predictors of reading ability. *Reading Research Quarterly* 23:304–19.

Bowers, P., and Wolf, M. 1993. Theoretical links among naming speed, precise timing mechanisms, and orthographic skill in dyslexia. *Reading and Writing: An International Journal* 5: 69–85.

Bradley, L., and Bryant, P. E. 1983. Categorizing sounds and learning to read: A causal connection. *Nature* 301:419–21.

Bradley, L., and Bryant, P. E. 1985. *Rhyme and Reason in Reading and Spelling.* Ann Arbor: University of Michigan Press.

Brady, S. A., and Shankweiler, D. P. (Eds.) 1991. *Phonological Processes in Literacy: A Tribute to Isabelle Y. Liberman.* Hillsdale, NJ: Lawrence Erlbaum Associates.

Cardon, L. R., Smith, S. D., Fulker, D. W., Kimberling, W. J., Pennington, B. F., and DeFries, J. C. 1994. Quantitative trait locus for reading disability on chromosome 6. *Science* 266:276–9.

Compton, D. L., Olson, R. K., DeFries, J. C., and Pennington, B. F. 2000. Are all RAN created equal? Comparing the relationships among two different formats of alphanumeric RAN and various word reading skills in normally achieving and reading disabled individuals. Manuscript submitted for publication.

Cornwall, A. 1992. The relationship of phonological awareness, rapid naming, and verbal memory to severe reading and spelling disability. *Journal of Learning Disabilities* 25:532–8.

Davis, C. J., Knopik, V. S., Olson, R. K., Wadsworth, S. J., and DeFries, J. C. submitted. Etiology of covariation between reading performance and rapid automatized naming: A twin study.

DeFries, J. C., Filipek, P. A., Fulker, D. W., Olson, R. K., Pennington, B. F., Smith, S. D., and Wise, B. W. 1997. Colorado Learning Disabilities Research Center. *Learning Disabilities* 8:7–19.

DeFries, J. C., and Fulker, D. W. 1985. Multiple regression analysis of twin data. *Behavioral Genetics* 15:467–73.

Denckla, M. B., and Rudel, R. G. 1976. Rapid "automatized" naming (R.A.N.): Dyslexia differentiated from other learning disabilities. *Neuropsychologia* 14:471–9.

Dunn, L. M., and Markwardt, F. C. 1970. *Examiner's Manual: Peabody Individual Achievement Test.* Circle Pines, MN: American Guidance Service.

Felton, R. H., and Brown, I. S. 1990. Phonological processes as predictors of specific reading skills in children at risk for reading failure. *Reading and Writing: An Interdisciplinary Journal* 2:39–59.

Fisher, S. E., Marlow, A. J., Lamb, J., Maestrini, E., Williams, D. F., Ricjardson, A. J., Weeks, D. E., et al. 1999. A quantitative-trait locus on chromosome 6p influences different aspects of developmental dyslexia. *American Journal of Human Genetics* 64:146–56.

Fulker, D. W., Cherny, S. S., and Cardon, L. R. 1995. Multipoint interval mapping of quantitative-trait loci using sib pairs. *American Journal of Human Genetics* 56:1224–33.

Grigorenko, E. L., Wood, F. B., Meyer, M. S., Hart, L. A., Speed, W. C., Shuster, A., and Pauls, D. L. 1997. Susceptibility loci for distinct components of developmental dyslexia on chromosome 6 and 15. *American Journal of Human Genetics* 60:27–39.

Hall, J. H., LeDue, C. A., Watson, A. R., and Roter, A. H. 1996. An approach to high throughput genotyping. *Genome Research* 6:781–90.

Hayduk, L. 1987. *Structural Equation Modeling with LISREL: Essentials and Advances.* Baltimore, MD: The Johns Hopkins University Press.

Idury, R. M., and Cardon, L. R. 1997. A simple method for automated allele binning in microsatellite markers. *Genome Research* 7:1104–9.

Liberman, A. M., and Shankweiler, D. P. 1979. Speech, the alphabet and teaching to read. In *Theory and Practice of Early Reading*, eds. L. Resnick and P Weaver. Hillsdale, NJ: Lawrence Erlbaum Associates.

Lovett, M. W., Steinbach, K. A., and Frijters, J. C. 2000. Remediating the core deficits of developmental reading disability: A double-deficit perspective. *Journal of Learning Disabilities* 33:334–58.

Manis, F. R., Doi, L. M., and Bhadha, B. 2000. Naming speed, phonological awareness, and orthographic knowledge in second graders. *Journal of Learning Disabilities* 33:325–33.

Manis, F. R., Seidenberg, M. S., and Doi, L. M. 1999. See Dick RAN: Rapid naming and the longitudinal prediction of reading subskills in first and second graders. *Scientific Studies of Reading* 3:129–57.

Mann, V. 1984. Review: Reading skill and language skill. *Developmental Review* 4:1–15.

McBride-Chang, C., and Manis, F. R. 1996. Structural invariance in the associations of naming speed, phonological awareness, and verbal reasoning in good and poor readers: A test of the double deficit hypothesis. *Reading and Writing: An Interdisciplinary Journal* 8:323–39.

Meyer, M. S., Wood, F. B., Hart, L. A., and Felton, R. H. 1998. Selective predictive value of rapid automatized naming in poor readers. *Journal of Learning Disabilities* 31:106–17.

Murphy, L. A., Pollatsek, A., and Well, A. D. 1988. Developmental dyslexia and word retrieval deficits. *Brain and Language* 35:1–23.

Neale, M. C., Boker, S. M., Xie, G., and Maes, H. H. 1999. *Mx: Statistical Modeling.* Box 126 MCV, Richmond, VA 23298: Department of Psychiatry. 5th Edition.

Neale, M. C., and Cardon, L. R. 1992. *Methodology for Genetic Studies of Twins and Families.* Dordrecht: Kluwer.

Olson, R., Forsberg, H., Wise, B., and Rack, J. 1994. Measurement of word recognition, orthographic, and phonological skills. In *Frames of Reference for the Assessment of Learning Disabilities: New Views on Measurement Issues*, ed. G. R. Lyon. Baltimore, MD: Paul H. Brookes Publishing Co.

Olson, R., Wise, B., Conners, F., and Rack, J. 1990. Organization, heritability, and remediation of component word recognition and language skills in disabled readers. In *Reading and Its Development: Component*

Skills Approaches, eds. T. H. Carr and B. A. Levy. San Diego: Academic Press.

Olson, R., Wise, B., Conners, F., Rack, J., and Fulker, D. 1989. Specific deficits in component reading and language skills: Genetic and environmental influences. *Journal of Learning Disabilities* 22:339–48.

Plomin, R., DeFries, J. C., and McClearn, G. E. 1990. *Behavior Genetics: A Primer*. San Francisco: W. H. Freeman and Company.

Rack, J. P., Snowling, M. J., and Olson, R. K. 1992. The non-word reading deficit in developmental dyslexia: A review. *Reading Research Quarterly* 27:29–53.

Scarborough, H. S. 1998. Predicting the future achievement of second graders with reading disabilities: Contributions of phonemic awareness, verbal memory, rapid naming, and IQ. *Annals of Dyslexia* 48:115–s36.

Shankweiler, D. and Liberman, I. Y. 1989. *Phonology and Reading Disability: Solving the Reading Puzzle*. Ann Arbor: University of Michigan Press.

Share, D. L. 1995. Phonological recoding and self-teaching: Sine qua non of reading acquisition. *Cognition* 55:151–218.

Siegel, L. S., and Ryan, E. B. 1988. Development of grammatical-sensitivity, phonological, and short-term memory skills in normally achieving and learning disabled children. *Developmental Psychology* 24:28–37.

Snowling, M. J. 1987. *Dyslexia: A Cognitive Developmental Perspective*. Oxford: Basil Blackwell.

Snowling, M. J. 1991. Developmental reading disorders. *Journal of Child Psychology and Psychiatry* 32:49–77.

Stanovich, K. E. 1988. The right and wrong places to look for the cognitive locus of reading disability. *Annals of Dyslexia* 38:154–77.

Stanovich, K. E. 1992. Speculations on the causes and consequences of individual differences in early reading acquisition. In *Reading Acquisition*, eds. P. B. Gough, L. C. Ehri, and R. Treiman. Hilldale, NJ: Lawrence Erlbaum Associates.

Stanovich, K. E., and Siegel, L. S. 1994. Phenotypic performance profile of children with reading disabilities: A regression-based test of phonological-core variable-difference model. *Journal of Educational Psychology* 86:24–53.

Stevenson, J., Pennington, B. F., Gilger, J. W., DeFries, J. C., and Gillis, J. J. 1993. Hyperactivity and spelling disability: Testing for shared genetic aetiology. *Journal of Child Psychology and Psychiatry and Allied Disciplines* 34:1137–52.

Torgesen, J. K., Wagner, R. K., and Rashotte, C. A. 1994. Longitudinal studies of phonological processing and reading. *Journal of Learning Disabilities* 27:276–86.

Vellutino, F. R., and Scanlon, D. M. 1987. Phonological coding, phonological awareness, and reading ability: Evidence from a longitudinal and experimental study. *Merrill-Palmer Quarterly* 33:321–63.

Vellutino, F. R., Scanlon, D. M., Sipay, E. R., Small, S. G, Pratt, A., Chen, R., and Denckla, M. B. 1996. Cognitive profiles of difficult-to-remediate and readily remediated poor readers: Early intervention as a vehicle for distinguishing between cognitive and experiential deficits as basic causes of specific reading disability. *Journal of Educational Psychology* 88:601–38.

Wagner, R. K., and Torgesen, J. K. 1987. The nature of phonological processing and its causal role in the acquisition of reading skills. *Psychological Bulletin* 101:192–212.

Walsh, D., Price, G., and Gillingham, M. 1988. The critical but transitory importance of letter naming. *Reading Research Quarterly* 23:108–22.

Wechsler, D. 1974. *Examiner's manual: Wechsler Intelligence Scale for Children - Revised.* New York: The Psychological Corporation.

Wolf, M. 1991. Naming speed and reading: The contribution of the cognitive neurosciences. *Reading Research Quarterly* 26:123–41.

Wolf, M. 1999. What time may tell: Towards a new conceptualization of developmental dyslexia. *Annals of Dyslexia* 49:3–28.

Wolf, M., and Bowers, P. G. 1999. The double-deficit hypothesis for the developmental dyslexias. *Journal of Educational Psychology* 91:415–38.

Wolf, M., Bally, H., and Morris, R. 1986. Automaticity, retrieval processes, and reading: A longitudinal study of average and impaired readers. *Child Development* 57:988–1000.

AUTHOR NOTE

The Colorado Learning Disabilities Research Center is supported in part by program project and center grants from the National Institute of Child Health and Human Development (HD-11681 and HD-27802). We would like to acknowledge the invaluable contribution of staff members of the many school districts and of the families who participated in this study.

Section • III

Implications for Intervention

Chapter • **14**

The Use of Fluency-Based Measures in Early Identification and Evaluation of Intervention Efficacy in Schools

*Edward J. Kame'enui, Deborah C. Simmons,
Roland H. Good III, and Beth A. Harn*

In a paper entitled, "Naming-speed processes, timing, and reading: A conceptual review," Wolf, Bowers, and Biddle (2000) make a bold call for a "more differentiated view of reading failure and, very importantly, a more comprehensive approach to reading intervention." These researchers assert that such an approach to reading intervention will require, at minimum, the use of (a) naming-speed measures (e.g., RAN) to aid the early identification of students at risk for a double deficit in reading (i.e., phonological processing deficit and a naming-speed deficit), and (b) interventions that focus strategically on the development of fluency and automaticity in the component skills of reading. In this paper, we offer a modest and partial response to the call of Wolf, Bowers, and Biddle (2000). Although this response is incomplete, it offers an important rendering of what is possible and perhaps what is on the horizon for practitioners, researchers, and stakeholders who share a keen interest in the prevention of reading failure. Our response to the call for a differentiated and comprehensive approach to reading intervention examines the linkage of dynamic, fluency-based assessment (Good, Simmons, and Smith 1998) with research-based interventions (National Research Council 1998; National Reading Panel 2000; Simmons and Kame'enui 1998), and high-stakes, standards-based outcomes in the complex "host environments" known as schools (Kame'enui and Simmons 1998).

In this chapter, we examine the role of fluency in identifying kindergarten children with potentially serious reading difficulties and in evaluating the efficacy of school-based interventions. Our goal is to explore and expose the critical and changing role of fluency in the development of the component foundational skills in beginning reading, including phonological awareness (e.g., phonemic segmentation), alphabetic understanding (e.g., knowledge of how sounds and letters relate and their primary role in word recognition), word recognition, and comprehension. This "changing concept of fluency" is in contrast to the traditional role assigned to fluency in the reading research as the primary and "immediate result of word recognition proficiency" (National Reading Panel 2000). A fundamental principle in the connected-text fluency research is that such practice facilitates the rapid integration of the component skills necessary for comprehension. For example, oral reading fluency correlates robustly ($r = .80$) with comprehension (Fuchs, Fuchs, and Maxwell 1988; see Markell and Deno 1997). In our analysis, the value of fluency is not limited to reading connected text quickly and accurately. Instead, it incorporates the development of the component skills of beginning reading such as phonemic awareness and letter-sound association, and the need for a high criterion level of proficiency. Moreover, it is predicated on the proposition that fluent performance of complex skills and higher-level processes (e.g., word recognition and reading comprehension) requires fluency in the component skills and lower-level processes (Logan 1997). Several recent fluency studies have targeted word recognition and demonstrated gains in connected text fluency and comprehension (Levy, Abello, and Lysynchuk 1997; Lovett, Steinbach, and Frijters 2000). Berninger et al.'s research (this volume) offers important empirical and conceptual distinctions between readers who meet the criteria for a rate disability only (i.e., accurate, but very slow readers), in contrast to those who meet the criteria for an automaticity disability (i.e., inaccurate and slow on component alphabetic skills, strategic processing, and executive functions). Wolf et al. (2000) and others (Torgesen 1998) note that interventions that address automaticity in the sublexical and lower-level processes that service word- and text-level processing have received little sustained attention.

To address the role of fluency in the early identification of serious reading problems and the evaluation of early intervention efficacy in schools, we examine two related topics. First, we discuss the role of fluency in the development of foundational skills (e.g., phonemic segmentation and nonsense word fluency) in beginning reading. Second, we assess and examine the efficacy of three different interventions designed to increase beginning reading skills of kindergarten students identified as at risk of reading difficulties. In doing so, we employ a set of fluency-based measures to evaluate intervention effects.

THE ROLE OF FLUENCY IN THE DEVELOPMENT OF FOUNDATIONAL SKILLS IN BEGINNING READING

Good, Simmons, and Smith (1998) argued that current assessment practices in early literacy fail to make the necessary and important linkage between assessment and intervention. Too often these practices assess latent constructs hypothesized to be related to reading, instead of assessing reading directly. In addition, they do not assess reading performance frequently, and they fail to assess the progress students make during their ongoing reading experience. Instead of these practices, Good et al. (1998) recommended employing an assessment system that meets the following six criteria: "(a) identify children early who are experiencing difficulty acquiring early literacy skills; (b) contribute to the effectiveness of interventions by providing ongoing feedback to teachers, parents, and students; (c) evaluate the effectiveness of interventions for individual students; (d) determine when student progress is adequate and further intervention is not necessary; (e) identify accurately children with serious learning problems; and (f) evaluate the overall effectiveness of early intervention efforts."

To evaluate the role and relation of fluency in the development of foundation skills in beginning reading, we employed a set of fluency-based measures called the Dynamic Indicators of Basic Early Literacy Skills (DIBELS) (Kaminski and Good 1996) which were developed and validated for use with children in kindergarten and early first grade. These fluency-based measures assess students' early literacy skills dynamically as they change over time. As such, these measures are sensitive to student literacy growth, easy and efficient to administer (e.g., each measure is a one-minute, fluency-based measure), capable of repeated and frequent administration (e.g., the Phonemic Segmentation Fluency measure has 25 alternate forms of equivalent difficulty), and cost effective (Good, Simmons, and Smith 1998). Dynamic Indicators of Basic Early Literacy Skills are not designed to serve as a comprehensive or diagnostic reading assessment tool. Rather, they are intended to "provide a fast and efficient indication of the academic well-being of students with respect to important early literacy skills" (Good, Simmons, and Smith; see recent Fuchs and Fuchs 1999, for a review of DIBELS). An important consideration is the relation of fluency-based measures, such as DIBELS, and nonfluency-based measures (e.g., Yopp-Singer) with RAN. In this paper, we explore these correlates and discuss their importance to the design of reading interventions.

USING FLUENCY-BASED MEASURES TO EXAMINE THE EFFICACY OF THREE EARLY READING INTERVENTIONS

To further explore the utility of fluency in early reading development, we examined three interventions designed explicitly to promote the development of foundational skills in beginning reading. A pretest, post-test, comparison group design with random assignment of subjects to groups was used to examine the effects of type of instruction on the reading development of kindergarten students identified as at-risk for reading difficulties. Type of instruction served as a between-subjects factor with three levels: Phonological Awareness-Spelling (PAS), Phonological Awareness-Storybook (PASB), and the Sounds and Letters and Story Thinking modules from the Open Court's Collection for Young Scholars (OC; Adams et al. 2000).

Participants

Kindergarten children from two school districts in the Northwest were screened for inclusion in the study. Three hundred and twenty-eight kindergarten students from five elementary schools in one school district, and 113 students from two elementary schools in another school district were screened in September, 1999 on two fluency-based measures, the Letter Naming Fluency (LNF) DIBELS Measure (Kaminski and Good 1996), and the Onset Recognition Fluency (OnRF) DIBELS Measure (Kaminski and Good 1996; 1998).

To participate in the intervention study, students were required to obtain a raw score of 11 or less on the Onset Recognition Fluency (OnRF) DIBELS Measure, and six or less on the Letter Naming Fluency (LNF) DIBELS Measure. In addition, students were excluded from the study if they had one of the following: (a) severe hearing or vision problems, (b) significant attendance concerns, (c) received English as a second language services, or (d) displayed significant disruptive behavior problems. Of the 541 kindergarten students screened for the study, 117 students were identified as at risk for reading disabilities or reading failure.

Initial probes for LNF and OnRF were administered to all students in September and the Peabody Picture Vocabulary Test-Revised (PPVT-R) in October of kindergarten. During the course of the study, student mobility was approximately 25%, which is characteristic of the district's overall mobility rate. Of the 117 students identified at the outset of the study, 87 were present for pretest and post-test assessments. Important initial concerns were whether groups were equivalent at pretest, whether attrition was systematic, and whether attrition affected group equivalence. Means and standard deviations on September measures for students completing the study and for students who were lost to attrition are reported in table 1. To examine group equivalence and the effects of attrition, a two-way, between-subjects, multi-variate analysis of variance was conducted using the Pillai's trace test statistic. The dependent variables were the fall measures of PPVT-R, LNF, and OnRF. The independent variables were group and attrition status. The interaction between group and attrition status was not statistically significant, indicating that group equivalence was not affected by attrition, $F(6, 208) = 0.40$, $p > .20$. The main effect of the group variable also was not statistically significant indicating that groups were equivalent on the fall measures, $F(6, 208) = 1.32$, $p > .20$. Finally, attrition status was not statistically significant, indicating that attrition did not systematically affect high or low performing students, $F(3, 103) = 0.68$, $p > .20$.

Table 1. Effects of Attrition on Intervention Group Equivalence

		OC		PAS		PASB	
		Complete	Attrit	Complete	Attrit	Complete	Attrit
	n	27	10	29	8	31	6
CA	Mean	66.8	69.6	67.6	65.5	67.9	70.1
	SD	3.7	4.5	4.4	2.1	4.1	7.3
PPVT	Mean	93.2	88.2	90.6	85.1	92.0	92.2
	SD	11.6	14.2	14.4	13.3	13.8	9.8
LNF	Mean	2.3	1.3	2.9	2.3	2.5	3.2
	SD	1.8	1.3	2.9	2.8	2.3	2.8
OnRF	Mean	5.6	5.9	7.2	7.6	6.5	8.0
	SD	3.5	1.5	4.0	3.9	3.2	4.8

Note. The LNF and OnRF were administered in September and the PPVT-R in October.

Measures

To evaluate the role of fluency in the development of foundation skills in beginning reading, we used four types of measures: (a) fluency-based measures of early literacy (i.e., Dynamic Indicators of Basic Early Literacy Skills, DIBELS; Kaminski and Good 1996); (b) a non-fluency measure of phonological awareness (i.e., Yopp-Singer Test of Phoneme Segmentation; Yopp 1995); (c) a receptive vocabulary measure (Peabody Picture Vocabulary Test-Revised 1981); and (d) a measure of rapid automatized naming (i.e., RAN Objects; Denckla and Rudel 1974; 1976). Figure 1 describes a schedule of the measures. A brief description of each measure follows.

Fluency-based Measures

Letter Naming Fluency (LNF) DIBELS Measure (Kaminski and Good 1996)   The LNF measure is a standardized, individually administered test used to assess the accuracy and fluency with which students name rows of randomly presented letters. A child's knowledge of letter names has consistently been found to be one of the best predictors of later reading performance (Adams 1990; Ball and Blachman 1991). On the LNF task, students are given an 8.5" x 11" sheet of paper with randomly ordered letters from the entire alphabet, both upper and lower-case, and asked to name as many of the letters as they can in one minute. The final score is the number of letters correctly named in one minute. Test-retest and alternate form reliability of the LNF measure averages above .95, and predictive validity coefficients with other reading criterion measures range from .59 to .90 (Kaminski and Good 1996).

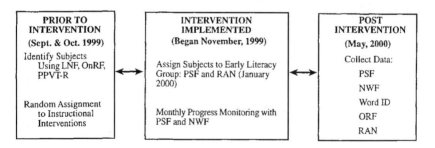

Figure 1.   Schedule of Study Activities and Measurement
Note. LNF = Letter Naming Fluency, OnRF = Onset Recognition Fluency, PSF = Phonemic Segmentation Fluency, NWF = Nonsense Word Fluency, Word ID = Woodcock Reading Mastery Word Identification subtest, ORF = Oral Reading Fluency, RAN=Rapid Automatized Naming

Onset Recognition Fluency (OnRF) DIBELS Measure (Kaminski and Good 1996; 1998; Laimon 1994)   The OnRF is a standardized, individually administered measure of phonological awareness that assesses a child's ability to recognize and produce the initial sound in an orally presented word. The examiner presents four pictures to the child, names each picture, and then asks the child to identify (i.e., point to or say) each of three pictures that begins with the same sound the examiner produces orally. The child is also asked to produce orally the onset for an orally presented word that matches one of the given pictures. The examiner calculates the amount of time taken to identify/produce the correct sound and converts the score into the number of onsets correct in a minute. Alternate form reliability of the OnRF measure is .65 and test-retest reliability ranges from .65–.90 (Kaminski and Good 1996).

Phonemic Segmentation Fluency (PSF) DIBELS Measure (Kaminski and Good 1996)   The PSF measure is a standardized, individually administered test of phonological awareness. The PSF measure assesses a student's ability to segment three and four phoneme words into the individual phonemes fluently. The PSF measure has been found to be a good predictor of later reading achievement and is intended for use with students from the winter of kindergarten to the middle of first grade (Kaminski and Good 1996). Because of its alternate forms, the PSF measure was used as a progress monitoring measure once a month and a post-test measure.

The PSF task is administered orally by an examiner presenting words of three to four phonemes. It requires the student to produce verbally the individual phonemes for each word. For example, the examiner says "sat" and the student needs to say "/s/ /a/ /t/" to receive the total possible points. After the student responds, the examiner presents the next word; the number of correct phonemes produced within one-minute determines the final score. Alternate form reliability for the PSF measure is reported to be .88, and one-year predictive validity with other reading measures range from .73–.91 (Kaminski and Good 1996).

Nonsense Word Fluency (NWF) DIBELS Measure (Kaminski and Good 1996)   The PSF measure is a standardized, individually administered test of letter-sound correspondence and of the ability to blend letters into words in which letters represent their most common sounds. The student is given a 8.5" x 11" sheet of paper with randomly ordered VC and CVC nonsense words (e.g., sig, rav, ov), and asked to produce verbally the individual letter sound or read the whole nonsense word. For example, if the stimulus word is "vaj" the student could say /v/ /a/ /j/ or say the word /vaj/ to obtain a total of three letter sounds correct. The student is allowed one-minute to produce as many letter-sounds as he or she can, and the final score is the number of letter-sounds produced correctly in one minute. Alternate form reliability for the NWF measure ranges from .67 to .87, and concurrent validity studies with the readiness sub-tests of the Woodcock-Johnson Psychoeducational Test ranges from .35 to .55. The NWF was used once a month from January to May to monitor the progress of all students.

Non-fluency Measure

Yopp-Singer Test of Phoneme Segmentation (Yopp 1995)   The Yopp-Singer Test of Phoneme Segmentation is a standardized, individually administered test designed to assess a child's "ability to separately articulate the sounds of a spoken word in order" (Yopp 1995). The examiner says a word and the child is required to break the word into its individual phonemes in the order presented in the word. This is an untimed measure, and the final score is the total number of words segmented correctly out of the 22 words administered. Reliability information on the Yopp-Singer is reported as .95 and the correlation with the Comprehensive Test of Basic Skills reading cluster in first grade was .43.

Receptive Vocabulary Measure

Peabody Picture Vocabulary Test-Revised (PPVT-R; Dunn and Dunn 1981)   The PPVT-R is an individually administered, standardized measure that assesses children's receptive vocabulary by asking them to identify one of four pictures that best represents the verbally presented word given by the examiner. Words are presented until the child responds incorrectly to six of eight items in a row. The number of correctly identified vocabulary words is then transformed to standard scores. The PPVT-R has consistently been found to identify students with language difficulties accurately and is appropriate for use with the age-range of students in the present study (Salvia and Ysseldyke 1988; Sattler 1988). Test-retest reliability for the PPVT-R is reported to be .77. Although the manual does not provide validity information, the test is the most commonly administered measure of receptive vocabulary and considered to be a sound technical device (Salvia and Ysseldyke 1988).

Rapid Automatized Naming Measure

The RAN measure used in this study was modeled after the measure developed by Denckla and Rudel (1974, 1976) as a measure of naming speed. Three measures of RAN were administered: object, number, and letter-naming. All of the measures were serial-list naming tasks, which are used most frequently as naming speed measures (Bowers and Swanson 1991; Wolf and Bowers 2000; Wolf and Obregon 1997). The measures require students to name as quickly as possible a visual array of five objects (i.e., chair, hand, ball, dog, star), five numbers (i.e., 2, 4, 7, 6, 9), and five letters (i.e., o, a, s, d, p) repeated ten times in random order on separate sheets of paper. On each measure, the array is presented in ten rows with five stimuli (i.e., either objects, numbers, or letters) per row. Standardized procedures were used in the administration of this task. Prior to beginning the timed portion of the task, students were asked to name the first row of the array to determine knowledge of the stimuli. If the child was not able to name the first row correctly, the timed portion of the task was not administered because the task was designed to measure speed at naming known stimuli. The score obtained from the administration was the total time taken to name the 50 items as measured by a stopwatch (i.e., time in seconds). Split-half reliability coefficients for these types of measures average .91 (Torgesen and Davis 1996), and test-retest reliabilities range from .87–.92 (McBride-Chang and Manis 1996).

Of the 117 students identified in the fall, 93 were able to identify objects accurately and the RAN Objects measure was administered to them; six students have moved since the RAN administration. More than half of the students in the sample were unable to identify letters and numbers accurately in January; therefore, RAN letters and numbers were not used as variables in the study.

Procedures for Intervention

Students were randomly assigned to one of the three instructional interventions and all received instruction 30 minutes a day, five days a week, from November 1, 1999 to mid May, 2000. The instruction was implemented as a supplement to the regular half-day of kindergarten instruction and occurred during extended school hours (i.e., either before or after the regular kindergarten instructional day). A trained teacher or teaching assistant provided instruction to groups of 4 to 5 students in a classroom at the child's school. Depending on the number of students identified as at risk, some schools had more intervention groups than others (e.g., a high of seven and a low of three intervention groups per school). Each school had all three instructional treatments represented, and if the number of students warranted, schools were randomly assigned additional instructional treatments across the seven schools to equalize the total number of instructional treatments in the study.

Phonological Awareness with Spelling Instruction (PAS)   The PAS instructional group consisted of two, 15-minute instructional emphases. The first instructional emphasis focused on developing phonological awareness and alphabetic understanding through explicit, systematically designed instruction. The scope and sequence of the PAS lessons followed the curriculum design and direct instruction principles of effective instruction discussed by Simmons and Kame'enui (1998) and Carnine, Silbert, and Kame'enui (1997). Activities for the first fifteen minutes of instruction focused on developing students' phonological awareness of sounds in words by systematically scaffolding the skills of identifying first sounds in words, discriminating sounds, blending, and segmenting. A second emphasis was alphabetic understanding in which students were explicitly and systematically taught letter names, letter sounds, VC (vowel consonant), CVC, and CVCC word types, and sentence reading.

The second fifteen minutes of the PAS intervention focused on developing children's phonological awareness skills by reinforcing and extending phonological awareness instruction and alphabetic skills through beginning spelling instruction. Research has indicated that spelling skills can be used to promote beginning reading (Adams 1990; Ehri and Wilce 1987). The spelling curriculum begins with children tracing and writing letters introduced during the first part of the intervention and then progresses to children writing initial sounds of words, initial and final sounds in words, and then all sounds in CVC words. Effective instructional and curriculum design principles were followed in the development and implementation of this curriculum as well.

Phonological Awareness with Storybook Instruction (PASB)   The PASB instructional group also consisted of two, 15-minute, instructional sections. The first fifteen minutes included the same phonological awareness and alphabetic understanding intervention as the PAS group. The second fifteen minutes of instruction focused on developing vocabulary and awareness of story structure through a repeated storybook reading intervention.

The repeated storybook intervention was based upon research by Dickinson and Smith (1994) and Senechal and Cornell (1993). Over 50 storybooks were read to students in which systematic instruction on identifying characters, characters' problems, story resolution, and oral retell was promoted. In addition, the development of a child's expressive and receptive vocabulary through the strategic teaching of selected vocabulary words in the stories was emphasized. Before a story was read to a child for the first time, target words important to the story were taught, practiced, and reinforced through specific activities within the story and across lessons. Review lessons were completed after every two books to provide students additional practice on using the new vocabulary and oral retelling skills.

Open Court-Reading (OC)   The OC instructional group used the Open Court Reading Series Sound and Letters and the Story Thinking modules as curriculum materials (Adams et al. 2000). The Open Court reading program has been recognized by the American Federation of Teachers as a "promising program for English and Language Arts due to its instructional focus on effective research-based beginning reading skills" (American Federation of Teachers 1999). The Sounds and Letters module focuses on developing phonological awareness, beginning handwriting, and reading decodable texts through a variety of instructional activities.

The Story Thinking module involved the teacher interactively reading stories with the children. During the interactive "Read-Aloud" activities children were asked to predict events, answer factual information questions, state what happened in the story, and discuss how the story concluded. Vocabulary from the story was also practiced during the reading of each story.

RESULTS AND DISCUSSION

Relation of Fluency to Foundational Skills in Beginning Reading

A correlation matrix including means, standard deviations, and relations among the main variables is displayed in table 2. Following, we highlight critical findings relevant to correlates of the foundational skills of beginning reading. The two phonemic segmentation measures (PSF-DIBELS and Yopp-Singer) administered in January were highly correlated (.77) confirming the relation of fluency and non-fluency based measures of phonemic segmentation. The phonemic segmentation tasks of both measures are similar in structure, and the primary differences reside in the scoring metric and the timing component (i.e., PSF is a one-minute timed measure and the Yopp-Singer is an untimed measure). The strength of the correlation suggests they measure much of the same construct. This finding seemingly offers practitioners with an alternative (i.e., one-minute fluency measure) for assessing students more frequently and efficiently. Fluency measures such as the phonemic segmentation fluency measure of DIBELS are one-minute indicators of

Table 2. Means, Standard Deviations, and Intercorrelations of Language, RAN, Phonological Awareness, and Alphabetic Principle Variables

Variable	Mean	Std Dev	October			January				April
			PPVT	RANOBJ	YOPP/SING	OnRF05	LNF05	PSF05	NWF05	PSF08
PPVT	91.9	13.2								
RAN Objects	36.8	9.7	.09							
Yopp-Singer	7.1	6.8	-.07	.33*						
OnRF Jan.	22.8	10.6	.01	.32*	.54*					
LNF Jan.	19.9	13.4	-.06	.55*	.51*	.48*				
PSF Jan.	26.0	17.6	-.08	.31*	.77*	.57*	.59*			
NWF Jan.	7.9	8.2	-.04	.37*	.54*	.39*	.71*	.57*		
PSF April	38.1	15.3	.01	.26*	.47*	.59*	.42*	.57*	.40*	
NWF April	23.1	12.9	-.12	.50*	.48*	.43*	.75*	.55*	.68*	.53*

*p < .05.

phonological awareness and they include multiple alternate forms. In contrast, the Yopp-Singer, on average, takes approximately 3 to 4 minutes to administer and has only one or two forms.

The correlation between the RAN Objects measure and the Yopp-Singer and PSF were similar and significant (.33 and .31). In the overall analysis, the relation of RAN and measures of phonemic segmentation accounted for approximately 10% of the variance. This finding suggests the modest, yet significant, correlation of a RAN measure (objects) with two phonological measures (Yopp-Singer and PSF). In addition, the moderate-to-strong correlation between the PSF and Yopp-Singer measures of phonemic segmentation administered in January with the NWF measure administered in April (.55 and .48, respectively) provide further support that phonemic segmentation is a correlate of early word recognition and that PSF and Yopp-Singer are functioning similarly.

The high correlation of letter naming fluency (LNF) and RAN Objects in January (.55) seemingly confirms the relation of print-based fluency measures. The role of RAN in the early foundations of reading is further documented in the relation of RAN Objects (January) to nonsense word reading (NWF). In January, this relation is small to moderate (.37); however, in April, the strength of the relation of RAN Objects to nonsense word fluency increases to .50 and both correlations are statistically significant at the .05 level. Finally, the patterns of relation among letter naming fluency and nonsense word fluency are strong and consistent. The January correlation of LNF with NWF is .71, and increases to .75 in April. The strength of these relations suggests the importance of learners' ability to recognize letter names and letter sounds automatically.

In summary, rapid automatized naming as assessed through RAN Objects evidenced small to moderate, yet significant, correlations with component skills of early reading including phonemic segmentation and nonsense word reading. The strength of the relation was lower with measures of phonemic segmentation (PSF) (.26–.33) than with print-based measures of letter naming fluency (LNF) (.55) and nonsense word fluency (NWF) (.37–.50), with RAN accounting for approximately 10% of the variance on phonemic segmentation, 30% of LNF, and 25% of NWF.

In a regression analysis, we further explored the interrelations among RAN, a non-fluency-based measure of phonemic segmentation (Yopp-Singer), and a fluency-based measure of phonemic segmentation (DIBELS-PSF). The separate and unique contribution of phonemic segmentation as assessed by the Yopp-Singer to phonemic segmentation fluency (PSF) was confirmed. Students' performance in January, 2000 on RAN Objects and the Yopp-Singer was used to predict January phonemic segmentation performance. As revealed in table 3, RAN and Yopp-Singer combined accounted for 59% of the variance in PSF. When RAN Objects was entered first in the regression analysis, it accounted for 10% of the variance, and Yopp-Singer accounted for an additional 49% of the variance when added in step 2. When the Yopp-Singer was entered first, it accounted for all 59% of explained variance, and RAN Objects added in step 2 explained 0% additional variance. Thus, although RAN Objects is related to both the Yopp-Singer and PSF, RAN Objects' relation to PSF is neither greater in magnitude nor different in kind from RAN Objects' relation to the Yopp-Singer. The fluency component of PSF appears to facilitate measurement of the construct of phonological awareness. Phonemic Segmentation Fluency (PSF) does not appear to operate as a generalized fluency measure. The absence of a nonfluency-based measure of nonsense word reading precluded extension of the regression analysis to nonsense word reading.

Using Fluency-Based Measures to Examine the Efficacy of Three Early Reading Interventions

Students' trajectories of progress on phonological awareness and alphabetic skills were examined using hierarchical linear modeling (HLM) procedures (Bryk and Raudenbush 1992; Bryk, Raudenbush, and Congdon 1996) conducted at two levels. At level 1, the intercept and slope parameters of individual student growth curves or learning trajectories are estimated on a student-by-student, within-student basis. At level 2, differences between students' slope and intercept estimates are modeled on a between-student basis. Students were assessed once per month from January through April, so each student had four repeated assessments with which to model an individual learning trajectory. At level 1 of the HLM, students' scores on the repeated measures of PSF and NWF were

Table 3. Contribution of Rapid Automatized Naming and Letter Naming Fluency to Phoneme Segmentation Fluency Scores in January

Model			R^2 Change	F Change
Model 1:	Step 1:	RAN Objects	.10	20.05*
	Step 2:	Yopp-Singer	.49	101.02*
Model 2:	Step 1:	Yopp-Singer	.59	120.28*
	Step 2:	RAN Objects	.00	0.78

Note. All measures administered in January. Total $R^2 = .59$, $df = 1$ and 84.
*$p < .05$.

predicted from the intervention month. Month was coded as January (-3), February (-2), March (-1), and April (0). In this way, the intercept of the learning trajectories corresponds to the students' predicted performance in April. Slope then corresponds to rate of change per month.

Initial concerns in HLM procedures are to ensure that a reliable estimate of intercept and slope is obtained, and that there is significant variability in subjects' intercept and slope to be modeled. For PSF, intercept estimates had a reliability of .84, and the reliability of slope estimates was .55. For NWF, the intercept had a reliability of .89, and the slope reliability was .46. Although reliability standards for growth curves have not been firmly established, these reliabilities are sufficient for research purposes. The mean intercept for the PSF learning trajectories was 37.50 (SD = 14.18), and the variability in PSF intercepts was significantly different from 0, $x^2(86) = 553.06$, $p < .05$. The mean slope for the PSF learning trajectories was 4.25 correct phonemes per month (SD = 3.62), and the variability in PSF slopes also was statistically significant, $x^2(86) = 192.22$, $p < .05$. For the NWF learning trajectories, the mean intercept was 24.42 (SD = 12.11) and the mean slope was 4.95 correct letter sounds per month (SD = 2.14). The variance in intercepts and slopes also was significantly different from 0, $x^2(86)$ = 770.82, $p < .05$, and $x^2(86) = 160.60$, $p < .05$, respectively. Reliable growth curve parameter estimates and significant variability in parameter estimates are necessary for level 2 analyses to identify variables that account for differences in students' learning trajectories. These assumptions were met and analyses proceeded to level 2.

The HLM level 2 analyses proceeded in three basic steps. The first step was to examine the relation of the January administration of RAN Objects and LNF, singly and combined, to the intercept and slope of students' learning trajectories. The second step was to examine the contribution of RAN and LNF in the context of January phonological awareness to explain differences in students' learning trajectories from January through April. The third step was to examine the contribution of intervention groups to differences in students' learning trajectories. The results of several level 2 models predicting growth trajectories are summarized in table 4. The first model is a null model where no level 2 variables are included. The null model provides a baseline estimate of the variability in slopes and intercepts that might potentially be explained by level 2 variables. The PSF measure provides an estimate of phonological awareness learning, and NWF provides an estimate of alphabetic learning.

Table 4.   Contribution of Rapid Automatized Naming and Fluency to Phonological Awareness Learning Trajectories

Model	Intercept (April)			Slope		
	Unexplained Variance	Explained Variance	Percent Explained	Unexplained Variance	Explained Variance	Percent Explained
Null Model	201.2	0.0	0%	13.1	0.0	0%
Model 1: RAN[a]	181.9	19.3	10%	13.1	0.0	0%
Model 2: LNF[b]	155.3	45.9	23%	12.1	1.0	8%
Model 3: RAN + LNF[b]	156.5	44.7	22%	12.3	0.8	6%
Model 4: Yopp[b] + OnRF[b]	100.0	101.2	50%	8.9	4.2	32%
Model 5: Yopp[b] + OnRF[b] + LNF	98.9	102.2	51%	8.8	4.3	33%
Model 6: Group[c]	156.0	45.2	22%	12.6	0.5	4%
Model 7: Yopp[b] + OnRF[b] + Group[d]	81.7	119.5	59%	7.9	5.2	40%

Note. Negative variance estimates reported as 0.

[a]Regression coefficient is significant for intercept, $p < .05$, but not for slope.

[b]Regression coefficient is significant for intercept and slope, $p < .05$.

[c]For intercept, PAS and PASB are significantly greater than OC, $p < .05$. No other differences are significant.

[d]For intercept, PAS and PASB are significantly greater than OC, $p < .05$. For slope, PAS is significantly greater than OC, $p < .05$. No other differences are significant.

Learning of Phonological Awareness

A first, key question addressed in this paper is the relation of rapid automatized naming (RAN) to learning trajectories in phonological awareness and the alphabetic principle. A first model of interest includes RAN Objects administered in January as a predictor of intercept and slope. RAN Objects accounted for about 10% of the differences in intercepts for the learning trajectories. In this case, the intercept was specified to represent an estimate of April performance for each of the groups. Thus, RAN Objects provides a significant but modest prediction of outcomes for the interventions. Rapid Automatized Naming Objects was not related to the slope of the learning curves.

Next, the joint contribution of RAN Objects and LNF was examined. The Letter Naming Fluency measure shares many characteristics of the RAN Letters in that it is a timed task involving letter naming, and is correlated .55 with the RAN measure. However, the LNF does not presuppose that students have learned the letter names. For example, in this study, RAN Letters was not administered to 49 of the 87 students because they did not meet the letter knowledge criteria for administering RAN Letters. Thus, a low score on LNF represents a combination of inaccurate responses and non-fluent responses. In model 2, January LNF was examined in isolation as a predictor of learning trajectories. In model 3, the January LNF and RAN Objects measures were combined as predictors of learning curves. Letter Naming Fluency as a predictor explains significant variability in intercepts (23%) and slopes (8%). Once LNF is included in the model, the RAN Objects measure does not add additional explained variance for either the slope or the intercept. In addition, the regression coefficient for RAN Objects is non-significant in a model with LNF. Thus, LNF appears to capture the variance explained by the current RAN estimate, which is based on RAN Objects, and to explain additional variance. A hypothesis consistent with this pattern of results is that LNF is assessing both the key general fluency characteristic of RAN with the addition of specific print-related knowledge.

A second step in the analysis examined the contribution of fluency in the context of phonological awareness skills in January when the Yopp-Singer and OnRF measures were administered. Model 4 represents the relation of the January measures of phonological awareness to the PSF learning trajectories. Model 5 includes both January phonological awareness measures and LNF. January phonological awareness (Yopp-Singer and OnRF) explained 50% of the variability in intercepts, and 32% of the variability in slopes.

Once January Yopp-Singer and OnRF were entered in the model, LNF did not account for any unique or separate variability, and did not contribute to the explained variance.

A final step in the HLM analysis was to examine the effects of intervention group. Group was examined in isolation in model 6, and the effect of group in the context of January phonological awareness was examined in model 7. Group differences explained 22% of differences in intercepts, and 4% of differences in slopes. Furthermore, group effects contributed significant explained variance in the context of January phonological awareness on the Yopp-Singer and OnRF. The PSF learning trajectory for each group is illustrated in figure 2.

The PSF learning trajectories are based on the model including OnRF and the Yopp-Singer as predictors of both the intercept (estimated performance in April) and the slope of the trajectory. The predicted April performance of both PAS (Phonological Awareness with Spelling Instruction) and PASB (Phonological Awareness with Storybook Instruction) was significantly greater than the predicted April performance of the OC (Open Court) intervention. The PAS and PASB versions were not significantly different from each other. Differences in slope were less pronounced, and only the PAS and OC slopes were significantly different, favoring the PAS. The PASB was not significantly different in slope from either the PAS or the OC groups. The level 2 regression equations

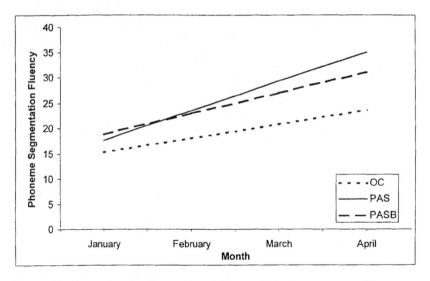

Figure 2.   Learning trajectories of intervention groups on Phoneme Segmentation Fluency.

predicting the slope and intercept of students' learning trajectories based on between-subjects variables are presented in table 5.

It is interesting to note in this model that the Yopp-Singer has a significant negative regression weight predicting the slope of the trajectory, indicating that higher scores on the Yopp-Singer are associated with a less steep learning trajectory of phonological awareness on repeated PSF measures. However, the OnRF measure has a significant, positive regression weight, indicating that higher scores are associated with a steeper learning trajectory on PSF as would be expected. In contrast, when predicting April performance (intercept), both the Yopp-Singer and OnRF have positive regression weights. One hypothesis that may account for this pattern is that both the Yopp-Singer and OnRF are related to phonological awareness in similar ways, but the Yopp-Singer may be more sensitive to differences at the upper end of the range of phonological awareness while the OnRF may be more sensitive to differences at the lower end of the range. For example, the 25th percentile of the Yopp-Singer was 0 for this sample, while the median was 5. For the OnRF measure, the 25th percentile was 15 and the median was 25. On the OnRF measure, a score of 25 is near the maximum range of the measure and distinctions between higher scores may not be meaningful. Thus, for children with high phonological awareness, differences between scores on OnRF may be approaching ceiling effects limiting the rate of growth of the phonological awareness trajectory, while differences between Yopp-Singer scores may not reveal ceiling effects.

Learning of Alphabetic Principle

Similar to learning phonological awareness, the first, key question addressed in this paper is the relation of rapid automatized naming (RAN) and general fluency to learning trajectories. The results of several level 2 models predicting parameters of NWF learning trajectories are reported in table 6. In models 1 through 3, the contributions

Table 5. Contribution of Rapid Automatized Naming and Fluency to Alphabetic Principle Growth Trajectories

Parameter	Level 2 Regression Equation
PSF Intercept	$\hat{\beta}_{0(i)} = 38.5 + 0.5\,(YS - \bar{Y}_{YS}) + 0.6\,(OnRF - \bar{Y}_{OnRF}) - 7.5 I_{OC} + 4.0 I_{PAS}$
PSF Slope	$\hat{\beta}_{1(i)} = 4.1 - 0.4\,(YS - \bar{Y}_{YS}) + 0.1\,(OnRF - \bar{Y}_{OnRF}) - 1.3 I_{OC} + 1.7 I_{PAS}$
NWF Intercept	$\hat{\beta}_{0(i)} = 23.4 + 0.7\,(LNF - \bar{Y}_{LNF}) - 1.5 I_{OC} + 4.4 I_{PAS}$
NWF Slope	$\hat{\beta}_{1(i)} = 4.3 + 0.1\,(LNF - \bar{Y}_{LNF}) + 0.3 I_{OC} + 1.8 I_{PAS}$

Note. Yopp-Singer (YS), OnRF, and LNF are centered around their grand means for the HLM analysis. I_{OC} is an indicator variable for the Open Court group, and I_{PAS} is an indicator variable for the Phonological Awareness plus Spelling group.

Table 6. Contribution of Rapid Automatized Naming and Fluency to Alphabetic (NWF) Principle Learning Trajectories

Model	Intercept (April)			Slope		
	Unexplained Variance	Explained Variance	Percent Explained	Unexplained Variance	Explained Variance	Percent Explained
Null Model	146.7	0.0	0%	4.6	0.0	0%
Model 1: RAN[b]	108.4	38.4	26%	3.4	1.2	25%
Model 2: LNF[b]	50.1	96.6	66%	3.1	1.5	33%
Model 3: RAN + LNF[b]	49.8	97.0	66%	2.9	1.7	37%
Model 4: Yopp + PSF[b]	92.5	54.2	37%	3.9	0.6	14%
Model 5: PSF[a] + LNF[b]	47.2	99.5	68%	3.1	1.4	31%
Model 6: Group[c]	123.2	23.5	16%	3.6	1.0	22%
Model 7: LNF[b] + Group[d]	45.8	101.0	69%	2.7	1.9	41%

Note. Negative variance estimates reported as 0.

[a]Regression coefficient is significant for intercept, p < .05, but not for slope.

[b]Regression coefficient is significant for intercept and slope, p < .05.

[c]For intercept and slope, PAS is significantly greater than OC and PASB while OC and PASB are not significantly different, p < .05.

[d]For intercept, PAS is significantly greater than OC and PASB, p < .05. For slope, PAS is significantly greater than PASB, p < .05. No other differences are significant.

of RAN Objects and LNF are considered in isolation and in combination. Both RAN and LNF explain significant and substantial differences in intercepts and slopes in isolation. However, when combined, only the LNF regression coefficients are significant, and addition of RAN does not explain substantially more of the variability in intercept and slope than LNF in isolation. Thus, similar to phonological awareness learning, LNF appears to represent the key general fluency characteristics of RAN Objects, with the addition of specific print-related knowledge.

A second step in the HLM analyses is a consideration of the role of January phonological awareness as estimated by the Yopp-Singer and a January PSF measure. The PSF measure explained significant and substantial differences in the intercept and slope of the NWF learning trajectories, and the Yopp-Singer did not add to the PSF with respect to the amount of variance explained. However, a comparison of models 5 and 2 indicates a pattern counter to the findings for phonological awareness learning trajectories. Inclusion of January phonological awareness on the PSF did not add substantially to the variance explained by LNF in isolation. In the combined model 5, the regression coefficient for PSF was significant for intercepts, but the addition of PSF only explained an additional 2% of the variance in intercepts.

As a final step in the analysis of the alphabetic principle learning trajectories, the effect of intervention group was examined. Group differences explained 16% of differences in intercepts, and 22% of the differences in slope of learning. Furthermore, group effects contributed significant explained variance in the context of LNF. The NWF learning trajectory for each group is illustrated in figure 3.

The NWF learning trajectories are based on the model including LNF as a predictor of both the intercept (estimated performance in April) and the slope of the learning trajectory. The predicted April performance of the PAS was significantly greater than the predicted April performance of the OC and PASB intervention groups. In addition, the slope of the PAS group was significantly steeper than the slope of the PASB group. The OC and PASB groups were not significantly different from each other in either intercept or slope. The level 2 regression equations predicting the slope and intercept of students' learning trajectories based on between-subjects variables were presented in table 5.

Summary

Three general findings emerge from this examination of learning trajectories. First, RAN Objects as a general fluency measure was

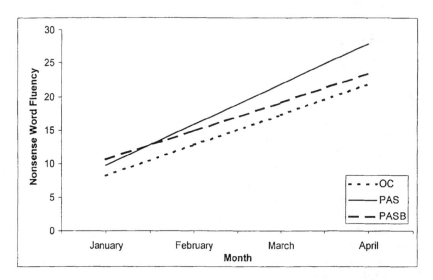

Figure 3.   Learning trajectories of intervention groups on Nonsense Word Fluency.
[a]Nonsense word fluency scores represent the number of correct letter-sounds a student reads in VC (vowel consonant) or CVC words in one minute.

related to predicted outcomes for both phonological awareness and alphabetic principle, but was only related to slope for alphabetic principle. Second, LNF consistently accounted for the RAN relations, and explained additional variance. In other words, when LNF was included in prediction models, RAN provided redundant information. The most noticeable difference between the phonological awareness and alphabetic principle learning trajectories was in the role of LNF and January phonological awareness. Letter naming fluency (LNF) was necessary in models of alphabetic principle learning, but redundant in models of phonological awareness learning. Conversely, January phonological awareness was necessary in models of phonological awareness learning, but redundant in models of alphabetic principle learning. Finally, all of the intervention groups displayed strong, positive learning trajectories, with the PAS group consistently robust. In particular, the PAS group was on track for established phonological awareness (35 to 45 correct phonemes per minute on the PSF measure) by the end of kindergarten. All three groups appeared to be making adequate progress toward established alphabetic principle by midyear of first grade (40 to 50 correct letter sounds per minute on the NWF measure).

REFERENCES

Adams, M. J. 1990. *Beginning to Read: Thinking and Learning about Print.* Cambridge, MA: MIT Press.

Adams, M. J., Bereiter, C., Brown, A., Campione, J., Carruthers, I., Case, R., Hirshberg, J., McKeough, A., Pressley, M., Roit, M., Scardamalia, M., and Treadway, J., G. H. 2000. *Open Court Reading.* Columbus, OH: SRA.

American Federation of Teachers 1999. *Building on the Best, Learning from What Works: Even Promising Reading and English Language Arts Programs.* Washington DC: Author.

Ball, E. W., and Blachman, B. A. 1991. Does phoneme awareness training in kindergarten make a difference in early word recognition and developmental spelling? *Reading Research Quarterly* 26(1):49–66.

Bowers, P. G., and Swanson, L. B. 1991. Naming speed deficits in reading disability: Multiple measures of a singular process. *Journal of Experimental Child Psychology* 51:195–219.

Bryk, A. S., and Raudenbush, S. W. 1992. *Hierarchical Linear Models: Applications and Data Analysis Methods.* Newbury Park, CA: Sage.

Bryk, A. S., Raudenbush, S. W., and Congdon, R. T. 1996. *Hierarchical Linear and Nonlinear Modeling with the HML/2L and HLM/3L Programs.* Chicago: Scientific Software International.

Carnine, D. W., Silbert, J., and Kame'enui, E. J. 1997. *Direct Instruction Reading,* 3rd ed. Upper Saddle River, NJ: Merrill/Prentice–Hall.

Denckla, M. B., and Rudel, R. G. 1974. "Rapid automatized naming" of pictured objects, colors, letters, and numbers by normal children. *Cortex* 10:186–202.

Denckla, M. B., and Rudel, R. G. 1976. Naming of objects by dyslexic and other learning-disabled children. *Brain and Language* 3:1–15.

Denckla, M. B., and Rudel, R. G. 1976. Rapid automatized naming (R.A.N.): Dyslexia differentiated from other learning disabilities. *Neuropsychologia* 14:471–9.

Dickinson, D. K., and Smith, M. W. 1994. Long-term effects of preschool teachers' book readings on low-income children's vocabulary and story comprehension. *Reading Research Quarterly* 29(2):105–22.

Dunn, L., and Dunn, L. 1981. *Peabody Picture Vocabulary Test—Revised.* Circle Pines, MN: American Guidance Service.

Ehri, L. C., and Wilce, L. S. 1987. Cipher versus cue reading: An experiment in decoding acquisition. *Journal of Educational Psychology* 79(1): 3–13.

Fuchs, L. S., and Fuchs, D. 1999. Monitoring student progress toward the development of reading competence: A review of three forms of classroom-based assessment. *School Psychology Review* 28(4):659–71.

Fuchs, L. S., Fuchs, D., and Maxwell, L. 1988. The validity of informal reading comprehension measures. *Remedial and Special Education* 9(2): 20–9.

Good, R., III, Simmons, D. C., and Smith, S. 1998. Effective academic interventions in the United States: Evaluating and enhancing the acquisition of early reading skills. *School Psychology Review* 27(1):45–56.

Kame'enui, E. J., and Simmons, D. C. 1998. Beyond effective practice to schools as host environments: Building and sustaining a school-wide intervention model in reading. *Oregon School Study Council (OSSC) Bulletin* 41(3).

Kaminski, R. A., and Good, R. H., III 1996. Toward a technology for assessing basic early literacy skills. *School Psychology Review* 25(2):215–27.

Kaminski, R. A., and Good, R. H., III 1998. Assessing early literacy skills in a problem-solving model: Dynamic indicators of basic early literacy skills. In *Advanced Applications of Curriculum-based Measurement*, ed. M. R. Shinn. New York: Guilford.

Laimon, D. E. 1994. The effects of a home-based and center-based intervention on at-risk preschool children's early literacy skill. Unpublished Doctoral Dissertation, University of Oregon, Eugene.

Levy, B. A., Abello, B., and Lysynchuk, L. 1997. Transfer from word training to reading in context: Gains in reading fluency and comprehension. *Language Disability Quarterly* 20:173–88.

Logan, G. D. 1997. Automaticity and reading: Perspectives from the instance theory of automation. *Reading and Writing Quarterly* 13:123–46.

Lovett, M. W., Steinbach, K. A., and Frijters, J. C. 2000. Remediating the core deficits of developmental reading disability: A double-deficit perspective. *Journal of Learning Disabilities* 33(4):334–58.

Markell, M. A., and Deno, S. L. 1997. Effects of increasing oral reading: Generalization across reading tasks. *The Journal of Special Education* 31(2):233–50.

McBride-Chang, C., and Manis, F. 1996. Structural invariance in the associations of naming speed, phonological awareness, and verbal reasoning in good and poor readers: A test of the double deficit hypothesis. *Reading and Writing* 8:323–39.

National Reading Panel 2000. Teaching children to read: An evidence-based assessment of the scientific research literature on reading and its implications for reading instruction [on-line]. Available: http://www.nichd.nih.gov/publications/nrp/smallbook.htm

National Research Council 1998. *Preventing Reading Difficulties in Young Children*. Washington, DC: National Academy Press.

Salvia, J., and Ysseldyke, J. E. 1988. *Assessment in Special and Remedial Education*, 4th ed. Boston: Houghton-Mifflin.

Sattler, J. M. 1988. *Assessment of Children*, 3rd ed. San Diego, CA: Riverside Publishers.

Senechal, M., and Cornell, E. H. 1993. Vocabulary acquisition through shared reading experiences. *Reading Research Quarterly* 28(4):360–74.

Simmons, D. C., and Kame'enui, E. J. (Eds.) 1998. *What Reading Research Tells Us about Children with Diverse Learning Needs: Bases and Basics*. Mahwah, NJ: Lawrence Erlbaum Associates.

Torgesen, J. K. 1998. Catch them before they fall: Identification and assessment to prevent reading failure in young children. *American Educator* 22(1):32–9.

Torgesen, J. K., and Davis, C. 1996. Individual difference variables that predict response to training in phonological awareness. *Journal of Experimental Child Psychology* 63:1–21.

Wolf, M., and Bowers, P. G. 2000. Naming-speed processes and developmental reading disabilities: An introduction to the special issue on the double-deficit hypothesis. *Journal of Learning Disabilities* 33(4):322–24.

Wolf, M., and Bowers, P. G. 1999. The double-deficit hypothesis for the developmental dyslexias. *Journal of Educational Psychology* 91(3):415–38.

Wolf, M., and Obregon, M. 1997. The "double-deficit" hypothesis: Implications for diagnosis and practice in reading disabilities. In *Readings on Language and Literacy*, ed. L. Putnam. Boston: Bookline Books.

Wolf, M., Bowers, P. G., and Biddle, K. 2000. Naming-speed processes, timing, and reading: A conceptual review. *Journal of Learning Disabilities* 33(1):387–407.

Yopp, H. K. 1995. A test for assessing phonemic awareness in young children. *The Reading Teacher* 49(1):20–8.

AUTHOR NOTE

The contents of this document were developed in part for the Office of Special Education Programs, U.S. Department of Education under Contract Numbers H023C980156 and H324M980127. This material does not necessarily represent the policy of the U.S. Department of Education, nor is the material necessarily endorsed by the Federal Government.

Chapter • **15**

Principles of Fluency Instruction in Reading:
Relationships with Established Empirical Outcomes

Joseph K. Torgesen,
Carol A. Rashotte, and
Ann W. Alexander

The focus of this chapter is on methods to prevent or remediate reading fluency problems in children who are at risk for, or experiencing, reading difficulties. Our interest in this problem was stimulated by the recent experience of providing intensive remediation to a group of 8- to 10-year-old children with severe reading disabilities. In this study (Torgesen et al. 2001), we provided 67.5 hours of highly skilled, one-to-one instruction to 60 children who had been selected because of significant difficulties acquiring word-level reading skills. These children were taught using two different instructional methods that produced essentially the same effects on reading growth. Both methods provided systematic instruction in phonemic decoding and orthographic reading skills, although they differed in the extent and depth of instruction. The methods also differed in the amount of time spent reading and writing connected text.

The children began the study as very poor readers with general intellectual ability at the low end of the average range (average Verbal IQ = 92.6). Their average standard reading scores as measured by the Woodcock Reading Mastery Test-Revised (Woodcock 1987) were very low: phonetic decoding was 69.3, word identification accuracy was 67.6, and passage comprehension was 82.6. The interventions provided to these children were very effective in improving the accuracy of their reading skills. Figure 1 shows growth over time on a combined measure of word reading accuracy and passage comprehension. Prior to our intervention, the children had received special education instruction in a resource room setting for an average of 16 months. During this time, they made negligible improvement in their standard scores on this measure of broad reading ability. However, they made dramatic improvement during our intervention, and these gains remained stable, with slight improvement, over the two-year period following the cessation of the intervention. It should be pointed out that figure 1 reports reading standard scores; improvement in these scores means that the children were becoming better readers *relative to the average performance of children their age.* In other words, the interventions significantly "closed the gap" in reading skills for these children. By any normal standard, the interventions employed in this study can be considered very effective in increasing the reading ability of a sample of children with severe reading dis-

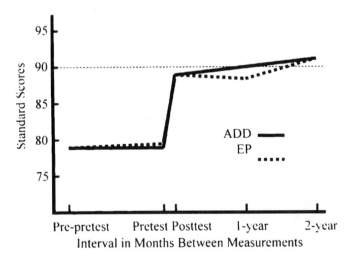

Figure 1.   Standard Scores on the Broad Reading Cluster before, during, and following the intensive intervention (from Torgesen et al. 2001). Intensive remedial instruction for children with severe reading disabilities: Immediate and long-term outcomes from two instructional approaches. *Journal of Learning Disabilities* 34:33–58.

abilities. One caveat about these results, however, is that the reading fluency scores of the children showed virtually no improvement compared to their scores for reading accuracy. For example, on the Gray Oral Reading Test-Revised (Wiederholt and Bryant 1992), standard scores for reading accuracy went from 75.6 to 90.9 at the two year follow-up point, while scores for rate went from 71.4 to 71.7. Thus, while the children attained text reading accuracy scores in the low end of the average range, their scores for reading fluency were still almost two standard deviations below average for children their age. Although the interventions we provided enabled children to accurately read and understand more difficult text, they read this text at a rate substantially slower than other children their same age.

This large discrepancy between improvements in reading accuracy and reading rate raised obvious questions for us about the nature of the reading interventions in our study. The discrepancy may also suggest that it is fundamentally more difficult to "normalize" reading rate in older children than it is to bring their reading accuracy and comprehension into the normal range. We hope to present information in this chapter that will help to clarify the different instructional issues involved in remediating rate versus accuracy problems in older children with severe reading disabilities.

WHAT DO WE MEAN BY READING FLUENCY?

Before we address some of those instructional issues however, we will first clarify what we mean by the term "reading fluency." In a recent review of research in this area, Meyer and Felton (1999) define reading fluency as the ability to read connected text "rapidly, smoothly, effortlessly, and automatically with little conscious attention to the mechanics of reading, such as decoding." Others suggest definitions of reading fluency that go substantially beyond reading rate, to include grouping words into meaningful phrases as one reads (Aulls 1978), prosodic reading (Allington 1983), or reading with the kind of intonation and stress that maximizes comprehension (Rasinski 1990). After reviewing a broad range of definitions of fluency, Hudson, Mercer, and Lane (2000) concluded that the richest interpretation of the concept would be to define it as "accurate reading at a minimal rate with appropriate prosodic features (expression) and deep understanding."

The latter definition suggests that the concept of fluency should be applied to the entire reading process from word identification to identification of word meanings, to construction of phrase and passage level meaning. We would not argue with this as an ultimate definition of fluent reading. After all, the primary purpose of learning to read is to get meaning from text, and individual differences in speed of all the processes referred to in this more inclusive definition could theoretically influence overall reading fluency. However, for purposes of exposition and measurement in this paper, we will focus on a much narrower definition of fluency. We will borrow the definition of fluency proposed by proponents of curriculum based assessment, which defines fluency as rate and accuracy in oral reading (Hasbrouk and Tindal 1992; Shinn et al. 1992). This definition is appropriate for this chapter because it describes the behaviors on which our sample of severely reading disabled children were obviously different from their age-peers, because it can be reliably measured, and because it is consistent with the theoretical focus of definitions of dyslexia which stress the role of word-level reading difficulties as the primary bottleneck to good reading growth in these children (Lyon 1995).

Although our definition of reading fluency is narrow when compared to the one offered by Hudson, et al. (2000), previous research has shown that direct measures of reading rate are highly correlated with measures of more complex reading outcomes. For example, Fuchs, Fuchs, and Maxwell (1988), reported that a measure of oral reading rate for text correlated .91 with reading comprehension scores from a widely used standardized measure in a sample of middle-school and junior high school students with reading disabilities. In fact, the measure of reading rate was more strongly related to the standardized measure of silent reading comprehension than were several different informal (and probably less reliable) measures of reading comprehension. Further, Jenkins et al. (2000) have recently reported that measures of oral reading rate were more highly correlated with reading comprehension scores than were measures of silent reading rate in a sample of children whose reading skills varied across a broad range. Again, this outcome may have been influenced by differences in reliability between measures of silent and oral reading rate, but this does not diminish the potential importance of oral reading rate as a significant dimension of reading performance.

A Model of Reading Fluency to Help Focus Intervention

As we think about the kind of interventions that may be most effective for reading fluency problems, we need to work within a model of reading fluency that identifies the major factors that are potentially responsible for a low score on a measure of reading rate. Logical analysis suggests the following primary components that might underlie individual differences in reading fluency as we have defined it:

1. Proportion of Words in Text That Are Recognized as Orthographic Units   Reading rate will be limited if the text we are reading contains a high proportion of words that are not in our sight vocabulary.

2. Variations in Speed with Which "Sight Words" Are Processed   Individual differences on this dimension might be caused by variability in the number of times the word has actually been recognized in text (practice effects) or by fundamental differences in processing speed. Within this latter category of constitutionally based differences in speed of processing, we would include both more central word identification processes that would influence both oral and silent reading rate, and more peripheral processes such as articulation rate that might most heavily influence oral reading rate.

3. Speed of Processes That Are Used to Identify "Novel" Words   When words that are not recognized as orthographic units are encountered in text, they must be identified by a variety of means that often involve conscious analysis. The most common of these methods involve phonetic decoding, recognition by analogy to known words, and guessing from the context or meaning of the passage.

4. Use of Context to Speed Word Identification   Although passage context does not play a large role in increasing word reading fluency for skilled readers (Stanovich and Stanovich 1995), it does provide useful support for younger and poor readers (Ben-Dror, Pollatsek, and Scarpati 1991; Pring and Snowling 1986). There may be important differences among young children and poor readers in ability to use context that are related to individual differences among them in reading fluency. One thing that might underlie differences in the ability of poor readers to use context as an aid to increasing their word reading fluency is the extent of their vocabulary and background knowledge. Children who are more adept at constructing meaning because of a larger knowledge base may experience a stronger beneficial effect of context on reading fluency than those who are less able to construct the meaning of a passage.

5. Speed with Which Word Meanings Are Identified   As long as children are under obligation to be actively thinking about the meaning of what they are reading, speed of identification of word meanings may play a role in limiting oral reading fluency. On a test like the Gray Oral Reading Test-Revised, children know they will be expected to answer comprehension questions following their reading of the passage. Thus, differences in rate may be partially the result of individual variation in the rate that meanings for words can be accessed.

If we are working to develop effective fluency interventions, and our time to intervene is limited (as it always will be), then we should start with interventions that will have the biggest payoff. They should focus on the factors that actually account for the most variance in fluency among children with reading disabilities. Since it is widely accepted that the most fundamental reading bottleneck for children with reading disabilities lies at the word, rather than the text, level of processing (Lyon 1995), we might expect most of the limitation in rate disabled readers to be caused by problems identifying individual words fluently, rather than in using text level features or semantic access problems.

FACTORS MOST RESPONSIBLE FOR FLUENCY PROBLEMS IN DISABLED READERS

As an introduction to this section, we first revisit the data from the remediation study we described in the beginning of the chapter, and then present some more systematic regression results from five studies. As a context for our further analyses of the results from the remediation study, we first present some information about reading rates in normally achieving children.

There is actually a great deal of variability in the recommended oral reading rates for students both across and within grade levels. For fifth graders and above (children similar to those in our remediation study), Rasinski (1999) cites recommended rates ranging from 108 to 185 words per minute. Using a formula that provides rates for different reading accuracy levels (99% word accuracy = independent reading, 90-98% = instructional, and below 90% = frustration) Raskinski determined a rate of 136 words per minute (wpm) or higher for fifth grade independent reading. Mercer et al. (in press) recommended 100 to 180 wpm for third through eighth grade reading fluency with grade level text.

The standard scores for reading fluency we used in our remediation study were obtained from the Gray Oral Reading Test—Revised (Wiederholt and Bryant 1992), which provided a direct comparison between reading rates of the children in our study with those obtained by children in a national standardization sample. We examined the rate at which children would have to read on the passages of the GORT-R to achieve an average score on the test. For students aged 10.6 to 10.11 to achieve a standard score of 100 for fluency, they would have to read at 137 to 150 wpm on each of the first seven stories.

We then examined the speed of reading for students in our remediation study on the GORT-3 story just prior to the last story on which they reached a ceiling because of too many word reading errors. Story levels ranged from Story 4 to Story 9. The average reading rate for the group was 78.3. Clearly, the students were reading at a rate well below expectations. However, the accuracy level was also more in line with an instructional level than an independent level. If we were to examine reading rate on passages where the children were reading at an independent level (two errors or fewer), would the rate still be slow and halting, or would it approach more normal fluency levels? Using the same subjects, but using the most difficult passage on which there were two or fewer errors (average story level was four), we found an overall reading rate of 122 wpm. This suggests that when the students were familiar with the words in a story, their fluency approached that of an average reader. However, when they encountered words they had to decode phonemically, or by some other conscious process, their overall fluency rate quickly declined. Because students are given 10 seconds to decode words on the GORT-3 before the examiner provides the word, it is easy to see how difficulty with just a few words could have a significant impact on reading rate.

The informal data from our remediation study suggests that the proportion of words in a passage that can be recognized easily by sight has a substantial effect on oral reading rate. This informal observation is consistent with the data in table 1 that more formally describes relationships between the reading fluency score on the GORT-3 and a variety of other potentially related skills and knowledge. The first column reports data from fifth grade children taken from a longitudinal study of 201 randomly selected children whose reading growth was followed from kindergarten through fifth grade (Wagner et al. 1997). The second column reports data from the 2-year follow-up assessment of children in the remediation study that has already been described in this chapter. Remediation study II (Rashotte, MacPhee, and Torgesen in press) provided 35 hours of small group instruction to children in grades 3 to 5 who were struggling to learn to read in the regular classroom. Prevention Study I (Torgesen et al. 1999), provided 88 hours of teacher- and aide-led instruction to children identified as the 12% most at risk for reading failure in kindergarten. The intervention lasted from kindergarten through second grade, and the data presented are from the follow-up scores at the end of fourth grade. Prevention Study II (Torgesen et al. 2000) provided 92 hours of

Table 1.   Correlations between text reading rate and component reading skills, phonological variables, and estimated verbal intelligence

	Longi-tudinal (5th grade)	Remed-iation I (5th–7th)	Remed-iation II (3rd–6th)	Preven-tion I (4th)	Preven-tion II (2nd)
Word Attack[1]	.66**	.50**	.63**	.74**	.69**
Word Identification[1]	.71**	.68**	.81**	.82**	.75**
Nonword Eff.[2]	.75**	.55**	.73**	.87**	.81**
Sight Word Eff.[3]	.82**	.71**	.81**	.88**	.89**
Phon. Aware.[4]	.53**	.54**	.53**	.56**	.44**
Rapid Naming (lets)[5]	.43**	.29*	—	.64**	.60**
Rapid Naming (digs)[6]	.44**	.28	.53**	.66**	.63**
Verbal IQ[7]	.62**	.13	.33*	.44**	.07
Text Fluency Range[8]	55-145	55-95	55-115	55-140	0-130

[1]The Word Attack and Word Identification sub-tests were both taken from the Woodcock Reading Mastery Test-Revised (Woodcock 1987).

[2]Non-word Efficiency Test from the Test of Word Reading Efficiency (Torgesen, Wagner, and Rashotte 1999).

[3]Sight Word Efficiency Test from the Test of Word Reading Efficiency.

[4]Phonological awareness was measured by the Elision sub-test of the Comprehensive Test of Phonological Processes (CTOPP) (Wagner, Torgesen, and Rashotte 1999).

[5]Rapid Naming of Letters sub-test from the CTOPP

[6]Rapid Digit Naming sub-test from the CTOPP

[7]Estimated verbal IQ was calculated somewhat differently across studies. For the longitudinal study it was estimated from the Vocabulary sub-test of the Stanford Binet (Thorndike, Hagen, and Sattler 1986). For remediation study I, it was the Verbal IQ score from the Wechsler Intelligence Scale for Children-Revised (Wechsler 1974) and for remediation study II, it was estimated from the Vocabulary sub-test of the Stanford Binet. For prevention study I it was estimated from the Vocabulary and Similarities sub-tests of the WISC-R, and for prevention study II, it was estimated from the Vocabulary sub-test of the Stanford Binet.

[8]This is the range of standard scores on the reading rate measure from the Gray Oral Reading Test-Revised. Standard scores were transformed to a mean of 100 and standard deviation of 15.

*$p < .05$, **$p < .01$

small group and computer based instruction to children identified as the 20% most at risk for reading failure at the beginning of first grade. The data are from the one year follow-up test at the end of second grade.

Table 1 indicates that most of the variables were consistently correlated with text reading rate when considered by themselves. The Sight Word Efficiency (SWE) measure, which assesses how many words from a list of increasingly difficult words a child can read in 45 seconds, was either most strongly related, or tied for most strongly related to text reading rate, across all the studies, and verbal ability showed the most variable relationship with reading rate across the studies. In order to determine which combinations of variables uniquely contributed to explaining the most variance in text reading rate, a series of multiple regressions were performed. In all cases except Remediation Study II, for which raw scores were not available, the variables entered first into the regressions were age and Sight Word Efficiency. We then examined whether any of the other variables explained significant additional variance in text reading rate. Finally, we identified the set of variables whose combined unique contributions explained the most variance in reading rate. The results of these regression analyses are reported below.

LONGITUDINAL STUDY

The Sight Word Efficiency (SWE) test accounted for 67% of the variance in Text Reading Rate. The only variables that were significantly related to Text Reading Rate with SWE in the equation were Non-word Efficiency (additional 1%), and the Verbal IQ measure (additional 6%). The combination of variables that uniquely explained the most variance were SWE and Vocabulary (73%). In order to determine whether Verbal IQ accounted for unique variance in text reading fluency for children whose fluency scores were below average, we selected children from the longitudinal sample whose range in rate scores was similar to the sample in the Remediation I study. This meant that children with rate scores of 100 or greater were eliminated from the sample. With this change, the relationships of most of the variables to Text Reading Rate dropped slightly. However, the relationships with Rapid Naming of Letters ($r = .50$) and Digits ($r = .48$) showed a slight increase, and the relationship with Verbal IQ was reduced by half ($r = .31$). In this case, Verbal IQ no longer explained additional variance in reading rate beyond that explained by the SWE measure (54%), and the combination of variables that uniquely explained the most variance were SWE and rapid naming rate for letters (56%).

REMEDIATION STUDY I.

The combination of age and Sight Word Efficiency explained 58% of the variance in Text Reading Rate. When entered after SWE, both the Word Identification measure (additional 6%) and the Word Attack measure (additional 4%) explained additional unique variance in reading rate. None of the other variables explained variance beyond that accounted for by the SWE measure. The combination of variables that uniquely explained the most variance was SWE and Word Identification (64%).

REMEDIATION STUDY II

Sight Word Efficiency explained 66% of the variance in text reading rate, and Word Identification (additional 10%), Word Attack (additional 2%), and Non-word Efficiency (additional 2%) all explained additional unique variance in the dependent variable. The combination of variables that uniquely explained the most variance was SWE and Word Identification (76%).

PREVENTION STUDY I

The combination of age and Sight Word Efficiency explained 78% of the variance in Text Reading Rate. The only variables that explained additional unique variance in reading rate were Non-word Efficiency (additional 2%), Rapid Naming of Letters (additional 1%), and digits (additional 1%). The combination of variables that uniquely explained the most variance in Text Reading Rate was SWE and Non-word Efficiency (80%).

PREVENTION STUDY II

The combination of age and Sight Word Efficiency explained 82% of the variance in Text Reading Rate. The only other variables that explained additional unique variance in reading rate were Non-word Efficiency (additional 1%), Rapid Naming of Letters (1%), and digits (1%). The combination of variables that uniquely explained the most variance in Text Reading Rate was SWE and Non-word Efficiency (83%). In discussing the results of these analyses, we will address the contributions of each of the variables to reading fluency one at a time.

Proportion of Words in Text that are Recognized as Orthographic Units

The most direct measure of the extent to which children could recognize words as orthographic units was the Sight Word Efficiency Measure. In order to obtain a high score on this measure, one must be able to recognize individual words very rapidly. The Word Identification measure also assessed this construct, and may have been particularly sensitive to the child's ability to identify more complex words accurately. What is clear from both the correlational and regression analyses is that the size of one's "sight vocabulary" is the variable most strongly related to text reading rate in both large random samples and in samples of children with reading disabilities. In the two remedial studies, it was the combination of the Sight Word Efficiency and Word Identification tests that uniquely explained the most variance in text reading rate.

Speed of Processes that are Used to Identify "Novel" Words

We did not have measures available for all of the potentially important processes in this area, but we did have good measures for phonemic decoding and letter identification processes. The Word Attack, Non-word Efficiency, and Rapid Naming speed for letters all assessed speed and accuracy of processes within this domain. In every study, one of these measures accounted for additional unique variance in text reading rate beyond that explained by the SWE measure. For the two prevention studies, it was the combination of Sight Word Efficiency and Non-word Efficiency that together explained the most variance in text reading rate.

Speed with Which Word Meanings are Identified

We obviously do not have fully adequate measures in this domain. However, the level of a child's verbal intelligence or extent of vocabulary as assessed by standardized measures does capture some of what is meant by this concept, if we can assume that children with more extensive vocabularies have had more exposures to a broader variety of words than other children (Cunningham and Stanovich 1998). Further, there is evidence that speed of verbal processing is substantially correlated with measures of verbal knowledge (Hunt, Lunneborg, and Lewis 1975). In the correlational analyses, this variable was significantly related to text reading rate in three of the five studies examined. However, it explained unique variance (beyond that explained by the SWE test) in text reading rate only in the longitudinal sample in which fluency scores covered the full range from extremely dysfluent to extremely fluent. Since it is likely that the causal relationship between text reading rate and richness of verbal knowledge is reciprocal, we also examined the influence of verbal ability on text reading rate in the longitudinal sample with verbal ability measured in the first grade, rather than concurrently with rate. For this longitudinal sample, the correlation between verbal ability measured in first grade and text reading fluency measured in fifth grade is .48, and first grade verbal ability explained additional variance in reading rate beyond that explained by concurrent Sight Word Efficiency scores (additional

2%). However, there is also evidence in this sample that the richness of a child's semantic network may be uniquely important to text reading efficiency only in older children at higher ranges of fluency. When children with above average fluency scores were eliminated from the sample, the correlation between verbal ability and fluency was cut in half (from .62 to .31), and verbal ability no longer explained unique variance in text reading rate. At lower levels of fluency, speed of recognition for individual words assumes primary importance in explaining individual differences in text reading rate. At these lower rates, size of vocabulary may influence reading rate through its relationship with the size of a child's sight word vocabulary. There is, for example, some evidence that children with large oral language vocabularies acquire "sight words" more readily than do children with more restricted vocabularies (Cunningham and Stanovich 1998; Torgesen et al. 2001).

General Naming Speed, or Speed of Processing

Our purest measure of the naming speed variable was rapid naming rate for digits. This variable is obviously similar to rapid naming rate for letters, and the relationships of these two variables to the dependent variable (text reading rate) were also very similar. However, since RAN for digits does not involve stimuli that are processed during reading, it serves as a better indicator than RAN for letters of speed-based processes that may be independent of reading related orthographic knowledge. That naming rate for digits was strongly correlated with text reading rate in all the studies but one indicates a potentially important contribution of general cognitive speed to text reading rate. That general cognitive speed did not contribute substantially to explaining variance in text reading rate beyond the variance accounted for by the Sight Word Efficiency measure should not be surprising, as the latter measure is also very likely sensitive to rate of processing differences among children. In the study in which rapid naming for digits was not significantly related to text reading rate (Torgesen et al. 2001), the most likely explanation is that students were more concerned about accuracy of word reading and comprehension than they were about reading rapidly, so that processing rate differences were less influential than they might otherwise have been.

OUTCOMES FROM FLUENCY ORIENTED INTERVENTIONS

The previous analyses suggest that the extent of one's "sight vocabulary" is certainly the most important factor explaining individual differences in reading fluency among children with reading disabilities. In all the intervention studies, speed or accuracy of phonetic decoding processes also helped to explain additional unique variance in fluency scores beyond that explained by sight word efficiency. It is interesting to consider these findings in light of outcomes from instructional or practice interventions that have focused on building reading fluency.

The oldest and most widely used method to increase reading fluency is the repeated reading technique (Meyer and Felton 1999). This is a straightforward practice/instructional technique in which the student repeatedly reads letters, words, phrases, or passages a specific number of times, or until fluency has reached a specified level. In the recent report of the National Reading Panel (National Reading Panel 2000), the repeated reading technique was found to be the only method for which there is consistent, positive support of effectiveness in increasing reading fluency.

Although repeated reading of connected text is the most commonly used application of the repeated reading technique, several kinds of focused, fluency-oriented practices have been found to produce gains in reading fluency. For example, both Tan and Nicholson (1997) and Levy, Abello, and Lysynchuk (1997) showed that practice reading single words generalized to increases in fluency for text containing those words. Further, when equivalent amounts of practice time were devoted to single word practice verses practice of the same words in context, both methods produced equivalent fluency increases on new passages containing the target words (Levy 1999). Methods that emphasize modeling and training of prosodic reading skills have not been found to be more effective in increasing fluency than those that simply have children reread passages an equivalent number of times (Young, Bowers, and McKinnon 1996).

The characteristics shared by most effective applications of the repeated reading technique include: (1) reading and rereading text a specified number of times or to a specified fluency criteria; (2) an actual increase in oral reading practice in a supported context using tutors or peers; (3) various types of feedback concerning accuracy and fluency of reading. In a recent demonstration of the effectiveness of the repeated reading technique over an extended period of time, Mercer et al., (in press) provided six minutes a day of repeated reading practice involving individual letters, phonograms, words, phrases, and passages to children with reading disabilities in a special education setting. The training, which was administered by an instructional aide, lasted for periods varying from 6 to 9 months to 19 to 25 months. Substantial gains in reading fluency and accuracy were demonstrated by almost all children in the study. Both Meyer and Felton (1999) and the report of the National Reading Panel (National Reading Panel 2000) contain much more extensive discussions of the repeated reading technique than can be provided in this chapter. Rasinski (2000) has recently described a variety of techniques for embedding opportunities for repeated reading practice within motivating and "authentic" reading contexts.

One interesting, but only partially answered question, concerns the mechanisms through which repeated reading practice has an impact on reading fluency. For example, repeated reading of text might have an impact on children's ability to use text level syntactic or symantic cues, it might help children develop more sensitivity to appropriate phrasing (prosody) as they read, or it might simply provide practice recognizing the individual words in the passage. The preponderance of evidence at this point suggests that the primary impact of repeated reading practice is to increase the speed with which individual words are recognized in text. For example, Rashotte and Torgesen (1985) demonstrated generalized gains in reading fluency after three weeks of repeated reading practice in a sample of children with reading disabilities, but only for passages that shared a substantial number of words with the practiced passages. In a similar vein, Faulkner and Levy (1999) produced evidence suggesting that for poor readers, the primary impact of the repeated reading technique is to improve the efficiency with which they process individual words in text. When this positive evidence is considered along with the failure to find differences between single word and text reading practice (Levy 1999), and the failure of practice in prosodic reading to produce stronger fluency gains than simple rereading of passages (Young, Bowers, and McKinnon 1996), it is apparent that the primary locus of the repeated reading effect is on individual word reading efficiency. Whether the technique is primarily useful in helping children acquire orthographic representations for previously unknown words, or whether it produces increases in the speed with which previously known words are identified is not clear from the research, but it seems likely that both types of effects would be present.

A relatively new approach to fluency training for children with reading disabilities, called RAVE-O (Wolf, Miller, and Donnelly 2000), provides training and practice to increase the richness of children's semantic networks in addition to practice to improve the speed of their text-based word identification processes. The idea of the semantic training is to improve children's ability to access rapidly the meaning of words in a variety of contexts. This approach is currently being evaluated in an ongoing series of studies, and preliminary reports (Wolf et al. 2000) that have shown that children receiving the RAVE-O intervention made significant gains in oral reading accuracy and fluency, as well as comprehension, when compared to children who received a math and study skills intervention. When compared to an instructional condition that emphasized phonetic decoding accuracy and word reading strategies, the RAVE-O students still showed greater gains in fluency, although the differences were smaller than in comparison to the math and study skills group. From the design of current studies, it is not possible to determine whether the semantic training component of RAVE-O contributes directly to these effects on fluency, or whether they are produced primarily by the lexical and sublexical repeated reading practice that is part of the program.

Our earlier analyses of the component reading and cognitive skills related to text reading fluency indicated that extent of vocabulary was uniquely related to fluency only at higher levels of fluency. Individual differences at lower ranges of fluency appeared to be primarily the result of differences among children in the efficiency with which they could identify the words in the passage. If this conclusion is supported in other analyses, it would not be surprising if the component of the RAVE-O intervention that is most effective in producing fluency gains for children with reading disabilities is the part that focuses on improving speed and accuracy of individual word identification. It also leaves open the clear possibility that, as children's word reading difficulties are more fully remediated, the semantic components of the intervention may be more important in producing additional gains in reading fluency.

INDIVIDUAL DIFFERENCES IN READING PRACTICE AS A LOCUS FOR FLUENCY PROBLEMS IN CHILDREN WITH READING DISABILITIES

Two obvious and related consequences of failure to acquire early reading skills at a normal rate are relative limitations in overall time spent reading, and more specifically, in the amount of practice reading individual words. For example, Allington (1977) found that children who needed reading practice the most (those with the poorest initial reading skills) actually received the least amount of time in actual reading during the school day. In a later study, Allington (1984) showed that children in low reading groups read as few as 16 words in a week of instruction, while children in high reading groups read as many as 1,933 words per week. Beimiller (1977-1978) has reported similar ability group differences in amount of actual practice in reading that is available to children in early elementary school.

These differences in reading practice opportunities are not restricted to the period of beginning reading instruction, but may actually become more pronounced as children get older. For example, Nagy and Anderson (1984) estimated that good readers may read as many as one million words a year both in and out of school, while less skilled readers may read as few as 100,000—a tenfold difference in the amount of word reading practice. More recently, Cunningham and Stanovich (1998) reported evidence suggesting enormous differences in the amount of reading done by 5th grade good and poor readers outside of school. For example, a child at the 90th percentile of reading ability may read as many words in two days as a child at the 10th percentile reads in an entire year outside the school setting. Differences in reading practice vary directly with the severity of a child's reading disability, so that children with severe reading disabilities receive only a very small fraction of the total reading practice obtained by children with normal reading skills.

Extensive exposure to text through wide and deep reading practice is essential to growth in the number of words that children can recognize orthographically. The best current theory of the way that children acquire the fully specified orthographic representations that enable fluent reading (Ehri 1998; Share and Stanovich 1995) requires that individual words be identified accurately on a number of different occasions during text reading. If words are not identified accurately in sufficient numbers of repetitions, then accurate orthographic representations are not formed, and words must be recognized through analytic means (phonemic analysis, analogy, context) that take more time than recognition on the basis of a unitized orthographic representation. Thus, one of the principle characteristics of most children with reading disabilities after the initial phase in learning to read is a severe limitation in the number of words that can be recognized instantly, without use of analytic processes (Rashotte et al. in press; Torgesen et al. 2001; Wise, Ring, and Olson 1999).

We have seen from our earlier analyses (table 1) that inefficiency in identifying single words is the most important factor in accounting for individual differences in text reading fluency in samples of children with reading disabilities. We also saw in our analyses of data from Remediation Study I that the reading fluency problems of these children were particularly pronounced for passages closer to their grade level expectancy that contained many words they could not easily identify.

When these findings are combined with the fact that the number of less frequent words (words children are less likely to have encountered before in text) increases rapidly after about third grade level (Adams 1990), it is easy to see why it is so difficult for children who have failed in reading for the first three or four years of school to close the gap in reading fluency with their normally achieving peers. If successively higher grade level passages include increasing numbers of less frequent words, and normal readers are continually expanding their sight vocabularies through their own reading behavior, it should be very difficult for children, once significantly behind in the growth of their sight word vocabulary, to close the gap in reading fluency. Such "catching up" would seem to require an extensive period of time in which the reading practice of the previously disabled children was actually *greater* than that of their peers. Even if word reading accuracy is dramatically increased through the more efficient use of analytic word reading processes (Torgesen et al. 2001), reliance on analytic processes will not produce the kind of fluent reading that is supported by orthographic word recognition processes.

The difficulties involved in "closing the gap" in reading fluency once children have experienced severe reading difficulties for several years is illustrated graphically in figure 2. Prior to intervention at grade four, children with dyslexia are very inaccurate readers and receive only a small fraction of the amount of practice in reading words obtained by children with normally developing reading skills. Both the inaccuracy in decoding new words in text and limitations in the number of word reading trials that children with dyslexia actually experience lead to a significantly slowed

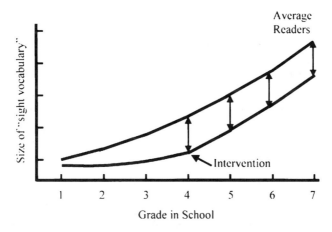

Figure 2. Projected growth in "sight vocabulary" of normal readers and disabled children before and after remediation.

rate of acquisition for new sight words. Thus, by grade four, when interventions that help them become more accurate, independent readers occur, they have a large relative deficit in the size and range of their sight word vocabulary when compared to average readers. If we make the generous assumption that, following intervention, they begin to read as much as average readers, we could speculate that they will form new orthographic representations (acquire sight words) at about the same rate as children with average reading skills. However, average readers can be expected to continue to form orthographic representations at a high rate during the late elementary school and middle school years. Thus, unless our remediated children with dyslexia receive more intensive, or more focused reading practice during these years, they will not "close the gap" in the number and range of words that can be recognized easily and fluently by sight. At each successively higher grade level, average readers will be able to identify a higher proportion of words in text at a single glance, and they will continue to be more fluent readers than the children with dyslexia who may now be accurate readers (because of more effective analytic word reading strategies), but whose sight word vocabulary will remain relatively deficient compared to average readers.

The foregoing analyses suggests that approaches emphasizing the prevention of reading disabilities, in which good reading ability is supported from the very beginning of reading instruction, may be the most effective way of eliminating reading fluency problems. In table 2, we present data from four intervention studies that are consistent with this idea.

Two of these studies in table 2 provided remedial interventions for children who were experiencing reading difficulties in 3rd through 6th grades, and two involved preventive interventions that were provided to children identified as at-risk for reading difficulties on the basis of poor performance on pre-reading and phonemic processing measures. Remediation study I (Torgesen et al. in press) has already been extensively discussed in this chapter, and Remediation study II (Rashotte et al. in press) was described briefly when table 1 was presented. The pretest standard scores are provided for both remediation studies to indicate differences in the level of severity of reading impairment before intervention in the two samples of children. Both Prevention studies were also briefly described earlier. The outcomes for Prevention Study I (Torgesen et al. 1999) are provided for immediate post-test at the end of second grade and for the two year follow-up at the end of fourth grade. The data from Prevention Study II (Torgesen et al. 2000) are from the one year follow-up test at the end of second grade.

Table 2. Differences in outcome for reading rate in prevention vs. remediation studies

Reading Measure	Studies						
	Remed-iation I		Remed-iation II		Preven-tion I		Preven-tion II
	(67.5 hours)		(35 hours)		(88 hours)		(92 hours)
	Pre	2yr foll.	Pre	Post	2nd	4th	2nd
Text Rate[1]	71.3	71.7	77.3	85.3	93.3	96.8	94.3
Text Accuracy[1]	75.8	91.0	89.5	98.3	96.7	98.5	96.2
Word Attack[2]	69.3	91.9	82.3	99.5	101.1	99.8	104.7
Word Ident.[2]	67.6	85.5	87.9	94.7	100.7	95.6	102.7
Passage Comp.[2]	82.6	95.8	93.1	104.7	94.2	87.5	95.9
Est. Verbal IQ[3]	93.1	101.5	89.4	95.7			

[1]Text rate and accuracy measures were from the Gray Oral Reading Test-Revised (Wiederholt and Bryant 1992). Standard Scores were transformed to have a mean of 100 and a standard deviation of 15 for purposes of comparison with other measures.

[2]The Word Attack, Word Identification, and Passage Comprehension tests were all taken from the Woodcock Reading Mastery Test-Revised (Woodcock 1987).

[3]Estimated verbal IQ was calculated somewhat differently across studies. For remediation study I, it was the Verbal IQ score from the Wechsler Intelligence Scale for Children-Revised (Wechsler 1974) and for remediation study II, it was estimated from the Vocabulary sub-test of the Stanford Binet (Thorndike, Hagen, and Sattler 1986). For prevention study I it was estimated from the Vocabulary and Similarities sub-tests of the WISC-R, and for prevention study II, it was estimated from the Vocabulary sub-test of the Stanford Binet.

The major observation from table 2 is that preventive studies do not show the large differences in outcomes for accuracy and fluency that are manifest in the remediation studies. One possibility might be that noticeable impairments in fluency do not begin to emerge in children with reading disabilities until late elementary school. However, the data from Prevention Study I show that this group of highly at-risk children actually improved their standard scores in rate from second to fourth grade. It is also possible that the children in the prevention studies, because they were identified by risk status rather than actual reading failure, may not have been as severely impaired as those in the remediation studies. This may clearly be true for Remediation Study I which intervened with children in the bottom 2% of reading skill, but it is less likely for the comparison with Remediation Study II, which served children in roughly the bottom 16% of reading skill. Additionally, a control group in Prevention Study I that received a variety of school-based interventions, but no research-based interventions, obtained a standard score of 81.7 on the fluency measure. Furthermore, a group of children from the large longitudinal study described earlier (Wagner, Torgesen, and Rashotte 1994; Wagner et al. 1997) who were selected by the same criteria in kindergarten as those in Prevention Study I, but who received no research-based interventions, obtained a standard score of 76 on the rate measure at the end of 5th grade. Thus, these comparisons suggest that early interventions that help to equalize the early reading practice between children at-risk for failure and normal learners by helping the at risk children keep pace in the development of early word reading skill, may eliminate many of the reading fluency problems of older children with reading disabilities. The comparisons also suggest that one of the major reasons for the seriously impaired fluency of older children in remediation studies is that they are simply not able to make up for the huge differences in reading practice that occur during the time they are poor readers.

CONCLUDING COMMENTS

The goal of this chapter was to consider information and ideas that may help to focus our efforts in studying ways to prevent or remediate reading fluency problems in children with reading disabilities. One conclusion from a comparison of outcomes between preventive and remedial studies is that it may be much easier to prevent reading fluency problems from arising than to remediate them once they are established in older children. The differences between outcomes of prevention and remediation studies are understandable in terms of current theories about the growth of orthographic reading skills. These theories suggest that the enormous reading practice differences that occur between disabled and normal readers produce large differences in the number of words that can be recognized as orthographic units in a single glance. Because one of the primary factors that limits reading fluency is inefficiency in recognition of individual words, this huge difference in "sight word" vocabulary can account for most of the fluency differences between disabled and normal readers. If prevention studies are successful in providing accurate word reading strategies for at-risk children from the beginning of reading instruction, they may help to eliminate many of the differences in cumulative reading practice that are a likely source of older disabled children's continuing fluency problems.

For children with reading disabilities who have limited sight word vocabularies and limited proficiency in decoding novel words, it seems that the first target of intervention should be to increase the accuracy of their individual word reading skills. As children read more accurately, they will receive more practice trials in which individual words are pronounced correctly, and should thus add to the vocabulary of words they can recognize by sight. This is clearly what happened to the children in our first remediation study (Torgesen et al. 2001). Although they were not able to add words to their sight vocabulary fast enough to "close the gap" in fluency relative to average children their same age, they did become able to read increasingly difficult passages containing familiar words at relatively fluent rates. The most successful fluency intervention described to date, repeated reading, is effective because it provides the kind of repeated exposure to words that leads either to the formation of new orthographic images or increases efficiency of access to images already formed. If, as some have suggested (Wolf and Bowers 1999), many reading disabled children have special difficulties in forming orthographic images of words in addition to problems acquiring phonetic decoding skills, repeated reading practice may be particularly effective because it concentrates exposure to specific words over a relatively short span of time. Simply providing more reading opportunities for these children may not be sufficient to increase their sight vocabulary at an acceptable rate, because, at higher grade levels, the less frequent words they are trying to learn occur at such infrequent intervals in text (Adams 1990). An important question for future research is how to increase the efficiency of reading practice for children whose reading accuracy problems have been remediated through successful interventions. In other words, how should practice be engineered and focused so that it produces accelerated growth in the fluent word reading processes that are the most critical factor in oral reading fluency?

REFERENCES

Adams, M. J. 1990. *Beginning to Read.* Cambridge, MA: MIT Press.

Allington, R. L. 1977. If they don't read much, how they ever gonna get good? *Journal of Reading* 21:57–61.

Allington, R. L. 1983. Fluency: The neglected reading goal in reading instruction. *The Reading Teacher* 36:556–61.

Allington, R. L. 1984. Content coverage and contextual reading in reading groups. *Journal of Reading Behavior* 16:85–96.

Aulls, M. S. 1978. *Developmental and Remedial Reading in the Middle Grades.* Boston: Allyn and Bacon, Inc.

Beimiller, A.1977–1978. Relationships between oral reading rates for letters, words, and simple text in the development of reading achievement. *Reading Research Quarterly* 13:223–53.

Ben-Dror, I., Pollatsek, A., and Scarpati, S. 1991. Word identification in isolation and in context by college dyslexic students. *Brain and Language* 40:471–90.

Cunningham, A. E., and Stanovich, K. E. 1998. What reading does for the mind. *American Educator* 22(1–2):8–15.

Ehri, L. C. 1998. Grapheme-phoneme knowledge is essential for learning to read words in English. In *Word Recognition in Beginning Reading*, eds. J. Metsala and L. Ehri. Hillsdale, NJ: Lawrence Erlbaum Associates.

Faulkner, H. J., and Levy, B. A. 1999. How text difficulty and reader skill interact to produce differential reliance on word and content overlap in reading transfer. *Journal of Experimental Child Psychology* 58:1–24.

Fuchs, L. S., Fuchs, D., and Maxwell, L. 1988. The validity of informal measures of reading comprehension. *Remedial and Special Education* 9:20–28.

Hasbrouk, J. E., and Tindal, G. 1992. Curriculum based oral reading fluency for students in grades 2 through 5. *Teaching Exceptional Children* 24:41–44.

Hudson, R., Mercer, C. D. and Lane, H. 2000. Exploring reading fluency: A paradigmatic overview. Unpublished manuscript. University of Florida, Gainesville, FL.

Hunt, E., Lunneborg, C., and Lewis, J. 1975. What does it mean to be high verbal? *Cognitive Psychology* 7:194–227.

Jenkins, J. R., Fuchs, L. S., Espin, C., van den Broek, P., and Deno, S. L. 2000. Effects of task format and performance dimension on word reading measures: Criterion validity, sensitivity to impairment, and context facilitation. Paper presented at Pacific Coast Research Conference, San Diego, CA, February.

Levy, B. A., Abello, B., and Lysynchuk, L. 1997. Transfer from word training to reading in context: Gains in reading fluency and comprehension. *Learning Disability Quarterly* 20:173–88

Levy, B. A. 1999. Learning to read: Context doesn't matter. Paper presented at the Society for the Scientific Study of Reading, Montreal.

Lyon, G. R. 1995. Towards a definition of dyslexia. *Annals of Dyslexia* 45:3–27.

Mercer, C. D., Campbell, K. U., Miller, M. D., Mercer, K. D., and Lane, H. B. in press. Effects of a reading fluency intervention for middle schoolers with specific learning disabilities. *Learning Disabilities Research and Practice*.

Meyer, M. S., and Felton, R. H. 1999. Repeated reading to enhance fluency: Old approaches and new directions. *Annals of Dyslexia* 49:283–306.

Nagy, W., and Anderson, R. C. 1984. How many words are there in printed school English? *Reading Research Quarterly* 19:304–30.

National Reading Panel 2000. Teaching children to read: An evidence-based assessment of the scientific research literature on reading and its implications for reading instruction. National Institute of Child Health and Human Development, Washington, D.C.

Pring, L., and Snowling, M. 1986. Developmental changes in word recognition: An information-processing account. *Quarterly Journal of Experimental Psychology* 38A:395–418.

Rasinski, T. V. 1990. Investigating measures of reading of fluency. *Educational Research Quarterly* 14:34–44.

Rasinski, T. V. 1999. Exploring a method for estimating independent, instructional, and frustration reading rates. *Journal of Reading Psychology* 20:61–9.

Rashotte, C. A., and Torgesen, J. K. 1985. Repeated reading and reading fluency in learning disabled children. *Reading Research Quarterly* 20: 180–202.

Rashotte, C. A., MacPhee, K., and Torgesen, J. K. in press. The effectiveness of a group reading instruction program with poor readers in multiple grades. *Learning Disabilities Quarterly*.

Rasinski, T. V. 2000. Speed does matter in reading. *The Reading Teacher* 54:146–51.

Share, D. L., and Stanovich, K. E. 1995. Cognitive processes in early reading development: A model of acquisition and individual differences. *Issues in Education: Contributions for Educational Psychology* 1:1–57.

Shinn, M. R., Good, R. H., Knutson, N., Tilly, W. D., and Collins, V. L 1992. Curriculum based measurement of oral reading fluency: A confirmatory analysis of its relation to reading. *School Psychology Review* 21:459–79.

Stanovich, K. E. and Stanovich, P. J. 1995. How research might inform the debate about early reading acquisition. *Journal of Research in Reading* 18:87–105.

Tan, A., and Nicholson, T. 1997. Flashcards revisited: Training poor readers to read words faster improves their comprehension of text. *Journal of Educational Psychology* 89:276–88.

Thorndike, R. L., Hagen, E. P., and Sattler, J. M. 1986. *Guide for Administering and Scoring the Stanford-Binet Intelligence Scale: Fourth Edition.* Chicago: Riverside Publishing.

Torgesen, J. K., Alexander, A. W., Wagner, R. K., Rashotte, C. A., Voeller, K, Conway, T. and Rose, E. 2001. Intensive remedial instruction for children with severe reading disabilities: Immediate and long-term outcomes from two instructional approaches. *Journal of Learning Disabilities 34:33–58.*

Torgesen, J. K., Wagner, R. K., Rashotte, C. A., and Herron, J. 2000. The effectiveness of teacher supported computer assisted instruction in preventing reading problems in young children: A comparison of two methods. Unpublished manuscript, Florida State University, Tallahassee, FL.

Wagner, R. K., Torgesen, J. K., and Rashotte, C. A. 1994. The development of reading-related phonological processing abilities: New evidence of bi-directional causality from a latent variable longitudinal study. *Developmental Psychology* 30:73–87.

Wagner, R. K., Torgesen, J. K., Rashotte, C. A., Hecht, S. A., Barker, T. A., Burgess, S. R., Donahue, J., and Garon, T. 1997. Changing causal relations between phonological processing abilities and word-level reading as children develop from beginning to fluent readers: A five-year longitudinal study. *Developmental Psychology* 33: 468–479.

Wechsler, D. 1974. *Wechsler Intelligence Scale for Children: Revised.* New York: The Psychological Corporation.

Wiederholt, J. L., and Bryant, B. R. 1992. *Gray Oral Reading Test-3.* Austin, Texas: Pro-Ed.

Wise, B. W., Ring, J., and Olson, R. K. 1999. Training phonological awareness with and without explicit attention to articulation. *Journal of Experimental Child Psychology* 72:271–304.

Wolf, M., and Bowers, P. G. 1999. The double-deficit hypothesis for the developmental dyslexias. *Journal of Educational Psychology* 91:415–38.

Wolf, M., Miller, L., and Donnelly, K. 2000. Retrieval, Automaticity, Vocabulary, Orthography (RAVE-O): A comprehensive, fluency-based reading intervention program. *Journal of Learning Disabilities* 33:375–86.

Woodcock, R. W. 1987. *Woodcock Reading Mastery Tests-Revised.* Circle Pines, MN: American Guidance Service.

Young, A. R., Bowers, P. G., and McKinnon, G. E. 1996. Effects of prosodic modeling and repeated reading on poor readers' fluency and comprehension. *Applied Psycholinguistics* 17:59–84.

Chapter • **16**

Moving The Bottom: *Improving Reading Fluency*

Betty Ann Levy

One of the most exciting recent developments in the area of reading disability has been a renewed interest in the acquisition of reading *fluency*. For several decades, researchers have focused on the almost universal deficit in phonological awareness and phonological processing shown by poor readers. Most poor readers exhibit difficulty in performing auditory tasks that require them to respond to the individual segments that make up spoken words. There is now general agreement that these problems in responding to individual auditory segments constitute a core reading deficit (e.g., Felton 1993; Foorman et al. 1997; Levy and Lysynchuk 1997; Olson et al. 1997). However, reading is a multifaceted skill and this strong focus on the phonological deficit may have led us to overlook a second deficit. The work of Bowers, Wolf and their colleagues (Bowers 1995; Bowers et al. 1994; Bowers and Wolf 1993; Wolf 1991) highlights this oversight. They pointed out that some children show a deficit that is marked by slow performance on a rapid automatized naming (RAN) task. This deficit explains variance in reading ability even when the variance due to phonemic awareness has been removed. The interesting aspect of this second deficit is that it is rate limiting. That is, this deficit appears to affect processes that are critical to the *rapid*, automatic word recognition that is necessary for *fluent* reading. In the remainder of this paper, I will describe work from my laboratory

that focused on understanding processes related to the development of reading speed and on our training studies with children
experiencing problems in developing reading fluency.

Following Ehri (1992), Levy (1999) suggested that after the
child sets up basic representations of printed words, the access
paths to these words must become automated, so that fluent reading can develop. Ehri argued that initially in solving the "print
problem," children must acquire basic connections between representations of orthographic patterns and their phonological equiva-
lents. Once these connections have been strengthened, the system
can automatically process print in larger orthographic units, sometimes even as large as words. It is this freeing from the need to
"sound out" every phoneme that allows the child to move from
the initial stage of slow laborious reading to the stage of fluent and
rapid reading. But what experiences are optimal in moving to reading fluency? Stanovich (1986) argued that children who learn to
read early and easily enjoy reading and are motivated to read on
their own, thus give themselves many hours of practice, beyond
the formal instruction received in school. Children who have difficulty in acquiring basic word recognition skills are not motivated
to read and thus fail to provide themselves with this additional
reading practice. Across time their exposure to print becomes much
less than that of their peers who enjoy reading. We know that exposure to print improves general verbal abilities, including reading
(Cunningham and Stanovich 1991; Stanovich and West 1989). But,
what kinds of practice will improve reading fluency?

PRACTICE: WORDS OR CONTEXTUAL READING

When children begin to read, they experience print in many different ways. Each of these experiences leaves a memorial representation that potentially can be used to improve reading skill on
subsequent occasions. That is, the memorial representation
formed during a reading experience may be recruited to aid later
reading fluency. Over the past few years, my students and I have
used transfer of skill across reading experiences to explore growth
in reading fluency. Our basic interest is in the development of skill
from one print experience to another. Are there optimal conditions for transfer to later fluent reading? To put this work in an
educational context, consider the whole language emphasis on
contextual reading. This position basically argues that children
should learn to read words in context because the contextual sur-
round supports word recognition, thus relieving the child from
the need to sound out every word. Fluent reading, they argue,

does not require the detailed analysis of each individual word. Words read in "word drills" will not help later contextual reading, because words read in texts and from single word displays are processed differently.

What evidence is available to support the view that reading in context leads to better word recognition skill? The now classic work of Goodman (1965) indicated that children who failed to read words presented in a word list were often able to read many of those words when they occurred in a story context. These data are consistent with the view that contextual support facilitates word recognition. However, these results have been questioned by Nicholson (1991), who showed that contextual gains are limited mainly to poor readers and very young readers. They are not shown by the most fluent child readers. These data suggest that contextual support is used in the service of poor word recognition skill, not in aid of fluent recognition. But does contextual reading benefit poor readers in their quest for fluency. Dahl (1979) argued that it does. Over an 8-month period, Dahl trained poor readers in grade 2 to read a set of passages, each to a criterion speed of 100 words per minute. This repeated reading procedure led to more fluent reading of many stories. One control group of children, matched for reading level, received an equivalent amount of reading practice, but they read single words, not texts. A second matched control group received only classroom instruction over the 8-month period. Dahl reported improvements in word identification and in comprehension, as measured by a cloze procedure, for the text-trained children. However, the word-trained children were equivalent to the classroom controls. These data support the view that contextual reading practice is more optimal for developing reading fluency than word recognition practice alone. Dahl argued that practice with words in context "gives the child the opportunity to integrate the subskill" (p. 62). Word practice alone does not provide this opportunity to improve the integration of skills needed for fast reading with comprehension.

However, following the logic of the LaBerge and Samuels (1974) model of automatization of word recognition, Samuels (1979) credited these same rereading benefits for texts to the automatization of word recognition, thus freeing the reader to devote processing resources to comprehension. Along the same lines, Rashotte and Torgesen (1985) reported that transfer occurred across different passages in a repeated readings paradigm only when the different passages had a high overlap of words. When different passages used largely different words, then training on one passage transferred little benefit to the reading of a later passage. As in the Samuels' work, the medium of transfer of reading skill appeared to be more fluent word recognition, not some general skill in integrating subskills needed for fluency. However, Fleisher, Jenkins, and Pany (1979) again raised the possibility that word practice was not sufficient to develop text reading fluency. They reported two studies in which poor readers in grades 4 and 5 were first given practice reading a set of words that were in fact the words of a short story (approximately 75 words long). Children practiced the words until all words could be read within one second. Then, each child read two short passages, one containing the trained words and one of equal difficulty in which none of the trained words occurred. Although in the first study, the story with the trained words was read faster than the control story with untrained words, this reading rate benefit was not found in the second study. Neither study showed any benefit to comprehension for the story with the trained words. These findings again suggested that word practice may be insufficient to enable more fluent text reading.

In Levy, Abello, and Lysynchuk (1997), we explored factors that might limit the conclusions drawn by Fleisher et al. We used basically the same paradigm as Fleisher et al., with word reading practice followed by story reading. In one study, we divided our forty poor readers in grade 4 into two groups, using a median split on a measure of rapid automatized naming (RAN). Following Bowers (1993), our logic was that poor readers with a naming speed problem may need much more practice than fast namers to improve their fluency. Perhaps fast namers would show transfer from word training to text reading fluency, while slow namers would not. Like Bowers (1993), we found that the slow namers were also the slowest text readers. However, slow namers gained just as much from practice on word naming as fast namers. Further, both groups showed improved text reading speed and improved text comprehension for the story that contained the trained words. This study suggested that it is possible to improve word recognition skill and that this improvement can enable improved speed and comprehension, even for the least fluent children. Our study differed from that of Fleisher et al. in a few, possibly critical, ways. First, we used longer passages (288 words each) to encourage meaning processing. Also, our stories were at or below the readers' reading level, so that when the words were read by the child there was some possibility that the message would be understood. Fleisher et al. used passages that were above the reading level of the participants, thus limiting the comprehension processing that was possible. We also used a time limit for each word during training in order to force even the slowest children to read as fast as possible. The main points we took from this study were that naming speed is a good indicator of word recognition difficulty and that improving word recognition speed will improve fluency of later text reading, contrary to the beliefs forwarded by the whole language philosophy.

In a recent paper, Bourassa et al. (1998) reported that for poor readers, practice at any linguistic level will lead to improved reading at other levels. Thus, practice in reading words in one story will improve the reading rate and comprehension of a different story that has a lot of the same words. Following Rashotte and Torgesen (1985), we argued that this transfer in fluency must be mediated at the word recognition level. This word recognition improvement was indicated by a further study showing that words trained in a story context are later read faster and more accurately from single word displays. Thus, our work suggests that the reading fluency of poor readers is limited by their slow word processing rate. Reading experience, in or out of a text context, will improve this deficit. In one final study, Bourassa, Hutchison, Pilarsky and I tried to compare more directly the benefits of practice to later story reading, when the practice occurred either in the context of a word game or in the context of a story. In this study, twenty-four good and twenty-four poor comprehenders in grade 4 participated in two yoked experiments. We chose these reader groups based on their performance on the Passage Comprehension sub-test of the Woodcock Reading Mastery Test. Good comprehenders had a mean comprehension score of 112.5 (range 109-126), while the poor comprehenders had a mean of 83.5 (range 69-89). As would be expected, the good comprehenders also had better word recognition skills, as indicated by the Word Identification sub-test of the Woodcock test (good: mean 111.8, range 92-127; poor: mean 87.3, range 63-108). Both groups participated in two studies separated by two to three weeks. Order of experiments and stories used in the transfer measures were counterbalanced across both groups, so that the critical fluency measures were not confounded with differences in materials across studies. Both studies contained a training phase and a transfer phase. The *transfer* phase was identical in the two studies. In each case, participants read two stories, each 279 words in length, twice in succession, followed by six comprehension questions that were asked and answered orally. All stories were at the grade 3.5 reading level. For one transfer story, the 108 content words (nouns, verbs, adjectives, adverbs) had all occurred in the training phase. For the control story, none of its content words had occurred during training. Two sets of training/control stories were used so that materials could be counterbalanced across experiments. The critical measures were the speed and accuracy of reading the two stories and the comprehension of the stories as measured by question answering.

The critical difference between the two studies was in the way the content words had been learned during training. In the *word training* study, the 108 content words from the critical transfer story were presented in a "stop the clock" computer game. Children were encouraged to read the words as quickly as possible so they would be at their best naming time. Words appeared on a computer screen one at a time. Naming time was measured from the onset of a word until the child's response activated a voice key that stopped the computer clock. The computer then recorded that time and displayed it on the screen for the child. Each word was repeated 13 times during training, with the entire word set being read before the next repetition began. Word order was randomized on every repetition. This training encouraged fast individual word recognition; the question was whether this training would show the same benefit to reading the transfer text as the story training task. In the *story training task*, children read a story four times in succession that contained all 108 content words (often with multiple repetitions) of the critical transfer story. This training, then, provided practice with the transfer story's words, but in a totally different story context. This practice provided experience in word recognition and in reading the words to integrate with comprehension processes, consistent with the whole language preferences for optimal reading training. Does this contextual reading, compared with word training, lead to more fluent reading of the transfer story?

Looking first at the *training* data, figure 1 shows that over the thirteen training repetitions in the "stop the clock" game both good and poor comprehenders learned to read the 108 target words faster, with the poor comprehenders gaining more than 100 milliseconds per word. Figure 2 shows that both groups also gained in reading accuracy during the training phase, with poor comprehenders showing dramatic learning. Thus simple practice or repetition in a naming game led to impressive gains in word recognition skill, particularly for the poor readers.

Tables 1 and 2 show the training data for the four readings of the training story. Table 1 shows that reading time for the story decreased over re-readings for both skill groups, with the poor comprehenders showing an impressive gain of almost 90 seconds across the four readings. Table 2 show that accuracy also improved over readings, with the poor comprehenders again showing the

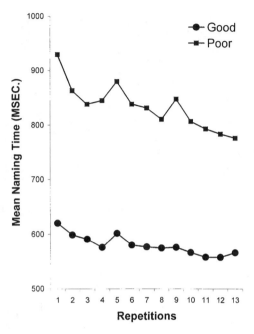

Figure 1.   Mean naming times (in seconds) for good and poor readers during word training.

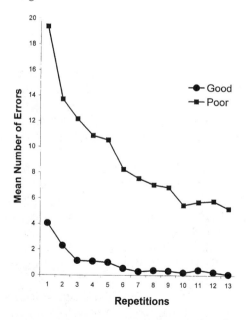

Figure 2   Mean number of naming errors for good and poor readers during word training.

Table 1. Mean Reading Times (in seconds) Across Four Repeated Readings During Training

	Repetitions			
	1	2	3	4
Good Readers				
Mean	156.5	133.7	122.5	1116.2
SD	40.5	34.4	31.2	25.6
Poor Readers				
Mean	311.2	264.3	243.4	223.4
SD	100.0	106.6	101.6	87.6

Table 2. Mean Number of Errors Across the Four Repeated Readings During Training

	Repetitions			
	1	2	3	4
Good Readers				
Mean	7.0	4.5	3.0	2.6
SD	3.7	3.1	2.1	2.2
Poor Readers				
Mean	28.2	21.7	17.6	16.5
SD	19.0	16.9	15.7	14.7

most dramatic improvement with practice. Thus, as in the word training task, simple repeated experience led to marked improvement in reading fluency, even for the most impaired children. The question is whether these different training regimes, both of which improved reading of the trained materials, show differential transfer to reading the transfer story that contained the 108 overlapping words.

Table 3 presents the mean reading time for the 279-word transfer stories (one containing the trained words and one with no trained words), on both the first and second reading of each story. As is clear from this table, both good and poor comprehenders, on both readings, read the story with the trained words faster than the story that contained untrained content words. Poor comprehenders showed the largest gains due to training. What is particularly striking, however, is the similarity of the reading times for Word and Text conditions. The Untrained values show that the texts yielded the same baselines prior to training. The Trained times show that the transfer benefit to reading speed was the same, whether training had occurred in a speeded word game or in

Table 3. Mean Reading Time in Seconds for the Two Readings of the Transfer Passage

First Reading

	Trained		Untrained	
	Words	Text	Words	Text
Good Readers	129	131	142	143
Poor Readers	239	242	282	280

Second Reading

	Trained		Untrained	
	Words	Text	Words	Text
Good Readers	113	118	122	123
Poor Readers	211	218	237	244

a different story context. Table 4 shows the same picture for reading accuracy of the transfer story: equivalent gains for the two training conditions. Taken together, these data suggest that practice in reading words, in or out of a text context, leads to improved reading fluency when those words are encountered later in a story. Reading practice in either form helps poor readers access words more rapidly and accurately. There is no evidence that contextual reading provides a greater benefit in improving fluency.

Finally, table 5 presents the mean number of comprehension questions answered after two readings of the transfer stories. Neither skill group in either training condition showed improved comprehension. This may have been partly due to the two readings prior to comprehension testing. Any differences due to training may have been negated by the rereading. Taken together, these data provide support for improvements in reading fluency with practice, particularly for poor readers. Context is not an

Table 4. Mean Number of Errors for the Two Readings of the Transfer Passages

First Reading

	Trained		Untrained	
	Words	Text	Words	Text
Good Readers	4.0	4.6	6.4	7.0
Poor Readers	12.9	17.0	27.0	29.8

Second Reading

	Trained		Untrained	
	Words	Text	Words	Text
Good Readers	3.1	3.1	4.1	3.9
Poor Readers	11.0	14.5	21.0	25.5

Table 5. Comprehension Questions Correct (*N* = 6)

First Reading

	Trained		Untrained	
	Words	Text	Words	Text
Good Readers	4.3	4.6	4.0	4.6
Poor Readers	3.3	2.8	2.9	3.0

Second Reading

	Trained		Untrained	
	Words	Text	Words	Text
Good Readers	3.1	4.8	5.1	4.6
Poor Readers	3.8	3.8	4.0	3.5

essential, or even an optimal, component of the experience. One might have expected context to show its maximal benefits in comprehension, yet there were none. It could be argued that the word task provided more practice (13 repetitions of the 108 content words) than the story task (4 readings, but with a varying number of repetitions of each target word within the story) so that it is surprising that story reading was as beneficial. However, it should be noted that story training was so slow for the poor readers that in terms of total training time there was little difference between the two conditions. Poor readers struggled laboriously to read passages (we provided assists after intervals of 1.5 seconds so that comprehension was not disrupted). It is a difficult and time-consuming experience. It appears to offer few additional benefits compared with a word game that the child can complete in short, enjoyable sessions. At least early in reading acquisition, it seems reasonable to improve fluency with as little struggle as possible. After all, we want poor readers to feel successful and we want them to enjoy reading stories. Making sure that they can read the content words of a story fluently *before* they try to understand the message may be a wise educational step.

From our research on reading practice, we conclude that practice or repeated exposure is important in speeding access to representations of printed words. This speeded access is critical to the development of reading fluency. Children who are poor readers, even the slowest namers as indicated by a RAN measure, benefit from repeated practice. In fact, these slow children showed some of the most dramatic gains in reading speed. From an educational perspective, one of the most important findings was that a variety of different experiences can lead to the development of fluency. Contrary to some earlier views, there is transfer of learning across linguistic levels and contexts. Speeded access can be developed in word games or in text reading situations. Thus creative teachers can develop an array of situations in which children will encounter target words, knowing that all of these experiences will help the child meet the ultimate challenge: to read a text fast and accurately while fully comprehending the message.

FORMING INITIAL REPRESENTATION

Although the research discussed above suggests that reading exposure and practice is important in speeding the processing of print, thus making reading more fluent, it is important to note that this work addressed *fluency*, not learning to read unfamiliar words. That is, these children were already readers and the materials were selected to be at or below the child's reading level. We were interested in how practice *automated* access to representations, not in how the print representations were initially acquired. I will suggest that these two phases of development respond to different learning conditions.

Our interest in the formation of representations for words encountered in print began with studies of optimal methods for setting non-readers on the path to reading. Following Adams (1990), we argued that young children should not learn to read by "gagging on print." Before they are asked to read printed text, they should be able to read 80 to 90 percent of the words on the page. Thus, the first task is to set up a print vocabulary with enough words to get the young reader started. Levy and Lysynchuk (1997) compared segmentation and whole word methods for teaching non-readers in kindergarten and grade 1 to read their first words. Our interest was in methods that led to rapid acquisition, with good retention and good generalization to reading orthographically related words. Guided by the earlier work of Goswami (1986, 1988, 1990a, b), Bruck and Treiman (1992), and Olson and Wise (1992), we compared word learning when the training emphasized different segment sizes. Eighty-three children in grade 1 and 17 children in kindergarten, selected because they read essentially no words, were divided into five groups. Four groups received daily training over a five week period in reading a set of 32 words. The fifth group was a standard classroom control that did the pretests and post-tests only. All trained groups learned to read the same 32 words, but the presentation conditions differed. In the Rime group, for the first 15 days of training, four words with the same rime (e.g., four igs: fig, rig, big, dig) were presented together on separate cards. The "ig" segment was colored in red, while the onsets were in black. This presentation therefore provided four family words with the shared orthographic unit highlighted in red ink. This method was used for the presentation of all eight rime families on each training day. On the first reading, the experimenter segmented each word into its onset and rime and then blended the two segments. Thereafter, the child attempted to segment and blend with corrective feedback maintaining these segments. After 15 days of reading all 32 words per day in this fashion, the red highlighting was dropped but the rime-blocking was retained for a further ten days of training. Generalization was tested the day after the end of training. It consisted of reading 32 new words and 32 non-words that shared the trained rimes. One week after training ended, retention was tested by asking the child to read all 32 trained words presented in a random order and with no colored highlighting.

The same basic procedure was used for the Onset group, except that the four words presented together during training shared an onset and the shared onset was highlighted in red ink. For the Phoneme condition, the four words presented together were unrelated, but for each word the individual phonemes were in different colors and the modeling and feedback were consistent with phoneme sounding and blending. For the Whole Word condition, the four words presented together were unrelated, each was printed in black ink, and the modeling and feedback were at the whole word level. Thus the four methods differed in both blocking of words during training and in the size of the segments taught. The basic findings were that the three segmentation methods (onset, rime, phoneme) led to similar rapid acquisition, all being better than whole word repetition. Retention and generalization mirrored learning. These data suggested that during the initial word learning phase of reading acquisition, whole word practice is NOT optimal, contrary to the benefits of this method during automatization, as discussed in the first section of this paper.

To examine this matter more closely, we next explored the effectiveness of the methods described above (except that the onset/rime split was done only with rime blocking) for children in grade 2 who were already reading considerably below the level of their peers. In a study reported by Levy, Bourassa, and Horn (1999), 128 of the poorest readers in grade 2 were selected over a two year period. These 128 poor readers were divided by a median split into the slowest and fastest namers on a RAN task. The 64 slow RAN and the 64 fast RAN poor readers were matched on their phonemic awareness ability. Each RAN group was then divided into four subgroups: one control group and three training groups, with 16 children per group. Using essentially the same blocking and highlighting methods described above, groups received onset/rime, phoneme, or whole word training. The control group received an equal number of sessions doing arithmetic problems. The important findings were that the slow RAN children learned more slowly irrespective of method used. However, they were particularly *disadvantaged* when whole word repetition was used. This finding somewhat surprised us; we thought that perhaps these children would gain more from word repetition practice, as they had in the earlier automatization study. As an educational note, it is not uncommon for resource teachers to ask children with reading problems to repeatedly read Dolsch word lists; this remedial teaching may be the *least* effective way to help these children acquire new words. The results suggested that these larger orthographic units present representational difficulties for children who are particularly slow processors. Note that while our fast and slow RAN groups did not differ in phonemic awareness skills, both groups were poor on these tasks relative to age expectations. Thus, the slow RAN children studied here are probably most like Bower and Wolf's (1993) double-deficit children, while the fast RAN children are most like their single deficit (phonological processing) group. Consistent with this notion, the slow RAN group were the worst readers as indicated by the Woodcock word identification test and by their pre-training ability to read the experimental word set.

The study described above suggests that, as with the non-readers studied by Levy and Lysynchuk (1997), segmentation methods lead to the best learning even for these very delayed readers in grade 2. However, it also raises the issue of *why* slow RAN children are so disadvantaged when faced with whole words. The same learning challenge should have been present in the onset-rime condition, where larger orthographic units were also trained, yet performance was much better with this segmentation training. Why was this larger orthographic unit (the rime) easier to learn? In considering this matter, we noticed that the onset/rime and whole word conditions differed, not only in the segment size highlighted and pronounced during training, but also in the words blocked together. In the onset/rime training, four words that shared the same rime unit were learned together. The rime unit was printed in red ink for each word in order to highlight the analogous unit across the four words. However, in the whole word condition, the four words presented together shared no orthographic unit. Across the entire word set, there was equivalent experience with each rime, but the rhyming words occurred randomly across the training set, not blocked as in the onset/rime condition. Could the benefit for the onset/rime over the whole word condition for the slow RAN children have resulted from the blocking, rather than the segmentation per se? Could it be that these children simply fail to perform internal analyses of the whole word displays so that the internal orthographic units are never "seen"? When words with a similar internal unit are blocked and/or highlighted, thus drawing attention to orthographic analogies in words, then even slow RAN children might represent them. What additional advantage, if any, comes from oral segmentation and blending?

In a study that we just completed (Levy et al. in preparation), we assessed the importance of orthographic blocking and high- lighting, even when the oral segmentation was always at the whole word level. In this study, we screened 809 children to find a sample of 80 grade 2 poor readers who met the same criteria as the slow RAN children in the Levy, Bourassa, and Horn (1999) study. These children were divided into five groups, 16 per group, with the groups matched on phonemic awareness (low), RAN score (slow), and reading level. The groups were statistically equivalent on all of these measures to the slow RAN children in the rime group studied by Levy et. al. (1999). This allows us to compare di- rectly the "whole word" training results in this study with the rime training results reported by Levy et. al. (1999). In the new study, four groups were trained to read the same 48-word set used by Levy et. al. (1999). The fifth, control, group again received an equivalent number of training sessions, but doing arithmetic prob- lems. The four training groups differed in how the word set was presented. However, an important feature of this study is that the *only* response modeled by the experimenter or given by the child was at the *whole word* level, for *all* groups.

The four training conditions were formed by the factorial combination of two variables: Blocking (Unblocked vs. Blocked) and Highlighting (Unhighlighted vs. Highlighted). Blocked re- ferred to the 48 words being presented in the 12 rime-family blocks, one family at a time. Unblocked meant that the 48 words were presented in four-word sets where no two words from the same family occurred within a set. Highlighted refers to the color coding of rime segments, while Unhighlighted refers to the whole word being presented in a randomly selected color. Thus the *Unblocked-Unhighlighted* condition was identical to the Whole Word condition used in Levy et. al. (1999). Here, the four words learned together were unrelated, with each printed in a randomly chosen color; all responses were with the word name. In the *Blocked-Unhighlighted* condition, the four words learned together were from the same *rime* family, but each word was printed in a random color so that the similar orthographic unit was not color coded. Again, all responses were with the word name. In the *Unblocked-Highlighted* condition, each four-word set was again unrelated, but across the set of 48 words, the rime was color coded. For each word, the rime was in colored ink and the onset was in black ink. Each rime was always in a specific color (i.e. "igs" were in red, "ames" were in blue, irrespective of which family instance that rime occurred in). This condition drew attention to the rimes, but the color code was not blocked so that the child had to figure out the color analogies. Only word names were used in oral responding. Finally, in the *Blocked-Highlighted* condition the four members of each rime family were presented together, with the rime unit printed in red and the onset in black. This presentation method was exactly like the rime condition in Levy et al. (1999), except that there the experimenter modeled onset/rime segmentation and blending while the child responded in the same fashion. In Levy et al. (in preparation) the oral responses of both the experimenter and the child were the whole word names. As in our earlier work, color training was discontinued after 15 days; there were then 5 days with all words printed in black ink, but blocking remained in the appropriate conditions. Retention, where the child read all 48 words in random order, occurred one week after the end of training. Generalization, tested with the reading of 48 different words and 48 non-words with the same rime endings, occurred the day after the end of training.

The main findings are easily summarized. Figure 3 shows the acquisition curves over the 20 days of training for the four whole word conditions (colors were discontinued at trial 16). As is clear from this figure, blocking led to faster learning but highlighting had no additional effect. That is, when the family instances occurred together in training, there was no additional benefit of also highlighting the shared orthographic unit. Similarly, when the family instances were scattered across the set of 48 items, then coloring the rime units was again of no benefit. These observations were supported by reliable effects of trials and of blocking, with no main effect or interaction involving highlighting, in the analyses of variance. However, orthographic blocking clearly facilitated learning for these children. This finding supports the view that these children fail to analyze word units spontaneously and "see" the repeated segments when these occur distributed across learning. However, when the shared orthographic unit is made more "visible" through blocking, then these children *can* process larger units and learning is facilitated. Thus, the deficit suffered by slow RAN children cannot be that the system cannot process letters fast

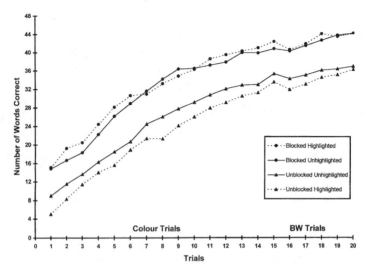

Figure 3.   Mean number of words read correctly during training for the four training conditions.

enough to allow unitization to occur. Rather, the system appears to fail to respond to segment similarity unless these segments are obvious in the print.

Although it is clear that orthographic blocking itself is sufficient to facilitate learning in these slow RAN children, we wondered whether adding phonological segmentation to orthographic blocking added further support for learning. In the blocked conditions in this experiment, no phonological segmentation occurred. To examine this issue, we compared the rime condition from Levy et. al. (1999) with the whole word conditions from the present experiment. Remember that we matched the present groups with the groups from Levy et. al. on all selection criteria to enable these comparisons. Figure 4 contains the same four acquisition curves for the whole word groups, as well as the acquisition curve for the rime condition from Levy et al. The two conditions that were *identical* in presentation format, differing only in oral response, were the Rime and the Blocked-Highlighted conditions. Figure 4 suggests that there was a trend for some additional benefit due to the oral segmentation in the Rime condition. However, this trend did not approach statistical reliability. Perhaps with a larger sample, the benefit would be reliable, but the striking thing is how much of the benefit is carried by orthographic blocking alone. These children seem to have their deficit in "seeing" bigger units; if the units are "visible" they can be processed and learning is benefitted.

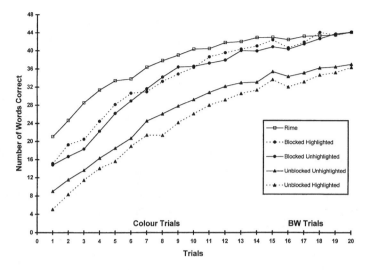

Figure 4.   Mean number of words read correctly during training, with the rime group. From Levy et al. (1999) included.

Although these acquisition data indicated that "orthographic visibility" enhanced learning, the retention and generalization data suggest some cost of this more rapid learning. Retention data, taken one week after training ended, was the first time the blocked groups now saw the trained word set in a random order. All trained groups read more words than the control group (minimum of 31 versus about 6). However, when trial 20 of acquisition was used as a co-variate in order to control for differences in the number of words originally learned, then retention in the two blocked conditions was reliably worse than in the two unblocked conditions. A similar comparison of the blocked conditions with the rime condition from Levy et. al. (1999) showed no differences between groups. Thus, in all conditions using blocking, retention suffered compared with unblocked learning. The same basic cost of blocking, with adjustments for trial 20 in learning, was found in generalization. For both word and non-word generalization tests, the blocked conditions showed poorer performance than the unblocked conditions. These findings suggest that although the segment similarity led to faster acquisition of the trained words, the rime segment was not well abstracted from the trained items. It was insufficient to support good generalization of that unit to new instances. Performance in the rime condition from Levy et. al. (1999) was better than for the blocked conditions in the present study for the non-word generalization test, but not reliably so for the word generalization test. Thus, the inclusion of phonological segmentation may have led to better abstraction of the ortho-graphic/phonological units, improving generalization to new items. Clearly, processes related to generalization need to be explored further.

These retention and generalization data point out a caution in believing that orthographic visibility is sufficient to decrease the deficit suffered by children at the bottom of the reading distribution. They may well need orthographic support to "see" the units during acquisition, but then also need phonological support to improve retention and generalization of these larger units. These findings are consistent with the superiority of segmentation training over whole word training for all poor readers and for beginning readers in our earlier studies. This final study sheds some light on the orthographic needs of these children. Their problem with larger units appears to lie in the manner in which they analyze print. They fail to "see" larger orthographic patterns, not because the system cannot process multi-letter units, but because these children do not normally approach the print in this way. Visual pattern support within the print itself can help these children read more normally.

DISCUSSION AND CONCLUSIONS

In the first section of the paper, we argued that fluency, even for the poorest readers, was related to the speed of reading individual words. Reading practice with words, in or out of a text context, is beneficial in automating word recognition. The improvement in word recognition speed is mirrored in improved text processing speed and accuracy. This improved fluency enables, but does not directly cause, better comprehension. Comprehension relies on other limiting processes as well. However, this automatization at the word processing level, through whole word practice, applies to a later stage of reading when the reader has already represented the words in memory; word reading practice facilitates speed in accessing these representations. In the second part of the paper, we argued that whole word reading is *not* an optimal method for acquiring initial word representations. For both beginning readers and poor readers, we found that segmentation methods were superior to whole word repetition in acquiring new print vocabulary. In fact, for those at the bottom of the reading distribution, the double-deficit children, whole word repetition was the least helpful form of practice. In the last study described above, we found that these slow RAN children benefitted from print in which larger orthographic units within words were made more visible in the print. These children are the ones who have the worst prognosis for developing fluent text reading and they need help with both visual and auditory processes, because these support reading developments. Our training work is consistent with the available literature showing that these children have difficulty in orthographic processing (Bowers and Wolf 1993; Manis, Seidenburg, and Doi 1999), and orthographic processing has been clearly linked with reading fluency (e.g., Barker, Torgesen, and Wagner 1992). It seems clear that understanding the mechanisms whereby orthographic processing limits the development of fluency is of major importance.

It has been difficult to determine the underlying mechanism that causes the deficit in orthographic processing. Bower and Wolf (1993) originally hypothesized that the deficit indexed by slow RAN was related to slow letter processing. They argued that children who are slow namers are very slow in processing single letters (see also Bowers this volume). When the timing of letter identification is slow, then mechanisms that associate letters into larger orthographic units is disrupted, so that larger units are not well represented. As Ehri (1992) has argued, fluent reading relies on rapid access to larger units, sometimes at the whole word level. Wimmer (this volume) shows, even in a shallow orthography like that used in German, where grapheme to phoneme correspondence presents no problem, reading skill still correlates with RAN. Wimmer argues that this correlation is related to poor orthographic pattern representation that is required for fluent processing in larger units. The effectiveness of our visual pattern manipulations in improving learning is consistent with these notions.

Bowers, Sunseth, and Golden (1999) provided some support for the slow letter processing account. However, somewhat surprisingly, their slow RAN children appeared to be able to offset that problem when letters appeared in strings that approximated English orthography. This finding suggests that orthographic knowledge, once attained, is used to speed letter perception, even for children with the speed deficit. Could the problem be located largely in the *formation* of higher-order units? Bowers and Newby-Clark (2000) argued for such a position. They suggested that exposure or practice must be more extensive before such units are formed for children who are slow letter processors. The data presented in the second section of this paper indicate that it may not be the amount of exposure or practice that is important; it may be the *type* of exposure that determines the speed of forming orthographic units. The work of Levy et al. (1999) and of Levy et. al. (in preparation; summarized above) shows that slow RAN children can acquire new print vocabulary but at rates determined by the method of instruction. Two factors are implicated. First, the "orthographic visibility" in the print. Blocking words with shared orthographic units appears to be sufficient to help these children to "see" and process letter *patterns* more rapidly. Second, segmentation methods that highlight the larger units, and relate the orthographic unit to its pronunciation, may be important in abstracting and representing larger units so that they can be retrieved for use in reading new words containing those units. This latter suggestion requires further testing.

These notions have some kinship with those of Manis, Seidenburg, and Doi (1999) who argued that the naming speed deficit is related to forming new *arbitrary* associations, but not to forming associations related to systematic rules. They liken slow RAN children to children with surface dyslexia who have difficulty reading exception, but not regular, words. They suggest that for exception words, the regular spelling/sound relations are violated, so new arbitrary associations must be formed between letter patterns and their pronunciation. Thus, they locate the problem in forming new representations. However, the data we presented on rime units is not consistent with the notion that the relations must be arbitrary. In fact, one value of onset/rime units is that they can regularize spelling/sound relations that are irregular at the phoneme level. For example, sounding out "brought," "sought," or "wrought," is difficult at the phoneme level, but quite regular at the onset/rime level. Of course, during acquisition, all alphabetic associations are initially arbitrary. The "rules" make them systematic once the coding scheme is acquired. Perhaps our "orthographic visibility" manipulations are a simple way to teach regularity, so that the difficulty with arbitrary relations is overcome (see also Manis this volume).

Finally, Wolf, Bowers, and Biddle (2000) have suggested that the orthographic deficit may be related to a problem in central timing that causes global deficits in tasks that require rapid timing, as in language processing for fluent reading. Our data clearly do not address such a notion directly. However, we do note that if a visual manipulation is sufficient to influence such a central processing mechanism, then defining the problem early in development and offering orthographic support to offset the timing problem is critical. We need to help these children form letter pattern representations so that the development of fluency is not impaired. Further exploration of the role of "orthographic visibility" in supporting early reading for children with the "double deficit" may help to clarify the visual processes underlying the RAN deficit.

REFERENCES

Adams, M. J. 1990. *Beginning to Read: Thinking and Learning about Print.* Cambridge, MA: MIT Press.

Barker, T. A., Torgesen, J. K., and Wagner, R. K. 1992. The role of orthographic processing skills on five different reading tasks. *Reading Research Quarterly* 27:334–45.

Bourassa, D. C., Levy, B. A., Dowin, S., and Casey, A. 1998. Transfer across contextual and linguistic boundaries: Evidence from poor readers. *Journal Of Experimental Child Psychology* 71:45–61.

Bowers, P. G. 1993. Text reading and rereading: Determinants of fluency beyond word recognition. *Journal of Reading Behavior* 25:133–53.

Bowers, P. G. 1995. Tracing symbol naming speed's unique contributions to reading disability over time. *Reading and Writing: An Interdisciplinary Journal* 7:1–28.

Bowers, P. G., Golden, J., Kennedy, A., and Young, A. 1994. Limits upon orthographic knowledge due to processes indexed by naming speed. In *The Varieties of Orthographic Knowledge I: Theoretical and Developmental Issues*, ed. V. W. Berninger. Dordrecht, Netherlands: Kluwer.

Bowers, P. G. and Newby-Clark, E. 2000. The role of naming speed within a model of reading acquisition. *Reading and Writing: An Interdisciplinary Journal.* In press.

Bowers, P. G., Sunseth, K., and Golden, J. 1999. The route between rapid naming and reading progress. *Scientific Studies of Reading* 3:31–53.

Bowers, P. G., and Wolf, M. 1993. Theoretical links among naming speed, precise timing mechanisms, and orthographic skill in dyslexia. *Reading and Writing: An Interdisciplinary Journal* 5:69–85.

Bruck, M., and Treiman, R. 1992. Learning to pronounce words: The limitations of analogies. *Reading Research Quarterly* 27:375–88.

Cunningham, A. E., and Stanovich, K. E. 1991. Tracking the unique effects of print exposure in children: Associations with vocabulary, general knowledge, and spelling. *Journal of Educational Psychology* 83:264–74.

Dahl, P. R. 1979. An experimental program for teaching high speed word recognition and comprehension skills. In *Communication Research in Learning Disabilities and Mental Retardation*, eds. J. E. Button, T. C. Lovitt, and T. D. Rowlands. Baltimore: University Park Press.

Ehri, L. C. 1992. Reconceptualizing the development of sight word reading and its relationship to recoding. In *Reading Acquisition*, eds. P. G. Gough, L. C. Ehri, and R. Treiman. Hillsdale, NJ: Lawrence Erlbaum Associates.

Felton, R. H. 1993. Effects of instruction on decoding skills in children with phonological processing problems. *Journal of Learning Disabilities* 26:583–89.

Fleisher, L. S., Jenkins, J. R., and Pany, D. 1979. Effects on poor readers' comprehension of training in rapid decoding. *Reading Research Quarterly* 15:30–48.

Foorman, B. R., Francis, D. J., Winikates, D., Mehta, P., Schatschneider, C., and Fleisher, J. M. 1997. Early interventions in children with learning disabilities. *Scientific Studies of Reading* 1:255–76.

Goodman, K. S. 1965. A linguistic study of cues and miscues in reading. *Elementary English* 42:129–34.

Goswami, U. 1986. Children's use of analogy in learning to read: A developmental study. *Journal of Experimental Child Psychology* 42:73–83.

Goswami, U. 1988. Orthographic analogies and reading development. Quarterly *Journal of Experimental Psychology* 40A:239–68.

Goswami, U. 1990a. Phonological priming and orthographic analogies in reading. *Journal of Experimental Child Psychology* 31:323–40.

Goswami, U. 1990b. A special link between rhyming skill and the use of orthographic analogies by beginning readers. *Journal of Child Psychology and Psychiatry* 31:301–11.

LaBerge, D. and Samuels, S. J. 1974. Toward a theory of automatic information processing in reading. *Cognitive Psychology* 6:689–718.

Levy, B. A. 1999. Whole words, segments, and meaning: Approaches to reading education. In *Converging Methods for Understanding Reading and Dyslexia*, eds. R. M. Klein and P. A. McMullen. Cambridge, MA: MIT Press.

Levy, B. A., Abello, B., and Lysynchuk, L. 1997. Transfer from word training to reading in context: Gains in fluency and comprehension. *Learning Disabilities Quarterly* 20:173–88.

Levy, B. A., Bourassa, D. C., and Horn, C. 1999. Fast and slow namers: Benefits of segmentation and whole word training. *Journal of Experimental Child Psychology* 73:115–38.

Levy, B. A. and Lysynchuk, L. 1997. Beginning word recognition: Benefits of training by segmentation and whole word methods. *Scientific Studies of Reading* 1:359–87.

Manis, F. R., Seidenburg, M. S., and Doi, L. M. 1999. See Dick RAN: Rapid naming and the longitudinal prediction of reading subskills in first and second graders. *Scientific Studies of Reading* 3:129–57.

Nicholson, T. 1991. Do children read words better in context or in lists? A classic study revisited. *Journal of Educational Psychology* 83:444–50.

Olson, R. K. and Wise, B. W. 1992. Reading on the computer with orthographic and speech feedback. *Reading and Writing: An Interdisciplinary Journal* 4:107–44.

Olson, R. K., Wise, B. W., Ring, J., and Johnson, M. 1997. Computer-based remedial training in phonemic awareness and phonological decoding: Effects on posttraining development of word recognition. *Scientific Studies of Reading* 1:235–53.

Rashotte, C. A., and Torgesen, J. K. 1985. Repeated reading and reading fluency in reading disabled children. *Reading Research Quarterly* 20:180–202.

Samuels, S. J. 1979. The method of repeated readings. *The Reading Teacher* 32:403–8.

Stanovich, K. E. 1986. Matthew effects in reading: Some consequence of individual differences in the acquisition of literacy. *Reading Research Quarterly* 21:360–407.

Stanovich, K. E. and West, R. F. 1989. Exposure to print and orthographic processing. *Reading Research Quarterly* 24:402–33.

Wolf, M. 1991. Naming speed and reading: The contribution of cognitive neurosciences. *Reading Research Quarterly* 26:123–41.

Wolf, M. and Bowers, P. G. 1999. The double-deficit hypothesis for developmental dyslexia. *Journal of Educational Psychology* 91:415–38.

Wolf, M., Bowers, P. G., and Biddle, K. 2000. Naming speed processes, timing, and reading: A conceptual review. *Journal of Learning Disabilities* 33:387–407.

AUTHOR'S NOTE

This work was supported by grants from the Social Sciences and Humanities Research Council of Canada. We thank the Hamilton-Wentworth Catholic District School Board, and their principals, teachers, parents, and students, for their participation in the research discussed in this paper.

CODA

Chapter • 17

Processes Underlying Timing and Fluency of Reading:
Efficiency, Automaticity, Coordination, and Morphological Awareness

Virginia W. Berninger, Robert D. Abbott,
Felix Billingsley, and William Nagy

In the late nineteenth century, Edwin Abbott Abbott, a theologian and Shakespearean scholar, published *Flatland* in which Flatlanders, who live in a 2-dimensional world, fly into a rage when Spacelanders, who live in a 3-dimensional world, suggest that there is another dimension of space. Likewise, Spacelanders fly into a rage when evidence of a fourth dimension—time is presented (Abbott 1894, cited in Hoffman 1998), presumably by Timelanders. During the twentieth century, the idea of a fourth dimension of time, even after Einstein made a strong case for it, met with much resistance (Hoffman 1998).

Similar to the resistance of Flatlanders and Spacelanders to the suggestion that another relevant dimension exists, some reading researchers have sometimes been reluctant to take into account variables other than a phonological core deficit in reading disability, for which substantial evidence exists. This reluctance is understandable in the context of the mindset of 19th and 20th century science that placed high regard on parsimony and the one best explanatory mechanism. However, at the dawn of the 21st century, a paradigm shift is occurring in many scientific fields away from Occum and his razor to development of models that deal with the multiple dimensions of complex systems (Gallagher and Appenzeller 1999). In this chapter, we propose multiple processes underlying timing and fluency, including morphological awareness, that contribute to reading and its disorders—not as better explanations than phonological processes and deficits, but rather as other relevant variables to be considered along with the phonological ones in understanding the complexities of the functional system for reading.

Evidence exists that normal and disabled readers differ in temporal parameters of word recognition in English (Compton and Carlisle 1994) and in languages with a more transparent orthography than English such as German (Wimmer and Mayringer this volume). The argument that precision timing (Bowers and Wolf 1993) is irrelevant to reading disability because neurologists have not found an internal clock localized somewhere in the brain is not compelling. Just as a memory engram has never been found in the brain despite considerable evidence for short-term, long-term, and working memory systems, timing mechanisms, too, may be emergent properties of the working brain. Minsky (1986), for example, proposed a model of brain functioning in which different mental processes are on different time scales, yielding a multi-scale temporal geometry of mind based on non-linear momentary time, which underlies the linear, unidimensional real time humans perceive at a conscious level. The notion that mental processes may occur on different time scales is beginning to be investigated empirically in cognitive neuroscience (e.g., Breznitz in press and this volume; Posner and McCandliss 1999). Timing mechanisms may not be orchestrated by a masterclock, but rather may be negotiated locally as many different mental processes, which, sensitive only to change in their own neural networks, create connections with each other electrochemically.

Table 1 illustrates the potential temporal complexity in language systems. Stimulus inputs, internal processing, and response production all have temporal parameters. Rate of the incoming speech signal can influence speech perception (e.g., Tallal 1980; Tallal et al.1993). Persistence of the incoming visible language signal (e.g., Lovegrove 1993; Lovegrove, Martin, and Staghuis 1986) or rate of change in visual gradients (fast or slow changing parameters of stimuli) (e.g., Lubs et al. 1991) can influence written word perception. Efficiency of the language processing systems can place rate constraints on processing and production (Perfetti

Table 1. Temporal Parameters of Functional Language Systems

Stimulus Input	Processing	Response Production
Temporal parameters of speech	Pathways for slow-changing and fast changing stimuli	Rate of production
Temporal parameters of written language	Rate constraints on specific language operations due to efficiency (speed) of system	Coordination of serial elements in production
	Pathways for automatic and strategic processing	
	Temporal constraints in working memory	
	Layers of language in word learning and processing (phonological, orthographic, and morphological)	
	Executive functions for coordinating component processes	

1985). Working memory has limited temporal coordination capacity as well as limited space resources; instructional programs that teach to all components of a functional system close in time (within the same instructional session) are likely to overcome the limited temporal coordination capacity and create functional connections among all the components in the language system (Berninger 1999). The degree to which language processes are automatized affects rate of processing and rate of responding. Rate of responding plays a critical role in learning language by ear and mouth (e.g., Garvey and Berninger 1981) and language by eye and hand (e.g., Berninger et al. 1992). Executive functions guide the serial organization of responses in real time (e.g., Lashley 1933).

Given this temporal complexity, researchers and clinicians should be cautious in drawing inferences about fluency solely on the basis of total time for a response or rate of responding (frequency of a behavior in a constant time interval). In this chapter, we first report data supporting specific timing deficits rather than a general timing deficit in reading and writing disability. Then we propose a scheme that combines behavioral observation with time scores or that combines behavioral observations and time scores with brain imaging paradigms to draw inferences about possible processes underlying observed slow responding. Then we discuss why morphological awareness may be an important language process contributing uniquely to the timing and fluency of reading. Next we discuss two treatment studies we have conducted aimed at increasing reading fluency. Following that, we examine why the Rapid Automatic Naming (RAN) task (Wolf, Bally, and Morris 1986) and Rapid Automatic Switching (RAS) task (Wolf 1986) are such robust markers of dyslexia in light of the processes underlying timing and fluency discussed throughout the chapter. Finally, we suggest future directions for treatment research on reading fluency.

GENERAL OR SPECIFIC TIMING DEFICITS?

Fluency of one component in a functional reading system may not predict fluency of another component of the reading system or of components in the writing system. Three measures of reading fluency (oral reading of graded passages, of real words in a list, and of pseudo-words in a list) and of writing fluency (of alphabet letters from memory, copying text, and composing) were in the phenotyping battery of our family genetics study. Based on discrepancy from Verbal IQ, of the 102 probands, 54 had three reading fluency deficits (with comorbid writing fluency deficits ranging from three for 17, to two for 14, to one for 14, to zero for 9 children); 21 had two reading fluency deficits (with comorbid writing fluency deficits ranging from three for 2, to two for 7, to one for 6, to zero for 6 children); 22 had one reading fluency deficit (with comorbid writing fluency deficits ranging from three for 3, to two for 4, to one for 7, to zero for 8 children); and 5 had zero reading fluency deficits (with comorbid writing fluency deficits ranging from three for 1, to one for 1, to zero for 3 children). Only 16% of the sample had deficits in all three reading fluency skills, and there was considerable variability in individual profiles as to which reading fluency and/or writing fluency skills were affected. Thus, individuals with specific reading and/or writing disability did not appear to be characterized by a general timing deficit (cf. Chiappe et al. in press) but rather specific timing deficits, which may be the outcome of deficits in precise timing mechanisms underlying reading and writing (cf. Bowers and Wolf 1993).

DIFFERENTIATING EFFICIENCY, AUTOMATICITY, AND COORDINATION

Time scores (total time for response or rate of responding) may reflect the net effect of cascading processes in table 1, including temporal constraints in processing stimulus input, in language processing operations, and in response production. However, in our treatment studies, we have observed three subtypes of dysfluent readers (see table 2) that suggest possible processes that could be contributing to slow oral reading; each of these subtypes, based on behavioral observations, points to different potential causal mechanisms for slow reading.

Processing rate or efficiency of the system. The first subtype's oral reading was very accurate, but painfully slow. We could establish a basal level (below which their performance was consistent) for accuracy but not for rate. These children's reading system functioned well in that they rarely made errors, but their system was not efficient (Perfetti 1985)—these children worked very slowly to accomplish the goal of accurate reading. These children are rarely identified by schools as having a reading disability because state-approved measures for qualifying for special education services typically rely only on accuracy measures and not rate measures. That is why Kame'enui et al.'s research (this volume) on validating assessment measures for reading rate is so important for early identification of students who are accurate, but not fluent, in their reading. Children who are accurate, but slow, may not be able to keep up with assignments in the classroom.

Automaticity of processing. The second subtype's oral reading was both inaccurate and slow, but associated with very specific kinds of errors: false starts, hesitations (often with filled pauses, e.g., um), and repetitions. Although these children's oral reading reflected knowledge of spelling-phoneme correspondences, it also reflected inordinate difficulty in committing word recognition to automatic pilot. However, they were able to self-monitor to detect and self-correct errors, suggesting that their executive functions were intact. (In this chapter we will use the terms executive functions, executive management, self-regulation, coordination, and executive coordination synonymously to refer to mental processes for coordinating and regulating other mental processes).

Table 2.   Hypothesized Processes Underlying Timing and Fluency

Process	Oral Reading Rate	Hypothesized Brain Locus
Efficiency	accurate but slow	cerebellum (precise timing)
Automaticity	slow with false starts, filled pauses, repetitions but good monitoring	striatum and/or insula
Executive Function (temporal coordination)	slow with inattention to detail within words and order across words, poor monitoring	left frontal

Executive coordination.   The third subtype's oral reading was both inaccurate and slow, but associated with a different pattern of errors. These children made many errors marked by inattention to orthographic and morphological features of words, inattention to serial order of words in sentences, inattention to the prosody or music of the language (Erekson 1999), and inattention to self-monitoring of meaning. They appeared to have difficulty with the executive management of language processes within and across words and rarely self-corrected errors, indicating that they were not self-monitoring. For example, one boy read "these pieces" for "this piece" and "carefully" for "careful," and read a word that came at the end of a sentence in the middle of the sentence. Sometimes this pattern occurred without the error types of the second subtype, suggesting that the problem was specific to the executive coordination system, but sometimes the two kinds of errors both occurred, suggesting that both automaticity and executive coordination were affected.

Each of these subtypes was slow and dysfluent, but in the first case, as a result of verbal inefficiency, in the second case, because of lack of automaticity, and in the third case, as the result of difficulty in temporal coodination of multiple language processes (and possibly co-occurring problems in automaticity). Oral reading rate alone was not sufficient to differentiate among these potential contributing mechanisms—error analysis was also needed.

Differentiating among the potential processes may have instructional implications. For the first subtype, merely practicing reading may be sufficient to increase efficiency because these children are basically accurate and merely need repeated exposure to printed words to create more rapid retrieval and production routines. Research should address the questions of whether repeated reading of the same text at a child's instructional level is sufficient or whether repeated reading of many texts (in which the same words are encountered in many different contexts) at a child's independent level is necessary to increase verbal efficiency (Perfetti 1985) of students who are accurate, but slow. For the second subtype, merely practicing reading may not be sufficient because a faulty brain mechanism for creating direct associations between stimuli and responses interferes with creation of automatic connections, no matter how many practice trials are taken. Children in this second subtype may have difficulty with direct access to or direct retrieval of lexical items and benefit from precision teaching in which rate aims and performances are carefully monitored and they receive precise feedback on a daily basis for both rate (e.g., White 1986) and resistance to distractibility (e.g., Binder,

Haughton, and VanEyk 1990). For the third subtype, explicit instruction in metacognitive strategies for self-monitoring and self-correction may increase the likelihood that executive management of reading will become coordinated in time and self-regulated. In sum, efficient, automatic, and coordinated/focused responses are faster than inefficient, strategic, or uncoordinated/inattentive responses, but time per se does not differentiate among these potential processes underlying timing and fluency; error types must be considered along with response times.

Brain imaging research may provide validation for these proposed processes, just as it has for other processes with a neural basis. For example, brain imaging has provided evidence for separate neural systems for processing fast-changing and slow-changing visual (Eden et al. 1996) and auditory (Livingstone et al. 1991) stimuli, and for the "what" and "where" components of the visual system (Ungerleider and Mishkin 1982) and the auditory system (Kaas and Hackett 1999). Brain imaging may demonstrate that separate neural systems exist for rate or efficiency of the language system (Perfetti 1985), for automatic reading that does not require conscious attention (LaBerge and Samuels 1974), and for self-regulated, temporally coordinated reading that reflects the prosody of the language (Erekson 1999; Strecker, Rosner, and Martinez 1998). Although parsimony may not be a reasonable criterion for scientific research on complex functional systems, such research still requires rigorous testing of hypotheses. In the appendix to this chapter, a set of experiments is described for systematically teasing apart the processes underlying the timing and fluency of oral reading. Each experiment is designed to test hypotheses by combining functional brain imaging and treatment research in order to make causal inferences about brain-behavior relationships in which the functional, working brain is both an independent and a dependent variable (Berninger and Corina 1998; Richards et al. 2000). Speculations about potential brain loci (also see table 2) are based on existing research, but such research would most likely show that more brain loci are involved in the circuitry for the various processes than are proposed.

CIRCLE OF CONNECTIONS IN WORD LEARNING

Figure 1 portrays the systems model guiding our treatment, family genetics, and brain imaging research on learning to read and spell single words. The architecture consists of an orthographic layer (0), a phonological layer (P), and a morphological layer (M). In some ways this architecture is similar to connectionist models that

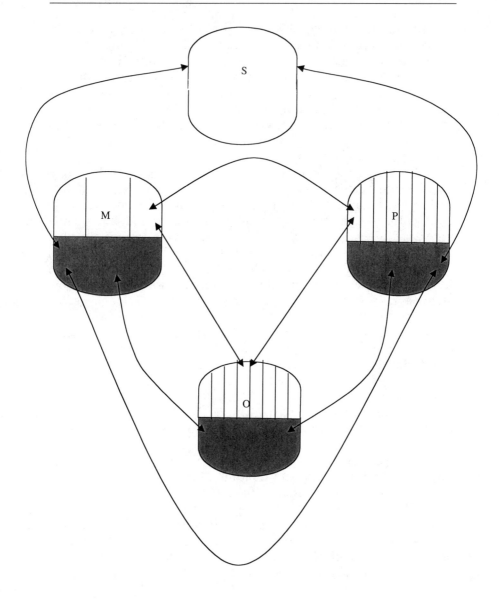

Key: See text for discussion of structure within layers and interconnecting arrows be-
tween layers
O = Orthographic Layer
P = Phonological Layer
M = Morphological Layer
S = Syntactic Layer (Contest Processor)

Figure 1.   Word Learning: Circle of Connections

aim to be computationally explicit (e.g., Harm and Seidenberg 1999). However, our model differs in some ways. First, we focus specifically on the morphology of lexical items (e.g., stems, inflectional suffixes, prefixes, derivational suffixes) rather than general semantics that also encompasses world knowledge about lexical items (e.g., that a cat has fur, four legs, etc.). Morphology has connections to semantics, especially in word stems, but has additional meaning encapsulated in the linguistic units of the lexical item. These linguistic units in the morphological layer have connections to the orthographic and phonological layers as well as to the syntactic layer discussed next. Second, not only the semantic (in our case morphological), but also the phonological layer has connections with context, which is conceptualized as syntactic structures for processing more than one word. However, the syntactic layer connects the individual words with the discourse processor for larger units of text (cf. Kintsch 1998). Third, each of these layers has a lexical-level processor (solid lower half) and a sublexical processor (vertical slots in upper half) (Berninger, Abbott, Thomson, and Raskind 2001); these are not separate routes but rather different levels of representation that become coordinated over time. Fourth, and most importantly, the goal of the model is to be instructionally explicit and to be explicit about the kinds of assessment information needed to be instructionally explicit. To accomplish this goal, the model aims to integrate what is known about assessment and intervention for aural/oral and written language. Results of our assessment and intervention research indicate that the language by ear, language by mouth, language by eye, and language by hand systems draw on this Circle of Connections in common and unique ways in word learning (Berninger 2000). Despite the differences between connectionist models that aim to be computationally explicit and that aim to be instructionally explicit, these models are complementary, rather than competing, alternatives that may inform each other.

Initially, our research focused on the orthographic and phonological layers and multiple orthographic-phonological connections at the lexical and sublexical levels (e.g., Berninger 1994; Berninger and Abbott 1994). More recently, our research focuses on each of the layers and their bidirectional connections in word learning at the lexical and sublexical levels: orthographic-morphological, orthographic-phonological and morphological-phonological. For the orthographic layer, the sublexical slots correspond to 1- (e.g., *a*) or 2- (e.g., *aw*) letter functional spelling units that can be recoded as phonemes. For the phonological layer, the sublexical slots correspond to phonemes, onset/rimes, or syllables. Thus the sublexical slots in the orthographic and phonological layers do not always correspond in a simple 1-to-1 manner. For the morphological layer, the sublexical slots correspond to prefixes, stems, and inflectional or derivational suffixes. The connections between the morphological and phonological layers may be neutral (e.g., *lovely*, in which the suffix does not affect the phonology of the stem) or complex (e.g., *national*, in which the suffix does affect the phonology of the stem) (Carlisle 2000; Fowler and Liberman 1995). Each layer (orthographic, phonological, and morphological) has both short-term and long-term memory representations and both procedural (computational) and informational (content) representations.

Relationships may exist between physiological mechanisms of the visual system and the orthographic layer (e.g., significant relationships between the magnocellular system and orthographic choice test, Stein, personal communication, June 24, 2000) and between the physiological mechanisms of the auditory system and the phonological layer, but further research is needed on this issue. At the phenotypic level, each of the layers in figure 1 are orchestrated flexibly, singly, or in combination, to participate in different components of the functional reading system (Berninger et al. 2000). At the genotypic level, however, genetic constraints appear to operate in the lexical levels of the phonological layer and the orthographic layer and in the sublexical connections between the phonological and orthographic layers (Raskind et al. 2000); work in progress is examining whether the morphological layer and its connections are also genetically constrained. Compared to matched controls, subjects with dyslexia are inefficient at the metabolic level during phonological processing (Richards et al. 1999) and show less blood oxygenation level dependent (BOLD) response in insula (and other areas) during lexical access tasks that probably involve both the morphological and phonological layers of aural language (Corina et al. in press); they also differ in BOLD response during phonological processing (Corina et al. in press).

Parts of this model were validated in an early intervention study for 128 at-risk beginning readers (see Berninger, Abbott, Brooksher et al. 2000, for description of the early intervention) that included instructional components aimed at the phonological and orthographic layers. Both sublexical connections (1- or 2-letter spelling units and phonemes) and lexical connections resulted in transfer to untrained words. Children also learned to *read* words when sublexical connections were taught between letters and phonological rime/onset units (Berninger, Abbott, Brooksher et al. 2000), letters and oral syllables (Berninger et al., submitted), or between letters and morphemes (Abbott and Berninger 1999), but alphabet principle alone (Berninger et al. 1999) was effective: there was never any added effectiveness for training one of these other connections over and beyond alphabet principle. However, children learned to *spell* real words and transfer words better when orthographic-phonological connections were taught between onset-rime units *and* lexical units (Berninger, Vaughan et al. 1998) or between spoken and written syllables (Berninger, Vaughan et al. 2000) in addition to alphabet principle. These conclusions, which illustrate that spelling is not the inverse of reading (Read 1981), apply only to *accuracy* of reading or spelling English. The following findings point to the conclusion that efficiency, automaticity, and executive coordination, although not depicted graphically in figure 1, contribute in important ways to the Circle of Word Learning.

Aggregation analyses performed in the family genetics study on paired measures of accuracy and of efficiency (rate) of phonological decoding showed a familial aggregation pattern consistent with a genetic basis for efficiency of phonological decoding in addition to the genetic basis it shares with accuracy of phonological decoding (Hsu et al. submitted). As shown in table 3, an orthographic composite, a phonological composite, Verbal IQ (an index of morphological processing), time score for rapid automatic naming of letters (RAN), and attentional ratings were significantly correlated with slopes of individual hierarchical linear modeling (HLM) growth curves for each student. In addition, RAN for letters also accounted for unique variance in real word reading, and attention ratings also accounted for unique variance in both real word and pseudo-word reading. The RAN findings suggest that automaticity of orthographic-phonological connections affects growth in word learning, whereas the attention findings suggest that coordination of attentional processes, so the student can focus, stay on task, and switch task as needed, also affects growth in word learning.

Further support for the relevance of automaticity and coordination mechanisms to learning written language comes from additional analyses of this sample. Deficit groups were defined on the basis of performance below a cut-off of -1 standard deviation on orthographic, phonological, or rapid naming (RAN)/rapid alternating switching (RAS) skills (Stage et al. in press). Rapid automatized naming requires naming of stimuli in a single category (e.g., letters), whereas RAS requires naming of stimuli that alternate across categories (e.g., letters and numbers). When mean growth (based on slopes of individual growth curves) was compared for a no

Table 3.   Predicting Growth Curve Slopes on Standardized Measures of Phonological Decoding and Real Word Reading

	WRMT-R Word Attack			WRMT-R Word Identification		
	Overall Equation $3.04^a + 4.50^a$ Time	Co-efficient	t	Overall Equation $7.0^a + 11.58^a$ Time	Co-efficient	t
Univariate Predictors of Slope						
Orthographic Composite	.56	2.22^c		2.14	4.99^a	
Phonological Composite	.711	3.37^b		1.56	4.18^a	
RAN Letters Time	−.03	−4.42^a		−.10	−7.84^a	
Attention Rating	.77	5.04^a		1.96	7.80^a	
Verbal IQ	.04	2.49^c		.09	3.42^b	
Multivariate Unique Predictors of Slope						
Orthographic Composite	−.15	−.28		−.22	−.35	
Phonological Composite	.16	.45		.20	.35	
RAN Letters Time	−.01	−1.07		−.06	−2.81^b	
Attention Rating	.57	2.10^c		1.59	3.74^a	
Verbal IQ	.03	1.27		.07	1.75	

$^a p < .001$
$^b p < .01$
$^c p < .05$

Note: Attention rating was based on tutor's appraisal of student's selective, sustained, and switching attention.

deficit group ($n = 15$), a RAN/RAS only deficit group ($n = 59$), a RAN/RAS + Phonological deficit group ($n = 24$), a RAN/RAS + Orthographic deficit group ($n = 18$), and a RAN/RAS + Orthographic + Phonological deficit group ($n = 7$), there were main effects for both real word and pseudo-word reading. For real word reading, the no deficit group was significantly different from all other groups, all of which included a RAS or RAS deficit. For pseudo-word reading, the no deficit and the RAN/RAS deficit groups were significantly different from all the other deficit groups. Thus, a single deficit was sufficient to impair real word reading, whereas a double deficit or triple deficit was likely to impair pseudo-word reading. In addition, in this sample of at-risk beginning readers, RAN/RAS for letters *and* orthographic coding of 2-letter spelling units in written words in short-term memory differentiated students whose growth curves showed significant growth in both real word reading and pseudo-word reading from those whose growth curves showed significant growth in real word reading only. Thus, automaticity of coding 1- and 2-letter units may play an important role in learning phonological decoding.

However, efficiency, automaticity, and executive coordination may not be the only processes contributing to reading fluency. According to the morphological fluency hypothesis, which we recently tested, the morphological layer contributes uniquely to reading fluency over and beyond the sizable contribution of the accuracy of orthographic-phonological connections. To test this hypothesis, the last and first authors constructed the University of Washington Morphological Awareness Battery, which included the Morphological Signals Test, The Decoding Fluency Test, and The Morphological Spelling Test. These tests and the Word Attack Subtest of the Woodcock Reading Mastery Test-Revised (WRMT-R) (Woodcock 1987), a measure of phonological decoding, were given to at-risk 2nd grade readers and at-risk 4th grade writers in the third or fourth month of the school year.

For the Morphological Signals Test, the examiner read orally four word choices that were also presented visually to the student along with a written sentence with a missing word. The child did not have to decode the word to choose which of the alternatives, based on grammatical information in the suffix, belonged in the blank, given the syntax of the sentence. Word choices were blocked by the degree to which existing representations in the morphological layer could be consulted. One block consisted of real words (e.g., *happiness*). One block consisted of real stems and suffixes that when combined were plausible but improbable (e.g., *smallness*). One block consisted of pseudo-morphs with a pseudo-word stem and a real suffix (e.g., *zutness*). See Nagy, Diakidoy, and Anderson (1983) for other research with these kinds of stimulus words. The score was the total correct across all three blocks.

For the Decoding Fluency Test, children were instructed to read a list of words as quickly and accurately as they could. Lists blocked polysyllabic words by developmentally appropriate inflectional suffixes (e.g., tense or number markers) or prefixes. The score was the average rate of accurate responding (number of words read correctly divided by the total time per block). This test differed from the Morphological Signals Test in three ways. First, this test required reading, but the Signals Test did not. Second, this test had time pressure, but the Signals Test did not. Third, this test did not assess morpho-syntactic knowledge, but the Signals Test did.

The Morphological Spelling Test required children to write words from dictation. The words were selected to reflect the kinds of morphological knowledge children normally acquire in the first through fourth grade range. (See Nagy, Osborn, and O'Flahavan 1994, for normal development of morphological knowledge.)

As shown in table 4, zero-order correlations were significant for accuracy of phonological decoding and decoding fluency, and for morphological awareness (based on the Signals Test) and decoding fluency. Correlations may be higher for words with inflectional suffixes than words with prefixes because the Signals Test contained only words with derivational suffixes. Multiple regressions showed that phonological decoding (entered first) but also morphological awareness (entered second) contributed unique variance to decoding fluency (table 4). Likewise, as shown in table 5, zero-order correlations were significant for accuracy of phonological decoding and spelling, and for morphological awareness (based on the Signals Test) and spelling. Multiple regressions showed that phonological decoding (entered first) but also morphological awareness (entered second) contributed unique variance to spelling (table 5). Thus, although connections between the orthographic and phonological layers in figure 1 may account for accuracy of word learning, the quality of representations in the morphological layer in figure 1 may affect the fluency of word reading.

However, fluency is a multi-dimensional concept (Rasinski 1990), which may operate differently at the word, sentence, and text levels (Erekson 1999; Strecker et al. 1998). We propose that *automaticity is most relevant to direct access and retrieval of single lexical items* from the mental lexicon, *whereas executive coordination is*

Table 4. **Predicting Speed of Decoding Polysyllabic Words on UW Decoding Fluency Test from Phonological Decoding and Morphological Awareness Alone or Combined ($N = 98$ 2nd and 94 4th graders)**

	Decoding Time	
	Words with Inflectional Suffixes	Words with Prefixes
Univariate Phonological Decoding (WRMT-R Word Attack)	−.56[a]	−.41[a]
Morphological Awareness (UW Morphological Awareness SignalsTest)	−.45[a]	−.34[a]
Multivariate Change in R^2		
Phonological Decoding Entered First	.31[a]	.17[a]
Combined Phonological Decoding + Morphological Signals	.03[b]	.02[b]

[a]$p < .001$
[b]$p < .05$

Table 5. Predicting UW Morphological spelling Test from Phonological Decoding and Morphological Awareness Alone or Combined (*N* = 98 2nd and 94 4th graders)

	Spelling
Univariate Phonological Decoding	.76[a]
(WRMT-R Word Attack)	
Morphological Awareness	.58[a]
(UW Morphological Awareness SignalsTest)	
Multivariate Change in R^2	
Phonological Decoding Entered First	.58[a]
Combined Phonological Decoding + Morphological Signals	.04[a]

[a]$p < .001$

most relevant to the sentence level in which words are serially ordered according to syntax and should be read aloud in a manner that reflects the prosody of the language (phrasing, stress, expression, pitch, juncture, and intonation). Executive coordination also applies to the orchestration of multiple language processes, not just lexical access. However, inefficiency in the language processing system may slow down sublexical as well as lexical and sentence level processes independent of problems in automaticity or executive coordination; and individuals with high verbal efficiency may engage in strategic, non-automatic processing very rapidly (cf. Perfetti 1985). Not all fast processing is automatic. Zutell and Rasinki's (1991) fluency scale includes pace, smoothness, and prosody. Their pace may reflect efficiency (rate) in our scheme, and their smoothness and prosody may be captured in our executive coordination at the sentence level.

INSTRUCTIONAL INTERVENTIONS FOR ENHANCING FLUENCY

A variety of approaches to increasing speed or fluency of oral reading are reported in the literature, either as a means to fluency for fluency sake or as a means to reading comprehension. In one approach (e.g., Levy, Abello, and Lynsynchuk 1997), words are pretrained before reading them in text and are trained to a specified fluency standard (i.e., rate of production). In another approach, rate of text reading is accelerated by forcing participants to read at the fastest rate they exhibited during self-paced reading (e.g., Breznitz 1987, 1997b, 1997c). In both these approaches, rate becomes an independent as well as dependent measure (Breznitz 1997a). At issue is whether there is an optimal rate of oral reading that promotes efficient processing. However, each language system has constraints as to how fast it can function, no matter how much training it has; pushing it beyond that rate may cause it to function poorly or even break down. In yet another approach, the same text is read repeatedly. Repeated reading, but not modeling prosody, leads to reading gains in disabled readers (Young, Bowers, and MacKinnon 1996). We used repeated reading in our design experiments based on all the necessary components of the reading system to bring many reading disabled children up to grade level (Berninger 1998); many disabled readers can improve their reading rate through repeated readings.

Two additional approaches to enhancing fluency were used in recent studies. In the first we compared a commercially available program that is widely used in the schools to build fluency to a combination of that program with explicit alphabet principle training. In the second study we compared training alphabet principle using accuracy only instructions and probes with training alphabet principle using rate plus accuracy instructions and probes.

Repeated Reading versus Combined Repeated Reading and Alphabet Principle

Thirty two children from our family genetics study were randomly assigned to one of two conditions (Berninger, Abbott, Abbott et al. in press) and participated in 13 individual one-hour long tutorial sessions. In the first treatment condition, 16 students used the *Read Naturally Program*, which is designed to promote fluency by rereading high interest passages at the student's instructional level (*Read Naturally* 1997). Students graphed times for cold readings (first time) and hot readings (subsequent times), answered comprehension questions, and summarized the passage. In the second treatment condition, in addition to those activities, 16 students received explicit training in alphabet principle using the *Talking Letters Program* (Berninger 1998). To equate time across treatments, the *Read Naturally* only group also did filler activities involving jokes and riddles.

ANOVA with repeated measures on time (sessions) and a between-subjects variable (Repeated Reading Only vs. Combined Repeated Reading + Alphabet Principle) resulted in two significant 2-way interactions. Those who received the combined treatment gained 1.6 instructional levels (based on an oral reading rate criterion) in *Read Naturally* by posttest, whereas the repeated reading only group gained only 0.6 instructional levels. Also, the combined group gained 5.3 points on oral reading comprehension, whereas the repeated reading only group lost 2 points. Thus, for children with reading disability, repeated reading alone may not be the best way to increase their oral reading fluency and reading comprehension. These children also seem to benefit from combining explicit alphabet principle training with repeated readings.

Efficiency of Alphabet Principle

Given the finding that efficiency of pseudo-word reading may have genetic constraints beyond those in accuracy of pseudo-word reading (Hsu et al., submitted), the first and third authors evaluated whether a modification of the precision teaching technique of setting time goals (e.g., Lindsley 1964, 1990; Johnson and Laying 1992, 1996; Kelly 1996; White and Haring 1976) would enhance efficiency of pseudo-word reading. Second grade at-risk readers were randomly assigned to a Zip Group that practiced alphabet principle with accuracy instructions or to a Zap Group that practiced alphabet principle with rate and accuracy instructions. The Zip and Zap Groups did not differ in accuracy of real word or pseudo-word reading or rate of pseudo-word reading prior to treatment. Instruction and practice were spaced over a period of 4 months in the middle of the school year rather than massed in a few weeks (Dempster 1988). Spelling units in *Talking Letters* (Berninger 1998) were divided into four sets that were each practiced six times in rotating order. They were taught using the same procedures as in Berninger, Abbott, Brooksher et al. (2000). Following each of 24 group instructional sessions, all students were given individual probes on spelling-phoneme associations in isolation and in application of these to "Jabberwocky" words (pseudo-words); both kinds of probes were graphed. Those given only accuracy instructions graphed their accuracy in each individual probe session and were encouraged to set goals to increase their accuracy the next time. Those given rate and accuracy instructions graphed their rate in each individual probe session and were encouraged to set goals to increase rate while maintaining accuracy the next time.

Results were analyzed for those students who were underachieving in reading accuracy relative to Verbal IQ prior to treatment. ANOVA yielded a significant main effect for time $F(1,12) = 9.39$, $p = .01$, and a significant interaction for treatment group x time, $F(1,12) = 7.5$, $p = .018$, on standard scores for age on the WRMT-R Word Identification subtest, a measure of real word reading. The Zap group that received both rate and accuracy instructions and feedback improved 6.7 points, but the Zip group that received only accuracy instructions and feedback improved only 0.4 points. Both groups improved on standard scores for age on WRMT-R Word Attack (accuracy of pseudo-word reading), $F(1,12)$ = 6.39, p = .027, but neither improved on efficiency (rate) of pseudo-word reading or Gates MacGinitie (MacGinitie 1989) reading comprehension. Thus, application of rate goals to alphabet principle resulted in improved real word reading, but application of accuracy goals appeared sufficient to increase accuracy of phonological decoding. We speculate that gains were not observed in efficiency of phonological decoding because, in second graders with severe reading disability, accuracy gains may need to be consolidated before gains in speed occur with resultant transfer to comprehension. Perhaps a more classic application of precision teaching methodology, with standard celeration charts and aim and remediation lines (see White 1986), would have increased the rate of reading sooner.

RAPID AUTOMATIZED NAMING AND RAPID ALTERNATING SWITCHING AS WINDOWS ON TIMING AND FLUENCY

The validity of RAN as a phenotypic predictor of reading disability and response to intervention is well established (see Wolf, Bowers, and Biddle 2000, for a review, and Manis and Freedman, and Wimmer and Mayringer this volume), but what the RAN task measures is not fully understood. Does it measure the temporal dimension as implied in "rapid" versus "slow"? Does it measure "automaticity" as in direct, unconscious access that does not require strategic, multi-step, controlled, and conscious processing? Does it measure retrieving lexical-level phonological "name" codes (most names of letters or numbers have two or more phonemes)? Or, does it measure the executive function of coordinating all these processes in time? Or, is it, as we suspect, a measure of all of the above?

In both our early intervention studies and family genetics study, the RAN or RAS deficit occurs more often than phonological or orthographic deficits. For example, in a sample of 128 first graders at-risk for reading disability, 108 had a RAN/RAS deficit, singly or in combination with an orthographic or phonological deficit (Stage et al. in press). In a sample of 102 probands with diagnosed reading disabilities and 118 of their parents who were also affected, 83.3% of the children had a RAN/RAS deficit and 56% of their affected parents had a RAN/RAS deficit. Moreover, children and adolescents in the family genetics study who had comorbid reading and math disability differed from those who had reading disability only on RAN/RAS, but not on Verbal IQ or phonological skills (Busse et al. 1999). Thus, a RAN/RAS deficit may affect automaticity and coordination in other academic or developmental domains (see Waber this volume). Similar to the children whose RAN deficit predicted keyboarding problems (Bowers this volume), RAN/RAS also predicted writing disabilities in the Busse et al. study.

Yet, when we used generalized estimating equations in aggregation analyses to identify which of the 24 measures in our phenotyping battery were the most promising genetic candidates based on parent-parent, parent-offspring, and sibling-sibling correlations, *RAN* measures, which may be an operational measure of automaticity, did not show the family pattern associated with a genetic basis, but *RAS* measures, which may be an operational measure of executive coordination, did show a family pattern suggestive of a genetic basis (Raskind et al. 2000). This pattern of results does not mean that RAN does not have a genetic basis (see Compton et al. this volume), but rather that it is not the most promising genetic candidate in our current data set: phonological short-term memory, phonological decoding, and written spelling are the strongest genetic candidates in our current data set (Raskind et al. 2000). Yet, RAN/RAS deficits, as measured by the same stimulus cards, instructional procedures, and norms used in the research program of Wolf and colleagues, are the most prevalent language deficits in our family genetics study and early intervention study—this is the paradoxical puzzle that we set out to solve.

Our first clue that an executive function for self-regulation or coordination of mental processes may be the genetic culprit in RAS came from confirmatory factor analyses and structural equation modeling at the phenotypic level (Thomson et al. submitted). Confirmatory factor analyses showed that parent ratings of items (like "stays focused on tasks" versus "is like a motor always on the go") loaded on separate factors for Inattention (self-regulation of covert mental activity) and for Hyperactivity (self-regulation of overt behavior). The Inattention Factor had a significant, direct path to the RAN/RAS Factor and the Orthographic Factor, both of which have visible language input, but not to the Phonological Factor, which has auditory language input. The Hyperactivity Factor had no significant, direct paths to any of the language factors (orthographic, phonological, or RAN/RAS).

Our second clue that Inattention ratings may be the genetic constraint in RAS (not RAN) came from aggregation analyses. Inattention ratings for nuclear family members were highly consistent with a genetic basis.

Our third clue that an executive, self-regulation function for attention to visible language may be genetically constrained came from additional aggregation analyses in which generalized estimating equations were used to analyze *pairs of measures* (Hsu et al. submitted). When parents' retrospective self-ratings of their own inattention and their ratings of their children's inattention were partialed out of Wolf's RAS or the Gray Oral Reading Test, Third Edition, Rate (Wiederholt and Bryant 1992) in aggregation analyses performed on paired measures, there was a family aggregation pattern consistent with a genetic basis for the contribution of inattention to RAS and oral reading rate. These findings, which are consistent with executive function disorder in reading disability (Swanson 1993, 2000), may explain why instructional interventions that direct struggling readers' *attention to the orthography* of written words are proving effective (Levy this volume; McCandliss et al. 1999). Color coding of 1- and 2-letter spelling units in alphabet principle also seems to be effective in directing beginning readers' attention to relevant orthographic information (Berninger, Abbott, Brooksher et al. 2000).

In sum, full understanding of dyslexia seems to require, in addition to the language layers depicted in figure 1, consideration of efficiency (fast, accurate processing), automaticity (fast processing that involves direct access without attentional resources), naming (and its possible neurological basis in insula, see appendix), and executive coordination of multiple language processes. Thus, we propose that the reason that the deceptively simple RAN/RAS measures developed by Denckla and Rudel (1976) and Wolf and colleagues (e.g., Wolf et al. 1986; Wolf 1986) are such powerful behavioral markers of neurological mechanisms in dyslexia is that they have a broad window for assessing all these underlying mechanisms. Both RAN and RAS require direct access to names in the lexical level of the phonological layer. The time score for RAN reflects both the efficiency (speed) and automaticity (direct access) of integrating the orthographic and phonological layers in figure 1. The time score for RAS, on the other hand, assesses the time costs in coordinating the process of switching between categories while simultaneously integrating those same layers.

Different individuals may be slow on RAN or RAS for different reasons. To tease apart which of the potential mechanisms may be contributing may require additional assessment information. The bottom line, however, is that RAN and RAS deficits should not be ignored. They are not synonymous with phonological deficits, which have different genetic and neurological bases, but should be taken as seriously as phonological deficits in school-age children with learning problems, especially when they occur in conjunction with rate disabilities in reading or writing.

FUTURE RESEARCH ON FLUENCY

Clearly, additional research is needed on how to increase rate of reading in children at-risk for developing adequate efficiency, automaticity, or executive coordination; see National Institute of Child Health and Human Development (2000), Stahl, Heubach, and Crammond (1997), and Kuhn and Stahl (2000) for overviews of research to date on fluency. Torgesen, Rashotte, and Alexander's results (this volume) speak to the importance of early intervention in speed of reading, as well as accuracy of reading, during developmentally critical phases of reading acquisition, because there may be a critical time period during which fluency (not necessarily accuracy) of reading can be accomplished (Abadzi 1996). Measures being validated by Kame'enui et al. (this volume) can be used to assess development of efficient as well as accurate reading during this critical period.

In future research, participants might be differentiated as to whether they are slow and accurate, slow and inaccurate, fast and accurate, or fast and inaccurate, based on group norms on psychometric tests or curriculum based measures. Those who are slow might be further classified according to the scheme in table 2. Research should address the optimal time needed to practice fluency; given the attentional problems we have observed in our samples of at-risk readers, it is interesting that Binder (1976) found that practice durations as short as 3 to 5 minutes slowed rate and increased off-task and disruptive behaviors, but behavior improved when duration was shortened to one minute or less and fluency goals also improved when students worked for shorter intervals. Research is also needed on decision rules for when to make the transition from accuracy to fluency goals (see White 1985). Should fluency training begin when accuracy is between 67% to 83% and fluency is 20 behaviors a minute? Should it continue until a fluency criterion of 100 behaviors a minute is reached? Is there value in over learning or practice beyond a 100% accuracy criterion? (Doughtery and Johnston 1996). A thorny issue is whether fluency should be assessed at a child's instructional level for accuracy, which would necessitate using reading measures at different levels for children of the same age, or only at a single instructional level for accuracy with children carefully selected to represent only that level, which would allow the same reading measures to be used with all children in a sample to assess fluency. That is, can fluency be measured validly apart from a common metric for accuracy? There is no reason to believe that fast, inaccurate reading is fluent reading.

Of special interest is whether there is a qualitative shift in fluency as children make the transition from learning to read to reading to learn (Chall 1979). This shift is often observed between third and fourth grade around the tenth birthday. Ability to form integrated visual images of words has been found to occur at about age 10 (Posner and McCandliss 1999). Perhaps this ability to form such lexical level representations in the orthographic layer is necessary for children to make the transition from decoding fast and efficiently to recognizing words automatically. Different kinds of mechanisms may underlie fast word recognition—often referred to as "sight words" (even though phonological naming as well as visual processes are involved)—fast, efficient phonological decoding, and/or direct, automatic lexical retrieval. Automatic, direct access is efficient, but fast, efficient processing is not necessarily automatic. Fast, efficient processing may involve several steps, conscious attention, and strategies, but automatic processing always involves a single, direct step, unconscious attention, and canned routines. Beginning readers may be fast and efficient but may not be automatic until they undergo the qualitative shift in fluency around fourth grade. Recent findings that accuracy (not speed) of single word recognition and speed of text reading predict reading comprehension in fourth graders (Jenkins et al. submitted) are intriguing, given that speed of single word recognition predicted comprehension in second graders (Berninger et al. submitted). This fluency transition may also involve a shift from word-level efficiency to word-level automaticity and to sentence-level executive coordination. However, word-level efficiency may continue to increase after the shift to word-level automaticity (see Stanovich 1990). The point is that efficiency and obligatory automaticity may be separable processes on their own developmental trajectories. Longitudinal research is needed to determine when, in development, efficiency and automaticity of single word reading asymptote and reach levels typical of adult skilled readers.

Additional research is also needed on the recent finding (Breznitz in press, this volume), based on electrophysiological studies, which are more sensitive to timing parameters than current fMRI, that, compared to normal readers, subjects with dyslexia have difficulty in synchronizing the different time scales for the auditory-phonological and visual-orthographic layers of the word learning module (see arrows between these layers in figure 1), and their auditory-phonological processing is slow. What instructional techniques would facilitate the temporal coordination of these different systems so that connections can form between the orthographic and phonological layers that are not only accurate, but also efficient in the early learning stages and automatic later in reading development? Is this asynchrony in coordinating different time scales due to ectopias (neural migration errors) (Rosen et al. this volume) that interfere with normal wiring of neural pathways between the orthographic and phonological layers? Or, are there abnormalities in white matter in the pathways between these layers (Poldrack this volume) that interfere with the temporal coordination of the layers? Is synthetic phonics effective in teaching children with dyslexia, because the feedback in phonological short-term memory speeds up the processing of the auditory-phonological layer?

Future instructional research on fluency should focus on the fluency of specific component skills in the reading and writing systems because components of a functional system can show considerable intra-individual differences in their fluency. In addition, fluency outcomes should be evaluated on the basis of (a) retention, (b) maintenance of performance, (c) endurance or resistance to distraction, and (d) application or transfer to training (Binder, 1996). Both near transfer and far transfer of tool skills (elementary components) to more complex behaviors (Johnson and Laying 1992) should be assessed. In addition, longitudinal studies are needed to generate developmental norms for the following metrics of oral reading fluency: (a) mean rate (words per minute) or total response time for a passage of constant length at different ages until performance asymptotes and is comparable to adult skilled performance (a possible index of efficiency); (b) standard deviations for rate or total time across repeated readings of the same passage at a given age level for the same age levels as in (a), which are a possible index of automaticity when standard deviations stabilize; and (c) qualitative judgments of smoothness and expression of prosody (a possible index of executive coordination or syntactic processing).

SUMMARY AND CONCLUSION

Clearly much work remains to understand the temporal dimensions of fluency in functional language systems, which have multiple components that interact in complex ways in momentary and real time.

APPENDIX

Efficiency

Lovett (1987) distinguished between readers who are disabled in accuracy of word recognition (who are invariably also slow in reading) and those who are disabled only in rate of word recognition (who are age- or grade-appropriate in accuracy of word recognition). Students can be identified who meet the criteria for accuracy disability and for rate disability. They can be imaged while performing oral reading tasks in the functional magnetic resonance imaging (fMRI) magnet (using Eden et al.'s 1999, interleaving technique to avoid motor artifact). We predict that brain differences will be found in angular gyrus (Pugh et al. 2000) and cerebellum for those who are both accuracy and rate disabled, but that brain differences will be found in cerebellum (Eden et al. Fawcett and Nicolson, and Ivry, Justus, and Middleton this volume) for those who are only rate disabled. Half of each disability group can be randomly assigned to treatments that work on accuracy only (e.g., alphabet principle training) or rate only (e.g., repeated readings with rate goals). After treatment participants can be reimaged. We predict that the accuracy disability group that receives accuracy training will show changes in angular gyrus, but that the accuracy disability group that receives rate training will not show changes there. We also predict that the rate disability group that receives rate training will show changes in cerebellum, but the rate disability group that received accuracy training will not show changes there.

Automaticity

Mishkin and Appenzeller (1987) reported evidence for two neural pathways in the visual system of primates: a relatively direct behavioral pathway for automatic, in-out processing and a more circuitous cognitive pathway for strategic processing (cf. Shiffrin and Schneider's 1977 distinction between automaticity and controlled processing). Berninger (1999) speculated that the written language systems in humans also have separable neural mechanisms for automatic access and retrieval of items and for active, strategic construction of ideas or text. Students can be identified who meet the criteria for rate disability only (see above) and for automaticity disability. In contrast to the rate disabled who are accurate but very slow readers, the automaticity disabled are also very slow, make errors that include hesitations (with or without filled pauses), false starts, repetitions (reflecting problems in automatic access to words), yet frequently self-correct, reflecting spared strategic processing and executive functions. They can be imaged while performing oral reading tasks in the magnet (using Eden et al.'s 1999, interleaving technique to avoid motor artifact). We predict that brain differences will be found in cerebellum for those who are rate disabled, but that brain differences will be found in striatum (Mishkin and Appenzeller 1987) or insula (Corina et al. in press; Hynd et al. 1990; Paulesu et al. 1996; Pennington et al. 1999; Posner and McCandliss 1999), a brain structure associated with naming (Semrud-Clikeman et al. 1991), for those who are automaticity disabled. Half of each disability group can be randomly assigned to treatments that work on rate only (e.g., repeated reading and setting rate goals) or automaticity only (e.g., using connectionist principles of paired associations of spelling-phoneme correspondences, Berninger, Abbott, Brooksher et al., 2000). After treatment, participants can be reimaged. We predict that the rate disability group that receives rate training will show changes in cerebellum, but that the rate disability group that receives automaticity training will not show changes there. We also predict that the automaticity disability group that receives automaticity training will show changes in striatum or insula, but the automaticity disability group that received rate training will not show changes there.

Executive Coordination

Wood et al.'s observation (this volume), that reading is as much like walking as it is like talking, suggests that the language and non-language systems may share executive functions for coordinating serial elements of motoric behavior (Lashley 1933). Oral reading draws upon both language and oral-motor systems. Students can be identified who meet the criteria for automaticity disability only (see above) and for executive coordination disability without co-occurring automaticity disability. In contrast to the automaticity disabled who are very slow readers, make errors reflective of difficulty in automatic access to the mental lexicon, and are good self-monitors, the executive coordination disabled are very slow, make errors that reflect difficulty with coordination of linguistic information within and across words, and are not good at self-monitoring. They can be imaged while performing oral reading tasks in the magnet (using Eden et al.'s 1999, interleaving technique to avoid motor artifact). We predict that brain differences will be found in striatum or insula for those who are automaticity disabled, but that brain differences will be found in left frontal areas (Lashley 1933) for those who have disabilities in executive functions. Half of each disability group can be randomly assigned to treatments that work only on automaticity (e.g., using connectionist principles of paired associations of spelling-phoneme correspondences) or only on executive functions (e.g., explicit instruction in metalinguistic awareness and self-monitoring strategies). After treatment participants can be reimaged. We predict that the automaticity disability group that receives automaticity training will show changes in striatum or insula, but that the automaticity disability group that receives metalinguistic awareness and self-regulation training will not show changes in these areas. We also predict that the executive coordination disability group that receives metalinguistic awareness and self-regulation training will show changes in left frontal areas, but that the executive coordination disability group that receives automaticity training will not show changes there.

REFERENCES

Abadzi, H. 1996. Does age diminish the ability to learn fluent reading? *Educational Psychology Review* 8:373–96.

Abbott, Edwin A. 1894. *Flatland: A Romance in Many Dimensions*. Harper Collins, 1983.

Abbott, S., and Berninger, V. 1999. It's never too late to remediate: A developmental approach to teaching word recognition. *Annals of Dyslexia*.

Berninger, V. 1994. *Reading and Writing Acquisiton: A Developmental Neuropsychological Perspective*. Madison, WI: Brown and Benchamark.

Berninger, V. 1998. *Process Assessment of the Learner (PAL): Guides for Intervention*. San Antonio, TX: The Psychological Corporation.

Berninger, V. 1999. Coordinating transcription and text generation in working memory during composing: Automatized and constructive process. *Learning Disability Quarterly* 22:99–112.

Berninger, V. 2000. Development of language by hand and its connections with language by ear, mouth, and eye. *Topics in Language Disorders* 20:65–84.

Berninger, V., and Abbott, R. 1994. Multiple orthographic and phonological codes in literacy acquisition: An evolving research program. In *The Varieties of Orthographic Knowledge I: Theoretical and Developmental Issues*, ed. V. Berninger. The Netherlands: Kluwer Academic Publishers.

Berninger, V., Abbott, R., Abbott, S., Graham, S., and Richards, T. in press. Writing and reading: Connections between language by hand and language by ear. To appear in *Journal of Learning Disabilities*.

Berninger, V., Abbott, R., Brooksher, R., Lemos, Z., Ogier, S., Zook, D., and Mostafapour, E. 2000. A connectionist approach to making the predictability of English orthography explicit to at-risk beginning reader: Evidence for alternative, effective strategies. *Developmental Neuropsychology* 17(2):241–71.

Berninger, V., Abbott, R., Thomson, J., and Raskind, W. 2000. Language phenotypes for reading and writing disability: A family approach. *Scientific Studies in Reading* 5:59–105.

Berninger, V., Abbott, R., Zook, D., Ogier, S., Lemos, Z., and Brooksher, R. 1999. Early intervention for reading disabilities: Teaching the alphabet principle within a connectionist framework. *Journal of Learning Disabilities* 32(6):491–503.

Berninger, V., and Corina, D. 1998. Making cognitive neuroscience educationally relevant: Creating bi-directional collaborations between educational psychology and cognitive neuroscience. *Educational Psychology Review* 10:343–54.

Berninger, V., Vaughan, K., Abbott, R., Brooks, A., Abbott, S., Reed, E., Rogan, L., and Graham, S. 1998. Early intervention for spelling problems: Teaching spelling units of varying size within a multiple connections framework. *Journal of Educational Psychology* 90:587–605.

Berninger, V., Vaughan, K., Abbott, R., Brooks, A., Begay, K., Curtin, G., Byrd, K., and Graham, S. 2000. Language-based spelling instruction: Teaching children to make multiple connections between spoken and written words. *Learning Disability Quarterly* 23:117–135.

Berninger, V., Abbott, D., Vermeulen, K., Ogier, S., Brooksher, R., Zook, D., and Lemos, Z. 2000. Comparison of fast and slow responders: Implications for the nature and duration of early reading intervention. Submitted.

Berninger, V., Yates, C., Cartwright, A., Rutberg, J., Remy, E., and Abbott, R. 1992. Lower-level developmental skills in beginning writing. *Reading and Writing: An Interdisciplinary Journal* 4:257–80.

Binder, C. 1996. Behavioral fluency: Evolution of a new paradigm. *The Behavior Analyst* 19:163–97.

Binder, C., Houghton, E., and VanEyk, D. 1990. Increasing endurance by building fluency. Precision teaching attention span. *Exceptional Children* 22(3):24–27.

Bowers, P., and Wolf, M. 1993. Theoretical links between naming speed, precise timing mechanisms, and orthographic skill in dyslexia. *Reading and Writing: An Interdisciplinary Journal* 5:69–85.

Breznitz, Z. 1987. Increasing first graders' reading accuracy and comprehension by accelerating their reading rate. *Journal of Educational Psychology* 79:236–42.

Breznitz, Z. 1997a. Reading rate acceleration: Developmental aspects. *The Journal of Genetic Psychology* 158(4):427–41.

Breznitz, Z. 1997b. Effects of accelerated reading rate on memory for text among dyslexic readers. *Journal of Educational Psychology* 89:289–97.

Breznitz, Z. 1997c. Enhancing the reading of dyslexic children by reading acceleration and auditory masking. *Journal of Educational Psychology* 89:103–13.

Breznitz, Z. in press. Asynchrony of visual-orthographic and auditory-phonological word recognition processes: An underlying factor in dyslexia. *Journal of Reading and Writing*.

Busse, J., Thomson, J., Abbott, R., and Berninger, V. 1999. *Cognitive Processes Related to Dual Disability in Reading and Calculation*. Boston: American Psychological Association.

Carlisle, J. 2000. Awareness of the structure and meaning of morphologically complex word: Impact on reading. *Reading and Writing: An Interdisciplinary Journal* 12:169–90.

Chall, J., 1979. The great debate: Ten years later, with a modest proposal for research stages. In *Theory and Practice of Early Reading*, Vol. I, ed. L. Resnick and P. Weaver. Hillsdale, NJ: Lawrence Erlbaum Associates.

Chiappe, P., Stringer, R., Siegel, L., and Stanovich, K. In press. Why the timing deficit hypothesis does not explain reading disability in adults. *Reading and Writing: An Interdisciplinary Journal.*

Compton, D., and Carlisle, J. 1994. Speed of word recognition as a distinguishing characteristic of reading disabilities. *Educational Psychology Review* 6:115–40.

Corina, D., Richards, T., Serafina, S., Richards, A., Steury, K., Abbott, R., Echelard, D., Maravilla, K., and Berninger, V. in press. An fMRI study of auditory word processing in dyslexic children. Neuroreport.

Dempster, F. 1988. The spacing effect: A case study in failure to apply the results of psychological research. *American Psychologist* 43:627–34.

Denckla, M. and Rudel, R. 1976. Rapid "automatized" naming (RAN.): Dyslexia differentiated from other learning disabilities. *Neuropsychology* 14:471–9.

Doughtery, K., and Johnston, J. 1996. Overlearning, fluency, and automaticity. *The Behavior Analyst* 19:289–92.

Eddington, Sir Arthur 1920. *Space, Time, and Gravitation.* Cambridge University Press.

Eden, G., Joseph, J., Brown, H., Brown, C., and Zeffiro, T. 1999. Utilizing hemodynamic delay and dispersion to detect fMRI signal change without auditory interference: The behavior interleave gradients technique. *Magnetic Resonance Medicine* 41:13–20.

Eden, G., Van Meter, J., Rumsey, J., Maisog, J., Woods, F., and Zeffiro, T. 1996. Abnormal brain processing of visual motion in dyslexia revealed by functional brain imaging. *Nature* 383:66–69.

Erekson, J. 1999. Sound meanings: The role of prosody in children's comprehension of text and developing sense of voice. National Reading Conference Symposium on Reconciling the Cognitive and the Social in Conceptualizations of Reading.

Fowler, A., and Liberman, I. 1995. The role of phonology and orthography in morphological awareness. In *Morphological Aspects of Language Processing*, ed. L. B. Feldman. Hillsdale, NJ: Erlbaum.

Gallagher, R., and Appenzeller, T. 1999. Beyond reductionism: Introduction to special issue on complex systems. *Science* 284:79.

Garvey, C. and Berninger, V. 1981. Timing and turn-taking in children's conversations. *Discourse Processes* 4:27–57.

Harm, M., and Seidenberg, M. 1999. Phonology, reading acquisition, and dyslexia: Insights from connectionist models. *Psychological Review* 106:491–528.

Hoffman, P. 1998. *The Man Who Loved Only Numbers.* New York: Hyperion.

Hsu, L., Wijsman, E., Berninger, V., Thomson, J., and Raskind, W. 2000. Familal aggregation analysis of paired correlated measures for automaticity, phonological short-term memory, and executive function subtypes in dyslexia. Submitted.

Hynd, G., Semrud-Clikeman, M., Lorys, A., Novey, E., and Eliopulus, D. 1990. Brain morphology in developmental dyslexia and attention deficit disorder/hyperactivity. *Archives of Neurology* 47:919-26.

Jenkins, J., Fuchs, L., Espin, C., van den Broek, P., and Deno, S. 2000. Effects of task format and performance dimensions on word reading measures: Criterion validity, sensitivity to impairment, and context facilitation. Submitted.

Johnson, K., and Laying, T. 1992. Breaking the structuralist barrier: Literacy and numeracy with fluency. *American Psychologist* 47:1475–90.

Johnson, K., and Laying, T. 1996. On terms and procedures: Fluency. *The Behavior Analyst* 19:281–8.

Kaas, J., and Hackett, T. 1999. "What" and "where" processing in auditory cortex. *Nature Neuroscience* 2:1045–6.

Kelly, R. 1996. A functional analysis of the effects of mastery and fluency on maintenance. DAI-A57/02, p.639.

Kintsch, W. 1998. *Comprehension: A Paradigm for Cognition.* New York: Cambridge University Press.

Kuhn, M., and Stahl S. 2000. Fluency, A review of developmental and remedial practices. CIERA Report #2-008, March 31.

LaBerge, D., and Samuels, S. 1974. Toward a theory of automatic information-processing in reading. *Cognitive Psychology* 6:293–323.

Lashley, K. S. 1933. Integrative functions of the cerebral cortex. *Psychological Review* 13:1–42.

Levy, B. A., Abello, B., and Lysynchuk, L. 1997. Transfer from word training to reading in context: Gains in reading fluency and comprehension. *Learning Disability Quarterly* 20:173–88.

Lindsley, O. 1964. Direct measurement and prosthesis of retarded behavior. *Journal of Education* 147:62–81.

Lindsley, O. R. 1990. Precision teaching: By teachers for children. *Teaching Exceptional Children* 22(3):10–15.

Livingston, M., Rosen, G., Drislane, F., and Galaburda, A. 1991. Physiological and anatomical evidence for a magnocellular deficit in developmental dyslexia. *Proceedings of the National Academy of Sciences* (USA) 88:7943 7.

Lovegrove, W. 1993. Visual transient system deficits in specific reading disability. New Orleans: Society for Research in Child Development.

Lovegrove, W., Martin, F., and Slaghuis, W. 1986. A theoretical and experimental case for a visual deficit in specific reading disability. *Cognitive Neuropsychology* 3:225–67.

Lovett, M. 1987. A developmental approach to reading disability: Accuracy and speed criteria of normal and deficient reading skill. *Child Development* 58:234–60.

Lubs, H., Duara, R., Levin, B., Jallad, B., Lubs, M., Rabin, M., Kushch, A., and Gross-Glenn, K. 1991. Genetics, behavior, and brain imaging. In *The Reading Brain: The Biological Basis of Dyslexia*, eds. D. Duane and D. Gray. Timonium, MD: York Press.

MacGinitie, W. 1989. *Gates MacGinitie Reading Tests*, Third Edition. Chicago, IL: Riverside.

McCandliss, B., Sandak, I., Beck, I., Perfetti, C., and Schneider, W. 1999. Inroads into reading acquisition failures: Relating alphabetic decoding instruction to changes in behavioral and fMRI measures. Society for Scientific Studies in Reading. Montreal.

Minsky, M. 1986. *The Society of Mind.* New York: Simon and Schuster.

Mishkin, M. and Appenzeller, T. 1987. The anatomy of memory. *Scientific American* 80–89.

Nagy, W., Diakidoy, I., and Anderson, R. 1983. The acquisition of morphology: Learning the contribution of suffixes to the meanings of derivatives. *Journal of Reading Behavior* 25:155–70.

Nagy, W., Osborn, J., Winsor, P., and O' Flahavan, J. 1994. Structural analysis: Some guidelines for instruction. In *Reading, Language, and Literacy*, eds. F. Lehr and J. Osborn. Hillsdale, NJ: Lawrence Erlbaum Associates.

National Institute of Child Health and Human Development. 2000. Report of the National Reading Panel. Teaching Children to Read. An evidence-based assessment of the scientific research literature on reading and its implication for reading instruction. Reports of subgroups. National Institutes of Health.

Paulesu, E., Frith, U., Snowling, M., Gallagher, A., Morton, J., Frackowiak, R., and Frith, C. 1996. Is developmental dyslexia a disconnection syndrome? Evidence from PET scanning. *Brain* 119:143-57.

Pennington, B., Filipek, P., Lefly, D., Churchwell, J., Kennedy, D., Simon, J., Filley, C., Galaburda, A., Alarcon, M., and DeFries, J. 1999. Brain morphometry in reading-disabled twins. *Neurology* 53:723-29.

Perfetti, C. 1985. *Reading Ability*. New York: Oxford University Press

Posner, M., and McCandliss, B. 1999. Brain circuitry during reading. In *Converging Methods for Understanding Reading and Dyslexia*, eds. R. Klein and P. McMullen. Cambridge, MA: MIT Press.

Pugh, K., Mencl, W., Shaywitz, B., Shaywitz, S., Fullbright, R., Constable, R., Skudlarski, P., Marchionne, K., Jennet, A., Flectcher, J., Liberman, A., Shankweiler, D., Katz, L., Lacadie, C., and Gore, J. 2000. Task-specific differences in functional connections within posterior cortex. *Psychological Science* 2:51–56.

Rasinski, T. V. 1990. Investigating measures of reading fluency. *Educational Research Quarterly* 14:37–44.

Raskind, W., Hsu, L., Thomson, J., Berninger, V. and Wijsman, E. 2000. Family aggregation of dyslexia phenotypes. *Behavioral Genetics* 30:385–96.

Read Naturally 1997. Turman Publishing, 2329 Kressin Ave., Saint Paul, MN 55120.

Read, C. 1981. Writing is not the inverse of reading for young children. In *Writing: The Nature, Development, and Teaching of Written Communication*, Vol. 2, eds. C. H. Frederickson and J. Dominick. Hillsdale, NJ: Lawrence Erlbaum Associates.

Richards, T., Corina, D., Serafini, S., Steury, K., Dager, S., Marro, K., Abbott, R., Maravilla, K., and Berninger, V. 2000. Effects of phonologically-driven treatment for dyslexia on lactate levels as measured by proton MRSI. *American Journal of Radiology* 21:916–22.

Richards, T., Dager, S., Corina, D., Serafini, S., Heidel, A., Steury, K., Strauss, W., Hayes, C., Abbott, R., Kraft, S., Shaw, D., Posse, S., and Berninger, V. 1999. Dyslexic children have abnormal chemical brain activation during reading-related language tasks. *American Journal of Neuroradiology* 20:1393–8.

Semrud-Clikeman, M., Hynd, G., Novey, E., and Eliopulos, D. 1991. Dyslexia and brain morphology: Relationships between neuroanatomical variation and neurolinguistic tasks. *Learning and Individual Differences* 3:225–42.

Shiffrin, R., and Schneider, W. 1977. Controlled and automatic information processing: II. Perceptual learning, automatic attending, and a general theory. *Psychological Review* 84:120–90.

Stage, S., Abbott, R., Jenkins, J., and Berninger, V. 2000. Predicating response to early reading intervention using Verbal IQ, reading-related language abilities, attention ratings, and Verbal IQ-word reading discrepancy. *Journal of Learning Disabilities*.

Stahl, S., Heubach, K., and Crammond, B. 1997. Fluency oriented reading instruction. National Reading Research Center NRRC. *Reading Research Report* No. 79, Winter.

Stanovich, K. 1990. Concepts in developmental theories of reading skill: Cognitive resources, automaticity, and modularity. *Developmental Review* 10:72–100.

Strecker, S., Rosner, N., and Martinez, M. 1998. Toward understanding oral reading fluency. In *47th Yearbook of the National Reading Conference*, National Reading Conference, eds. T. Shanahan and F. Rodriguez-Brown. National Reading Conference.

Swanson, H.L. 1993. Executive processing in learning disability subtypes. *Journal of Experimental Child Psychology* 56:87–114.

Swanson, H.L. 2000. Working memory, short-term memory, speech rate, word recognition, and reading comprehension in learning disabled readers: Does the executive system have a role? *Intelligence* 28:1–30.

Tallal, P. 1980. Auditory temporal perception phonics and reading disabilities in children. *Brain and Language* 9:192–8.

Tallal, P., Galaburda, A., Llinas, R., and von Euler, C. 1993. *Temporal information processing in the nervous system: Special reference to dyslexia and dysphasia.* New York: The New York Academy of Sciences.

Thomson, J., Abbott, R., Busse, J., Hartman, R., Prather, T., Raskind, W., and Berninger, V. 2000. Self-regulation of attentional and motor activity and its relationship to language and academic skills in dyslexia. Submitted.

Ungerleider, L. and Mishkin, M. 1982. Analysis of Visual Behavior In *Two Cortical Visual Systems*, eds. D. Ingle, M. Goodale, and R. Mansfield. Cambridge, MA: MIT Press.

White, O. 1985. Decisions, decisions...*B.C. Journal of Special Education* 9:305–20.

White, O. 1986. Precision teaching—Precision learning. *Teaching Exceptional Children* 52:522–534.

White, O., and Haring, N. 1976. *Exceptional Teaching.* Columbus, OH: Charles Merrill.

Wiederholt, J., and Bryant, B. 1992. *Gray Oral Reading Test,* Third Edition (GORT3). Odessa, FL: Psychological Assessment Resources.

Wolf, M. 1986. Rapid alternation stimulus naming in the developmental dyslexias. *Brain and Language* 27:360–79.

Wolf, M., Bally, H., and Morris, R. 1986. Automaticity, retrieval processes, and reading: A longitudinal study in average and impaired reading. *Child Development* 57:988–1000.

Wolf, M., Bowers, P., and Biddle, K. 2000. Naming-speed processes, timing, and reading: A conceptual review. *Journal of Learning Disabilities* 33:387–407.

Woodcock, R. 1987. *Woodcock Reading Mastery Test-Revised.* Circle Pines, MN: American Guidance.

Young, A., Bowers, P., and MacKinnon, G. 1996. Effects of prosodic modeling and repeated reading on poor readers' fluency and comprehension. *Applied Psycholinguistics* 17:59–84.

Zutell, J. and Rasinski, T. 1991. Training teachers to attend to their students' oral reading fluency. *Theory into Practice* 30:212–7.

ACKNOWLEDGMENTS

The research reported in this chapter was supported by P50 33812-05 and HD 25858-10 from the National Institute of Child Health and Human Development. The authors thank Joanne Carlisle for helpful discussion in refining the model for Circle of Connections in Word Learning; Jennifer Thomson, Wendy Raskind, Li Hsu, and Ellen Wijsman for their contributions to this chapter from the perspective of family genetics; Todd Richards and David Corina for their contributions from the perspective of functional brain imaging; and Joe Jenkins for insightful comments on an earlier draft. They thank Greg Daigle for preparing figure 1. The authors are also grateful to Maryanne Wolf, organizer of the Timing and Fluency Conference, for her vision and leadership to the field in stimulating research on the role of timing and naming in reading and reading disorders.

Index